OXFORD ADVANCED HISTORY

GERMANY

1858-1990 | **Hope, Terror and Revival**

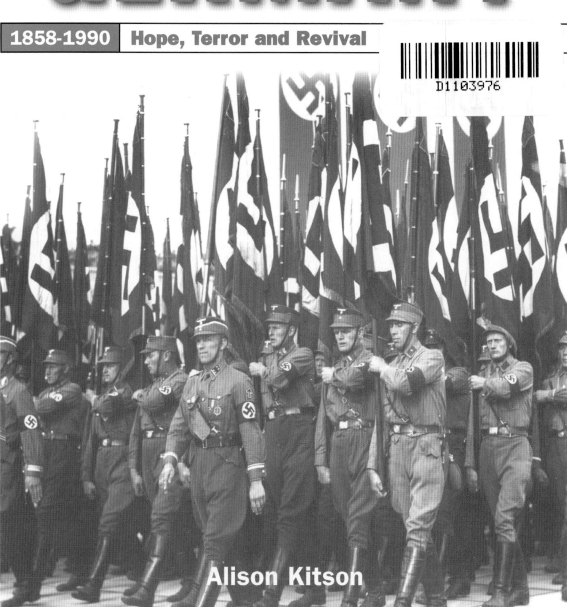

Alison Kitson

OXFORD
UNIVERSITY PRESS

OXFORD
UNIVERSITY PRESS
Great Clarendon Street, Oxford OX2 6DP

Oxford University Press is a department of the
University of Oxford.
It furthers the University's objective of excellence
in research, scholarship, and education by
publishing worldwide in Oxford New York
Athens Auckland Bangkok Bogotá Buenos Aires
Cape Town Chennai Dar es Salaam Delhi
Florence Hong Kong Istanbul Karachi Kolkata
Kuala Lumpur Madrid Melbourne Mexico City
Mumbai Nairobi Paris São Paulo Shanghai
Singapore Taipei Tokyo Toronto Warsaw with
associated companies in Berlin Ibadan

Oxford is a registered trade mark of Oxford
University Press
in the UK and in certain other countries

British Library Cataloguing in Publication Data
Data available

ISBN: 978 0 19 913417 5

15 14 13 12 11

Printed in China by Printplus

Designed by Peter Tucker, Holbrook Design
(info@holbrook-design.co.uk)
Maps by Jeff Edwards

This book is dedicated to my parents

I would like to thank the following people for their advice and support in
writing this book: Katharine Burn, Marian Hodgkin, Peter Oxley, Martin
Roberts, Andy Crawley, Julian Critchley, Kevin and Jake Burrell, the fellows
of Newnham College, Cambridge, and my students at Cheney school,
Oxford.

Acknowledgements

The author and publisher would like to thank Katharine Burn, Series
Consultant, for her valuable input and advice during the development
of this project.

The author and publisher would like to thank the following for their
permission to reproduce the following photographs:
AKG, London: 23crb, 47bc, 49bl, 52cla, 52bc, 66ca, 101tr,113cla, 117crb,
126tl, 130ca, 132bc, 133cla, 133clb, 164ca, 169bcr, 179tr, 185br, 205cra,
219br, 221clb, 226ca, 226cb, 242c, 255cla, 281cra, /Berlin/SMPK,
Nationalgalerie: 109tl, /Erik Bohr: 108tr, /© DACS 2001: 179bc, 218tr,
/Erich Lessing/Galerie der Stadt Stuttgart: 92ca, clb, crb; © Associated
Newspapers/David Low/Evening Standard/Centre for the Study of
Cartoons & Caricature, University of Kent, Canterbury: 161crb, 231clb,
235cra; Bildarchiv Preussischer Kulturbesitz: 270bl, 276clb, 285tl, 292ca
/© DACS 2001: 97br; Bridgeman Art Library/ Marianne Brandt/Fine Art
Society, London, UK/Private Collection: 108tc, /© DACS 2001/Private
Collection: 108crb; © Corbis: 117cl, 177br, /Austrian Archives: 93cl,
/Bettmann: 16tl, /Hulton-Deutsch Collection: 184bl, 251tl; Mary Evans
Picture Library: 8bc, 52cra, 70bl, 70br, 79cr, 79br, 80bl, 90tl, 105bl,
112clb, 112crb, 116tr, 117tl, 117cra, 130br, 133bl, 151br, 166crb, 168cla,
184cra, 186bl, 189tl, 193cra, 193bl, 197clb, 214bl, 222bl, 256cla;; Hulton
Archive: 42tl, 58clb, 70ca, 82bl, 87br; Illustrated London News: 116cl,
116br, 180cb; Keystone Pressedienst: 193br, 270cla, 270br, 282crb,
283clb, 289cla, 289crb, 291cr, 292bl, 292br; David King Collection/©
DACS 2001: 136cla, 147tr; Kladderadatsch: 18clb, 28cl, 36clb, 43br; Kurt
Klamann/ Die Auferstehung from Windstarke 12, Eine Auswahl Neuer
Deutscher Karikaturen, publisher Verlag der Kunst, 1953/Photo Randy
Bytwerk, Calvin College German Propaganda Archive: 279cra;
Popperfoto: 15cla, 128tl, 133tl, 214ca, 214br, 252clb, 258c; Punch Ltd:
84crb, 232tl; Rasse, Blut und Gene: Geschichte der Eugenik und
Rassenhygiene in Deutschland (Suhrkamp 1981) by P.Weingart, J.Krol
and K.Bayertz: 201bc; Rex Features: 284cb, 284cra, /Sipa: 283tc;
Tobis/Kobal Collection: 203tr; Topham Picturepoint: 148ca, 197crb;
Ullstein Bild: 32tl, 46cla, 60bl, 68bl, 158tr, 209tc, clb, crb; Wiener
Library Archives: 119br, 129tl.
A=above; c=centre; b=below; l=left; r=right; t=top

The author and publisher gratefully acknowledge permission to reprint
from the following copyright works: Alan Bullock: extracts from *Hitler: A
Study in Tyranny* (Hamlyn, 1973), reprinted by permission of the Octopus
Publishing Group. Victor Klemperer: extracts from *I Shall Bear Witness*
(Phoenix Press, 1999), by permission of the Orion Publishing Group Ltd.
Harry Kessler: extracts from *Diaries of a Cosmopolitan* (Weidenfeld &
Nicolson, 1971), by permission of the Orion Publishing Group Ltd.

We have tried to trace and contact all copyright holders prior to
publication. If notified, by anyone we have not traced, we will be
pleased to rectify any errors or omissions at the earliest opportunity.

Contents

Meeting examination criteria: a map of this book

Chapter		EDEXCEL	OCR	AQA
1	The unification of Germany	AS: Unit 3 (Bismarck and the Unification of Germany)	AS: Module 2586 (Germany 1862–90) A2: Module 2589 (Bismarck & the Unification of Germany 1858–1871)	AS/A2: Alternative E Modules 1 & 4 AS: Alternative G Module 1
2	Bismarck 1871–1890	A2: Unit 4 (Bismarck & Germany 1871–90)	AS: Module 2586 (Germany 1862–90)	AS/A2: Alternative E Modules 1 & 4 AS: Alternative G Module 1
3	Wilhelmine Germany 1890–1914			AS/A2: Alternative E Modules 1 & 4 AS: Alternative G Module 1
4	The early years of the Weimar Republic 1918–1923	AS: Unit 2 (The Democratic Experiment 1918–1929)	AS: Module 2586 (Germany 1919–45)	A2: Alternative E Module 4 AS: Alternative G module 1 AS: Alternative J Modules 1 & 3
5	The 'Golden Years' 1924–1929	AS: Unit 2 (The Democratic Experiment 1918–1929)	AS: Module 2586 (Germany 1919–45)	A2: Alternative E Module 4 AS: Alternative G Modules 1 & 3 AS: Alternative J Module 1
6	The rise of the Nazi Party	AS: Unit 2 (The Democratic Experiment 1918–1929) AS: Unit 1 (The Rise of National Socialism up to 1933)	AS: Module 2586 (Germany 1919–45) AS: Module 2582 (Nazi Germany 1933–45)	A2: Alternative E Module 4 AS: Alternative G Module 3 AS: Alternative J Module 1
7	The collapse of the Weimar Republic	AS: Unit 1 (The Rise of National Socialism up to 1933)	AS: Module 2586 (Germany 1919–45) AS: Module 2582 (Nazi Germany 1933–45	A2: Alternative E Module 4 AS: Alternative G Module 3 AS: Alternative J Module 1
8	The creation of a Nazi dictatorship	AS: Unit 3 (Life in Hitler's Germany)	AS: Module 2586 (Germany 1919–45) AS: Module 2582 (Nazi Germany 1933–45)	A2: Alternative E Module 4 AS/A2: Alternative G Modules 3 & 4 AS: Alternative J Module 1
9	The Nazi State	AS: Unit 3 (Life in Hitler's Germany)	AS: Module 2586 (Germany 1919–45) AS: Module 2582 (Nazi Germany 1933–45)	A2: Alternative E Module 4 AS/A2: Alternative G Modules 3 & 4 AS: Alternative J Module 1
10	Social & racial policy in the Third Reich	AS: Unit 3 (Life in Hitler's Germany)	AS: Module 2586 (Germany 1919–45) AS: Module 2582 (Nazi Germany 1933–45)	A2: Alternative E Module 4 A2: Alternative G Module 4 AS: Alternative J Module 1
11	The Nazi economy	AS: Unit 3 (Life in Hitler's Germany)	AS: Module 2586 (Germany 1919–45) AS: Module 2582 (Nazi Germany 1933–45)	A2: Alternative E Module 4 A2: Alternative G Module 4 AS/A2: Alternative J Modules 1 & 4
12	Nazi foreign policy	A2: Unit 4 (German foreign policy 1933–39)		A2: Alternative E Module 6 A2: Alternative J Module 4
13	Popularity and resistance, 1933–45	AS: Unit 3 (Life in Hitler's Germany)	AS: Module 2586 (Germany 1919–45) AS: Module 2582 (Nazi Germany 1933–45)	A2: Alternative E Module 4 A2: Alternative G Module 4 AS: Alternative J Module 1
14	Interpretations of Nazism	A2: Unit 6 (Hitler and the Nazi State: Power and Control 1933–39)	AS: Module 2586 (Germany 1919–45)	A2: Alternative E Module 4 AS: Alternative G Modules 1 & 3 AS: Alternative J Module 1
15	The division of Germany 1945–1969			A2: Alternative G Module 4
16	Towards reunification			A2: Alternative G Module 6
17	The economic modernisation of Germany c.1880–c.1980			A2: Alternative G Module 4

* These provide examination-style questions   ** See page 6

5

Using this book

The way in which you use this book will obviously depend on the examination specification you are following, and the particular options within it that you have chosen to study. The contents map on pages 4–5 makes clear how different chapters relate to the main AS and A level specifications, while within each chapter a clear introduction and list of key questions outline how the main issues are dealt with. Concise conclusions are offered in the end of chapter summaries.

Where there are important differences of interpretation between historians, the main text will introduce you to these controversies and suggest further reading. However, there are also specific sections that focus on major historical debates. These explore the different reasons why historians have such conflicting views, and set out criteria that you will find helpful in comparing interpretations and assessing their value.

Key Skills

Since the study of history involves information gathering (i.e. research) and processing (assessing the value and implications of different kinds of evidence) in order to reach conclusions which you then have to communicate, it can obviously contribute significantly to the practice of two of the designated *Key Skills*: Communication and Information Technology. The spread of activities within this book has, therefore, been carefully planned to provide opportunities for you to develop and demonstrate these Key Skills.

The specifications for these Key Skills at level 3 are as follows:

Communication

C3.1a   Contribute to a group discussion about a complex subject.

C3.1b   Make a presentation about a complex subject, using at least one image to illustrate complex points.

C3.2   Read and synthesize information from two extended documents about a complex subject. One of these documents should include at least one image.

C3.3   Write two different types of documents about complex subjects. One piece of writing should be an extended document and include at least one image.

Information Technology

IT3.1   Plan and use different sources to search for, and select, information required for different purposes.

IT3.2   Explore, develop and exchange information and derive new information to meet two different purposes.

IT3.3   Present information for two different purposes and audiences. Candidates' work must include at least one example of text images and one example of numbers.

The contents map on pages 4–5 provides a clear indication of the pages where Key Skills activities can be found and which elements of the specifications they cover. A Key Skills logo on the page itself also indicates which activity is being referred to. These Key Skills activities arise naturally out of the work that you are doing and can be used as part of your teacher-assessed portfolio of evidence, demonstrating the application of these skills.

Spotlight

These sections provide opportunities for a detailed focus, either exploring significant issues within a chapter, or examining the impact of particular policies through specific case studies. They generally include a range of different kinds of source material, with structured questions and activities to help you to engage with the issues and reach your own conclusions.

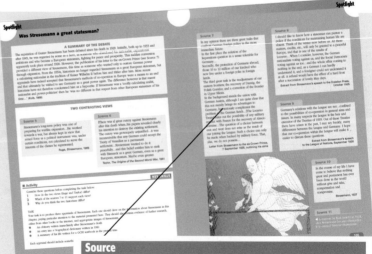

Source

A large number of sources are presented within each chapter. Primary sources give you access to the kinds of evidence on which our understanding of the period has been built, while extracts from historians' accounts give you an insight into their particular interpretation of events.

Note

These boxes provide additional information or reminders. They alert you to issues that may influence the judgements you may make about certain events, individuals or historical interpretations.

Activity

The activities include a range of exercises that will help you to make sense of all that you have read. Structured tasks encourage you to manipulate information – organising it in different ways – to complete summary charts; to analyse and compare different explanations, and to assess the consequences of particular developments. The activities take a variety of forms, including research work, decision-making exercises, role-play, discussion and debate, as well as exam-style sequences of structured questions and essays.

Think about

Most sources are linked to a 'think about' encouraging you to reflect on the evidence or historical interpretation offered. The questions posed help you to relate the source to your developing knowledge of the topic and to assess its value and implications.

'Think about' boxes relating to the main text also help you to think critically about what you are reading: making links, drawing comparisons and predicting likely outcomes.

Further reading

Suggestions here include texts written specifically for AS and A level students as well as accessible works by prominent historians. Some include guidance as to how the books might be read and which sections may prove particularly relevant or enjoyable. Where appropriate, the place of these books in key historical controversies is also made clear.

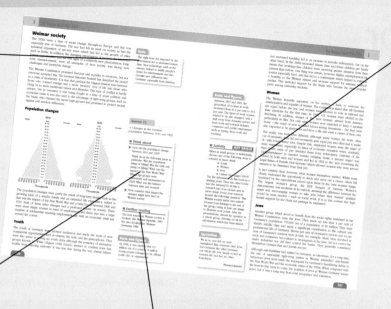

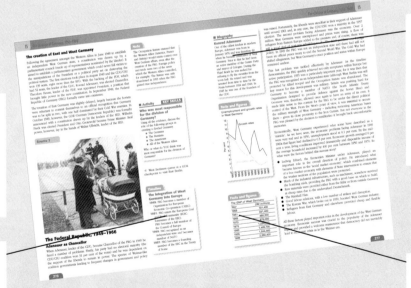

Cross reference

These boxes alert you to relevant sections elsewhere in the book that may extend or enhance your understanding of the text you are reading.

Biography

These boxes provide short biographies of key individuals, helping you to assess their significance, and to place specific actions or decisions in the context of their wider careers.

Timeline

These provide useful summaries of the main developments explained in the text. They help you to develop an overview of the particular issue or sequence of events and to locate particular incidents within a wider chronology.

Facts and figures

These boxes present statistical information or specific details to exemplify and substantiate more general claims made in the main text.

Examination-style exercises

Each chapter includes specific assessment exercises modelled on the details provided in AS and A level specifications and specimen papers. A large number of structured *document exercises* provide plenty of opportunity for exam practice, while those chapters that deal specifically with major issues of historical controversy include similar structured exercises focused solely on issues of historical *interpretations*.

Chapter 1

The unification of Germany

Nations are inventions, the products of particular historical circumstances and movements

Sheehan, *German History 1770–1866*, 1989

◀ A cartoon from 1867. France warns Prussia: 'Now you're big enough. You mustn't get any bigger. I'm telling you this for your own health.'

▼ King Wilhelm I of Prussia is proclaimed German Emperor (Kaiser) in the Hall of Mirrors at Versailles, on 18 January 1871, after the defeat of France in the Franco-Prussian War.

Introduction

In 1871 Germany united to become a single state. It had previously existed as many separate states. The unification of Germany has had an enormous impact, not just on German history but on the history of Europe since 1871. Without a single powerful German state, two world wars might never have happened and Hitler might never have risen to power. German unification is, therefore, one of the most important events of modern history. This chapter examines how and why Germany united. It also introduces one of the most important figures in German history, Otto von Bismarck. Bismarck has always provoked extreme responses from historians. He has been described as a hero, a brilliant statesman and politician, a ruthless opportunist and even as the man who made Hitler possible. Although he himself denied that individuals can shape history, his own actions and achievements proved otherwise.

Key questions

- What events between 1815 and 1871 led to German unification?
- Who was Bismarck and what were his aims?
- What role did each of the following play in the unification of Germany:
  - Prussia (the largest German state)
  - Economic growth
  - War
  - Nationalism
  - Liberalism
  - Bismarck
- Was Germany united by 'Blood and iron'?
- Was the unification of Germany inevitable?

An era of change

■ Think about

▶ Look at Source 1. According to the caption, why did France not want Prussia (the largest German state) to get any bigger?

▶ Do you think this was the real reason?

Facts and figures

1800 Travel from Paris to St Petersburg took 20 days

1813 The first gas lights installed in Pall Mall, London

1835 Invention of the electric telegraph

1840s First postage stamp available in Britain (Penny Black)

1860s Oil available for the first time

1877 Invention of the telephone

1880s Electricity widely available

1889 Invention of the internal combustion engine

1890s Introduction of gliding

1896 Invention of the radio

1900 Travel from Paris to St Petersburg took 30 hours

1903 The Wright Brothers flew the first petrol-driven aeroplane

Source 4

There is a dynamism about nineteenth-century Europe that far exceeds anything previously known. Europe vibrated with power as never before…its prime symbols were its engines – the locomotives, the gasworks, the electric dynamos…Europeans, in fact, were made to feel not only powerful but superior…for nineteenth-century man, power was the object of wonder and hope…

Davies, *Europe*, 1997

As Source 4 suggests, the nineteenth century was a time of enormous change in Europe. Society became less agricultural and more industrial; less rural and more urban. This was the era of steam engines, railways and, later, electricity. It was the era of machines that transformed production. It was the era of factories, built to house those machines. It was the era of urbanism as people flocked to the towns where the new factories were located. The impact of these changes cannot be overestimated.

Germany witnessed these changes as much as any country during the nineteenth century. Of great importance to its industrial development were improved communications. Better roads were built, canals were dug and, in particular, the railways arrived. The first line opened in 1835 and the railway system quickly expanded (despite doctors' health warnings of the dangers of travelling at such speed). German society also underwent an important change. The German people were no longer defined for life according to their status at birth. Instead, they were defined by their social class at any given point. It was, in consequence, easier to move between social groups and nobles were free to pursue middle-class professions – although moves in the opposite direction, from peasant upwards, remained less common.

Europe's population was expanding rapidly, increasing from around 150 million in 1800 to over 400 million by 1914. This created tensions everywhere, not least in overcrowded, unhygienic living conditions in the rapidly expanding towns. In Germany, much of the population growth was in the countryside and food supplies were becoming inadequate. Terrible epidemics of disease, such as cholera, brought demands for better public health provision. These demands came from the expanding working classes, which began to acquire political awareness and self-confidence due to their large numbers, their concentration in the towns and their poor treatment. They were often joined by the growing middle classes who, despite their wealth and importance as traders and industrialists, resented their lack of political power. The traditional aristocratic elites in Germany were more determined than those in many other countries to hold on to their privileges and power and they were often the ones least affected by the changes happening around them.

This was also an era of growing nationalism which was to blossom fully towards the end of the century. Uneven economic growth among neighbouring states created opportunities for the most successful states to expand, in order to satisfy the needs of a growing population, to supply enough raw materials for production and to secure new markets. Some states, though not Germany, looked outside Europe for this and built up huge empires which spanned continents. In Germany, voices demanding the unification of the country could be heard; their calls were finally answered in 1871.

> **Key term**
>
> **Nationalism**
> Strong feelings of loyalty between people who share race, language and culture. Also a desire in a people to defend their country and make it strong. The idea grew rapidly during the nineteenth century. At its worst it can lead to persecution of minority groups, such as Jews. It can also encourage expansion and war against other states. In its mildest form, however, it involves feelings of solidarity among a people and pride in their country. These feelings are more commonly termed patriotism today.

Germany 1815–1858

The German Confederation, 1815

Germany as a single country did not exist until 1871. Before the nineteenth century the area known as Germany consisted of over 350 different states, loosely linked by a common language. Some of the states were large kingdoms, such as Prussia and Austria, and others were little more than a city, ruled by noblemen. Together they formed part of the massive Holy Roman Empire, which also included extensive Austrian territories. This Empire, though vast, had little bearing on the states of which it was formed; it had no real political significance and disappeared after Napoleon invaded and defeated Austria and Prussia in 1805-6.

By the time of his own defeat in 1815, Napoleon had changed Germany for good. The hundreds of individual states had been reduced to just thirty-nine, although the largest two remained Austria and Prussia. In the Vienna Settlement of 1815, the German Confederation (Bund) was established, using the boundaries of the old Holy Roman Empire. This Confederation did not signal a unification of German people, not least because non-Germans were included – such as Italians – while groups of German-speakers were excluded (see Source 5). It was a federation of states rather than a federal state. In other words, the individual states remained independent and there was no overall head of the confederation. The Federal Diet which met at Frankfurt and was supposed to be the main decision-making body of the Confederation was really a chance for individual states to protect their own interests. Decisions were rarely made, as they depended on the unanimous approval of the member states.

> **Key term**
>
> **Federal**
> Where individual states are bound to a central government but also keep some of their own powers.

The main player in the creation of the Confederation was Prince Metternich, Foreign Minister of Austria. He saw Austria as the dominant influence in the Confederation. The idea of the Confederation was not to encourage unification. In fact, the intention of Metternich was the exact opposite. With an Austrian Empire full of different ethnic groups, the last thing he wanted to encourage was nationalism. If Germans were to unite then perhaps the Slovaks, Hungarians, Serbs, Croats and other groups in the Austrian Empire would also demand independent states.

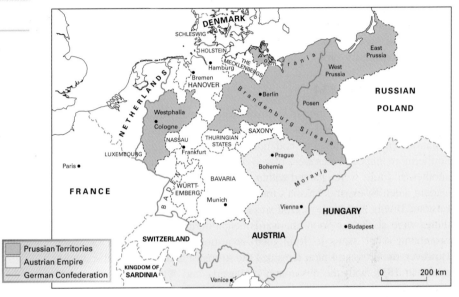

Note

The Austrian Empire contained all the lands ruled by the ruling house of Austria, but also Hungary, parts of modern day Italy and regions that have since become independent, such as the Czech Republic.

Source 5

▶ The German Confederation.

In fact, the calls for German unification at this point were muted and mainly restricted to the middle class. It was true, however, that the years of Napoleonic rule had encouraged the growth of two ideologies; nationalism and liberalism. Liberals were often nationalists, although the reverse was not always the case.

Key term

Liberalism
Belief in individual rights and freedom. Liberals supported free trade.

Source 6

... happiness and pleasure are not the highest aims of the people, but freedom. That is the will of God and reason ... the happiness and the greatness of a people depend only on the highest possible liberty of all citizens and the equality of all, established by laws they make themselves or that are made by their representatives ... An enthusiastic people which is willing to fight for such laws and for such a fatherland cannot be conquered ... and the most beautiful of all: Germans we are all together! ... that wonderful people from the Weichsel to the Vosges, from the North Sea over the Alps to Carpathia, made equal through speech, customs, and descent, all citizens of the Reich – a unified people of brothers is irresistible.

Extract from a speech by a nineteen-year-old student in 1820

■ Think about

▶ How does Source 6 combine both liberalism and nationalism?

In 1819, a member of a nationalist student group murdered Kotzebue, an anti-liberal playwright with Russian connections. This prompted Metternich to issue the Karlsbad decrees which imposed tighter control on education and censorship of publications less than 320 sides long. This latter measure led, not surprisingly, to successions of dull and excessively long books, whose length had been pointlessly extended in order to avoid censorship! The whole episode illustrated how fiercely Metternich opposed both liberalism and nationalism and in this attitude he was, for now, supported by Prussia.

Although Austria was the strongest, most dominant member of the Confederation, the territorial settlement at the Vienna Conference prepared the way for future changes to the balance of power. Prussia's population more than doubled with the acquisition of land to the west, including the Rhineland and Westphalia. Such gains brought with them better supplies of raw materials and more advanced industry. They also shifted Prussia's field of vision into the heart of Germany, as they came at the expense of losing Polish territory to Russia. This enabled Prussia, as the century progressed, to dominate Germany in a way that Austria could not. From now on, lesser German states would tend to look to Prussia for protection and not Austria.

The Zollverein, 1834

The complicated organization of Germany with its many independent states did little to promote internal trade within the Confederation. There was no common currency and no common system of weights and measures. Furthermore, import duties were placed on goods transported from one state to another, and tolls were charged within the states themselves. In 1818, Prussian leaders, keen to expand Prussia's trade and industry, established the Prussian Customs Union. A single, low tariff was charged at Prussia's border and internal duties were abolished. Soon afterwards neighbouring states joined this union, prompting other states to form their own unions elsewhere in Germany. However, the Prussian Union remained the strongest and gradually absorbed its rivals. In 1834, with the absorption of Bavaria and Wurttemberg, the union became known as the Zollverein (Customs Union). By 1836, the Zollverein included 25 states and a population of 26 million.

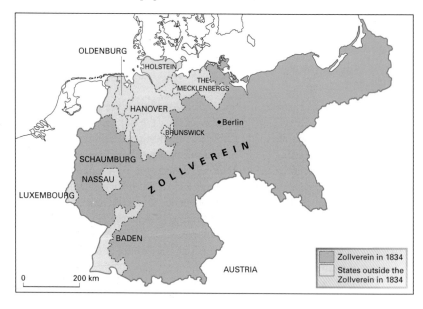

Think about

▶ Can you suggest any possible reasons why Austria was not included in the Zollverein?

Source 7

◀ The Zollverein.

Significantly, the Zollverein excluded Austria. In fact, Austria was invited to join it in the early stages but it refused, as it supported high tariffs, and in any case had a large home market of its own. Prussia, it has been argued, saw its opportunity to establish economic control over the Confederation and alienate Austria in its first step towards dominance over Germany. Certainly, the Zollverein greatly enhanced Prussia's influence over German affairs, to the extent that Austria later tried to join it. The Zollverein became a focal point for

German nationalism. If, nationalists argued, economic unity worked to everyone's advantage, why not go the next step and secure political unity as well? Whilst most historians acknowledge the important contribution the Zollverein made towards unification, not all of them believe that it inevitably led to such a development. The member states of the Zollverein remained protective of their own political independence, which was, if anything, increased by the boost to their revenues after 1834. In addition, many were still hostile to Prussia, and indeed fought against her in 1866.

Revolution, 1848–1849

1848 was a year of revolution in Europe. It started in France, where the French king, Louis Philippe, fled to England after students and workers took to the streets in Paris. News of the February Revolution spread quickly and provided the spark which ignited the passions of those in Germany who wanted change. The violent protests came from peasants and workers who demanded improvements to their daily lives. Hardship was common. In the Prussian countryside, much of the land was owned by the Junkers, who exploited their peasant labourers. Even where peasants were able to rent land, the cost was high. Bad harvests in 1846 and 1847 had not helped, and proved particularly disastrous in the context of a rising population.

Workers in the towns fared no better. The rising population led to overcrowded and unhygienic living conditions and conditions in the factories were equally squalid. The poor harvests raised the price of food and a recession in the textile industry in 1847 led to further difficulties. In such conditions, protests were by no means uncommon, even before 1848, but they were given more impetus by the events in France.

Rulers throughout Germany hastily made concessions to the revolutionaries. However, it was a different group that exploited the violence for political ends. The middle classes had grown in numbers and wealth by 1848, but were denied greater political power by the nobility who were fiercely protective of their privileges. Therefore it was among the middle classes that liberalism and nationalism had developed, and the time seemed ripe to pursue these aims more actively. Calls for an assembly to discuss and prepare for German unification were successful. The Diet of the Confederation agreed to be replaced by a '*Vorparlament*' or 'pre-parliament' and this body of 596 men met at Frankfurt in May 1848. Their common backgrounds and broadly common aims, however, concealed many different shades of opinion.

One of the key issues on which they disagreed was the boundary of this united Germany. There were two options. The first was to include German-speaking Austria (*Grossdeutschland* – Big Germany) and the second was to exclude it, leaving Prussia as the dominant state (*Kleindeutschland* – Little Germany). Slowly, after much discussion, a smaller Germany emerged as the favourite. By March 1849, the Frankfurt Parliament proposed a Constitution for a German Empire. The crown of this new Germany was offered to the King of Prussia, who refused to accept a thing 'moulded out of the dirt and dregs of revolution, disloyalty and treason'. What right, he argued, did these common men have to offer a king another crown? He was not the only ruler to reject the Constitution; the rulers of Saxony, Bavaria and Hanover did the same.

Why did the Frankfurt Parliament fail? On one level, it was because the rulers regained their confidence after the fright of 1848 and used the Prussian and Austrian armies to strengthen their position. On another level, however, it was because the liberals lacked the necessary backing. They were themselves afraid

Key term

Junkers

Prussian aristocrats from east of the River Elbe.

Note

Most of the members of the Frankfurt Parliament were middle class. In fact, its members were unusually well qualified – over 80% had university degrees. Most were teachers, lawyers, and professors and there were some writers and clergymen. Out of the 596 members, just 4 were artisans and one was a peasant, who was further disadvantaged by being a Pole from Silesia.

Quotation

The weaknesses of revolutionary forces in Germany were…evident from the start: it took a spark from outside to ignite the revolution; there was a range of forces with different aims exerting pressure on the regimes… Having withdrawn from the fray, rather than being defeated, conservative forces were able to observe the disarray and flailings of the revolutionary groups, and later to return to take control of the situation with their armed forces intact, and even strengthened by concessions to peasant demands.

Fulbrook, *A Concise History of Germany*, 1990

of the violence on the streets and could hardly claim to represent the protesters. One of the messages that north German liberals took away from this episode was the importance of securing Prussia's backing for any future unification proposal.

Why did Prussia grow in strength after 1850?

Meanwhile, the Prussian government took steps, in May 1849, to ensure that any further moves towards German union would be under its control. The Erfurt Union, consisting of Prussia, Saxony and Hanover, was led by Prussia, and membership was open to the other German states. Its purpose was to explore the issue of unification, but it failed, however, largely through Austrian opposition. In 1851 the German Confederation (still dominated by Austria) was fully re-established and Prussia was forced to abandon alternative unification plans which Austria found unacceptable. However, Austria's triumph was short-lived as she was soon facing problems elsewhere. While the economy of the German Confederation as a whole flourished, Austria's did not (Source 8). In an increasingly industrial age, Austria's vast agricultural areas held back economic growth. In addition, her taxation system was outdated. Furthermore, Austria's involvement in military disputes with Italy and south-eastern Europe led to high expenditure on the army. In desperation, Austria attempted both to link her empire with the Zollverein and also to break the Zollverein up, but most of the German states preferred things as they were and Austrian plans were rejected.

Austria also lost an important ally during this period. During the Crimean War (1854–1856), Austria wavered between offering her support to Russia and to Britain and France. By the end of the war she had alienated Russia without securing the backing of either Britain or France and was, therefore, left isolated.

Meanwhile, Prussia went from strength to strength. Its industrial growth far outstripped that of Austria and in the space of ten years it doubled, as indeed did foreign trade.

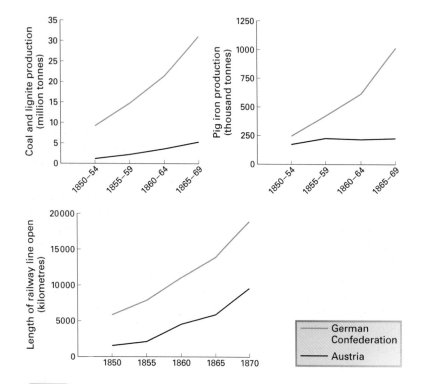

■ **Think about**

▶ How did the economic growth of the German Confederation and Austria differ?

▶ What impact do you think this had on relations between the German Confederation and Austria?

Note

Another factor in Prussia's growing economy was her advanced education system. Elementary education had been made compulsory in 1812 and soon afterwards, technical institutions were established.

Source 9

▲ The Prussian War Minister, von Roon.

■ Activity

The year is 1862 and the English Ambassador to Prussia is preparing a report. This report is intended to inform politicians in England how powerful the state of Prussia currently is.

Your task is to write this report, remembering to be as specific as possible in the details you provide. Your report should include the following areas:

● The Prussian economy
● Prussia's territory
● The power and strength of the Prussian monarchy
● Prussia's strength compared to Austria's
● Whether you think there will be some sort of German unification soon.

How can we explain such rapid industrial growth? The answer lies in a number of factors all of which interlink. The Zollverein provided a large free-trade area in Germany which brought many advantages. Trade outside the Confederation also increased and the result was more money to invest in further industrial projects. Rich coal and iron resources enabled the mining industries to flourish and the newly built railways, themselves a product of expansion, further stimulated the economy because of the ease of transporting materials and goods. The Prussian government supported this industrial growth. For example, the government offered money to struggling industries.

Nationalism

While Prussia's economy became increasingly modern and forward-looking, politically she remained, by contrast, conservative and backward-looking. Manteuffel, the Prussian Prime Minister, governed without parliament and rejected all calls for a more representative, democratic political system. Despite this, the liberals won a large majority in the Prussian Parliament in 1858. A year later the National Association (*Nationalverein*) was founded to provide a platform for liberal discussions. It called for a centralized government led by Prussia in the place of the German Federal Diet. Their programme stated that 'In the present circumstances effective steps for the attainment of this aim can originate only with Prussia.' But how widespread was nationalism at this point? Although growing in middle-class circles and promoted through celebrations of German culture, it is unlikely that it ever really filtered down to the ordinary people. And whilst growing pressure from the liberals was a factor in unification, it can hardly be argued that unification came as the result of widespread, fervent nationalism throughout Germany.

Why was there a constitutional crisis in Prussia?

In 1858 King Friedrich Wilhelm IV suffered a series of strokes. His brother, Wilhelm, became regent and then King Wilhelm I when Friedrich Wilhelm died three years later. The new king was 64 years old and a devout Protestant, believing his power came from God. He was also a military man, convinced that a stronger army was essential to Prussia's greatness. When, in 1859, war broke out between France and Austria over the issue of a united Italy, a stronger Prussian army seemed even more crucial. With war on its doorstep, Prussia needed to be in a position to defend itself, and even exploit opportune circumstances. He asked the War Minister, von Roon, to strengthen the army and a bill was prepared to send to the Prussian Parliament in 1860. It proposed to increase the length of service in the army from two to three years and to abolish the Landwehr (a citizens' army, led mainly by middle-class officers). The cost of these changes would be high and the Parliament, now dominated by liberals, refused to approve a budget for the changes unless significant alterations were made. The new King was faced with a difficult decision. Either he abdicated or he accepted that Prussia's military affairs were beyond his control. He could tolerate neither option. This is what we describe as a 'constitutional crisis', when the constitution itself does not present any obvious solutions to such a deadlock. The only possible solution was to appoint a chief minister who might somehow be able to get the bill passed by the Prussian Parliament. Von Roon persuaded the King to meet the Prussian Ambassador to Paris and by the end of the meeting the King had a new Minister-President, Otto von Bismarck. It was 1862 and the beginning of a new era.

What were Bismarck's aims?

▲ Otto von Bismarck.

■ Historical debate

Historians have debated whether or not Bismarck had fixed aims. In his memoirs, which he wrote after he resigned his post in 1890, Bismarck creates the impression that he had a plan from the beginning. This may, however, be an attempt to enhance his own reputation. At the other extreme, the historian A.J.P. Taylor has argued that Bismarck improvized his policies day by day. There was no fixed plan, but Bismarck was brilliant at exploiting circumstances. Otto Pflanze, who has written a massive three-volume biography of Bismarck, proposes an alternative interpretation. While Bismarck had very real aims, he adopted what Pflanze terms a 'strategy of alternatives'. In other words, Bismarck kept his options open about how and when to achieve his aims.

Who was Bismarck?

Otto von Bismarck was born in 1815. His father was a Junker and a relatively uneducated man. His mother came from an educated middle-class background. She was intelligent and ambitious for her children and Bismarck was sent to boarding school at an unusually young age. Bismarck did not enjoy school. On leaving, he decided to study at Gottingen University where he was something of a misfit. He did not quite belong to either the aristocratic or the middle-class circles, though he chose the former. He disliked the lack of good manners and breeding amongst the middle class. He also disliked their seriousness. After university he entered the civil service. It was during this period that he fell desperately in love with an English girl, Isabella Loraine-Smith. He followed her around Germany and lost his job in the process, only to be jilted when she married someone else. He returned to the family estates which he ran successfully, despite his reputation as 'wild Bismarck' who had a liking for wine and women. During this time he read and travelled widely and continued to form his political ideas. The turning point came when he met Marie von Thadden in 1842. She was a devout Protestant and set out to 'save' Bismarck. He in turn was converted. Unfortunately, Marie died in an epidemic, an event which apparently had Bismarck praying for the first time in fifteen years. Soon afterwards he proposed to Marie's close friend, Johanna and she accepted. She provided Bismarck with the comfort and stability he needed. In 1847 Bismarck became a Deputy in the Prussian United Diet. A year later his defence of the old order during the revolution led to his first major political appointment, as the Prussian Representative at the Diet in Frankfurt. Here he played a significant role in trying to exclude Austria from German affairs. In 1857 he became the Prussian ambassador to St Petersburg in Russia and then to Paris. It was from here that he was summoned in 1862 to meet with King Wilhelm I of Prussia.

Source 10

'In many domestic and foreign affairs and questions,' wrote a contemporary, 'Prince Bismarck likes to provide himself with an alternative in order to be able to decide the same in one of two opposed directions.' Frequently these alternatives were multiple solutions to a single political problem that could be simultaneously explored until the moment of final choice. Often they were multiple possibilities of alliance with opposed political forces between which a final choice had to be avoided as long as possible. In its many variations, the strategy of alternatives provided Bismarck with a means of navigating amid the shifting currents and treacherous eddies of the time stream. It enabled him to gain and retain the initiative. The knowledge that his quiver held more than one arrow gave him the confidence and sureness that most of his opponents lacked.

Pflanze, *Bismarck and the Development of Germany Vol I*, 1990

Source 11

Did he [Bismarck] foresee it [German unification] himself? Of all questions in Bismarck's career this is the most difficult to answer. He was always emphatic that he could not make events. He said once: 'Politics are not a science based on logic; they are the capacity of always choosing at each instant, in constantly changing situations, the least harmful, the most useful,'…When someone praised his direction of events between 1862-1871, he pointed to many mistakes that he had made and said: 'I wanted it like this, and everything happened quite differently. I'm content when I see where the Lord wishes to go and can stumble after him.' Was this false modesty?…Certainly there is not a scrap of evidence that he worked deliberately for a war with France, still less that he timed it precisely for the summer of 1870.

Taylor, *Bismarck, The Man and The Statesman*, 1955

Source 12

Bismarck was at pains always to insist that war for him was only a final resort, to be avoided thankfully if the desired result could be achieved by other means…On the other hand, at no time so far as is known, did he ask himself whether the very fact that his aims could be achieved only by war did not put a question-mark against those aims.

What, in the autumn of 1862, was it that he wanted to achieve? It is doubtful whether at this stage he had any more specific or distant aim than reducing Austria's pretensions [claims] to the leadership of Germany, and setting up some sort of North German Union dominated by Prussia.

Crankshaw, *Bismarck*, 1981

Source 13

'I shall soon', said in effect the Prussian statesman, 'be compelled to undertake the conduct of the Prussian Government. My first care will be to organize the army, with or without the help of the Landtag [Prussian Parliament]. The King was right in undertaking this task, but he cannot accomplish it with his present advisers. As soon as the army have been brought into such a condition as to inspire respect, I shall seize the first best pretext to declare war against Austria, dissolve the German Diet, subdue the minor states, and give national unity to Germany under Prussian leadership.'

Bismarck in conversation with Disraeli, a British politician, in 1862. The account comes from Count Eckstadt, the Saxon Ambassador to London

Source 14

…Prussia must gather and consolidate her strength in readiness for the favourable moment, which has already been missed several times; Prussia's boundaries according to the Vienna treaties are not favourable to a healthy political life; not by means of speeches and majority verdicts will the great decisions of the time be made – that was the great mistake of 1848 and 1849 – but by iron and blood…

Bismarck's speech to the Prussian Parliament, 1862

■ Questions

1 How do Sources 10, 11 and 12 differ in their interpretation of Bismarck's aims?

2 What light, if any, do Sources 13 and 14 shed on Bismarck's aims?

3 Can you suggest any reasons why historians hold different views on the question of Bismarck's aims?

■ Activity

You will need to read the rest of this chapter before attempting this activity.

Re-read the 'Historical Debate' box and Source 11. Your task is to write a review of A.J.P. Taylor's book for a historical journal. Using the information on these two pages and the rest of the chapter, you need to decide whether or not you agree with Taylor's argument. You must back up your reason with evidence. Remember that your intended audience will want to know if the book is worth reading!

How did Germany become united?

The problem with the Liberals

Bismarck's first task as Minister-President was to resolve the constitutional crisis over the army bill. In his memoirs he recounted his promise to King Wilhelm I:

Source 15

I succeeded in convincing him [the King] that, so far as he was concerned, it was not a question of liberal or conservative of this or that shade, but rather monarchical rule or parliamentary rule, and that the latter must be avoided at all costs, if even by a period of dictatorship. I said; 'in this situation I shall, even if your majesty command me to do things which I do not consider right, tell you my opinion quite openly; but if you finally persist in yours, I will rather perish with the King than forsake your majesty in the contest with parliamentary government.'

■ Further reading

As you can see from the previous spotlight, there are many biographies of Bismarck. Shorter biographies include:
Waller, *Bismarck*, 1985
Abrams, *Bismarck and the German Empire 1871–1918*, 1995

Bismarck addressed the crisis in a typically ruthless and uncompromising fashion. He argued that there was no provision within the Constitution for resolving disputes between the two houses of parliament. The matter was therefore for the King to decide. The army bill was never passed but was nevertheless implemented and funded through the collection of taxes. Relations between Bismarck and the liberals deteriorated and, by the end of 1863, Bismarck had practically established a dictatorship in Prussia. The liberals were still powerful, however, and won a large majority in the 1863 election. It took two successful wars to convince them to support Bismarck, an outcome that was perhaps not entirely unplanned. Although Bismarck had clear foreign policy aims in 1862, he also began to appreciate that internal unity was an important by-product of successful wars.

Source 16

◀ A cartoon from a liberal magazine. Bismarck is holding the Prussian Constitution and saying that he cannot rule with it.

■ Think about

▶ What point is the cartoonist in Source 16 trying to make?

▶ Why is it significant that this cartoon comes from a liberal magazine?

▶ What strikes you about Bismarck's use of the word "rule"?

Schleswig-Holstein

The two duchies of Schleswig-Holstein (see Source 5) were autonomous (self-governing) but under Danish sovereignty. Holstein contained mainly Germans and was part of the German Confederation, whilst Schleswig contained a mixture of Germans and Danes and was outside the Confederation. In 1863 King Frederick of Denmark died, leaving no immediate heirs. As agreed by the Great Powers in 1852, he was succeeded by Christian of Glucksburg whose

Note

This was agreed by Britain, France, Russia, Prussia, Austria and Sweden.

Note

The British politician, Palmerston, made the joke that only three people ever understood the Schleswig-Holstein issue: Prince Albert who was dead, a German professor who had gone mad and Palmerston himself, who had forgotten what it was about anyway.

Quotation

I am certainly no Bismarck enthusiast, but he has the ability to act... I look forward to the future with pleasure. There is something invigorating, after fifty years of peace, in a day like the battle of Dupple [against the Danes] for the young Prussian troops. One feels as if all one's nerves had been refreshed.

Extract from a letter written by a German Liberal, April 1864

Note

Bismarck was fortunate in 1866; Russia was unlikely to support Austria and an alliance with Italy was concluded. Bismarck somehow managed to secure the neutrality of France, although Napoleon III was signalling his support to both Prussia and Austria. However, it was not Napoleon's intention at this point to become involved in a war. He was much more interested in securing the best territorial position for France.

Note

The Prussian victory at Koniggratz was not a foregone conclusion, despite Prussia's military superiority. A recent interpretation suggests that the outcome was partly dependent on the blunders of the Austrian command.

right to become King arose from his marriage to King Frederick's first cousin. Holstein refused to accept Christian on the grounds that his inheritance came through the female line. Meanwhile, Christian annexed Schleswig to the Danish crown. The Federal Diet demanded armed intervention but Bismarck called instead for joint action by Prussia and Austria alone.

The Danes were quickly defeated and, in the Treaty of Vienna in October 1864, they surrendered all rights to both duchies. However, Austria and Prussia held different views about the next step. Austria would have been happy to see the duchies remain autonomous, whereas Bismarck clearly had plans to annex the territories to Prussia. An agreement (the Gastein Treaty) was finally reached in 1865. Holstein would be administered by Austria and Schleswig would be governed by Prussia. At Austria's insistence, the duchies would remain under a joint sovereignty, thereby preventing full annexation to Prussia. Reluctant to go to war with Austria at this point, Bismarck accepted the decision. It was clear, however, that he expected further tensions to follow which would provide him with an opportunity to resolve the Austrian issue.

War with Austria

Tensions did indeed continue over the duchies of Schleswig and Holstein and Bismarck made clear at a meeting of the Prussian Crown Council that war against Austria was inevitable. Bismarck had planned for this confrontation for some time. 'Germany is clearly too small for us both' he had written in 1856. In 1866 the time was right not only to settle the disputes over the duchies but also to settle the future of Germany. The Prussian army, under the command of General von Moltke, was well trained and well equipped. In addition, it seemed highly unlikely that either Britain or Russia – still smarting after Austria's actions in the Crimean War – would get involved.

In April 1866, Bismarck concluded a secret alliance with Italy. He also increased tensions by proposing a new constitution to the Federal Diet which he knew would be unacceptable to the Austrians. Meanwhile, the majority of the smaller German states rallied to the Austrian cause, fearing Prussian domination. The years of economic union did not appear to have increased their support for Prussia.

In June, Austria broke the Gastein Treaty by placing the Schleswig-Holstein question under the control of the Federal Diet. Prussia responded by occupying Holstein. Surprised that this alone did not provoke a declaration of war, Bismarck presented a fuller version of his proposal to reform the Federal Constitution. Austria now called on members of the Confederation to mobilize their armies. Prussia declared the end of the German Confederation and her troops advanced.

Within seven weeks, the Austrian army was defeated at Koniggratz. Bismarck had no wish to go any further and had to restrain the King who wished to inflict more wounds on Austria and win Austrian territories. This, in Bismarck's view, would encourage Austria to ally with any potential enemy of Prussia, especially France. Bismarck, in tears, presented the King with an ultimatum: either war should end or he would resign. Finally, a peace settlement was agreed at Prague in August. No Austrian land was annexed by Prussia although Venetia was surrendered to the Italians. Prussia did, however, annexe Schleswig-Holstein, Hanover, Hesse-Kassel, Nassau and the city of Frankfurt, all of which had supported Austria in the war. Austria was forced to accept Prussian dominance in Germany and agreed to the creation of a North German Confederation.

Not only had Bismarck achieved his aim of dominance over Austria. The war had also brought about the collapse of the liberals' vote in the election of 1866. Bismarck finally ended the conflict over the army bill in Parliament by persuading the King to admit he was at fault and by successfully requesting Parliament's approval for his actions over the previous four years (see note). Even the liberals accepted such a move in the wake of military victory and with the prospect of unification.

Bismarck had gained significant victories, both inside and outside Prussia. But which victory had he put first in his planning?

Source 17

The war of 1866 was entered on not because the existence of Prussia was threatened, nor was it caused by public opinion and the voice of the people...but for an ideal end – the establishment of power...Prussia felt itself called upon and strong enough to assume the leadership of the German races.

Field Marshal Helmut von Moltke, 1866

Source 18

It had been he [Bismarck] who had possessed the temerity [cheek] to break with the traditions of Prussian diplomacy and to choose an anti-Austrian policy as the means of dividing the parliamentary opposition that was threatening to paralyse the Prussian Government when he came to power in September 1862...

Craig, *Germany 1866–1945*, 1981

The North German Confederation 1867

What had Bismarck achieved through war with Austria? Prussia now controlled four-fifths of the population, and most of the territory, north of the River Main. The annexation of Hanover, Nassau, Hesse-Kassel, Schleswig-Holstein and Frankfurt was carried out in a brutal fashion. They were not consulted at any stage and as one historian points out 'It was not unification, but conquest' (Stiles, 1986). However, there remained independent states in north Germany which were outside of direct Prussian control (Saxony was the most significant). These states were forced to become part of the North German Confederation which covered all of Germany north of the Main and was controlled by Prussia. This Confederation was probably never an end in itself, however. It was another important step towards unification of the whole of Germany. It was also, in its exclusion of Austria, a symbol of Prussian dominance. If Germany was to be united, then it would surely be under Prussian control.

The Constitution of the North German Confederation

The Constitution of the North German Confederation outlived the Confederation itself. It became the basis for the Constitution of the German Empire of 1871 and is, therefore, worthy of some comment. Bismarck worked hard to produce a constitution which would prevent a system of parliamentary rule but would provide enough popular participation in government to satisfy the liberals. He also worked hard to ensure Prussian dominance of the Confederation whilst reassuring the northern (and indirectly, southern) states that their independence would not be destroyed.

Note

The King was persuaded by Bismarck to accept an indemnity bill. This provided the Prussian Parliament's approval for all government expenditure for the previous four years. Historians have since criticized the liberals for agreeing to the bill, but in reality they had little choice. They agreed with Bismarck's economic and foreign policy and wanted to support any moves in the direction of unification.

■ Think about

▶ Do Sources 17 and 18 agree on the main motives behind war with Austria?

▶ From your own knowledge, what do you consider to have been Bismarck's main motive behind war with Austria?

Cross reference

See Source 21 on page 26 for a map showing the North German Confederation.

The new Constitution

Presidency President Chancellor Ministers	The King of Prussia was also President of the Confederation, and had the armed forces of the states under his supreme command. He was responsible for foreign affairs, declarations of war and dismissal of ministers. The Chancellor (Bismarck) was answerable only to the President.
BUNDESRAT (Federal Council) Representatives selected by each member state	States were allotted votes according to their size. Prussia had 17 votes out of 43 – not a majority but enough to prevent changes to the Constitution (which required a two-thirds majority). It initiated legislation (laws). It was led by the Chancellor.
REICHSTAG (Chamber of Deputies) 297 deputies voted in by universal male suffrage (all men over 25)	Deputies received no salary so tended to be wealthy. They had the right to veto legislation but not to initiate it. The liberals won two concessions: a secret ballot in elections and control over the annual budget. The latter was not a significant victory – most of the budget was spent on the army and was outside the Reichstag's control. It did win *some* control over the army though – from 1872, the amount spent on the army would be fixed by law.

■ Think about

▶ Who held the most power within the Constitution?

▶ How democratic was the Constitution? In other words, how much power did ordinary Germans have?

▶ Do you think the individual states would have been happy with their position in the Constitution?

Note

The four southern states outside the North German Confederation were:
- Baden
- Württemberg
- Hesse
- Bavaria

The Confederation was responsible for defence, foreign policy and economic matters such as customs and banking. The individual states kept their own rulers, their own parliaments and their own laws. Local taxation could be raised to pay for government services including education.

The Franco-Prussian War

The failure of economic union

There was still the issue of the southern states however. There was little support in these areas for a Prussian-dominated Germany and they defended their right to remain independent. The term used to describe this is particularism. Bismarck had used the Prague settlement to ensure that the southern states could not support either France or Austria against Prussia. Clauses were inserted into the peace treaties which put the armies and railways of the states under Prussian control in times of war. Quite why they accepted this is unsure, but it may have been due to their own distrust of France. In any case, it meant that the southern states were no longer a potential threat to Bismarck. He decided not to force the southern states to unite with the north at this point. It is probable that Bismarck hoped that economic unity would eventually lead to political unity.

The four southern states were allowed to join the Zollverein and, in June 1867, Bismarck forced them to accept a new Zollparlament (customs union parliament). This organization would be dominated by Prussia and would include members of the North German Reichstag and elected members of the southern states. However, if Bismarck hoped that this would smooth the path to political unity he was mistaken. Elections for the Zollparlament in the southern states produced a overwhelming majority of deputies who opposed political union. It was becoming clear that the evolution of political unity out of economic unity would take considerable time. Was Bismarck prepared to wait? Historians have disagreed about Bismarck's plans at this point. Did he see a war against France as the only way of luring the southern states into the

Confederation? His famous words at the time, in 1869, are perhaps the best indication of his intentions:

Source 19

That German unity could be promoted by actions involving force I think is self-evident. But there is a quite different question, and that has to do with the precipitation of a powerful catastrophe and the responsibility of choosing the time for it. A voluntary intervention in the evolution of history...results only in the shaking down of unripe fruit, and that German unity is no ripe fruit at this time leaps, in my opinion, to the eye. If the time that lies ahead works in the interest of unity as much as the period since the accession of Frederick the Great has done...then we can look to the future calmly and leave the rest to our successors...

Extract from a dispatch by Bismarck to the Prussian envoy in February 1869

■ Think about

▶ What was Bismarck's view of unification in 1869, according to Source 19?

▶ A year after this dispatch, Bismarck used a war against France as a way of speeding up unification. Does this mean that he was lying to the Prussian envoy?

Luxembourg: a dress rehearsal for war?

Napoleon III was eager to acquire territory on the west bank of the River Rhine, land that had formerly belonged to the French. He was disappointed that his neutrality in Prussia's war against Austria had not brought him any further towards this goal. Bismarck wanted, at this point, to keep the support of France. Apart from anything else, the Prussian army was not in a good enough state to face the French in a war. He pointed Napoleon away from the Rhine and towards Luxembourg. Luxembourg was a duchy under the sovereignty of the King of Holland but had also been made part of the German Confederation in 1815.

Napoleon succeeded in persuading the King of Holland to relinquish Luxembourg. When news reached the Reichstag there was uproar at the thought of France simply taking land which contained German speakers and which had Prussian troops stationed on it. Bismarck must have been prepared for this nationalist outburst and indeed may have encouraged it despite his earlier encouragement of Napoleon. However, he did not want to fight France and so he put the matter in the hands of the Great Powers. In London it was decided that Prussia should withdraw its troops stationed in Luxembourg (a significant gain for France) but that the duchy should remain independent of French control. This was, overall, a humiliating defeat for Napoleon.

What were Bismarck's aims in Luxembourg? To prevent the French from making territorial claims on Germany? Or to undermine French relations to the point where war was clearly on the cards? Or was he simply keeping all his options open?

■ Biography

Napoleon III

Emperor of France 1852-1870 and nephew of Napoleon Bonaparte. He was elected President in 1848 but staged a coup in 1851 which allowed him to remain as President for a further ten years. In 1852 he abolished the Second Republic and made himself Emperor of the Second Empire. He encouraged industrial expansion in an attempt to make France strong, but was unsuccessful in his foreign policy, especially against Prussia which defeated France in the Franco-Prussian War, 1870–71, leading to his abdication.

The Spanish Succession

An opportunity to provoke France – if this was indeed Bismarck's aim – came in 1870. Isabella, the Queen of Spain, had been forced to abdicate two years earlier. In 1870, the Spanish crown was offered to Prince Leopold, a member of the Prussian royal family. The prospect of a Hohenzollern on the Spanish throne was extremely alarming to France. Nevertheless, Bismarck pressured Leopold into accepting the crown in June 1870. This provoked France to such a degree that King Wilhelm in turn persuaded Leopold to step down, much to

Key term

Hohenzollern

The Hohenzollern dynasty ruled Prussia from 1701 to 1918 and the German Empire from 1871 to 1918.

Bismarck's distress. This was not enough to avert war, however. Gramont, the French Foreign Minister, insisted that Wilhelm should renounce Leopold's claim permanently which the Prussian King, independently of Bismarck, refused to do.

Bismarck received a telegram from the King outlining his meeting with the French Ambassador to Prussia, Benedetti, who had been sent by Gramont to put pressure on Wilhelm. The telegram became known as the Ems Telegram after the town of Bad Ems where the meeting took place. Although Bismarck did not add anything to the telegram, he edited words out to give the impression of an even firmer snub of the French by Wilhelm. He then ensured that the amended telegram was published in Berlin and abroad. Bismarck had obtained guarantees from the southern states that they would support him in a war against France. He was now, if not before, expecting a war.

The war

The Ems Telegram was the final straw for the French, and Napoleon declared war on 15 July 1870. Bismarck was in a strong position. Austria felt no obligation to support France after being let down in 1866. Nor was she prepared to risk a war without the support of Italy, who posed a threat to her southern borders. The German army (to all intents and purposes the Prussian army) was also in very good shape. Morale was high, leadership skilful and equipment effective, especially the new Krupp field batteries.

In September, after a series of swift victories, Moltke saw his chance to surround the French forces at Sedan. The French lost more than twice as many men as Germany and Napoleon III was captured. Despite this crushing defeat, France limped on until the fall of Paris in January 1871.

Source 20

▶ A woodcut from a painting by a German artist showing Napoleon III and Bismarck the day after Napoleon's capture by Bismarck at the Battle of Sedan. Bismarck is seated on the right.

Think about

▶ What impression of the French defeat does Source 20 convey?

The Treaty of Frankfurt, signed in May, was a harsh settlement for France. The French territories of Alsace-Lorraine were annexed to Germany (see Source 21) and an indemnity of five billion francs had to be paid over four years. This settlement ensured a lasting rivalry and hatred between the two countries. For the next thirty-eight years the French swore to seek revenge on Germany and regain the land France lost in 1871.

■ Historical debate

As we have already seen (pages 16–17) there is a debate about the nature of Bismarck's aims. It is difficult to deny that German unification was one of them (although at least one historian – **A.J.P. Taylor** – would challenge even this). Exactly how Bismarck intended to bring about unification is more difficult to pin down, however. Did Bismarck see a war against France as the only way? In his memoirs he wrote that 'a Franco-German war must take place before the construction of a united Germany could be realized' (Craig, 1981). This was, however, written with the benefit of hindsight and may have been an attempt by Bismarck to give his actions the impression of being well planned in advance. Other statements made at the time suggest that Bismarck was unsure about war, though was not ruling it out completely. His famous 'ripe fruit' speech (see Source 19) implied a wait-and-see policy. Not surprisingly, all this has led to a debate amongst historians. Some, such as **Eyck**, argue that Bismarck was indeed intending to fight France whilst others, such as **Kolb**, argue that France's reaction to the succession issue took Bismarck by surprise. **Craig** takes this even further by arguing that Bismarck did not want a war at all. **Carr** takes a moderate view, arguing that Bismarck was prepared to risk a war but tried to prevent it. A possible way through this debate is to remember **Otto Pflanze's** phrase 'a strategy of alternatives'. Perhaps it was a case of keeping all options open until the right option made itself clear.

> **Quotation**
>
> At least I am not so arrogant as to assume that the likes of us are able to make history. My task is to keep an eye on the currents of the latter and steer my ship in them as best I can.
>
> Bismarck

Document exercise: Bismarck and the war against France

Source A

War against France not certain

Unhappily I believe in a war with France before long – her vanity, hurt by our victories, will drive her in that direction. Yet, since I do not know of any French or German interest requiring a resort to arms, I do not see it as certain. Only a country's most vital interests justify embarking on war – only its honour, which is not to be confused with so-called prestige. No statesman has a right to begin a war simply because, in his opinion, it is inevitable in a given period of time…On the battlefield – and, what is far worse, in the hospitals – I have seen the flower of our youth struck down by wounds and disease…Such memories and sights would leave me without a moment's peace if I thought I had made the war for personal ambition or national vanity…You may rest assured that I shall never advise His Majesty to wage a war unless the most vital interests of the Fatherland require it.

Bismarck speaking to a conservative deputy in the Prussian Parliament in 1867

Source B

Bismarck amends the Ems Telegram

Having decided to resign, I invited [Roon] and Moltke to dine with me…both were greatly depressed…During our conversation I was informed that a telegram from Ems…was being deciphered…On a repeated examination of the document I lingered upon the authorisation of His Majesty, which included a command, immediately to communicate Benedetti's fresh demand and its rejection both to our ambassadors and the press. I put a few questions to Moltke as to the extent of his confidence in the state of our preparations, especially as to the time they would still require in order to meet this sudden risk of war. [Several] considerations, conscious and unconscious, strengthened my opinion that war could be avoided only at the cost of the honour of Prussia and of the national confidence in it. Under this conviction I made use of the royal authorisation communicated to me…to publish the contents of the telegram, and in the presence of my two guests I reduced the telegram by striking out words…

Bismarck, *The Man and the Statesman*, 1898

Source C

Bismarck reflects on the war

I assumed that a united Germany was only a question of time...I did not doubt that a Franco-German war must take place before the construction of a united Germany could be realised...I was at that time pre-occupied with the idea of delaying the outbreak of this war until our fighting strength should be increased.

Bismarck, *The Man and the Statesman*, 1898

Source D

Bismarck wanted to avoid war

It is always dangerous to speak with too great assurance of Bismarck's intentions, but the explanation given here [that Bismarck believed French politicians would block a war] is certainly more reasonable than the argument, often made, that he was seeking war with France from the beginning of the Spanish question. Throughout his life, Bismarck was an opponent of preventive war...If the trumpets of war were to sound in the spring of 1870, the initiative in his view would have to be France's, and he was confident that in the prevailing circumstances Napoleon would not give the necessary command.

Craig, *Germany 1866-1945*, 1981

Source E

Bismarck did want war

I personally feel convinced that Bismarck undertook it [support of Leopold] with the intention of putting Napoleon in a formidable dilemma: either to suffer a political defeat which would in the long run cost him his throne, or to wage war – and that he foresaw that Napoleon would prefer war. Therefore, responsibility for the war rests in the first instance with Bismarck. He is of course, not the only person responsible...[but] Bismarck alone kept the initiative by knowing beforehand how the others would react to his moves.

Eyck, *Bismarck and the German Empire*, 1968

■ Examination-style questions

1 Comprehension in context
   Using Source B and your own knowledge explain why Bismarck edited the Ems Telegram.

2 Comparing the sources
   How and why do Sources D and E differ in their interpretation of Bismarck's aims?

3 Assessing the sources
   How useful are Sources A and C when assessing Bismarck's aims?

4 Making judgements
   'Bismarck planned to use a war against France in order to unite Germany.' Using all the sources and your own knowledge, explain whether or not you agree with this statement.

■ Activity

Return to the Spotlight on pages 16–17. You now know enough about Bismarck to complete the activity.

Unification

Between the battle of Sedan and the fall of Paris, enthusiasm for the war amongst the southern states waned. Bismarck was concerned that they might withdraw their support. At the same time the southern states were increasingly of the opinion that they could not afford to remain isolated with such hostility between Germany and France. Having supported Bismarck, they were vulnerable to French reprisals. It was therefore useful for all concerned to see further political unity in Germany. One historian has claimed that unification was not planned before the war and that Bismarck '...pushed the south German states into the Reich not at all with a vision of a distant future, but solely to keep them in the war.' (Taylor, 1966) An alternative interpretation is that Bismarck, whether planning a war with France in advance or not, saw an opportunity once war had started to push for unification. He saw his opportunity to achieve his long-term ambition more quickly than might otherwise have been expected.

Source 21

◀ The unification of Germany 1867–1871.

One thing is certain, however. Although the war against France had aroused nationalist passions, the unification was carried out for practical rather than ideological reasons:

Source 22

On 18 January 1871, in a ceremony at Versailles, the German Empire was proclaimed, with rulers of the German states offering King Wilhelm I of Prussia the hereditary crown of a united Germany. Whatever nationalist mythology may subsequently have claimed, there was a great deal of grumpiness on all sides: reluctance on the part of princes, as well as a certain sulkiness on the part of the new Emperor himself. What had been engineered, under Bismarck's guidance, was effectively the extension of Prussian power rather than the expression of nationalist enthusiasm for a united Germany.

Fulbrook, *A Concise History of Germany*, 1990

Why was Germany united in 1871?

Timeline

1815 The Vienna Settlement
The German Confederation
created

1818 Prussian Customs Union set up

1834 The Zollverein (Customs
Union) created

1848 Revolution
Frankfurt Parliament fails to unite
Germany

1851 The German Confederation re-
established

1854–6 The Crimean War

1858 King Friedrich Wilhelm IV
replaced by his brother Wilhelm
as regent

1859 The Nationalverein founded

1860 von Roon presents the army
bill to the Prussian Landtag
(Parliament) which leads to a
constitutional crisis

1861 Wilhelm becomes King of
Prussia, aged 64

1862 Bismarck appointed Minister–
President of Prussia

1863 Bismarck practically establishes
dictatorship in Prussia

1864 Denmark defeated by Prussia

1865 Gastein Treaty – Prussia and
Austria agree to share Schleswig-
Holstein

1866 Austria defeated by Prussia

1867 North German Confederation
established
Indemnity bill ends the
constitutional crisis
Southern states join the Zollverein
Luxembourg crisis

1870 Spanish crown offered to
Prince Leopold
Ems Telegram
War with France

1871 Unification of Germany
France defeated by
Prussia/Germany
Treaty of Frankfurt

Further reading

You might like to follow up
Sheehan's argument in his book
German History 1770–1866, 1989.

■ Activity

Historians have disagreed about the relative importance of different factors contributing to German unification. German historians initially stressed the greatness of Bismarck. By 1919, however, a British economist, Keynes, was already challenging this with his statement 'The German Empire was not founded on blood and iron, but on coal and iron'.

In small groups, take one of the factors listed below and prepare a short presentation on its contribution to German unification. Try to convince the other groups that your factor was the most important. At the end of the presentations, take a class vote on the order of importance of all the factors.

● Bismarck

● Economy

● Prussian army

● Nationalism & liberalism

● Other countries (especially France and Austria)

Conclusions

Many factors contributed to the unification of Germany. The growing strength of Prussia, both economically and politically, was a major factor – perhaps *the* major factor. However, circumstances outside Germany also played a major role and enabled Bismarck to achieve unification sooner than perhaps even he expected. War against France certainly determined the timing of unification and in this respect, it could indeed be argued that Germany was united by 'blood and iron'. Historians are still arguing about whether or not German unification was inevitable. Most agree with Fulbrook (see Source 22) and argue that it was not. James Sheehan, for example, argues that it came as a surprise and a shock. Thomas Nipperdey, however, argues that unification was part of a natural and inevitable process and would have happened without Bismarck. For him, German unification was the result of increased German identity during the nineteenth century. On the whole, the evidence does not support Nipperdey. Germany did not unite because of popular pressure from the German people. It united because the smaller German states felt that they had little choice.

Chapter 2

Bismarck 1871–1890

Source 1

Source 2

Although his body was laid to rest, Bismarck's spirit has continued to haunt German history. Historians have argued over his achievements and his reputation, his motives and his methods. For most historians the unification of Germany has meant Bismarck. Innumerable books have been written about him. By 1895, five years after his resignation, there were already 650 biographies available. Twenty years later there were 3500 and the number has gone on increasing ever since.

Stiles, *The Unification of Germany 1815–90*, 1986

◀ A German cartoon from a liberal magazine in 1875 showing Bismarck as a weary Atlas supporting the burden of Germany. The German people in the foreground are saying that 'He cannot leave', and France and the Papacy in the background are looking pleased.

Introduction

In 1871 Germany became an Empire. In charge of this new Empire was Otto von Bismarck, Minister-President of Prussia and now Chancellor of Germany, a title he held until his resignation in 1890. Bismarck had already established a formidable reputation in Prussia. During the nineteen years as Chancellor, he asserted his own wishes and own particular methods just as completely over the new Empire. He was generally regarded as one of Europe's greatest statesmen by 1890. At home, he was less popular and few mourned his resignation. Nevertheless, he had achieved many of his aims. He had kept Germany out of war and had avoided unfavourable alliances being made against her. He had encouraged Germany to continue her industrial expansion and kept political power firmly in the hands of the Kaiser and the aristocracy. Not all of these seem like achievements to us now, however. Indeed, Bismarck's legacy has been debated at length by historians ever since the end of the Second World War. The chief question which has been asked is to what extent did Bismarck make Hitler's regime possible?

In this chapter, however, we concentrate on Bismarck's achievements and failures in his own time.

■ Think about

▶ How was Bismarck regarded by the German people, according to Source 1?

▶ Look carefully at the figures in Source 1. Do you think this cartoon is meant to represent the view of all German people?

Key questions

● How was the German Empire governed?
● What were Bismarck's aims in his domestic and foreign policy?
● How was Germany changing?
● Who opposed Bismarck and why?
● What were Bismarck's methods in his domestic and foreign policy?
● How successful was Bismarck?
● What was Bismarck's legacy?

A united Germany?

The unification of 1871

On 18 January 1871, King Wilhelm of Prussia became Kaiser Wilhelm I of a united Germany. The ceremony took place at the grand palace of Versailles. The German Empire consisted of 25 states and one administrative territory (the newly acquired Alsace-Lorraine). It was a joining together of the North German Confederation and four southern German states .

Note

The ceremony was held at Versailles, just outside Paris, to demonstrate that the war against France was effectively over and Germany had won.

To what extent did the ceremony at Versailles reflect a sense of pride and unity across those states which now shared a common name? Despite a common language and culture, Germany could hardly be described in 1871 as a country already 'united'. There was no national flag until 1892 nor a national anthem until 1919. Such was the lack of common national figures that artists generally had to carve statues of Bismarck for the country's monuments. Furthermore, there were important religious, ethnic and economic differences between the individual states. Protestantism, the most popular religion, was dominant in the north, whilst Catholicism was mainly found in the rural areas of the southwest and the Rhineland. Industrialization was most widespread in the north and west, whilst the economy of the south and east remained more agricultural. The Empire excluded German speakers (for example in Austria) and included non-German speakers (such as Poles and Danes). When Germany united in 1871 it was more the result of Prussian power than an expression of popular nationalism.

The Constitution of the Empire

The Constitution of the German Empire was modelled on that of the North German Confederation (see page 21). The differences were relatively minor and were designed to reassure the previously independent states, who feared a loss of their rights. The Bundesrat (Federal Council which represented the different states) now had greater authority. War could only be declared with its approval, rather than, as previously, under the sole authority of the King of Prussia. In addition, constitutional changes could be vetoed in the Bundesrat by 14 out of a total of 58 votes, rather than by two-thirds of the total votes as previously. This enabled the southern states to form a common front.

Individual states retained significant powers. They kept their own rulers, governments and parliaments and controlled the education, health and civil rights of their populations. Bavaria and Wurttemberg, amongst the last states to be included in a united Germany, were allowed to keep their own armies, even in peacetime. Germany was certainly a federal state:

Source 3

The constitutional position of the Federal Council [Bundesrat] in the North German Confederation, as well as in the German Empire, derives its peculiar character from the fact that its members are bound by the instructions issued to them by their governments and therefore do not, like the deputies in the Reichstag, represent the whole but only the state which nominated them.

Extract from a report by Bismarck to Wilhelm I, March 1871

Why were the individual German states given such important powers? Firstly, it was a way of reassuring the reluctant southern states and, therefore, of smoothing the transition to a united Germany. Secondly, it enabled Prussia, by far the largest and most powerful state, to assert its own wishes more effectively.

Without doubt, Prussia dominated the German Empire. The King of Prussia was also the German Kaiser, the Prussian Prime Minister was also the German Chancellor and the Prussian army was effectively the German army. In the Bundesrat, Prussia commanded seventeen out of fifty-eight votes and could, therefore, block changes to the Constitution single-handedly. With almost 30% of the votes, Prussia was rarely outvoted.

In Prussia, the parliament was elected under a three-class voting system, giving property-owners the greatest say. Members of the government, diplomats and army leaders were generally drawn from the Prussian landed elites (Junkers). Bismarck's own dislike of democracy is well documented. In 1862 he urged King Wilhelm to avoid parliamentary rule at all costs. Given Prussia's dominance over Germany, it was not surprising that the authoritarian model of Prussian government was adopted for the whole Empire. Whilst the German Constitution created, in theory, a constitutional monarchy, in practice it was extremely authoritarian:

- The Prussian elites dominated the Imperial government and army just as they did in the state of Prussia.
- The Kaiser himself had extensive powers including the control of foreign policy and the authority to appoint and dismiss ministers, including the Chancellor.
- The Bundesrat represented the states but could hardly be held to represent the people as a whole.

Note

President Ulysses S. Grant of the USA sent a telegram to Berlin congratulating Germany on its decision to be a federal state, just like America!

■ Think about

▶ How did the role of members of the Bundesrat and the Reichstag differ? (Note: see the diagram on p.21 if you are unsure about the meaning of these terms).

▶ Do you think a powerful Bundesrat made Germany more or less united?

Key terms

Parliamentary rule
Where parliament holds the balance of power and dictates the actions of the ruler.

Authoritarian
Keeping political power in the hands of the ruler and denying greater power to the people.

Constitutional monarchy
Where the ruler shares power with parliament according to principles laid down in the Constitution.

- The Chancellor, who directed the day to day affairs of the Empire, was responsible only to the Kaiser. If the Reichstag disapproved of the Chancellor there was nothing it could do. The members of the government did not reflect the political composition of the Reichstag.

It was, therefore, surprising that Bismarck approved the introduction of universal male suffrage for Reichstag elections. In fact, the apparent power held by the Reichstag seemed at odds with Bismarck's dislike of democracy. The Reichstag had the power to veto new laws, including the budget (though not necessarily the army budget). However, in practice, the power of the Reichstag was limited. It could not propose new laws itself, it had no control over who was appointed Chancellor and its control over the budget was minimal. Even the apparently democratic gesture of universal male suffrage had its weaknesses. Reichstag deputies received no salary and therefore needed private sources of income. It was consequently rare to find 'ordinary' Germans standing in Reichstag elections.

Was Germany a 'modern' state in 1871?

Germany's economy

Germany's economy underwent a fundamental change during the second half of the nineteenth century. An agrarian (farming) revolution which involved the purchase of new machinery to replace farmworkers, led thousands to seek employment in the towns. German (and most particularly, Prussian) industry grew rapidly and by 1900 challenged Britain's. It can certainly be claimed that Germany, in 1871, had an increasingly modern, industrial economy.

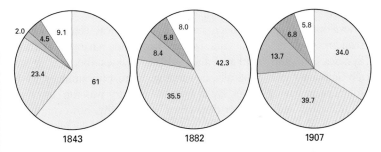

2.0 4.5 9.1 23.4 61	8.0 5.8 8.4 42.3 35.5	5.8 6.8 13.7 34.0 39.7
1843	1882	1907

☐ Agriculture and forestry
☐ Industry and crafts
☐ Commerce and communications
☐ Public and private services
☐ Domestic service

German society

The historian Hans-Ulrich Wehler claimed in 1973 that Germany had not modernized either politically or socially, despite the economic changes outlined above. Certainly, the power of the elites, both landed and industrial, remained formidable. Furthermore, social mobility – movement from one social class to another – was in theory possible but in practice rare.

Two groups which expanded due to industrialization were the working and middle classes. The working classes, who provided the manpower for industrial production, often worked in appalling conditions which could leave them ill or deformed. Their living conditions were no better – overcrowded, unhygienic and a haven for deadly bacteria.

Note

Bismarck was hugely important in the Empire. He held three important posts simultaneously: German Chancellor, Prime Minister of Prussia and Minister-President of Prussia.

Cross reference

See pages 14–15 for more information about Prussia's industrialization.

Facts and figures

The typical working day for industrial workers was 12 hours, six days a week. After 1873 many workers became unemployed or suffered a drop in wages. Potatoes and bread became the basic diet as few could afford meat.

Source 4

▶ The percentage distribution of workers in Germany, 1843–1907

Note

Wehler's book, *The German Empire*, was published in Germany in 1973. The first English translation appeared in 1985.

Source 5

◀ Workers' housing in Berlin in 1872, with new factories in the background.

The middle classes fared much better. Businessmen acquired wealth and status, though were still denied greater political influence. For Wehler, this was evidence that social structures had not modernized but tended to support the status quo. More recently, however, historians have argued that the middle classes were becoming more dynamic and involved in politics locally. They did not, however, gain greater political power at a state level, partly because they lacked unity.

Germany's political system

Economic development had not been matched by political change. Other industrial nations, such as Britain and France, had made changes to their political systems. As the working and middle classes became more economically important and politically demanding, more opportunities were provided for them to have a bigger say in how the country was run. In other words, industrialization led to greater democracy. In Germany, however, there were no moves towards real democracy and power remained largely in the hands of the unelected elites:

Source 6

> The political system was, in fact, an autocratic, semi-absolutist sham…because the real power relationships had not undergone any decisive alteration.
>
> Wehler, *The German Empire 1871–1918*, 1985

What did this mean for the future of Germany? Although the *Sonderweg* theory (see margin) is less popular than it was, it is generally agreed that the combination of an economically modern but politically backward state had serious repercussions on Germany. Bismarck spent a great deal of time trying to play different groups off against each other in order to isolate them. It has also been argued that he pursued a policy of colonial expansion as a means of uniting the people and diverting their attention away from political demands. This tactic was used increasingly after Bismarck's resignation and, it has been argued, was a factor in the outbreak of the First World War.

Note

The *Sonderweg*

The author of Source 6, Hans Ulrich Wehler, argued that Germany had followed a '*sonderweg*' or 'special path' from 1848 and that this helped to explain the rise of Hitler in the 1920s. The middle classes, despite growing in wealth and economic importance, did not gain more political power. The Prussian landed elites continued to dominate the key positions in the army, civil service and government and did all they could to protect their privileged position, aided and abetted by Bismarck, himself a Prussian aristocrat and opponent of democracy. After the collapse of the monarchy in 1918, the elites became more and more desperate to resist democracy and keep power for themselves, which, it has been argued, paved the way for Hitler's rise.

Bismarck and the Liberals 1871–1879

Political parties

On 21 March 1871 the new Imperial Reichstag met for the first time. The deputies were divided into six main groups which are summarized below:

- The most right-wing party was the **German Conservative Party**. Its supporters were mainly aristocrats, and in particular Junkers, the landed elite of Prussia. Its main aim was to protect the status quo and the interests of its supporters. The Prussian aristocracy had had a privileged and powerful position in Prussia and it did not want this to change.
- Another right-wing party was the **Free Conservatives**, whose support came from both landed and industrial elites. This party usually offered Bismarck strong backing.
- The **Centre Party** was founded in 1870 to represent the interests of German Catholics. Supporters came from a range of backgrounds. Its aims were quite conservative and traditional. It wanted to protect the rights of individual states and, of course, the Catholic Church.
- There were two liberal parties and the more right wing of these was the **National Liberal Party**. Its support came from educated and wealthy members of the middle classes. Their main aims were national unity, free trade and constitutional (rather than authoritarian) government. They were opposed to the idea of the Church having any power and influence over State affairs and they defended individual liberties.
- The **Progressive Party** was also liberal, but slightly to the left of the National Liberals. They shared many of the same aims but were in favour of giving parliament more power and were very suspicious of the army.
- The **Social Democratic Party** was founded in 1875. It was the joining together of previous socialist or workers' groups. It drew its support from the industrial working classes. Its aims were greater democracy and equality for all. Specifically it wanted to improve the lives of the working classes.

The support of the liberals

The National Liberals won 155 out of total of 399 seats in the first Reichstag elections of the Empire. Together with the Progressive Liberals and the Free Conservatives, they provided Bismarck with a comfortable majority. Until 1878, Bismarck could count on the support of the liberals. They strongly supported unification and backed policies aimed at reducing the differences between the individual states. This came at a cost however. Bismarck was not a liberal; his policies were motivated by circumstances rather than ideological conviction. For much of the 1870s it was useful to keep liberal support and for the most part, their aims and his coincided. Where they did not, the liberals tended to give way. In 1874, for example, they agreed to a septennial (seven year) rather than an annual army budget and even failed to block a Press Law which increased government censorship. This latter measure went totally against liberal ideas of individual rights such as free speech. The relationship between Bismarck and the liberals was one of compromise, but Bismarck never intended to let it control his policies.

Economic crisis

The economy of the Empire flourished following unification. The French paid their war indemnity punctually and this boosted government projects and military expansion. In addition, currency reform in 1871 added to the amount of money in circulation. All this led to much greater speculation. People took risks and invested money in newly founded companies which were promising

■ Think about

▶ Which parties were likely to support change?

▶ Which parties wanted Germany to remain as it was?

▶ Which parties could have worked together?

▶ Which parties would have opposed each other?

▶ From what you already know about Bismarck (see Chapter 1) which parties were most likely to offer him support?

Note

The matter of the military budget was a constant source of tension between the liberals and Bismarck. Given that military spending formed a huge part of the Empire's budget, the liberals wanted the army's budget to be controlled by the Reichstag. Bismarck, however, attempted to minimize any control the Reichstag might have.

rich profits. As one observer at the time put it 'A shower of gold rained down on the drunken city'. It was creating a bubble that could be burst at the first sign of a loss of confidence

The collapse of the Austrian stock market and a financial crisis in America in 1873 were enough to provoke a crisis. Bankruptcies followed in Germany and an economic depression set in. Economic growth did not recover fully until 1895. How did the depression affect Germany?

- Although weakened, the German economy was strong enough to withstand the depression. Large banks and businesses survived and swallowed up smaller bankrupted enterprises. The average rate of economic growth by the 1880s was 2.5 per cent a year, a healthy figure. Industrialization and urbanization both continued to increase.

- The depression led to increased pressure on the government for a protectionist economic policy. Many believed that only tariffs on imports would protect and secure a home market by pricing foreign competition more highly. The first pressure group campaigning to end free trade (the so-called Long-Name Society) was formed in 1871, but it was only after 1873 that more notice was taken of it. Bismarck knew that abolishing free trade could cost him the support of the liberals, He also knew, however, that tariffs would provide a welcome increase in revenue. Perhaps this was the time for Bismarck to break with the liberals.

- The campaign for protectionism led to an alliance between agricultural and industrial elites in 1877. German agriculture was beginning to suffer from foreign competition. American grain, for example, was robbing German producers of both foreign and home markets. Higher tariffs on foreign grain coming into Germany would encourage people to buy more local produce.

- Anti-Semitism increased as Jews were used as scapegoats for the economic problems. Their high profile in the stock market and banks made them vulnerable to the attack. For the first time, anti-Semitism became a political movement.

- Support for working-class associations grew after the crisis due to fear of unemployment and lower wages. In 1875, the Social Democratic Party was formed.

The *Kulturkampf*

Bismarck claimed that his primary aim as Chancellor was 'the creation and consolidation of Germany'. However, his domestic policies included attacks on a number of internal 'enemies of the state'. These so-called enemies included substantial minority groups such as Poles, Jews and socialists. The biggest group of all, however, was the Catholic Church in Germany. The attack on the Catholics became known as the *Kulturkampf* which translates as a 'struggle of civilizations' but was simply an attempt to discriminate against a single religious group.

Bismarck made clear his opposition to the newly formed Centre Party (which represented the Catholics – see page 33) as early as 1871. The appointment of Adalbert Falk to the post of Minister of Culture in Prussia signalled a more aggressive attack and the central element of the *Kulturkampf* was the Falk Laws of 1873 (commonly known as the May Laws). Under these laws, the Catholic Church became more closely controlled by the state. Under the measures brought in between 1873 and 1876, Jesuits were forced to leave Germany, Catholic schools were supervised by the state and civil wedding ceremonies were made compulsory.

Note

The territories of Alsace-Lorraine, which the Germans took from France as part of the Treaty of Frankfurt, contained rich mineral deposits. This was a further boost to economic growth.

Key term

Protectionism
When countries raise the duties on imports to encourage people to buy home-produced products.

Key term

Jesuits
Members of a particularly zealous order of Roman Catholic priests founded in 1534.

But why were the German Catholics identified as enemies? Firstly, Catholics were caught between two sources of authority, the German Kaiser and the Pope. In 1870, the Pope issued a proclamation declaring 'papal infallibility'. This meant that any statements he made on issues connected to Catholicism were beyond question. Catholics were not allowed to disobey the Pope even if that meant disobeying their King. The idea of a German owing allegiance to someone other than the Kaiser was difficult for Bismarck to accept. His fears were made worse by the fact that most Catholics lived in the south, an area least attracted by Germany unity and still a potential ally of Austria. He was not convinced that he could count on their support for the new Empire.

Bismarck's actions were not solely defensive, however. The liberals also loathed the Centre Party partly because of its lack of enthusiasm for national unity and also because they were opposed to any Church control over what they regarded as State matters. By attacking Catholicism, Bismarck hoped to secure stronger support from the liberals and in this he was right. However, by 1878 he was looking to the Centre Party for support in order to push through a new economic policy. Bismarck was, therefore, also playing political games.

Quotation

Politics is less a science than an art. It is not a subject that can be taught. One must have a talent for it.

Bismarck

Source 7

The question that confronts us becomes, in my opinion, distorted...if it is looked on as a confessional or religious one. It is essentially political. It is not a matter of an attack by a Protestant dynasty upon the Catholic Church, as our Catholic fellow-citizens are being told; it is not a matter of a struggle between faith and unbelief. What we have here is the age-old struggle for power, as old as the human race itself, between kingship and the priests, a struggle for power that goes back far beyond the coming of our saviour to this world...

Bismarck speaking to the Prussian Chamber of Peers, March 1873

■ Think about

▶ What light, if any, does Source 7 throw on Bismarck's motives for attacking the Catholics?

In the end, the *Kulturkampf* failed. If Bismarck was trying to weaken Catholicism, his policies had the opposite effect. Many Catholics made their feelings clear by refusing to celebrate national events or by flying the papal flag. Windthorst, the leader of the Centre Party, appealed to his fellow Catholics to express their opposition in elections. His appeal was successful as the figures in the margin demonstrate. The Centre Party had become the biggest party in the Reichstag by 1884.

By 1878, Bismarck was contemplating a change of economic policy which could lose him liberal support. In itself, this removed one of the reasons behind the *Kulturkampf* as the support of the liberals was no longer influencing Bismarck's policies. The growth of the Centre Party in the Reichstag also made the *Kulturkampf* politically unwise. The Centre Party was likely to support the new economic policy and this was too tempting for Bismarck. A new Pope in 1878, who held out an offer of friendship in exchange for an end to discrimination, provided Bismarck with a way out. In 1879 Falk was dismissed and his laws were abandoned with one or two exceptions. However, the *Kulturkampf*, which only ended completely in 1887, had a lasting impact on Bismarck's relations with the Centre Party. He could never rely on its support.

Facts and figures

Number of Centre Party deputies in the Reichstag, 1871–1890

Year	Deputies
1871	63
1874	91
1877	93
1878	94
1881	100
1884	99
1887	98
1890	106

The era of conservatism 1879–1890

The break with the liberals

As we have already seen, there was pressure on Bismarck to adopt a more protectionist economic policy. In 1878, Bismarck announced a bill in the Reichstag signalling an end to free trade. Not surprisingly, the liberals rejected the bill and it was defeated. Bismarck's only hope was to dissolve (close down) the Reichstag and hope that fresh elections would return a more supportive majority. There followed a stroke of good luck for Bismarck. Two assassination attempts on the Kaiser, both blamed incorrectly on the socialists, enabled Bismarck to appeal to national sentiments. Not surprisingly, the socialists lost seats in the election. More crucially, so did the liberals. The conservatives and the Centre Party were the main beneficiaries.

The National Liberals were at this point afraid of losing all influence over the government. Many went as far as supporting an Anti-Socialist Law which went against their liberal principles and also divided the party. Such was the division within the party that fifteen rebel members even voted in favour of protectionism. In the event, however, the bill ending free trade was passed by a majority consisting of Conservatives and the Centre Party. This was Bismarck's break with the liberals. It did not, however, ease Bismarck's relations with the Reichstag. The *Kulturkampf,* although now being dismantled, had made consistently good relations between the Centre Party and Bismarck unlikely. In addition, the division of the National Liberals had provided fewer right-wing liberals prepared to support Bismarck than he had hoped. Consequently, it was not until 1887 that Bismarck regained a clear majority in the Reichstag.

Meanwhile, Bismarck had to build on support from the Conservatives. The result was a move towards greater authoritarian and conservative policies. But socialist support was increasing at the same time. How could Bismarck contain forces demanding political change while attempting to defend traditional rights and privileges?

Source 8

◀ A cartoon from a German liberal magazine in 1879. Bismarck is at the wheel of the ship and the liberal spoke is saying to the smiling conservative and Centre Party spokes: 'Don't get cocky. When the wind shifts, I will be on top again.'

■ Think about

▶ How accurate is Source 8 as an interpretation of Bismarck's domestic policy?

Quotation

As he got older, Bismarck apparently became more and more difficult. One contemporary said of him 'It was always Me! Me! Me! And when that did not work, complaints about ingratitude and tears of North German sentimentality.'

Facts and figures

Number of Socialist deputies in the Reichstag 1871–1890

Year	Number
1871	2
1874	9
1877	12
1878	9
1881	12
1884	24
1887	11
1890	35

■ **Think about**

▶ On what grounds is Bismarck opposing the socialists here?

▶ From what you know of Bismarck's views, do you think that this was the main reason for Bismarck's opposition?

The attack on socialism

The elections of 1881 were effectively a defeat for Bismarck. He could by now only rely on the support of the German Conservatives and Free Conservatives, who only controlled 85 seats between them in the new Reichstag. Over three-quarters of the new deputies opposed the government. The National Liberals by this time had divided. The Secessionists, who represented the left wing of the party and were more fiercely opposed to Bismarck, won almost as many seats as the remaining National Liberals. Meanwhile, the National Liberals themselves were drifting further to the right and supported co-operation with the conservatives.

Bismarck also had to face a challenge from a different front: the socialists. The Social Democratic Party was formed in 1875 and represented the interests of the working classes. It stood for democracy and equality, neither of which Bismarck had any sympathy for. In the eyes of Bismarck, it also posed a possible international threat because socialism, like Catholicism, was an international movement. He was therefore alarmed at the growing power of the socialists in the Reichstag which reflected a widening of popular support. Bismarck used two assassination attempts on the Kaiser to push through an Anti-Socialist Law in 1878 banning all socialist meetings and publications. The Social Democratic Party, however, was still allowed to stand in Reichstag elections.

Source 9

For eleven years we have had the advantage of associating here with Social Democrats, and do you remember, gentlemen, of hearing, amid all the long speeches delivered in this place by socialists, a single one in which it was possible to discover the slightest shadow of a concrete idea or of a project for further action indicating what they actually intend to do when they shall have made a breach …in the existing social system? I recall nothing of the sort, and I believe I know the reason why these gentlemen are so carefully silent about the manner in which they intend to refashion the world when they are masters. It is because they do not know themselves. They can never keep the promises with which they have misled the people.

Bismarck in 1878

The Anti-Socialist Law lasted for 12 years and was as unsuccessful as the *Kulturkampf* in weakening Bismarck's 'enemies of the state'. The socialists grew in strength during the 1880s. Almost twice as many people voted for them in 1887 as in 1878. By 1890 there were 35 socialist deputies.

State socialism

Bismarck's social welfare programme stands out as his only positive response to social change. It provided sickness and accident insurance for the lowest paid workers and pensions for the over seventies and the permanently disabled. In fact, it was Bismarck's only enduring contribution to Germany, although he did not regard it so highly and made no mention of it in his memoirs. So what motivated Bismarck? It was possible that Bismarck did feel a genuine desire to help those in need, but as ever, political considerations were foremost in his mind. The measures were intended to win support from the working classes and discourage their demands for greater political power. They were also a way of robbing the Social Democratic Party of support by providing for the working classes at state level.

The socialists were unsure about how to react. Although they approved the measures, they were loath to support a regime which was trying to destroy them. In the end they approved the ideas behind the measures but rejected the actual bills unless amendments were made. Nevertheless, three laws were passed successfully. In 1883 a Health Insurance Law was brought in, followed by an Accident Insurance Law in 1884. In 1889 an old age pension scheme was introduced.

Germanization

Catholics and socialists were not the only groups identified as enemies of the state. Poles and Jews were also targeted by Bismarck, who embarked on a policy of 'Germanization'. He was, in part, responding to the demands of conservatives and knew that his policies would meet with their approval. In 1886 a Settlement Law encouraged German peasants to settle in the eastern Prussian provinces from which 16,000 Poles and Jews (with Russian citizenship) had been forced to leave. By 1885, more than 32,000 had left. Those Poles who remained suffered discrimination. Polish, for example, was no longer taught in schools. Similarly, French-speakers living in Alsace-Lorraine had to be taught in German and the Danes of Schleswig-Holstein suffered in similar ways.

Bismarck and the Reichstag

One of Bismarck's reactions to the hostile Reichstag of 1881 was to attempt to reduce its power. Its authority over the military was reduced but generally Bismarck was unsuccessful, despite threats to change the Constitution. Instead he focused on protecting the dominance of the Prussian conservative elites within the civil service and the army.

A sympathetic majority in the Reichstag only came as a result of tensions abroad. Bismarck exploited the Bulgarian Crisis (see p. 43) to create a war scare. In the elections of 1887, the Kartell (German Conservatives, Free Conservatives and National Liberals) won 220 seats whilst the socialists and new Freisinnige Party (made up of left-wing liberals) lost seats. Bismarck was able to push through a new septennial (seven year) military budget. His problems were not over, however. In March 1888 Kaiser Wilhelm I died and his eventual successor did not see eye to eye with the 'Iron Chancellor'.

Document exercise: Bismarck's domestic policy

Source A

Bismarck's political principles

I have often acted hastily and without reflection, but when I had time to think I have always asked: what is useful, effective, right, for my fatherland, for my dynasty...I have never been a doctrinaire liberal, reactionary, conservative – those I confess seem to me luxuries...Yes, I've no fixed opinions, make proposals, and you won't meet any objections of principle from me...My aim from the first moment of my public activity has been the creation and consolidation of Germany, and if you can show a single moment when I deviated from that magnetic needle, you may perhaps prove that I went wrong, but never that I lost sight of the national aim for a moment.

Bismarck to the Reichstag, 1881

Source B

Bismarck deals with the liberals and the socialists

▲ A cartoon from 1878 showing Bismarck dealing with the liberals and socialists, who are portrayed as pests.

Source C

Extracts from The Anti-Socialist Law, October 1878

Associations which further social-democratic, socialist or communist aims and thus threaten to overthrow the existing state and social structure are banned…Meetings in which social-democratic, socialist or communist tendencies..make their appearance are to be dissolved [closed down]…All printed matter in which social-democratic, socialist or communist tendencies appear…is to be forbidden.

Source D

Arguments in favour of State socialism

Anybody who has before him the prospect of a pension, be it ever so small, in old age or infirmity (illness) is much happier and more content with his lot…The state must take the matter into its own hands…as the right that men have to be taken care of when, with the best will imaginable, they become unfit for work. Why should the regular soldier, disabled by war, or the official, have a right to be pensioned in his old age, and not the soldier of labour? This thing will make its own way; it has a future.

Private conversation between Bismarck and his close friend, Moritz Musch

Source E

The limited success of State socialism

The system of social insurance which he [Bismarck] established was too little and too late. The lower classes wanted more than protection against out-and-out starvation. They wanted respect, equality and freedom…The defeat which the Chancellor suffered in the campaign against the socialists was all the more galling … because he had planned it with such care. He had sought to avoid the mistakes of the *Kulturkampf*. He had not relied on force exclusively, but had tried to win over the moderates in the opposing camp. And yet it had all been in vain…The ageing statesman now began to experience a recurrent mood of pessimism.

Hamerow, *The Age of Bismarck*, 1973

■ Examination-style questions

1 Comprehension in context
Using Source E and your own knowledge, explain what Hamerow means by 'the mistakes of the Kulturkampf'.

2 Comparing the sources
To what extent do Sources A and B offer similar interpretations of how Bismarck conducted his domestic policy?

3 Assessing the sources
How valuable is Source D in assessing the motives behind Bismarck's social welfare programme? Use both the source and your own knowledge in your answer.

4 Making judgements
'Bismarck's domestic policies failed to tackle the real issues facing Germany at that time'. How far do you agree with this statement?

Bismarck's foreign policy

The unification of Germany had a profound effect on the balance of power in Europe. The British politician, Benjamin Disraeli, declared in a speech to the House of Commons in February 1871 'You have a new world, new influences at work, new and unknown objects and dangers with which to cope...The balance of power has been entirely destroyed, and the country which suffers most...is England.' Britain feared that Germany would renew hostilities against both Austria and France to gain more power. In fact, Bismarck's primary aim for the next nineteen years was to avoid war at all costs. He wanted Germany to concentrate its efforts on strengthening its economy and functioning as a united state. He had no wish to gain greater territory. In 1888 he said:

Key term

balance of power
Ensuring that no single state in Europe dominated the others.

Source 10

What territory could she [Germany] think of annexing? She has enough of Poland already. By seeking fresh conquests, the German Empire would only be exposing itself to perpetual warfare with Russia and France, who is simply waiting for an opportunity for avenging Alsace and Lorraine. Under these circumstances warlike proposals...would not fit in with my programme.

Bismarck's intention to avoid war, however, was no guarantee that other states would avoid war with Germany. France, although weakened by the Franco-Prussian War, would soon recover and its desire for revenge on Germany would remain. At the heart of Bismarck's foreign policy until 1890 lay a determination to isolate France and prevent the unthinkable: an alliance between France and Russia (or even Austria) which would leave Germany exposed to the threat of a war on two fronts. The ideal solution was to conclude alliances with both Austria and Russia which would prevent such a nightmare from happening. The difficulty, however, lay in the hostility between Russia and Austria, making it difficult for Germany to establish good relations with both. Bismarck showed considerable diplomatic skill in addressing this issue, but his policies could not solve this basic problem.

Cross reference

See the map of Europe on page 26 for a sense of how Germany could become 'encircled' by enemies.

The Three Emperors League

In 1873 Germany, Russia and Austria formed the Three Emperors' League (*Dreikaiserbund*). Although this seemed to be the answer to all of Bismarck's problems, the League was little more than a sign of good intent. The three powers agreed to consult each other in the event of war and emphasized their desire for peace. Only two years later, however, the limitations of the League were apparent. Bismarck, alarmed by France's quick recovery and von Moltke's (mistaken) belief that France could overpower German forces, made threatening gestures to France. He used the press to imply that an attack on France was imminent. 'Is war in sight?' was the headline of one article. Bismarck hoped that Britain, alarmed at the prospect of another war, would pressure France into slowing down her rearmament programme. He was mistaken. Not only did Britain fail to respond in such a way, but the Russian Emperor visited the Kaiser in person to voice his concerns and Austria was no less unsympathetic. Bismarck was forced to stop his campaign.

Crisis in the Balkans, 1875–1878

The situation in the Balkans was very unstable. The Ottoman Empire which ruled the Balkans had been in decline since the end of the previous century. Meanwhile, the rise of nationalism in the nineteenth century had made the Balkan states hungry for independence. It was not, however, as simple a matter as the Ottoman Empire versus the Balkan states. The Great Powers also had vested interests in the area. Russia regarded itself as a defender of the Slav people. It also wanted to protect its own interests in the region by ensuring that its ships had clear access through the Mediterranean Straits (the Dardanelles, Sea of Marmara and Bosphorus) while access to potentially hostile powers was denied. One of these potentially hostile powers was Austria, which wanted to increase its own control over the region. This was partly a defensive measure to prevent nationalist groups in the Balkans from threatening the Austro-Hungarian Empire which itself consisted of many different ethnic groups.

In 1875 there were uprisings in Bosnia and Herzegovina. If the Ottomans had been forced to withdraw, Russia and Austria would have battled for power over the region. This would have put Germany into the impossible position of having to choose sides even though it needed to keep the support of both. Bismarck worked hard at a diplomatic solution to the crisis and in 1876 Austria and Russia drew up a plan to divide the Balkans in the event of a Turkish defeat. The Turks were not defeated, however, and Russia invaded Turkey in April 1877. This was despite the absence of any offer of support from Germany, much to Russia's irritation. Both Austria and Britain were alarmed at Russia's actions and the threat of war loomed over Europe. Bismarck once again attempted to settle the issue through diplomacy. In 1878 a congress was held in Berlin and Bismarck was in command. A settlement was reached which created lasting tensions. Russia gained land which it had lost in 1856 but the other decisions were less to its liking. Austria gained control over Bosnia-Herzegovina, Britain gained control over Cyprus while Bulgaria was partitioned (divided). Russia felt robbed by foreign powers which had not even fought in the recent conflict.

Note

Bismarck's taste in food was regarded with astonishment by the participants of the Berlin Congress. He apparently ate cherries and shrimps at the same time.

Source 11

▶ The Berlin settlement.

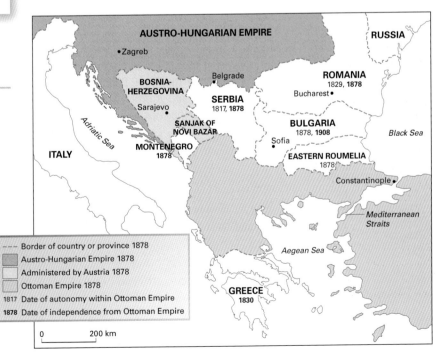

- - - Border of country or province 1878
Austro-Hungarian Empire 1878
Administered by Austria 1878
Ottoman Empire 1878
1817 Date of autonomy within Ottoman Empire
1878 Date of independence from Ottoman Empire

0   200 km

Source 12

◀ A painting of the Congress of Berlin, 1878. In the foreground from left to right are: Count Kalnoky, Prince Gorchakov (sitting), Disraeli, Count Andrassy, Bismarck and Count Shuvalov.

■ Think about

Prince Gorchakov of Russia wanted to distance himself from the unpopular peace reached at the Berlin Congress. On his return to Russia he blamed Count Shuvalov for the agreements which had been reached.

▶ To what extent does Source 12 confirm Gorchakov's story?

Note

Germany was not the first to introduce tariffs. Russian tariffs went up by 50% in 1877 which badly affected German trade.

Alliances

The Berlin Congress left Germany out of favour with Russia. Relations between the two countries were not helped by the introduction in Germany of tariffs on Russian products such as timber and corn. Nor were they helped by an anti-German press campaign by the Russians. A renewal of the Three Emperors League, which had collapsed during the Balkan crisis, looked unlikely.

Bismarck renewed his bid to isolate France and gain useful allies by suggesting a stronger alliance with Austria. The Dual Alliance was signed in 1879 and heralded a new era in diplomacy. This was an alliance which was signed in peacetime and was to last for 39 years. Each country promised help to the other in the event of a Russian attack. If either were attacked by another power then the other would remain neutral. Bismarck would have preferred not to have mentioned Russia specifically, due to the Kaiser's Russian sympathies, but Austria insisted so that the alliance did not appear to be anti-French.

How successful was this alliance? It strengthened Germany's position in Eastern Europe and held out the possibility of a renewal of the Three Emperors' League. This latter aim seemed to be fulfilled by the Three Emperors' Alliance of 1881 which included Germany, Austria and Russia. They agreed to remain neutral in any war with a fourth power and to consult each other about the Balkans. However, neither the Dual Alliance nor the Three Emperors' Alliance removed the basic antagonism between Russia and Austria over the Balkans. Bismarck was aware of the need to keep his options open:

Source 13

We cannot abandon Austria, but neither can we lose sight of the possibility that the policy of Vienna may willy-nilly abandon us. The possibilities which in such a case remain open to us must be clearly achieved and steadily borne in mind by German statesmen before the critical moment arrives…

Quotation

In 1880 Bismarck spoke to the Russian ambassador in Berlin of the 'importance of being one of three on the European chess-board. That is the invariable objective of all Cabinets and of mine above all others. Nobody wishes to be in a minority. All politics reduce themselves to this formula: to try to be one of three.'

In 1882, Italy joined Germany and Austria to form a Triple Alliance. Italy's main motive was to seek support in the event of a war with France over her colonies. The addition of Italy did not bring huge benefits to Germany – the alliance promised support to Italy in the event of a French attack, but Italy would only support Austria and Germany in the event of them being attacked by two powers at the same time. However, the support of Italy meant that Austria's southern borders were secure and this could strengthen Austria if a war with Russia were to break out. It also prevented an alliance between Italy and France.

The Bulgarian Crisis

In 1885 a war broke out between Bulgaria and Serbia. Russia supported Bulgaria (now ruled by Prince Alexander, the pro-Austrian nephew of the Russian Tsar), and Austria supported Serbia. The possibility of war caused Bismarck great anxiety. Austria, not strong enough to fight Russia alone, would almost certainly call on German assistance and this in turn could lead to an alliance between Russia and France. The appointment, in 1886, of Georges Boulanger as Minister of War in France made Bismarck even more nervous. Boulanger supported a policy of revenge against Germany and the recapture of Alsace-Lorraine.

Bismarck was therefore desperate to avoid a war. The Three Emperors' Alliance collapsed during the Bulgarian crisis and he was anxious to keep some kind of alliance with Russia. In June 1887 the two countries signed the Reinsurance Treaty in which they promised neutrality unless Germany attacked France or Russia attacked Austria. This removed the threat of a joint Russian-French attack on Germany. However, Bismarck also secretly recognized Russia's rights in Bulgaria and the Straits which ran contrary to his friendship with Austria. Bismarck was on dangerous ground and his agreement could encourage Russia to challenge Austria further in the Balkans. To prevent this, Bismarck persuaded Britain, Austria and Italy to sign a Mediterranean Agreement designed to prevent further Russian expansion into the Balkans. He also prevented German loans from reaching Russia which undermined her strength and ability to fight a war. Whilst this was a successful short-term measure it had an unfortunate long-term consequence. Russia looked to France for money and this was the beginning of an understanding between the two countries which was to fulfil Bismarck's nightmare.

Note

Summary of alliances

1873 Three Emperors' League (Germany, Russia, Austria)

1879 Dual Alliance (Germany and Austria)

1881 Three Emperors' Alliance (Germany, Russia, Austria)

1882 Triple Alliance (Germany, Austria, Italy)

1884 Three Emperors' Alliance renewed

1887 Reinsurance Treaty (Germany, Russia)

Source 14

▶ A German liberal cartoon from 1887, showing Bismarck's role in the Bulgarian Crisis. He is diverting the engine 'revenge' to clear the way for the engine 'peace'.

■ Think about

▶ Explain what the cartoonist in Source 14 means by diverting the engine from 'revenge' to 'peace'.

▶ Is this a fair interpretation of the events of 1887?

▶ Would the other states involved in the Bulgarian Crisis have agreed with this view?

Bismarck's Imperial policy

According to a report written by the British Ambassador to Berlin in 1871, Bismarck had made it clear in a conversation that he did not want Germany to acquire colonies, nor did he want to build a bigger navy. In 1884, however, Bismarck embarked on a policy of colonial expansion that was to see German territory increase significantly. Why did Bismarck change his mind so dramatically?

■ Historical debate

Historians have debated the reasons behind Bismarck's colonial policy at length. The main arguments that have so far been advanced can be summarized as follows:

1 Bismarck believed that time was running out for Germany because other powers were claiming all the available colonies for themselves.

2 Bismarck pursued colonial expansion as a way of diverting attention away from social tensions at home, leading to what is termed 'social imperialism'. Others argue that this policy only originated after Bismarck's resignation.

3 Bismarck was eager to please his conservative alliance and also saw colonial expansion as a way of reuniting the National Liberals around a common cause and encouraging their support of his policies.

4 Bismarck was pressured by those who claimed that Germany needed new markets for her products.

5 Bismarck had long-term plans for an empire but had been waiting for the right time.

6 Bismarck stumbled into colonial expansion just as he stumbled into everything else.

7 Bismarck believed that colonial expansion would demonstrate Germany's strength to others. It would also alienate Britain which could in turn help build a friendship with France.

It is likely that Bismarck pursued colonial expansion for a combination of reasons. The argument of social imperialism, first advanced by Wehler, as the sole reason for Bismarck's colonial policies now seems unlikely. Colonial expansion only generated real enthusiasm amongst those who stood potentially to profit from it and that excluded many of the people that Wehler claimed Bismarck was trying to woo through increased nationalism. It is likely, however, that domestic considerations were a significant factor in Bismarck's decision. The increased nationalism of the 1884 elections was to Bismarck's advantage.

Most German expansion was in Africa. A number of protectorates were established there including Cameroon, Togoland, German East Africa and German South West Africa. Many of these gains led to clashes with Britain but not to a closer relationship with France which regarded German activity in Africa with suspicion. Britain eventually recognized most of Germany's African possessions, as she was distracted by threats elsewhere in her Empire. However, German success in her new colonies was not great. Bismarck had hoped to adopt a 'hands off' policy by allowing chartered companies to run the new territories, but this proved impossible. The cost of quelling local

Note

The scramble for Africa
This is the term used to describe the frantic efforts by European states to claim what was left of Africa by the last quarter of the nineteenth century.

Key term

protectorate
A state that is controlled and literally 'protected' by another state.

opposition in East Africa alone cost nine million Reichsmarks and took two years. All in all, therefore, the colonies were both a political and economic disappointment. It was not surprising that Bismarck abandoned colonial expansion in 1888.

Document exercise: Bismarck's foreign policy

Source A
Bismarck's aims in his own words

Our main policy is and remains a policy of peace. We have no reason to want a war, and I do not see what we should have to gain by one…The pivot of our position, and with that of our whole policy, the point on which things turn, is our relationship with Russia. The French will only attack us if we let ourselves get embroiled [involved] with Russia, but then are certain to do so. As for the English, they have no reason at all for attacking us, even if they are beginning to envy our industrial and commercial progress…The ticklish factor in our connections with Russia is of course Austria. We cannot let Austria be overrun and shattered. But just as little must we let ourselves be dragged into war by her. To manoeuvre between these two crags is a matter of skill and a clear head, much the same qualities as are necessary to prevent two trains meeting in a head-on crash.

Source B
Friendship between Germany and Austria

If, contrary to expectations and against the sincere desire of both the High Contracting Parties [ie. Germany and Austria], one of the two Empires shall be attacked on the part of Russia, the High Contracting Parties are bound to assist each other with the whole of the military power of their Empire, and consequently only to conclude peace conjointly and by agreement.

Extract from the Dual Alliance, 1879

Source C
Friendship between Germany and Russia

Article 1: In case one of the High Contracting Parties [i.e. Germany and Russia] should find itself at war with a third Great Power, the other would maintain a benevolent neutrality towards it, and would devote its efforts to the localization of the conflict. This provision would not apply to a war against Austria or France in case this war should result from an attack directed against one of these two latter Powers by one of the High Contracting Parties.
Article 2: Germany recognizes the rights historically acquired by Russia in the Balkan Peninsula, and particularly the legitimacy [right] of her dominant and decisive influence in Bulgaria…

Extract from the Reinsurance Treaty, 1887

Source D

A friendship between France and Russia is broken up

▲ A French cartoon from 1890 about Bismarck's attempts to disrupt Franco-Russian relations.

Source E

A Historian's assessment

It was in foreign affairs that Bismarck was most competent and his achievements most impressive. The empire he had created was secure by 1890. In the previous twenty years he had won the respect of virtually everyone, but the trust of few...For nearly two decades his policy was reasonably peaceful, but it was also unsteady. He was acutely aware of the precarious situation of Germany in foreign affairs. He was ever on the alert for any threatening intrigue or even the suggestion of such. This made others wary of him in a period when he should have tried to win international confidence in his country.

Waller, *Bismarck*, 1985

■ Examination-style questions

1 Comprehending in context

Using Source A and your own knowledge, explain why Bismarck wanted to follow a policy of peace after 1871.

2 Comparing the sources

To what extent and why do Sources A and B offer different perspectives on who was Germany's most important ally?

3 Assessing the sources

How valuable is Source D in understanding the state of European diplomacy in 1887?

4 Making judgements

How far do you agree with the view that Bismarck was a diplomatic genius?

■ Activity

Using the timeline at the end of this chapter to help you, summarize Bismarck's foreign policy. Take each event included in the timeline and note down Bismarck's aims/motives and the outcome. You may wish to put this into a summary chart like the one below.

Event	Bismarck's aims or motives	Outcome

1 How successful do you think Bismarck's foreign policy was overall?

2 Was Germany in a strong position by 1890?

3 What problems remained?

4 How could these problems have been solved?

The fall of Bismarck

In 1888, the wife of the British Ambassador in Berlin declared that 'the Emperor…has allowed Prince Bismarck to have his own way in everything'. Certainly, Bismarck and Wilhelm I had their ups and downs and Bismarck often resorted to resignation threats and outbursts of tears to get his own way. But the relationship worked because the Kaiser had generally allowed Bismarck to make his own decisions. The death of Wilhelm I in 1888 was therefore a blow to Bismarck. The new King, Friedrich, reigned for just three months. After his death, his son (Wilhelm I's grandson) assumed the crown. Wilhelm II was 29 years old and a different character entirely from his grandfather. He was determined to make his mark and to rule Germany himself. Bismarck, now 73, certainly underestimated the new monarch.

A clash of personalities was not the only cause of poor relations, however. Bismarck and the new Kaiser disagreed over matters of policy. In particular, their views diverged over the issue of socialism. Wilhelm II favoured a policy of more social reform which would, he hoped, woo the working classes away from the Social Democratic Party. Bismarck, on the other hand, wanted to confront the Social Democrats by introducing a more aggressive anti-socialist bill which proposed to expel from their homes anyone under suspicion of socialist agitation. The bill was defeated and in the elections which followed, the left wing and Centre Party increased their seats at the expense of the conservatives. Most worryingly for Bismarck, the Social Democratic Party now had 35 deputies. Bismarck wanted to use the new Reichstag's refusal to support measures concerning the army and anti-socialism as an excuse to redraft the Constitution and substantially reduce the Reichstag's powers. In other words, Bismarck was planning a coup.

Note

Few in Germany mourned Bismarck's resignation; he had simply alienated too many people during his long period in office. The work of nationalist historians in Germany soon helped to transform Bismarck into a national hero, however, and by the time of his death in 1898, his popularity had reached new heights.

Source 15

▶ A cartoon called 'Dropping the Pilot' about Wilhelm II forcing Bismarck from office.

■ Think about

Source 15 comes from *Punch*, a British magazine.
▶ What does it tell us about the British view of Bismarck?
▶ How do you think other states reacted to Bismarck's fall?

Wilhelm II opposed such a plan. He already had an alternative Chancellor in mind, General von Caprivi, and he waited for the right moment. It came in March 1890 when Bismarck, desperately trying to gain support in the Reichstag, was even denied the support of the conservatives. Wilhelm gave Bismarck an ultimatum and Bismarck finally resigned on 29 March 1890. He left Berlin feeling very bitter. His attack on Wilhelm in his memoirs was so vicious that an agreement was made by his descendants to withhold publication of the worst chapters until after Wilhelm's death.

Spotlight

Bismarck's legacy

■ Historical debate

German historians initially regarded Bismarck as a hero and created a myth that the German Empire was the product of inevitable and natural forces. However, the rise of Hitler and the Second World War had a profound impact on historians' assessment of Bismarck. As early as 1950, connections were being made between Bismarck and Hitler. Historians began to question whether there was something more sinister behind Bismarck's 'rule' and German unification which paved the way for the horrors of the Third Reich. Was Bismarck guilty of stirring up a kind of nationalism which sought territorial expansion and increased anti-Semitism? Did his use of force against Austria and France in the 1860s signal to others that conflict and war was the way forward for Germany? Did his dislike of democracy and refusal to give greater political power to the expanding middle and working classes create tensions that inevitably led to the rise of Nazism?

More recent historians do not deny that Bismarck had a profound effect on the later development of Germany and even the rise of Hitler. But they have challenged the degree to which Bismarck made it inevitable. They have challenged the view that Germany under Bismarck was unlike anywhere else. They have challenged the view that the middle classes simply supported Bismarck and remained powerless (although they accept that political power largely remained in the hands of the elite). And they have challenged the view that unification was inevitable and the result of sinister forces which ultimately led to Hitler.

Perhaps the best way for you to assess Bismarck is to try and evaluate what he did or did not achieve in his own lifetime and in what state he left Germany. You may decide that he made many mistakes and left behind problems. But you may also decide that he also had some great achievements. Certainly, people in Germany, in the decade after his resignation, thought he had achieved a great deal. In an opinion poll in 1899 most people answered 'Bismarck' to the question 'Who is the greatest statesman of the century?', and the majority considered 1871–1890 to be the happiest period in the century.

Source 16

...the staggering course of the First World War and still more the Second World War makes it impossible to pass over in silence the query whether the germs of the later evil [i.e. Hitler] were not really implanted in Bismarck's work from the outset...One then breathes the atmosphere of the tragedy of history, of human and historical greatness, and also the problematical uncertainty which will ever hover around Bismarck and his work – while Hitler's work must be reckoned as the eruption of the satanic principle in world history.

Meinecke, *The German Catastrophe*, 1964

Source 17

The complexity of the structure of alliances which he erected was...a source of weakness as well as strength. It achieved the fundamental objective sought by the Chancellor, the maintenance of stability. But it also made that stability depend on a man of genius who was inimitable [unique] and irreplaceable.

Hamerow, *The Age of Bismarck*, 1973

Source 18

My entire life was spent gambling for high stakes with other people's money. I could never foresee exactly whether my plans would succeed...Politics is a thankless job, chiefly because everything depends on chance and conjecture. One has to reckon with a series of probabilities and improbabilities and base one's plans upon this reckoning...As long as he lives the statesman is always unprepared

Bismarck, *The Man and the Statesman*, 1898

Source 19

Once political and economic unification had been achieved, authoritarian and diversionary strategies were implemented to fend off the inevitable challenge of...modernizing forces. Parliament had been treated like an inconvenience... All this... achieved, however, was a temporary lull. Problems were swept under the carpet and social tensions were left to smoulder. By 1890 it was clear that the Bismarckian approach to domestic policy was no longer practicable and his departure left his successors with a legacy of unresolved problems.

Abrams, *Bismarck and the German Empire 1871–1918*, 1995

Source 20

Most of what Bismarck created disappeared within fifty years of his death. The country he united was divided after 1945...Prussia's eastern provinces, whose potential loss so concerned Bismarck, belong to Poland and Russia, and Prussia herself...has disappeared from the map...The constitution Bismarck drafted for a united Germany disappeared under the impact of the First World War...The monarchical order that he believed vital to the internal stability of the three central and east European empires has disappeared, and likewise the aristocratic latifundia [landed estates] that were its economic and social backbone...Bismarck would find little that is familiar in contemporary Germany – with one exception: The social insurance system...And yet, ironically, this was an achievement on which Bismarck placed little store..."

Pflanze, *Bismarck and the Development of Germany Vol. III*, 1990

Source 21

◀ A huge statue of Bismarck in Hamburg, carved in 1906.

Source 22

The supreme quality of Bismarck's statesmanship was his recognition that no policy could be pursued beyond a certain danger limit, and that it was essential to have alternatives ready for dignified retreat...Few politicians, in Germany or in other lands, have possessed such suppleness of mind...There was no causal chain linking Bismarck's technique of power politics and the ...resort to world conquest in the Nazi era. Bismarck's latterday champions...have stressed the extent to which Hitler's policies run directly counter [opposite] to all his precepts. Rightly they emphasise the limited character of Bismarck's ambitions for Germany...

Palmer, *Bismarck*, 1976

Source 23

The Empire Bismarck created survived for 47 years, slightly longer than Germany was divided after the Second World War...Bismarck's 'lesser German' unification [i.e. excluding Austria] was successful in achieving a national legitimacy [right] which it was beyond the capacity of two world wars and 40 years of division to extinguish.

Lerman 'Bismarckian Germany and the Structure of the German Empire' in Fulbrook (ed.), *German History since 1800*, 1997

Source 24

Under Bismarck's leadership the German nation had become united, strong and powerful. But the sense of freedom and individual independence of justice and humanity, had been lamentably [regrettably] weakened...It is therefore no mere chance that his work did not last, and that the Prussian crown and the Hohenzollern [Prussian royal family] dynasty...ceased to exist twenty years after his death.

Eyck, *Bismarck and the German Empire*, 1968

See the next page for the activity which goes with this spotlight.

1 Draw up a balance sheet of Bismarck's achievements and failures using the
tables below.

Start by using the sources on pages 48 and 49. If you have trouble finding
evidence to back up the points made by the different historians then this might
encourage you to reject their claims.

Then add to the tables using your own knowledge. It is very important that you
are able to support your own points with evidence! The timeline opposite might
help you.

Bismarck's Achievements	Evidence

Bismarck's Failures	Evidence

2 Get into small groups. Each group member should write an obituary of
Bismarck (written as if the year was 1898) from a different point of view.
Choose from the list below:

A Social Democrat

A Catholic

A Prussian aristocrat

A German nationalist

A French diplomat

3 Now write your own assessment of Bismarck's legacy. Structure your assessment
around the following question: 'Was Bismarck good for Germany?' *Note:* For
inclusion in your key skills portfolio, this assessment must be an extended piece
of writing (e.g. 3 pages or more) and should include at least one image (e.g. a
picture downloaded from the Internet, a chart or a table). When you have
finished, compare your interpretation of Bismarck with the other members of
the class. How far do you agree or disagree with each other?

Conclusions

It will be clear that Bismarck remains a controversial character. Although in
many ways he achieved his aims both in his domestic and foreign policy,
historians have questioned to what extent these aims were valid. By refusing to
allow a move towards democracy, was Bismarck simply creating tensions that
would explode after his lifetime? Did he ignore the ways in which Germany
was changing and try to hold the clock back? On the other hand, his social
welfare legislation was much more forward-looking and has outlived
everything else he left behind. Abroad he steadfastly pursued a policy of peace.
He did not yearn to make Germany bigger like later German leaders. Instead
he sought to strengthen the Germany that existed. Yet even in this respect his
legacy was unstable. The fundamental problems in Europe remained and
Bismarck left no one in his wake who possessed the skill to solve them. Yet for
all his failures, it is perhaps too harsh to judge him by the developments which
came later in Germany. Nothing was inevitable after Bismarck.

Timeline

YEAR	DOMESTIC POLICY	FOREIGN POLICY
1870	Pope proclaims 'papal infallibility' Centre Party formed	
1871	Unification of Germany National Liberals win 155 seats in Reichstag elections	
1873	Economic depression begins Kulturkampf begins with the Falk (May) Laws	Three Emperors' League between Germany, Austria and Russia
1874	Liberals agree to a new Septennat Press Law increases censorship	
1875	Social Democratic Party formed	'War in Sight' scare Uprisings in Bosnia and Herzegovina
1876		Austria and Russia agree to divide the Balkans between them in the case of a Turkish defeat
1877	Alliance between landed and industrial elites in favour of protectionism	Russia invades Turkey
1878	Bismarck announces a bill which signals an end to free trade Two assassination attempts on the Kaiser Socialists and liberals lose seats in the Reichstag elections Anti-socialist Law	Berlin Congress
1879	Falk Laws largely abolished Bismarck chooses the support of the Centre Party instead of the liberals	Dual Alliance between Germany and Austria
1881	Reichstag elections a disaster for Bismarck. Can only rely on the support of 85 out of 397 deputies	Three Emperors' Alliance between Germany, Austria and Russia
1882		Italy joins Germany and Austria in a Triple Alliance
1883	Health Insurance Law	
1884	Centre Party becomes the largest party in the Reichstag and conservatives also do well	Germany begins a programme of colonial expansion
1885		War breaks out between Bulgaria and Serbia
1886	Settlement Law encourages German peasants to settle in the eastern Prussian provinces	Appointment of Boulanger as the French Minister of War
1887	Bismarck's supporters gain seats in the Reichstag elections	Reinsurance Treaty between Germany and Russia German loans withheld from Russia
1888	Death of Kaiser Wilhelm I. His grandson becomes Kaiser Wilhelm II	Colonial expansion abandoned
1889	Old age pension scheme introduced	
1890	Socialists gain 35 seats in Reichstag elections Bismarck plans a coup against the Reichstag Bismarck resigns	

Chapter 3

Wilhelmine Germany 1890–1914

Source 1

▲ Kaiser Wilhelm II in military uniform in 1895.

Source 2

▲ The Krupp steel works in Essen in 1911.

Source 3

▲ A photograph taken in Berlin on 1 August 1914.

■ **Think about**

▶ What image do you think Kaiser Wilhelm II was trying to project of himself in Source 1?

▶ Source 3 was taken in 1914. Can you think of any reason why these young German men are cheering?

■ **Further reading**

For the most recent assessment of Kaiser Wilhelm II, see Clark, *Kaiser Wilhelm II*, 2001.

Source 4

Before our eyes yesterday an elevating ceremony was played out: before us stands the statue of Emperor Wilhelm I, the imperial sword raised in his right hand, a symbol of law and order. It reminds us all of other duties, of the serious struggle against the tendencies which are directed against the foundations of our existence as a state and a society. So, gentlemen, my appeal goes out to you now: Forward in the struggle for religion, for morality and order, against the parties of revolution!

Speech by Kaiser Wilhelm II in 1894

■ **Think about**

▶ What does Source 4 suggest about Wilhelm's aims?

Introduction

It was clear from the start of his reign that Kaiser Wilhelm II intended to rule Germany differently from his grandfather. Bismarck's resignation in 1890 ended what many Germans were soon to regard as a period of strength and stability. However, as you know, Bismarck's legacy was far from promising in several respects. He had ignored the consequences of many of the social and economic changes in Germany, attempting to isolate the 'threat' from the left whilst protecting authoritarian rule and the continued power of the elites. The new Kaiser failed to address these fundamental issues and the frequent changes of Chancellor (four between 1890 and 1914) left him with more direct power and influence than was intended by the Imperial Constitution. His own personality was badly suited to such power and he became increasingly preoccupied with foreign policy. By the beginning of the 1900s, the growing military power of Germany was used as a way of masking internal opposition by generating patriotic loyalties. This policy of papering over the basic cracks which were appearing within the political system was hardly to the long-term advantage of Germany. Of course, one of the key features of this period was that it ended with a world war. To what extent was this the fault of the Kaiser and his government?

Key questions

- How did Germany develop economically and socially during this period?
- To what extent did the Kaiser establish a 'personal rule'?
- Where did power really lie?
- How successfully did the government deal with political opposition?
- To what extent was foreign policy used to distract attention away from internal problems?
- How much responsibility should Germany bear for the outbreak of the First World War?

Kaiser Wilhelm II

Historians disagree about the importance of the Kaiser during this period. He has been regarded in two different ways: as crucial to an understanding of the events which followed his accession and also as a more marginal figure who was unsuccessful in fully asserting his power. However, it is certainly helpful to have a sense of his aims and personality and it would be hard to deny that his power and influence *were* important factors influencing German policy, even if the extent of them is in dispute.

Wilhelm was the son of a German father and an English mother (he was the grandson of Queen Victoria). He was born with a paralysed left arm and a defect in the balancing mechanism in his ear. As an adult, he still required assistance in dressing and cutting up food. Historians have speculated as to how this affected him as he grew up. Certainly he showed signs of needing to prove his own strength and power and from an early age showed a great interest in the military. As Kaiser he was rarely seen out of military uniform and he often chose soldiers to advise him. His moods were erratic and he was extremely sensitive to criticism from those around him, although this did not include sensitivity to public opinion in general. One of his closest advisers until 1894, Eulenberg, told one of the Kaiser's Chancellors:

Source 5

> Wilhelm takes everything personally. Only personal arguments will impress him. He likes to lecture others but will not allow himself to be taught. He cannot bear boredom; heavy-handed, stiff and pedantic people get on his nerves and can achieve nothing through him. Wilhelm II likes to shine and to do and decide everything by himself...To get him to accept an idea one has to pretend that the idea is his own...Never forget that HM [His Majesty] needs to be praised from time to time...You will always achieve all you desire so long as you do not omit to express your admiration whenever HM has earned it.
>
> Extract from Bülow's *Memoirs*, 1930–1931

Wilhelm was prone to outbursts of rage when things did not go his way. In another communication to Bülow (Chancellor 1900–1909), Eulenberg expressed his dismay that 'HM is no longer in control of himself when he is seized by rage'.

This unpredictable and at times unbelievable behaviour made him in many ways an unsuitable monarch. Certainly his chancellors frequently had to restrain him from making potentially disastrous decisions and found their own freedom for action hampered by his mood swings. However, Wilhelm was also lazy and uninterested in the day-to-day detail of government. He once boasted that he had never read the Imperial Constitution. In these circumstances, he could be swept along by others, especially in military matters. And yet he wanted to establish a 'personal rule' where he set the terms and directed policy with minimal contact with the Reichstag. He believed that his power came from God.

Germany 1890–1914

The economy

What kind of country did the new Kaiser rule over? In economic terms, Germany continued to flourish; indeed her industrial might expanded much further after 1890. Production of manufactured goods increased by a multiple of five compared to British production which merely doubled. By 1914 Germany produced two-thirds of Europe's steel and over half its coal. Germany also led the way in the newer industries of electrical goods, chemicals and steel.

Agricultural production was more patchy, but overall by 1914 Germany was producing a higher yield of crops than anywhere else in the world.

Several factors contributed to this economic growth, but it is worth highlighting particular factors here. Firstly, the population was expanding at an astonishing rate. The German population increased from 41 million to 67.7 million between 1871 and 1914. In France during the same period the population increased from 36 million to 40 million. This provided a vast labour force, much of which was located in towns and cities as more and more people left the countryside in search of work. Other factors included the sheer size of the German Empire (which provided a substantial home market for manufactured goods) and the expertise of the German banking system which granted generous long-term loans which in turn boosted investment.

■ **Think about**

▶ Does Source 5 support the view that the Kaiser controlled German policy?

Note

Foreign visitors were frequently stunned by Wilhelm's odd behaviour. The head of the Military Cabinet died of a heart attack after dancing for Wilhelm in a tutu.

Source 6

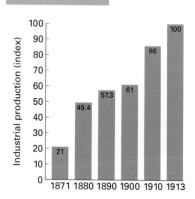

▲ The growth of German industrial production after unification, with 1913 as the base.

■ **Think about**

▶ What impact do you think this economic growth had on Germany's military potential and German society?

■ **Summary**

German society 1890–1914:

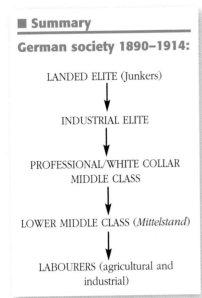

LANDED ELITE (Junkers)

↓

INDUSTRIAL ELITE

↓

PROFESSIONAL/WHITE COLLAR
MIDDLE CLASS

↓

LOWER MIDDLE CLASS (*Mittelstand*)

↓

LABOURERS (agricultural and
industrial)

Society

German society was clearly undergoing a period of profound change. The middle and working classes were swelling in number, whilst the economic power of the old land-owning elites was in decline. Industrial workers were beginning to acquire some sense of a common identity which was expressed in the growing popularity of the Social Democratic Party and the trade unions. German society remained, however, fundamentally divided along class, religious and geographical lines. Movement from one social class to another remained rare.

At the top of the social pyramid were the landed elites (Junkers) who, despite their declining economic power, remained the most privileged and powerful groups in political terms. They dominated appointments to the government, the army and the bureaucracy, and in Prussia they still dominated elections through the three-class voting system (see p. 30). Not surprisingly, they continued to defend their own interests and fight against the threat of greater democracy which could challenge their pre-eminent position in the government of Germany. Joining this land-owning elite in increasing numbers were the wealthy industrialists who, rather than challenging the power of the Junkers, instead sought to join their ranks. They too feared an extension in the power of the working class which could cut their profits, and were therefore commonly in tune with right-wing conservative politics. They even sought to copy the land-owning elite's lifestyle, for example by purchasing landed estates and securing army posts for their sons.

One rung down the social ladder were the less wealthy members of the middle class. Those involved in expanding professions, such as civil servants and academics, tended to support the status quo and offer support to the government. They were generally satisfied with the status they had achieved. The *Mittelstand* (lower middle class) were less happy, however. Craftsmen, shopkeepers and small farmers, for example, felt stranded between the industrial working class (who were gaining strength from trade unions and the Social Democrats) and the growing success and power of larger industrial concerns. This feeling of exclusion led them to question Germany's industrial age and turn to right-wing pressure groups who they hoped would restore Germany's 'traditional' values.

At the bottom of this hierarchy lay the labouring classes. Agricultural labourers found it increasingly difficult to earn a living. Many had become seasonal labourers and were dependent on finding alternative sources of employment to supplement their income. Not surprisingly, many labourers found their way to towns and cities to seek employment. For the industrial workers, now growing rapidly in numbers, employment was more stable and wages increasing. However, working and living conditions were poor and the rising cost of food and rents did little to help.

The political structure

The political structure established in 1871 (see pages 30–31) remained largely unchanged. The elites continued to dominate the government, and the Reichstag, although certainly becoming much more troublesome, could only exercise a negative influence on government policy (i.e. the power to block government policies).

Note

In East Prussia, cheap labour was sometimes brought in from Poland and Russia and, where peasants owned land, the practice of dividing it between their children was a further cause of poverty.

Source 7

Election results 1887-1912 (numbers of seats)

Party	1887	1890	1893	1898	1903	1907	1912
German Conservatives	80	73	72	56	54	60	43
Free Conservatives	41	20	28	23	21	24	14
National Liberals	99	42	53	46	51	54	45
Centre Party	98	106	96	102	100	105	91
Left Liberals	32	76	48	49	36	49	42
Social Democrats (SPD)	11	35	44	56	81	43	110
Minorities	33	38	35	34	32	29	33
Right-Wing Splinter Parties	3	7	21	31	22	33	19
Total	397	397	397	397	397	397	397

■ **Think about**

The Reich government generally looked for support from the conservatives and the National Liberals. The Centre Party often supported the government, but became increasingly critical of government policy in the early 1900s. The SPD, though more willing to work with the government than one might suppose, was hardly a source of support on which the government could – or would want to – rely. See page 33 for a summary of these political parties.

▶ What patterns of voting emerge from Source 7?

▶ Was this a pattern to be welcomed by the government?

One of the most striking features of these elections was the growing strength of the Social Democratic Party, which by 1912 had become the largest single party in the Reichstag. Despite the strong opposition to the party from both the government and the right, the SPD's programme was hardly revolutionary. Its manifesto of 1891 (the Erfurt Programme) signalled a basic intention to pursue reform within the existing parliamentary system. This was partly the result of pressure from the trade unions, most of which were led by social democrats who opposed revolutionary aims. Whilst the SPD refused to work with other parties, it continued to stand in elections and campaign legally for reform. One historian has described the government's failure to recognize the readiness of the socialists to work with it as a 'tragedy for Germany' (Craig, 1981).

Pressure groups

The weaknesses of the Reichstag led to a growth of pressure groups representing a range of different social groups:

Trade unions increased their membership considerably after 1890 and, by 1914, membership had risen to about 3.3 million. Their approach towards government was to work with it rather than to confront it and they focused their efforts on practical matters such as working hours, wages and conditions. Those workers who did not belong to a trade union (collectively known as the *Lumpenproletariat)* sometimes made more direct challenges to the government through spontaneous strikes, other illegal and even violent protests. They were not, however, supported by either the official trade unions or the SPD.

The Agrarian League was formed in 1893 by Junkers keen to see the restoration of protectionist measures to protect them from foreign competition. It soon became a major influence within the German Conservative Party. Attempts to secure the support of the peasants made some headway in the north but, in the south, the peasantry formed their own pressure groups – the Peasant Leagues. Their influence was particularly marked in Bavaria and the Centre Party, worried about the loss of the peasant vote, began to form its own Catholic Peasant Associations and became more supportive of protectionist policies.

Nationalist groups grew in number after 1890. They were largely an attempt by the ruling classes to secure support for naval expansion and a more aggressive foreign policy and did not pose a threat to the government. Their sources of support came mainly from the middle classes. The Navy League, one

Facts and figures

The number of strikes increased during this period – for example, there were three general miners' strikes (in 1889, 1905 and 1912). In 1910 nearly 700,000 workers were involved in more than 3,000 strikes. Most of the strikers were neither members of the SPD nor the trade unions.

Note

Women also formed pressure groups. There was inequality between men and women in all aspects of German life. Married women had no control over their property, did not receive equal pay and could not vote. Until 1908 they were not permitted to take part in any political activity. By 1914 there were two main women's organizations, the BDF (Federation of German Women's Associations) which was conservative in outlook, and the Socialist Womens' Movement which was much more radical.

Note

The Kaiser supported the social welfare measures brought in by Caprivi. He wanted to kill socialism with kindness – in other words, to make it difficult for the SPD to oppose the government.

Source 8

We must cry out, so that the whole nation hears us, we must cry out until it reaches the steps of the throne! But we must at the same time act, so that our cry does not once again die away unnoticed…we must bring things to a point where our district council presidents report to their superior: 'The greatest discontent dominates the farmers' circles', and their previous attitude, that was so well disposed to the government, has turned into the reverse…

Extract from an article written in 1892 by a Silesian tenant-farmer

of the most significant nationalist groups, had about 200,000 members by 1900. Anti-Semitic groups also grew in number and contested elections, although their impact on German politics was small.

In conclusion, we can see that although the *structure* of the political system remained the same, there were signs that the German people were becoming more politically active.

Domestic policy, 1890–1914

Caprivi

Bismarck's successor as Chancellor was Leo Graf von Caprivi, a man whom Wilhelm believed he could control but who in fact exercised a degree of independence. Caprivi embarked on a 'new course' intended to conciliate different political groups and achieve a workable government majority in the Reichstag. In 1891 he was able to implement a number of social welfare measures including limitations on child and female labour and working on Sundays. He followed this up with a series of trading treaties which offered lower duties on food to Germany's trading partners in exchange for easier access to foreign markets for manufactured goods.

What seemed on the surface to be sensible policies aimed at winning over the left and encouraging economic expansion led to Caprivi's downfall in 1894. The key problem was that Caprivi was alienating the elites by his social welfare reforms and upsetting the landed elites with his Tariff Act which left them much more vulnerable to cheap foreign food imports. It was this dissatisfaction which led to the creation of the Agrarian League in 1893. Nor were the socialists satisfied with the few measures which Caprivi had brought in – the left 'was not to be fobbed off with limitations on Sunday work and child labour' (Craig, 1981). The result was therefore a deadlock between government and the Reichstag, a situation which Caprivi had set out to avoid.

None of this was helped by Caprivi's unusual decision to relinquish the position of Prussian Prime Minister (a post which Bismarck had combined with Chancellor). Caprivi's replacement in this post was Count Botho zu Eulenberg, a favourite of the Kaiser. Eulenberg, a landed aristocrat himself, fully supported the conservative opposition to Caprivi and encouraged the Kaiser to ignore the wishes of his Chancellor. In 1894, amidst a wave of anarchy across Europe and an increase in SPD seats in the previous year's elections, Eulenberg pressed the Kaiser to implement an anti-socialist bill. Caprivi was presented with the subversion bill and refused to support it. The Kaiser's response was to threaten to rule without the Reichstag and it was only on Caprivi's insistence that the plan was dropped. By this time, however, Caprivi had lost too much favour amongst the ruling elites and was dismissed by the Kaiser along with Eulenberg (an illustration of the Kaiser's capricious nature).

Hohenlohe

Caprivi's successor was an elderly Bavarian gentleman named Prince Chlodwig zu Hohenlohe-Schillingsfürst. Hohenlohe was not a natural leader and made no decisive contribution to German politics. He represented industrialists and anti-socialists and much of his efforts were spent trying to get anti-socialist measures through the Reichstag, although this was more to satisfy the Kaiser than out of any burning desire on his part. However the subversion bill, presented to the Reichstag in 1895, was not passed.

From 1897 onwards, Hohenlohe, although still Chancellor for a further three years, was no longer at the heart of policy making. The Kaiser made three appointments during that year: Count Bernhard von Bülow as Foreign Secretary, Admiral von Tirpitz as Navy Secretary and Count Posadowsky-Wehner as Interior Minister. The first two appointments signalled the Kaiser's determination to focus increasingly on foreign policy. Certainly, Germany's foreign policy took on a much more aggressive character. The policy of *Weltpolitik* (World Policy) emerged in 1897, consisting of three main strands:

● Acquire more colonial territory
● Create a German-dominated economic zone in central and eastern Europe
● Expand the navy

This policy was immensely popular amongst the nationalist pressure groups such as the Pan–German League and was also popular with industrialists who saw the promise of new markets for their goods and new sources of raw materials. It also promised to fulfil the ambitions of the Kaiser and his closest ministers who wished to raise Germany's profile on the world stage.

The expansion of the navy had a profound impact on Germany's domestic and foreign policies. The Navy League, created in 1898, acted as a propaganda instrument to drum up popular, patriotic support for Germany's expanding fleet, and it met with success. Expansion of the navy proved more popular than the army, perhaps because it symbolized *German* growth (the army was still dominated by Prussia). Naval bills were passed by the Reichstag in 1898 and 1900, with the support of the Centre Party. However, naval expansion was not without its problems. For one thing, the cost of building such a powerful fleet was high. Secondly, it contributed significantly to deteriorating relations with Britain (see page 66).

Source 9

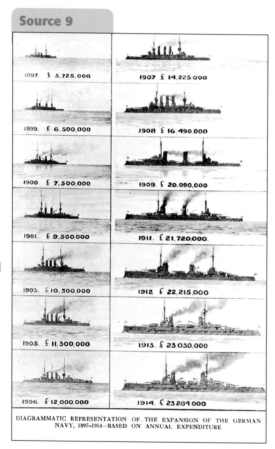

DIAGRAMMATIC REPRESENTATION OF THE EXPANSION OF THE GERMAN NAVY, 1897–1914—BASED ON ANNUAL EXPENDITURE

▲ A British diagram produced in 1914, showing the growth in the German navy since 1897.

■ **Think about**

This diagram of German naval expansion was produced in Britain.

▶ What does it suggest about Britain's response to German naval expansion?

▶ Why do you think it was produced?

The other significant political development during Hohenlohe's chancellorship was an attempt to achieve a 'marriage of iron and rye'. This involved an alliance between the landed and industrial elites which was described in 1897 as '*Sammlungspolitik*'. The alliance was hardly a stable one, however, and was based on the negative aim of suppressing socialism. The alliance of the conservatives and National Liberals (but not the Centre Party) was only briefly of much use. In the elections of 1898, only the Centre Party and the Social Democratic Party gained more seats with the *Sammlung* parties losing out.

Bülow as Chancellor

In 1900 Hohenlohe resigned and his place was filled by Bülow, who was by now exerting a good deal of influence on policy. Bülow faced two main problems on the domestic front. Firstly, his attempt to increase tariffs on foodstuffs did not go far enough to please the conservatives, while further alienating the socialists and Left Liberals who opposed the inevitable knock-on effect of higher food prices. Not surprisingly, the SPD again gained seats in the 1903 election. In the end, the tariff changes were supported by the Free Conservatives, the Centre Party and the National Liberals (the so-called black-blue alliance), but the 'marriage of iron and rye' was damaged.

The second problem facing Bülow was how to finance *Weltpolitik*. The government finances had been in deficit since 1900 and the biggest demands from the army and the navy had yet to be made. In 1905, Bülow proposed to raise indirect taxes and introduce an inheritance tax. Both measures created immediate opposition. Socialists and the Centre Party voted against raising indirect taxes which would increase the prices of goods purchased by the working people who could least afford them. Meanwhile, the inheritance tax was fiercely opposed by the conservatives, who weakened the proposal to such an extent that it was not worth implementing.

Bülow was facing a stalemate. The Centre Party was critical of the government's treatment of the native people of German South West Africa, where an uprising in 1904–1905 had been crushed, after reports reached them from Catholic missionaries. It had also denied the government support over the raising of indirect taxation. Bülow decided to break with them but faced the inevitable problem of forming a workable coalition in the Reichstag. He was helped by the election result of 1907 when the nationalist appeal of the government led to a drop in SPD seats and an increase in seats of the right-wing parties. Bülow proceeded to form the 'Bülow Bloc' consisting of conservatives and liberals. It was an uneasy alliance, however, with the Left Liberals demanding the kinds of social reform which the conservatives found intolerable.

The *Daily Telegraph* Affair

In 1908 a conversation took place between the Kaiser and a friend which was subsequently written up in the style of an 'interview' for the *Daily Telegraph*, in the hope that it might improve Anglo-German relations. In this 'interview' the Kaiser claimed that 'the prevailing sentiment amongst my own people is not friendly to England' but that the English were 'mad, mad as March hares' in believing that he himself wanted anything other than peace. Following the publication of the article, demands were made by the German press and the Reichstag for more control over the Kaiser's actions. Bülow – who claimed not to have read the article although it had been sent to him before publication – sided with the Kaiser's critics and tried to persuade the Kaiser to agree to more constitutional constraints on his behaviour. In the event, no changes to the constitution followed, demonstrating the Reichstag's divisions and essential weaknesses. The affair had, however, fatally undermined Bülow's relationship with the Kaiser. The support which he had gone to such lengths to secure was rapidly dwindling.

Bethmann Hollweg

In 1909 Bülow's fate was sealed by a further unsuccessful attempt to raise money for the military. The Bülow Bloc fell apart as the conservatives again rejected an inheritance bill, supported this time by the Centre Party which had been stung by the anti-Catholic tone of the 1907 election campaigns. The shortage in government finances remained and there was little prospect of a majority of support for the government. Bülow resigned.

His successor was Theobald von Bethmann Hollweg, an experienced administrator who sympathized with the policy of *Weltpolitik* and disliked democracy. However, his freedom for manoeuvre was restricted by previous policies and by the growing tensions that German actions had unleashed in Europe. He increasingly relied on the court, the army and the bureaucracy to support him in the face of continued opposition from the Reichstag. Only the patriotism generated by military expansion and the possibility of a threat from Russia enabled him to get anything through the Reichstag.

One of the few initiatives put forward by Bethmann Hollweg was a reform of the three-class voting system of Prussia which had long been on the political agenda. It further illustrated the deadlock in the Reichstag; the conservatives found it too threatening whilst the other parties found its moderation unacceptable. Bethmann Hollweg withdrew the bill in the face of such opposition. Two years later, in 1912, his opposition grew further with the SPD winning 110 seats in the election and becoming the single largest party in the Reichstag.

In the same year both the Navy Office and the War Ministry requested large increases in military expenditure. Initially Bethmann Hollweg resorted to a temporary measure of a tax on spirits to avoid a row over an inheritance tax, but a further request for money to fund the army's expansion forced the issue. This time, the inheritance bill was passed following the successful passage of the second army bill. Although it inevitably provoked opposition from the conservatives, the other parties rallied to the government to demonstrate their patriotism in the face of a perceived threat from Russia. The new tax had finally been achieved but the national debt remained high.

The Zabern affair

In 1913 an event occurred in the former province of France, Alsace, which was yet another example of the divisions within German society and the increasing breach between the government and its people. In this case, it was the army

■ **Activity**

Write a resignation letter from Bülow to the Kaiser explaining why you have resigned as Chancellor of Germany.

■ **Summary**

German Chancellors 1890–1917:

Caprivi: 1890–1894

Hohenlohe: 1894–1900

Bülow: 1900–1909

Bethmann Hollweg: 1909–1917

Source 10

◄ A photograph taken in Zabern in early 1914.

which provoked the affair by mistreating inhabitants of the town of Zabern. Rather than dismissing the commanding officers as was expected, the Kaiser merely transferred them to another area. This was as good as saying that the army was above the law and under the sole authority of the Kaiser. The public outcry illustrated that the status accorded to the military by the Kaiser was not acknowledged by the German people. Bethmann Hollweg received an enormous vote of no-confidence in the Reichstag (293 to 54 votes) but remained in office until 1917. Here again was a sign that the Reichstag was weak; the Chancellor remained unaccountable to the Reichstag and his authority came from the Kaiser alone.

Where did power lie in Wilhelmine Germany?

■ Historical debate

This has been the subject of considerable debate since the 1960s. The interpretations generally fall into four groups outlined chronologically:

Interpretations	Examples of historians
Some historians argue that Kaiser Wilhelm II established a personal rule in which he exercised considerable control over the direction of government policy. He set the terms and his chancellors were never able to assert power in the way that Bismarck had done previously. However, that is not to say that the Kaiser ruled well. His obsessive and unpredictable personality led to considerable errors of judgement, such as the *Daily Telegraph* affair. Nevertheless, in this 'individualist' interpretation, power lay with the Kaiser.	Röhl
An alternative interpretation – labelled 'structuralist' for convenience – argues that in fact power lay in the hands of the elites. The determination of the elites to cling on to power led to anti-socialist policies and eventually to foreign expansion in order to divert attention away from internal problems.	Wehler Berghahn
A more recent interpretation argues that we should stop focusing solely on the Kaiser or the elites and consider what was happening at the grass roots level. Rather than being manipulated, there were signs that the working and middle classes were beginning to assert themselves more effectively and that they were having an impact, however indirectly, on the direction of government policy.	Eley Blackbourn Evans
Most recently, there has been an attempt to find a way through these different interpretations. On the one hand, the Kaiser was never able to dominate the direction of foreign and domestic policy. On the other hand, the nature of the German Constitution meant that when no agreement between power blocks could be reached, the key decisions fell to him.	Clark

■ Activity KEY SKILLS

Compare the four Chancellors of Germany between 1890 and 1917. For each Chancellor, make notes under the following headings:
- Aims
- Successes
- Failures
- Why forced to resign

Using these notes, discuss whether or not you agree with the following statement:

'The problems encountered by the German government in its domestic policy between 1890 and 1914 were less to do with the Chancellors themselves and more to do with other factors.'
Note: For inclusion into your key skills portfolio, you will need to write up your answer to the question, including at least one image.

■ Activity KEY SKILLS

Read the historical debate on this page. Then arrange yourselves into four groups. Each group will consider one of the interpretations and look for evidence which *supports* it using the material in this chapter. You might also like to consider what evidence you could put forward to *undermine* the other three interpretations.

The groups will then take part in a debate, arguing either for or against the following motion:

'Power clearly lay in the hands of Kaiser Wilhelm II between 1890 and 1914.'

At the end of the debate, try to reach a consensus on where you think power did lie between 1890 and 1914.
Note: The class teacher may wish to tape/video the debate or make detailed notes to provide evidence for the key skills criteria.

Document exercise: Domestic policy 1890–1914

Source A

The policies of the SPD

...our tactics today cannot be the same as during the state of emergency. In any case we never gave up parliamentary activity and participation in daily politics even at the time; only the Party's principal task then had to consist of the bitterest, grimmest resistance against a government, which placed us outside the law, was trying to destroy us politically and individually, and hence with whom there could only be war, not negotiation. Nowadays it is different. The government has probably not given up the struggle against us. But the barbaric war of annihilation is over, and they have recognised us as a belligerent power and are conducting a civilised fight against us, in which, by our ability, we are in a position to achieve real successes.

A Bavarian Social Democrat outlines his party's policy in 1891

Source B

The views of Kaiser Wilhelm II

Public opinion didn't concern him. He knew that people didn't love him, and cursed him; but that wouldn't deter him. I then reminded the Emperor of the difference between Prussia and the Empire; said that in Prussia he had old rights which continued to exist, so far as the Prussian Constitution had not limited them...The Emperor interjected 'the Emperor hardly has any rights', which I attempted to refute. Besides, this was quite unimportant, said HM: the south German democratic states didn't worry him. He had 18 army corps and would make short work of the south Germans.

Report by Hohenlohe in 1897

Source C

Navy propaganda

...the concept of the navy has indeed, as Prince Bismarck once said, been the hearth around which the German attempts at unity have clustered and warmed themselves...It has also, however, been allotted the further task of overcoming the discord between the parties in the united German Empire, and directing the minds of the disputants towards a higher goal: the greatness and glory of the Fatherland. Today millions of our compatriots are spiritually alienated from the state and the prevailing economic order; the concept of the navy possesses the power...to revive the national spirit of the classes and fill them once again with patriotic loyalty and love for the Kaiser and Reich.

From an article written by the press bureau of the Imperial Army Office, 1900

Source D

The election results of the SPD (numbers of seats)

1887	11
1890	35
1893	44
1898	56
1903	81
1907	43
1912	110

Source E

The policies of the Centre Party

In the Reichstag new groups must be formed. The Centre Party will enter no permanent coalition, only such temporary combinations as may be necessary from time to time...There can be no question of a systematic opposition on our part against the government...The main thing is that everyone, without regard for party viewpoints, should unite in support of society and the government and protect them against attack.

Extract from the *New York Herald*, 1890 outlining the policy of Windhorst, leader of the Centre Party

■ **Examination-style questions**

1 **Comprehension in context**
Using Source B and your own knowledge, explain how Kaiser Wilhelm II viewed his own power.

2 **Comparing the sources**
To what extent do Sources A and E outline similar attitudes towards the German government?

3 **Assessing the sources**
How reliable is Source C about the likely effect of naval expansion on the German people?

4 **Making judgements**
Using all the sources and your own knowledge, explain how effectively Kaiser Wilhelm II and his government dealt with political opposition.

Foreign policy

'The war to end all wars'. This was how the First World War was to be described. Not surprisingly, the events leading up to it, and the question of who was most responsible, have generated considerable debate amongst historians. However, the purpose of this section is to explore German foreign policy between 1890 and 1914 and as such it should not be regarded as a comprehensive account of the origins of the war. The focus here is on Germany, but this should not be interpreted as suggesting that Germany was the *only* country responsible for war.

The end of Bismarck's diplomacy

Bismarck's primary aim in foreign policy had been to maintain the isolation of Germany's main enemy, France. This had involved alliances with Austria-Hungary (in the 1882 Triple Alliance, also involving Italy) and Russia (the Reinsurance Treaty of 1887). These two alliances stood uneasily together, however, as Austria-Hungary and Russia were unlikely to resolve their differences in the Balkans. In 1890, after Bismarck's resignation, Caprivi argued that an alliance with Russia was unacceptable in the light of Germany's close ties to Austria-Hungary and, consequently, the Reinsurance Treaty was not renewed. It is possible that it would not have lasted for long anyway, but this decision certainly had the effect of making Russia feel isolated, especially when the Triple Alliance was renewed in 1891. As a result, Russia was more inclined

Note

A summary of the historical debate surrounding the causes of the First World War can be found on page 69.

to respond to French pressure and in 1894 the Franco-Russian Alliance was signed. This seemed to fulfil Bismarck's 'nightmare of coalitions' in which Germany faced potential enemies on both sides. Certainly Germany's position in Europe made her vulnerable to encirclement and was a significant factor in the foreign policies that followed.

Although military plans were drawn up in case a two-front war did break out, Germany did not feel unduly alarmed at this point. One of the key miscalculations made by Germany was that Britain would remain aloof from alliances with France or Russia and that she would gradually be won over to Germany's side. This British alliance would help to neutralize any potential threat to Germany from France or Russia. However, because a British alliance was considered inevitable, it was treated with insufficient urgency. Indeed, in 1896 the Kaiser jeopardized relations with Britain by sending a telegram to Kruger, the Boer President, supporting the independence of the Transvaal in South Africa. Britain was offended as she was trying to defend her own position in the area.

Weltpolitik

By 1897 the Kaiser and his circle – which by now included figures such as Bülow and Admiral Tirpitz – had strong feelings that Germany should actively pursue a policy which would enhance its status as a world power.

> **Source 11**
>
> The times when Germany left the land to one of his neighbours, the sea to the other, and reserved heaven, where pure doctrine is enthroned, for himself (*Laughter – Bravo!*) – those times are past…We must demand that the German missionary and the German trader, German goods, the German flag and German ships in China are just as much respected as those of other powers. (*Lively Bravos!*)…we don't want to put anyone in the shade, but we demand our place in the sun too. (*Bravo!*) In East Asia as in the West Indies we will endeavour to safeguard our rights and our interests, true to the traditions of German policy, without unnecessary severity, but also without weakness. (*Lively applause.*)
>
> **Bülow speaking to the Reichstag after Germany acquired Kiaochov in China, 1897**

The policy of *Weltpolitik* was to dominate German foreign policy after 1897. It involved active colonial expansion and the creation of a strong navy. Its popularity derived from the economic opportunities of an overseas empire as well as nationalist ambitions for Germany to become a more powerful state on the world stage.

Historians have differed in their interpretation of *Weltpolitik*. Fritz Fischer, whose controversial claims about German foreign policy are summarized on page 69, argued in the 1960s that it represented the first step towards world status which would involve both colonial and European expansion. In other words, he saw it as the first step towards war. Other historians such as Wehler and Berghahn emphasize the extent to which *Weltpolitik* was driven by domestic concerns and was intended to distract the people away from internal disputes and encourage them to support the Kaiser and his government (Source 12).

Cross reference

Germany's military plan, known as the Schlieffen Plan is discussed in a margin note on page 68.

Note

Between 1890 and 1896 there was therefore no clear direction in foreign policy. During these years there were two main views on the future direction of Germany's foreign position. One was for Germany to dominate middle Europe economically, the other was for Germany to extend her ambitions and seek to gain world status by establishing a larger overseas empire. By 1896, the second view was emerging as the favourite.

■ Think about

▶ What do you think Bülow means in Source 11 by 'a place in the sun'?

▶ How would you describe the tone of this speech?

Note

Social Darwinism was the application of Darwin's biological theories of 'survival of the fittest' to society and politics. It was used to justify limited social reform, for example, because by providing for the poor, the 'unfit' might artificially survive and even thrive. Social Darwinism had a significant impact on relations between states. In order to 'survive', many believed that states had to prove their fitness and strength, for example by expansion and if necessary by war.

Weltpolitik therefore came into existence as a red herring of the ruling classes to distract the middle and working classes from social and political problems at home.

Geiss, *German Foreign Policy 1871–1914*, 1976

There are probably elements of truth to the last interpretation, termed 'social imperialism'. Certainly naval expansion stirred the patriotism of many and naval bills were passed without difficulty by an increasingly critical Reichstag. Fischer's argument is perhaps more difficult to defend. The chaotic and largely unsuccessful implementation of *Weltpolitik* undermines his theory that this was a coherent masterplan. The colonial gains in Africa, the Far East and the Pacific were small compared with other states and were too widely scattered to be defended properly. What is more, German naval expansion caused considerable alarm in Britain, whose naval fleet was the strongest in the world. This effect was not unintentional, the idea being to force Britain to acknowledge German power and accept that an alliance was in her best interests. This was a good example of how German foreign policy was mismanaged by using heavy handed and threatening tactics.

Meanwhile, Bülow continued to work on the assumption that Britain would eventually come round to Germany's way of thinking. Another opportunity to improve relations between the two countries was lost between 1898 and 1901. After clashes with France in North Africa and the threat that Russian expansion in the Far East posed to her empire, Britain felt isolated and looked to Germany for possible assistance. Her approach was ignored and Britain finally ended her 'splendid isolation' in 1902 with an anti-Russian alliance with Japan. This was followed shortly by a 'friendly agreement' between France and Britain known as the Entente Cordiale in 1904. Bülow's free hand policy had failed to keep Britain out of the arms of France and a Europe split in two was beginning to take shape. Only Russia's weakness, after the defeat of her war against Japan in 1905, offered any consolation to Germany.

The first Moroccan crisis

In 1905 France tried to extend her influence in Morocco. Germany argued that this would have illegal trading implications and the Kaiser went to Morocco himself to demand a settlement. This was another demonstration of heavy-handed methods and was intended as a show of strength which would convince France that it was Germany, and not Britain, that was the important ally. In the event, however, Britain supported France at the international conference held at Algeciras in 1906 and Germany was forced to back down. Germany was by now more isolated than ever and the Entente Cordiale was strengthened, not destroyed, by the crisis. In 1907 the Entente was extended to include Russia after Britain concluded territorial agreements with her. Although all the agreements involving Britain were not firm commitments, they nevertheless succeeded in splitting Europe in two, with the Triple Alliance on one side and the Triple Entente on the other.

Why did tensions continue to increase after 1907?

Three events in particular contributed to the increase in tension 1907–1912:

● A crisis in the Balkans in 1908–1909 which demonstrated where loyalties lay. Germany stood by Austria and forced Russia (still weak after the Japanese war) to back down in 1909, an event Russia was determined should never be repeated.

■ **Think about**

▶ Did the formation of alliances make war more or less likely?

- A naval race between Britain and Germany. The British government responded to fears that the German navy could overpower its own if measures were not taken. The Liberal government agreed to increase battleship production and the race was on. In 1909, negotiations were conducted between Britain and Germany, but made little progress. Relations between Germany and Britain were severely damaged.

Nr. 586 (Neujahrs-Nummer)   Stuttgart den 5. Januar   1909

DER WAHRE JACOB

1909

Der Schrecken Europas.   Mutter Europa: Gebt Obacht, Kinder, der böse Mann kommt!

Source 13

◀ A German newspaper cartoon published in January 1909 and called Europe's Terror. Mother Europe is saying to her children (the countries of Europe): 'Watch out children, the evil man is coming!' The man on horseback represents Germany.

■ Think about

▶ Why is it surprising that this cartoon was produced in Germany? Whose point of view might it reflect?

Source 14

Chart: Number of people in the navy (000's)

Year	Germany	Great Britain
1880		
1891		
1901		
1911		
1914		

Number of people in the navy (000's)
0 10 20 30 40 50 60 70 80 90 100 110 120 130 140 150

◀ The expansion of the German and British navies before the First World War.

■ Think about

▶ Do these figures back up the diagram on page 58?

- The second Moroccan crisis in 1911. French troops were sent to Morocco at the Sultan's request and Germany regarded this as a first step towards a French take-over which would contravene the agreement reached at Algeciras in 1906. As before, however, Germany had an ulterior motive. By sending a gunboat, the *Panther*, to Morocco, she was again demonstrating her strength. Secondly, it was hoped that the offer to recognize a French Protectorate in Morocco in exchange for land in the French Congo would gain some French goodwill. The results were disastrous for Germany. The British fleet was put on alert and Germany received considerably less land than she had requested. Furthermore, British and French ties were put on a firmer footing and a naval agreement between the two countries was concluded.

■ Activity

Summarize relations between Britain and Germany between 1890 and 1911. You could do this in several formats including a cartoon strip, a flow chart or a newspaper editorial written by either a German or British journalist. Your summary should demonstrate how Germany missed opportunities and how relations between the two countries deteriorated.

Weltpolitik had again failed to achieve its aims and Germany was more isolated than ever. By 1912, Europe was divided and an arms race was evident. Not only was the naval race reaching new proportions, but there was also an expansion in land forces in Britain, Germany, Austria and Russia. Germany was alarmed at the speed of the Russian recovery and calculated that Russian strength by 1917 would make it difficult to defeat her in a two-front war.

The outbreak of war: Germany's fault?

In December 1912 a meeting took place between the Kaiser and his senior military and naval advisers. The prospect of war was clearly on the cards. Germany was still at loggerheads with Britain and the outbreak of war in the Balkans made it seem increasingly likely that Germany would at some point be called upon to help her ally, Austria. During the meeting, war was regarded as likely, but it was also made clear that timing would have a role to play:

Think about

▶ Why do you think Moltke saw war as unavoidable in 1912?

▶ What views did the military and naval leaders have about the timing of war and why?

▶ Does this source provide conclusive evidence that war was being planned in advance?

> **Source 15**
>
> General von Moltke said that he believed a war was unavoidable. But we ought to do more through the press to prepare the popularity of a war against Russia, as suggested in the Kaiser's discussion. HM [the Kaiser] supported this and told the State Secretary [Tirpitz] to use his press contacts, too, to work in this direction. T[irpitz] made the observation that the navy would prefer to see the postponement of the great fight for one-and-a-half years. Moltke said the navy would not be ready even then and the army would get into an increasingly unfavourable position, for the enemies were arming more strongly than we, as we were very short of money. That was the end of the conference. The result amounted to almost nothing.
>
> **Extract from Admiral Müller's records of the war council meeting, 8 December 1912**

Evidently war, if it came, would be better in 1914 than in 1912. However, historians disagree about whether this document represents conclusive proof that Germany was *planning* a war from 1912. The Kaiser's moods were changeable and his ideas often unrealized – and Müller himself suggests that little was achieved at the meeting.

The assassination

In June 1914, the heir to the Austrian throne, Archduke Franz Ferdinand, was shot in Sarajevo by a Serb extremist. The events which followed appear, in retrospect, to have been under German control. At some point after the assassination, war was seen as inevitable, at least by the German military, and swift action seemed the best option.

Germany offered Austria a 'blank cheque' after the assassination – a promise of support no matter what happened. Without this guarantee, Austria would have hesitated to declare war on Serbia and risk fighting Russia. However, the offer of German support persuaded it to send a delayed ultimatum to Serbia which it expected to be refused, providing a further justification for war.

Source 16

The Kaiser authorised me to inform our gracious majesty that we might in this case, as in all others, rely upon Germany's full support...But it was in the Kaiser's opinion that this action must not be delayed. Russia's attitude will no doubt be hostile, but for this he had for years prepared, and should a war between Austria and Russia be unavoidable, we might be convinced that Germany, our old faithful ally, would stand at our side. Russia at the present time is in no way prepared for war, and would think twice before it appealed to arms... If we had really recognised the necessity of warlike action against Serbia, the Kaiser would regret it if we did not make use of the present moment, which is all in our favour.

Report from the Austrian Ambassador in Berlin to the
Foreign Minister in Austria, 5 July, 1914

Serbia did reject the ultimatum and on 28 July, Austria declared war on Serbia. It is clear that Germany had been pressing Austria to act quickly and ignore attempts at mediation by Britain. Three days later, Russian mobilization began. If the Schlieffen Plan (see margin note) was to be implemented, speed was essential. The dominance of the military leadership was clear. Attempts were made – successfully – to claim that the Russian mobilization was a virtual declaration of war on Germany and Germany's decision to declare war on Russia on 1 August and France two days later was greeted enthusiastically by many. The violation of Belgian neutrality provided the pretext for a declaration of war on Germany by Britain, who was in any case desperate to preserve a balance of power in Europe. War had begun.

■ Think about

The Kaiser had refused to offer unconditional support to Austria during the Balkan Wars 1912-13.

▶ Does Source 16 provide any clues as to why he was prepared to offer such support in 1914?

Note

The Schlieffen Plan was devised by General Schlieffen after the Dual Alliance between France and Russia in 1894. It addressed the problem of a two-front war. Schlieffen proposed that German troops should quickly defeat France (by marching through neutral Belgium) before Russia had a chance to mobilize fully. Within six weeks the French would be defeated and the German troops could then focus their efforts on the defeat of Russia. Significantly, this meant that speed was of the essence and explains why Germany declared war on Russia as soon as she received news of Russia's mobilization and then declared war on France.

Note

What was the role of Bethmann Hollweg in the outbreak of war? Certainly, he was eager to see Germany expand and he was aware of the strength of the German army. He was also, however, concerned about Russia's growing strength. In 1914 he saw an opportunity to split the Triple Entente over the Balkan issue. This was a miscalculation and Germany found herself at war with all the Triple Entente members in August 1914. However, it was a calculated risk, and Bethmann Hollweg accepted the need to move swiftly once Russia mobilized. War on such a scale may not have been deliberately planned, but nevertheless, Germany was prepared.

Source 17

◀ German mobilisation in August 1914.

Was the First World War Germany's responsibility?

Timeline

Germany 1890–1914

1890: Bismarck's resignation. Caprivi becomes Chancellor.
1891: Social welfare reforms; start of tariff reform.
1893: Agrarian League formed
1894: Hohenlohe becomes Chancellor; Dual Alliance between France and Russia
1897: Bülow appointed Foreign Minister; policy of *Weltpolitik* begins
1898: Creation of Navy League; first naval bill passed by Reichstag
1900: Bülow becomes Chancellor; government facing a budget deficit
1904: Entente Cordiale between France and Britain
1905: Bülow fails to solve the deficit problem; news of mistreatment of natives in SW Africa; first Moroccan crisis
1907: Formation of Bülow Bloc after general election; Entente Cordiale extended to include Russia
1908: The *Daily Telegraph* Interview
1909: Bethmann Hollweg becomes Chancellor; Germany forces Russia to back down in the Balkans; failed negotiations between Germany and Britain over the navy
1911: Second Moroccan crisis
1912: SPD becomes the single largest party in the Reichstag; war breaks out in the Balkans
1913: The Zabern affair
1914: Assassination of Archduke Franz Ferdinand, heir to the Austrian throne; Germany offers Austria the 'Blank Cheque'; war

■ Think about

At the Peace Conference in Versailles in 1919, German delegates were allowed no say, and in the final treaty were forced to sign a 'confession' that they started the war.

▶ If the delegates HAD been able to speak, what might they have said in their defence?

■ Historical debate

In the Treaty of Versailles of 1919, Germany was forced to accept the blame for starting the war in the famous 'war guilt clause'. However, up to the 1960s, the most popular interpretation of the war was that the Great Powers had stumbled into it and all shared the blame. The publication of Fritz Fischer's Griff nach der Weltmacht (Germany's aims in the First World War) in 1961 posed a fundamental challenge to this view. Fischer argued that Germany was largely to blame for the war which was the result of the expansionist aims of the German government. He also pointed to the continuities of this expansion ambition from 1897 (with Weltpolitik) to Hitler. This argument caused a storm of controversy and Fischer became a hated figure in some circles in Germany. Prominent German historians refused to shake Fischer's hand in public and the German government withdrew a grant to fund a lecture tour in America. Despite this opposition, Fischer's argument gained wide acceptance and it has certainly had a far-reaching impact on the historiography of the First World War. However, Fischer has been criticized for claiming too great a coherence to the foreign policy of Kaiser Wilhelm II and for relying on insubstantial evidence to prove his point. A twist in the Fischer thesis was advanced by historians of the 'new orthodoxy' such as Hans Ulrich Wehler who, whilst agreeing that Germany's responsibility for the war was the greatest, argued that it was domestic pressures rather than blatant expansionist aims that determined German foreign policy before 1914. With a budget deficit, an increasingly unmanageable Reichstag and a socialist movement growing in popularity and strength, diversionary tactics were chosen which would focus attention outside of Germany and generate popular support for an increasingly unpopular Kaiser and his government. More recently, historians have tended to acknowledge Germany's significant role in the outbreak of war, especially in 1914 itself, but also recognize the role of other factors, not least the other Great Powers. John Lowe, for example, identifies four main causes of war: the legacy of Weltpolitik, the growth of Russian power, nationalism in the Balkans and the inadequacy of German policy during the July crisis of 1914.

Conclusions

There was a lack of clear direction in domestic policy after 1890 and internal problems were at best dealt with superficially. The Reichstag was becoming more unmanageable, the working class was becoming more politically active and powerful and the government's budget deficit was not completely solved. The more aggressive foreign policy ushered in by the Kaiser had the dual effect of diverting attention away from these problems whilst also fulfilling ambitions to project Germany onto the world stage. Germany was, by this time, a world power in terms of her economic strength and the government wanted this to be reflected outside of Germany. The policy of Weltpolitik, however, created tensions in Europe which certainly contributed to the First World War. Whether Germany was primarily to blame for the war is a matter for debate, but it is hard to deny that her role was particularly significant in 1914 itself.

Chapter 4

The early years of the Weimar Republic 1918–1923

Source 1

▲ Street fighting in Berlin during the Spartacist uprising in 1919.

Source 2

▲ The German airforce is destroyed in 1919 as part of the terms of the Treaty of Versailles.

Source 3

▲ A German cartoon from 1923. The mother is saying: 'Don't worry children, father will soon be home with some potatoes…'

Introduction

Sources 1 to 3 are all images from the years 1918-1923. Together they create an impression of violence, humiliation and starvation. But to what extent is this an accurate image? It is all too easy to view the period known as the Weimar Republic, which began in 1919 and ended in 1933, merely as the prelude to Hitler's rule. Historians have searched endlessly for the clues to explain his rise to power. The answer must lie partly in the years before 1933. It is not surprising, therefore, that historians have often tended to concentrate on the more negative aspects of the Weimar Republic.

It is certainly true that the early years of Weimar up to 1923 were dogged with many problems. The humiliation of defeat in the war, the forced abdication of the Kaiser, political violence of all kinds, a detested peace treaty, a severe economic crisis, the invasion of a foreign power and the first attempt by a little known party, the Nazis, to take power all contributed to the instability of these years. One historian describes Germany by 1920 as 'one step from chaos' (Davies, 1996) whilst another writes that it is 'almost a miracle that the Weimar democracy succeeded in maintaining its existence during these years...' (Kolb, 1988).

Key questions

- What happened in the revolution of 1918?
- How was the new Republic run?
- How serious was the opposition to the new Republic?
- Was the Treaty of Versailles too harsh?
- Was the Weimar Republic doomed from the start?

The end of the war

Germany's defeat

By the summer of 1918 it was clear that Germany would lose the war. Despite advances on the Western Front in the early part of the year, the collapse of Bulgaria and the weakness of Austria left Germany ill-defended on her eastern side. Troops from the Western Front could not be spared and, to make matters worse, Germany's enemies were by now receiving support from America after she joined the war in 1917. By August 1918, the Allies had regained all the land lost during the previous three months. German territory was now under threat.

America offered her allies huge numbers of troops and vast amounts of vital supplies. Germany was fast running out of both. Although she lost fewer men (about 2 million) than some countries, she could not afford to split her army in half in order to fight effectively on two fronts, nor could she send men to fight without weapons. Britain's blockade of Germany during the last two years of the war severely restricted supplies to Germany. Not only did this affect the troops; it also led to severe food shortages in Germany. These were made worse by poor harvests in 1917 and 1918, and agricultural production in general fell. By 1918, Germany was producing only 50 per cent as much butter and 60 per cent as much meat as in pre-war years. Each German was receiving only 1000 calories a day towards the end of the war and as many as three-quarters of a million people died of starvation or malnutrition.

Towards an armistice

By September 1918, the German High Command accepted that the war was over. Plans were made to request an armistice with Wilson, the American

Further reading

For a good overview of the Weimar years, try:
Layton, *From Bismarck to Hitler: Germany 1890–1933*, 1995
Hiden, *The Weimar Republic*, 1974
For a more detailed account, see:
Kolb, *The Weimar Republic*, 1988
Feuchtwanger, *From Weimar to Hitler*, 1993

Note

A consequence of the Russian Revolution in 1917 was the ending of war between Russia and Germany. In the Treaty of Brest-Litovsk, March 1918, Russia lost all the gains she had made on her western side over several hundred years. Estonia, Latvia, Lithuania and Poland were given to Germany and Austria, whilst Finland, Georgia and the Ukraine became independent states.

President, who had already outlined possible peace terms, known as Wilson's 'Fourteen Points'. As a sign of good intent, reforms of the political system were begun, moving Germany further towards a parliamentary monarchy which the Allies would find more acceptable. The Reichstag was given greater political influence. Prince Max of Baden, Germany's new Chancellor from October, formed a government which met the approval of the biggest parties in the Reichstag and he was himself responsible to the Reichstag rather than to the Kaiser. Thus, a significant step away from autocratic rule was taken suddenly from within the Reichstag, not in response to popular demand.

The new government, under pressure from the High Command, asked Wilson for 'the immediate conclusion of an armistice on land, at sea and in the air.' The German people were stunned. Propaganda had convinced them that victory was within sight. Those who now accepted that defeat was the only possible outcome simply wanted the war to end.

Source 4

Germany's needs became ever more desperate. The bread got still worse, the milk got thinner; the farmers would have nothing to do with the towns. And would-be hoarders came home empty-handed; the men at the front were incensed…at the misery at home…For four years they had fought, on the Eastern Front, on the Western Front, in Asia, in Africa; for four years they had stood their ground in the rain and mud of Flanders…During the night of October 3rd the Peace Note was despatched to President Wilson. This unexpected bid for peace opened the eyes of the German people at last; they had had no idea of the impending catastrophe. So it was all for nothing – the millions of dead, the millions of wounded, the starvation at home. All for nothing…The people thought only of peace. They had been thinking of war too long, believing in victory too long. Why hadn't they been told the truth?

Extract from *I Was a German* by Ernst Toller, 1934

Revolution

The October reforms outlined above were one step towards a new, more democratic Germany but they could hardly be described as revolutionary. Although left-wing parties such as the SPD had been calling for changes to the political system for some time, the October reforms took them by surprise and were not the result of popular pressure. However, once the news of an impending armistice spread, the German people began to take matters into their own hands. On 28 October the High Seas Fleet was instructed by the Admiralty to sail into the Channel. This order had to be abandoned as sailors in Wilhelmshaven refused to carry out what they saw as a pointless suicide mission in a war already lost. A few days later, sailors mutinied at the port of Kiel and took control of the city. Their actions were imitated elsewhere in Germany. Workers' and soldiers' councils took control of various German towns and cities (see Source 5) and they met little resistance from the police. Their key demand was an end to the war but President Wilson's insistence on the resignation of those responsible for Germany's policy led to another demand: the abdication of the Kaiser.

(see Source 5)

Key term

Parliamentary monarchy

A parliamentary monarchy is where the king has to share some power with parliament.

Quotation

A prince had taken over from a count as Chancellor; from the point of view of the mass of the population nothing had changed.

The October Reforms described by Heiber, *The Weimar Republic*, 1993

■ Think about

Ernst Toller was a young poet and playwright who witnessed the events of 1919 first hand. He supported the communist cause and was imprisoned in 1919 for revolutionary activities.

▶ Compare Toller's reaction to peace with Adolf Hitler's (below). What are the similarities and differences between their reactions?

'Since I had stood at my mother's grave I had not wept…now I could not help it…so it all had been in vain…all the sacrifices…the hunger and thirst…the shame of indignation burned my brow.'

Adolf Hitler, *Mein Kampf*, 1925

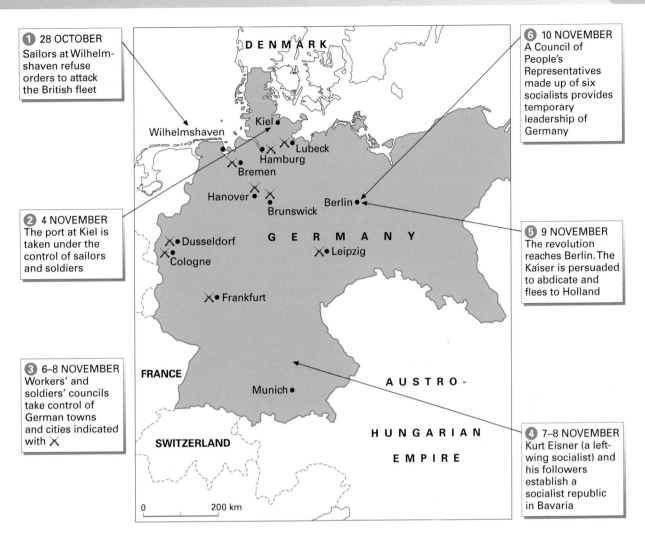

1 28 OCTOBER
Sailors at Wilhelm-shaven refuse orders to attack the British fleet

2 4 NOVEMBER
The port at Kiel is taken under the control of sailors and soldiers

3 6–8 NOVEMBER
Workers' and soldiers' councils take control of German towns and cities indicated with ×

6 10 NOVEMBER
A Council of People's Representatives made up of six socialists provides temporary leadership of Germany

5 9 NOVEMBER
The revolution reaches Berlin. The Kaiser is persuaded to abdicate and flees to Holland

4 7–8 NOVEMBER
Kurt Eisner (a left-wing socialist) and his followers establish a socialist republic in Bavaria

▲ Steps to revolution.

■ Biography

Friedrich Ebert (1871–1925)

Ebert was a saddler by trade but was elected to the Reichstag in 1912 and became President of the SPD the following year. He was appointed Chancellor after the revolution in 1918 and was made President in 1919. Between 1919 and 1925, he did all he could to protect the new Republic, crushing uprisings from the left and the right and earning the hatred of both.

By November, the revolutionary movement had spread to Berlin and Prince Max hurriedly persuaded the Kaiser to step down. Later that day, Phillip Scheidemann, a member of the Social Democratic Party, proclaimed Germany a republic from a window in the Reichstag. Friedrich Ebert was quickly appointed Chancellor. What followed was an attempt by the liberal and socialist parties to prevent the revolution from going any further. There was a very real fear that the workers' and soldiers' councils were the first step towards a communist take over as had happened in Russia in the previous year. In actual fact, the councils' members were far more moderate than was supposed and the Spartacus League, later to become the Communist Party in Germany, could muster the support of no more than about 1000 people at the end of 1918.

A Council of People's Representatives was approved by an assembly elected by Berlin workers and soldiers. It contained members of the SPD and the USPD (independent socialists who had broken away from the SPD during the war) and was intended to provide temporary leadership until an election for a new National Assembly was held. The revolution was over and any future changes would be decided through legal means. Meanwhile, an armistice was signed on 11 November and one of the deadliest wars in history came to an end. Most Germans were relieved that the war had ended, although nationalists accused the government of 'stabbing them in the back' by ending the war when Germany could, they believed, have gone on to win.

The Spartacist Rising

Although many Germans were relieved that the revolution had not gone any further, members of the Spartacus League remained deeply frustrated. They felt that Germany had lost a golden opportunity to transform itself into a fairer, more equal state in which power and wealth would be shared out amongst all the people and not just the privileged few. The founders of the Spartacus League, Rosa Luxemburg and Karl Liebknecht, both lost their lives in the struggle to achieve their aims.

Source 6

A study of the existing situation enables us to predict with certainty that in whatever country, after Germany, the proletarian revolution [revolution of the workers] may next break out, the first step will be the formation of workers' and soldiers' councils…On November 9th, the first cry of the revolution, as instinctive as the cry of a newborn child, was for workers' and soldiers' councils…[but] we have to recognize that these were no more than the first childish and faltering steps of the revolution, which has many difficult tasks to perform and a long road to travel before the promise of the first watchwords can be fully realized…How can we best deal with the situation with which we are confronted in the immediate future? Your first conclusion will doubtless be a hope that the fall of the Ebert-Scheidemann government is at hand and that in its place a socialist, proletarian, revolutionary government will be declared. For my part, I would ask you to direct your attention, not to the apex (top) but to the base…There is only one way of achieving the victory of the proletarian revolution. We must begin by undermining the Ebert-Scheidemann government by destroying its foundations through a revolutionary mass struggle on the part of the proletariat…first and foremost, we must extend the system of workers' councils in all directions.

Extracts from Rosa Luxemburg's founding manifesto of the KPD (German Communist Party), 31 December 1918

On 5 January, revolutionaries staged an uprising in Berlin, led by the USPD, the Spartacus League (by now part of the German Communist Party or KPD) and other revolutionary leaders. They occupied offices of middle-class newspapers and proclaimed the end of the Ebert-Scheidemann government, but most left after three days due to the lack of a clear strategy. Only the Spartacists fought on until they were brutally crushed by ex-soldiers known as the *Freikorps* (Free Corps) who were brought in by the government's defence minister, Gustav Noske. The use of ex-soldiers who had fought in the name of the Kaiser further discredited the government in the eyes of the revolutionaries. However, they had simply been overpowered and on 15 January, Luxemburg and Liebknecht were murdered by a group of officers. Ebert was said to be horrified and ordered an investigation into the murders.

The Weimar Constitution

Agreeing on a new constitution

Four days after the murder of the Spartacist leaders, elections were held for a National Assembly. The main job of this assembly was to draw up a new Constitution for Germany. The abdication of the Kaiser in November had left a power vacuum in Germany and it was now necessary to decide how

■ Biography

Rosa Luxemburg was born in Russian Poland but gained German citizenship through marriage. She was a revolutionary socialist and took part in the 1905 Russian Revolution. After spending the First World War in a German prison, she co-founded the communist Spartacus League in 1918 with **Karl Liebknecht** who was also a revolutionary. Liebknecht was elected to the Reichstag in 1912 as a member of the SPD but moved towards more radical politics. Both Luxemburg and Liebknecht helped to organize the Spartacist uprising in January 1919 and both were brutally murdered by members of the *Freikorps*.

■ Think about

▶ How does Luxemburg feel about the new Weimar Government in Source 6?

▶ How does she believe a 'proletarian revolution' will occur?

▶ How do you think Luxemburg wanted Germany to be run?

Note

The KPD refused to stand in the election in protest against the Republic.

the German Republic would be run and by whom. As you can see from the summary which follows, the main political parties had different ideas about this. However, the results of the election, in which all men and women over 21 could vote, boded well for the new Republic. The SPD, DDP and Centre parties between them polled 76 per cent of the vote, whilst nationalists polled only 10.3 per cent and the USPD 7.6 per cent. So the parties who were strongest in their support of the new Republic achieved a majority of the votes. Ebert was made president with fellow SPD member Scheidemann as Chancellor. In February, the new assembly met in Weimar, a small town in northern Germany, and work on the new Constitution began.

The main political parties in Weimar Germany

Z (Centre Party)	NSDAP (Nazis)
Formed in 1870 to protect Catholic interests. In favour of political reform and defended the Weimar Republic until 1930. Usually to the right of the DDP in its policies. Took part in Weimar governments up to 1932. Most support came from Catholic workers & middle class.	Formed in 1919 as the German Workers' Party. An extremely nationalist and racist party which opposed the Weimar Republic. Initially pursued violent methods of winning power but later focused on winning elections. Appealed to all sectors of society after 1929.
DNVP (German National People's Party) A nationalist party formed in 1918 to protect the interests of the land-owning class. Rejected the Republic, the Treaty of Versailles and democracy. Most support came from Junkers (landed nobility) and some urban lower middle class.	DVP (German People's Party) Formed in 1918, this was a right-wing liberal party which opposed the Weimar Republic in principle but took part in governments. Most support came from the upper middle class and employers. Led by Gustav Stresemann who became Chancellor and Foreign Minister.
DDP (German Democratic Party) A left-wing liberal party formed in 1918. Supported the Weimar Constitution but lost electoral support after 1919. Most support came from liberal intellectuals and businessmen.	SPD (Social Democratic Party) Formed in 1875, this socialist party was the Weimar Republic's strongest supporter. Received more votes than any other party up to 1932. Most support came from workers and lower middle class. Radical members were thrown out in 1917 and formed the USPD.
KPD (Communist Party) Formed in 1918 by the Spartacus League. Joined Comintern (international communist organization led by Russia) in 1919. Opposed the Weimar Republic and wanted to establish a communist state in Germany. Became more popular after 1929.	BVP (Bavarian People's Party) A Catholic Party representing Bavaria. Effectively a branch of the Centre Party, but willing to work with anti-democratic politicians in Bavaria in order to exclude the SPD.

■ Activity

1 Discuss the meaning of the following terms:
   Nationalist
   Socialist
   Communist
   Liberal
   Right-wing
   Left-wing

2 Which of the parties described here were left-wing? Which were right-wing? Which were in the middle? Place each party in order starting with the most left-wing and ending with the most right-wing.

3 What would each party want from the new constitution? Which parties wanted to destroy it?

4 Why would agreement on the new constitution be difficult to reach?

5 What kind of election results would have been disastrous for the Weimar Republic?

The Weimar Constitution

	Old Constitution	Weimar Constitution
Head of State	● Kaiser ● Inherited his position ● Could appoint and dismiss Chancellor and other ministers ● Could dissolve the Reichstag ● The Chancellor was responsible to him and no-one else ● Had the power to declare martial law and rule without the Reichstag 'if public security within the federal territories is threatened'	● President ● Had to be 35 or over ● Elected by men and women aged 20 and above every seven years ● Could be re-elected ● Could appoint and dismiss Chancellor and other ministers ● Could dissolve the Reichstag ● Could rule without the Reichstag in times of emergency (Article 48)
Reichstag (Parliament)	● Elected by all men aged 25 or over ● New laws required the approval of a majority of Reichstag deputies ● Shared power with the Bundesrat, which represented the German states ● Had no power over who was in the government (i.e. the ministers)	● Elected by all men and women aged 20 or over ● New laws required the approval of a majority of Reichstag deputies ● Reichstag could overrule the Reichsrat (see below) by a two-thirds majority ● The Chancellor and other ministers were responsible to the Reichstag – a vote of no confidence would force a resignation
States	● The Constitution begins 'His majesty the King of Prussia. His majesty the King of Bavaria; His majesty the King of Wurttemberg' ● Laws had to be passed by the Reichstag and the Bundesrat, which represented the German states ● The right to vote in many states (e.g. Prussia) was based on wealth	● The Constitution begins 'The German People' ● Reichsrat replaced the Bundesrat and still represented the German states but had less power ● Reichsrat could be overruled by the Reichstag (see above) or by a referendum (popular vote) ● Everyone aged 20 and above could vote in state elections
Civil Liberties	● Basic rights: 'There shall be a common citizenship for all Germans and the citizens of each member state shall be treated as natives in every other state.' ● No mention of social rights	● Basic rights: 'All Germans are equal before the law' ● Social rights included the freedom to: travel and live throughout Germany, exercise free speech, be free of censorship, follow any religion, negotiate for better working terms, receive an education, be treated equally no matter what, own property and be protected by the State

■ Activity

1 Identify the similarities and differences between the two Constitutions.

2 What were the most significant changes in your opinion? Why?

3 Were there any obvious weaknesses in the Weimar Constitution? Why do you think Article 48 was included? Why have some historians criticized its inclusion?

4 How would each of the political parties summarized on page 75 have reacted to the new Constitution? Write a newspaper article from the perspective of one of the parties outlining your response to the Constitution. Other members of the group could choose different perspectives.

5 'Overnight we have become the most radical democracy in Europe' (Ernst Troeltsch, *The German Democracy*, December 1918). Do you feel that this Constitution made Germany into a radical democracy? Give reasons for your answer.

■ PROPORTIONAL REPRESENTATION

The new Reichstag was to be elected using a system called PROPORTIONAL REPRESENTATION. This basically meant that seats in the Reichstag were allocated to the different parties according to the number of votes they received. Although this is a very fair electoral system in terms of making sure that everyone's vote counts, it rarely produces an overall MAJORITY in Parliament. In other words, no single party gets more seats in Parliament than all the other parties put together. In Weimar Germany, therefore, if a government was formed consisting of only the biggest party, then every time it wanted a law passed, all the other parties in the Reichstag could vote against it and it would fail. The answer to this problem is to form a COALITION. This is a government that contains more than one political party. The advantage of a coalition is that laws will get through the Parliament. The disadvantage is that members of the coalition may not agree on policies and there will be frequent changes in government.

■ Activity: choose your government!

1 Study the results of the 1920 election below. In pairs/groups, create a coalition government by selecting the parties you want to be represented in it. You must consider the following points very carefully:

● What combination of parties will give you a majority (more seats than the other parties put together)?
● Which party should your Chancellor come from?
● What combinations of parties might be able to work together (look back at the summary on p. 75)
● What problems would you still expect with your government?

Source 7

Elections for the Reichstag during the Weimar Republic (% of vote)

Party	1920	1924	1928	1930	1932 July	1932 Nov.	1933
NSDAP	–	3.0	2.6	18.3	37.3	33.1	43.9
DNVP	14.9	20.5	14.2	7.0	5.9	8.8	8.0
DVP	13.9	10.1	8.7	4.5	1.2	1.9	1.1
Z/BVP	17.9	17.3	15.1	14.8	15.9	15.0	14.1
DDP	8.3	6.3	4.9	3.8	1.0	1.0	0.9
SPD	21.6	26.0	29.8	24.5	21.6	20.4	18.2
USPD	17.9	0.30.	1	–	–	–	–
KPD	2.1	9.0	10.6	13.1	14.3	16.9	12.2
Turnout	79.1	78.8	75.6	81.9	84.0.	80.6	88.5

2 Now study the election results for the years after 1920.
● Between 1923 and 1928 the SPD refused to take part in a coalition. What problems do you think this caused and why?
● Look at the election results for 1930–1932. Why was it difficult to form successful coalitions?
● How would you describe the general trends in voting patterns between 1919 and 1932?

■ Conclusions

● The new Weimar Constitution brought democracy to Germany.
● The Reichstag had more power than before and was elected by universal male and female suffrage.
● Germany was still a federal country (individual states kept their own governments and parliaments) but the federal government in Berlin had more power over the states than before.
● An elected President replaced the Kaiser. The President was very powerful and could rule without the Reichstag in times of emergency, which would give him the power of a dictator. However, in the right hands, Article 48 could work to Germany's advantage by ensuring a swift response to a crisis. Only in the wrong hands could Article 48 become a threat to democracy.
● Proportional representation led to frequent changes of coalition governments.
● A large majority passed the Constitution. However, it was unlikely to please everyone because of the many different opinions held by the political parties. It was essentially a compromise.

Reactions to the Weimar Constitution

Source 8

At five o'clock this afternoon Ebert's swearing-in at the National Assembly... The house was crowded except for the seats belonging to the nationalists and independents... Ebert appeared on the stage in a frock coat, small, broad-shouldered with gold-rimmed spectacles...Ullstein's *Berliner Illustrierte* saw fit to publish today a photograph of Ebert and Noske in bathing trunks. The memory of the picture haunted the ceremony...Ebert made a speech. All very decorous but lacking go, like a confirmation in a decent middle-class home. The Republic should avoid ceremonies; they are not suited to this type of government. It is like a governess dancing a ballet. All the same, the whole occasion had something touching and, above all, tragic about it... Pondering the deeper significance of it can bring tears very close.

Count Harry Kessler, *The Diaries of a Cosmopolitan*, 1971

Think about

▶ Why do you think some seats were empty at the ceremony?

▶ What were Kessler's overall impressions of the ceremony?

▶ Why do you think Kessler was close to tears?

▶ Why do you think the *Berliner Illustrierte* published the photograph of Ebert and Noske in bathing trunks? (Note: for more information about Kessler, see page 110)

Timeline

1919: Spartacist uprising

1920: Kapp *Putsch*

Communist uprising in the Ruhr

1921: Assassination of Matthias Erzberger

1922: Assassination of Walther Rathenau

The National Assembly passed the Constitution by 262 votes to 75 but it pleased no one entirely. It was a compromise between the different parties, representing what most people found tolerable rather than what people really wanted. However, only the DNVP and DVP voted against it, signalling a desire by most of the other parties to co-operate with this democratic experiment. Unfortunately, the electorate as a whole did not feel as inclined to support the new Republic. The election of January 1919 proved to have been a high point in support of the Republic. The next election in 1920 saw a fall in the support for the pro-Weimar parties, whilst support for anti-Weimar parties such as the DNVP grew.

Meanwhile, it became clear that the Spartacist uprising was not the last attempt to bring down the government by violent means. In March 1920 the Ehrhardt Brigade, a unit of the *Freikorps* which had refused to disband, marched into Berlin and, under the leadership of Wolfgang Kapp, attempted to overthrow the government. The Kapp *Putsch* (uprising), as it became known, met with initial success. The Weimar government was unable to crush the Ehrhardt Brigade and President Ebert and his government were forced to flee to Dresden. The only weapons left in the government's hands were the workers in Berlin. It persuaded the trade unions to stage a general strike and, as a result, Berlin ground to a standstill. Kapp and his accomplice, General Luttwitz, were forced to surrender although, in contrast to the Spartacist uprising, they were barely punished. This not only demonstrated the right-wing bias of the courts; it also reflected the government's anxiety about losing valuable right-wing support. Two days later, the communists staged an uprising of 50,000 workers in the Ruhr. This time, the government was able to rely on the regular army which had proved so reluctant to crush the Kapp *Putsch* and the uprising was easily suppressed.

This was not the end of violent opposition. Assassinations of key government members carried out by the nationalists punctuated the next few years. In 1921 the victims included Matthias Erzberger, Germany's representative on the Reparations Commission, which was responsible for fixing the sum of money which Germany had to pay the Allies for war damage. In 1922, the unfortunate victim was Walther Rathenau, Germany's Foreign Minister.

The Weimar Constitution therefore had a mixed reception and did little to dampen opposition to the Republic from either side of the political spectrum.

However, was this the *fault* of the Constitution or was it simply inevitable given the circumstances? Clearly there were those who felt the Constitution was a mistake and indeed, many have since blamed the Constitution for the collapse of the Weimar Republic in 1933. However, this is not entirely fair. As we have seen, the Constitution was certainly a compromise. By giving the President the right to rule by decree, there was always the possibility that he might try to establish a dictatorship. However, this was not an unusual right in a democracy and in the correct hands, did not herald a return to dictatorship. Ebert, for example, used it wisely in 1923 to cope with a string of crises. Similarly, the use of proportional representation did not inevitably weaken government or encourage the growth of political extremes. The Nazis would have received similar results under a more traditional electoral system. On the other hand, the Weimar Constitution did not provide Germany with the kind of stable government necessary to see it through some difficult times and was open to misuse in the wrong hands. You will have an opportunity later to reflect on the role of the Constitution in the fall of the Weimar Republic.

Source 9

▶ Armed workers marching through Berlin as part of the Spartacist uprising in January 1919.

Source 10

▶ Freikorps soldiers march into Berlin as part of the Kapp Putsch in March 1920.

■ Think about

▶ Who posed the biggest threat to the Weimar Republic between 1919 and 1922 – the left-wing or the right-wing?

Document exercise: reactions to the Weimar Republic

Source A

Prince von Bulow expresses concerns about the Republic

But our new masters were equally unfit to govern. Most characteristic of their mentality was the speech from the Reichstag steps delivered by Scheidemann, an ex-imperial state secretary, who, in proclaiming the Republic, began his oration with the following: 'the German people have won all along the line'. A stupid lie! And a very cruel piece of self-deception! No, alas, the German people had not 'won' – it had been conquered, overpowered by a host of enemies, wretchedly misled politically, reduced by famine and stabbed in the back...The republic that emerged from our revolution was, as I have said, flatly amenable [acceptable]...its leaders the perfection of mediocrity. But at least there were no serious disorders.

Extract from the memoirs of Prince von Bulow, first published in 1931

Source B

The frightened middle class

The middle class is frightened and at its wits' end, not knowing what to do or where to turn; most of them are fluttering like birds who have fallen out of the nest and do not know where to go. They must be found another nest, and those who are simply asking all the time 'What is to happen now?' must be given the courage that comes to them only with being in a numerous company and having something to lean on...Social Democracy and Catholicism are two forces of immense importance...But Germany is Germany and anybody with his eyes open and able to look ahead cannot accept these two strong pillars as enough in the long run to give the needed support to a Republic – for the Republic has become the only possible thing...Thus it is necessary now to organize those strata of the non-Catholic middle-class who are at all inclined towards democratic ideas....

Theodor Wolff, *Through Two Decades*, 1936

Source C

The Communist threat

◀ This poster from 1919 says 'Vote Spartacist', and shows them crushing the Reichstag and the old order.

Doctor Kapp's proclamation, March 1920

The Reich and nation are in grave danger. With terrible speed we are approaching the complete collapse of the state and of law and order. The people are only dimly aware of the approaching disaster. Prices are rising unchecked. Hardship is growing. Starvation threatens…The Government, lacking in authority, impotent [powerless] and in league with corruption, is incapable of overcoming the danger…

■ Examination-style questions

1 Comprehension in context
Study Source A. Using the source and your own knowledge, why do you think Bulow objected to the phrase 'the German people have won all along the line'?

2 Comparing the sources
Study Sources A and B. What are the similarities and differences in their response to the new Republic?

3 Assessing the sources
How reliable is Source C as evidence about the extent and nature of opposition to the Republic?

4 Making judgements
'The Weimar Republic lacked popular support from the start'. Using all the sources and your own knowledge, explain how far you agree with this statement.

The Treaty of Versailles

On 18 January 1919, representatives from 32 states met to determine peace terms. Their task was enormous. Not only did the Treaty have to satisfy public demands that the aggressor be punished; it also had to meet the different demands of the three key players, France, Britain and America. And to make matters worse, it was of course also intended to prevent such a war from ever happening again. Not surprisingly, these tasks were in conflict with one another, not least the desire for revenge and the desire to avoid future war. That the Treaty was far from perfect is hardly surprising. Perhaps more surprising is that a treaty was drawn up at all.

The aims of the Big Three

By far the most influential powers represented at Versailles were Britain, France, America and Italy who together formed the Council of Four which met daily for over three months. After Italy walked out in protest, the 'Big Three' were left to thrash out the terms between them.

President Wilson of America had already outlined possible peace terms a year previously in his famous 'Fourteen Points'. They reflected Wilson's own interpretation of why the war started by calling for more openness in diplomatic relations, for a reduction in armaments and for the freedom to trade and navigate the seas without obstruction. He also called for 'A general association of nations to be formed to afford mutual guarantees of political independence and territorial integrity to great and small states alike.' In other words, Wilson believed that future wars could only be avoided with greater co-operation between nations. Of course, this depended on the readiness of nations to co-operate with one another and in this sense Wilson's vision was an

Facts and figures

The cost of the First World War was immense. Around 8 million soldiers died, a further 7 million were permanently disabled and 15 million were wounded. In addition, there were around 5 million civilian casualties in Europe (excluding Russia) who died mainly of disease and famine. The material cost was equally high. It has been estimated that the total cost of war, including the destruction of land and the cost of mobilization, was somewhere in the region of $260 billion.

■ Biography

Woodrow Wilson

was born in 1856 and was the American President between 1912 and 1920. Wilson's most famous achievements were the Fourteen Points and the League of Nations. He was the first American President ever to leave the country and negotiate a European peace but he suffered an isolationist reaction among American Republicans who wanted to avoid any future commitments in Europe. He suffered a stroke in 1919 and died in 1924. He once declared 'What is expected of me only God could perform.'

ideal which underestimated national feelings of pride, security and ambition. Nevertheless, his points provided a useful starting point and the League of Nations, set up to mediate between countries in disputes, owed much to Wilson's vision.

In terms of Wilson's feelings towards Germany, it is true that the Points did not outline specific punishment beyond the loss of land such as Alsace-Lorraine. It is unlikely that Wilson felt comfortable with the notion of revenge, although he did believe Germany should be punished and had to respond to an American public, which was increasingly hardline in its attitude to Germany. At the same time, however, the people of America were increasingly determined not to get embroiled in European disputes in the future. In the end the American Senate refused to ratify either the Treaty or America's membership of the League of Nations.

In Britain, Lloyd George had a similarly careful path to tread between his own aims and public opinion, although the two were not so different as has been supposed. His primary aims were to maintain a balance of power in Europe, eliminate Germany as a colonial and naval rival and gain a share of any money paid to the Allies by Germany. He agreed that Germany should accept blame for the war and therefore pay for war damage as well as lose land. However, too harsh a punishment could have the effect of weakening Germany to the extent that it would no longer provide any kind of barrier against Russia. With communism now established in Russia, the British were anxious to limit its impact on Europe; if Germany were pushed too far, it might even give in to communism herself.

France was in a different position to Britain. Its material losses were greater and it was geographically more vulnerable to future German attack. Clemenceau, the French Prime Minister, had security issues at the forefront of his mind. With the collapse of the Austro-Hungarian and Russian Empires, Germany could in theory assert its influence in Central Europe even more firmly. Now was the time to exploit German weakness and ensure future security. Clemenceau therefore called for a drastically reduced armed force in Germany, further losses of land on Germany's east and west borders, extensive payments to cover war damage and a firm anti-German alliance system which would centre around a stronger Poland. Although sympathetic to many of Clemenceau's arguments, an overly powerful France was as much of a threat to Lloyd George's concept of a balance of power in Europe as a strong Germany, and he therefore sought to water down some of Clemenceau's more extreme demands.

■ **Biography**

Lloyd George
was born in 1863 and was an MP for 55 years. He was Prime Minister from 1916–1922. A member of the Liberal Party, he never had the complete backing of his party and led a coalition government with the support of the Conservatives. He tended to neglect domestic issues in favour of foreign affairs which eventually lost him support. A notorious womanizer and a very strong character, he had enemies in high places who kept him out of office after 1922.

■ **Biography**

Georges Clemenceau
was born in 1841. He entered politics in 1870 when he became Mayor of Montmartre. He was without fear, fighting many duels in his life, and was passionate in his devotion to France. One of his primary aims as a politician was to recover Alsace-Lorraine from the Germans. At Versailles (aged 79) he fought tirelessly on France's behalf and demanded ruthless terms against Germany, although he was forced to compromise on all of them. During the peace conference he survived an assassination attempt but later that year lost support in elections and was forced to retire.

■ **Activity**

Design a political cartoon for a newspaper in January 1919. Your cartoon should illustrate the negotiation process at Versailles and give a sense both of the demands that the different countries were going to make and the likely clashes between them. Try **not** to draw the cartoon from a single country's perspective.

Source 11

◀ From the left, Clemenceau, Wilson and Lloyd George at Versailles, 1919.

The first 26 articles of the Treaty of Versailles contained the Covenant of the League of Nations. This was to be a permanent organization with 45 members, although it was hoped that this number would grow as former enemy powers were accepted into the League (Germany joined in 1926). Its primary purpose was to avoid conflict through peaceful negotiation and disarmament.

■ Activity

1 Discuss how each of the Big Three might have reacted to the final Treaty. How satisfied would they have been? What concerns might they have had?

2 Write an editorial for a French, American or British newspaper in July 1919. You have just heard the details of the Treaty. What views are your newspaper likely to have?

(*Note:* If you wish to write an editorial from a German perspective, you should read the section below on 'The reaction in Germany'.)

Note

The Versailles Treaty was only one of several treaties concluded between 1919 and 1920. Separate treaties dealt with the other defeated powers, Austria-Hungary, Bulgaria and Turkey. The complete disintegration of the Austro-Hungarian Empire was confirmed and new independent states emerged including Czechoslovakia and what was to become known as Yugoslavia. Meanwhile, nothing was done to restore lands forfeited by Russia in the Treaty of Brest-Litovsk leading to further new independent states including Poland, Finland, Estonia, Lithuania and Latvia. Self-determination (running your own country) was the order of the day. It has been argued that the creation of so many relatively weak and inexperienced nations left Central and Eastern Europe exposed to the aggression of the bigger powers.

The terms of the Treaty

Source 12

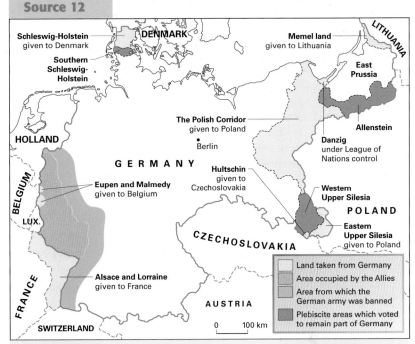

ARMED FORCES
The German army was not allowed to exceed 100,000. All tanks, military and naval aircraft, submarines and heavy artillery were forbidden. Six battleships only were permitted.

WAR GUILT
Known as the 'War–Guilt Clause', article 231 of the Treaty contained Germany's acceptance that she was responsible for the war. This clause made Germany liable for war damage costs.

REPARATIONS
The most contentious issue at Versailles was money. How much should and could Germany pay? A Reparations Commission was set up and in 1921 fixed the bill at £6,600 million.

The reaction in Germany

Germany was not permitted any representation at Versailles and was only summoned to receive a draft of the Treaty in May, at which point her protests were largely ignored. Not surprisingly, Germany felt aggrieved at this treatment, calling the Treaty a '*Diktat*', which echoed her complaints of a dictated peace. However, there was little she could do but accept the Treaty: her bargaining powers were non-existent in the light of her total surrender and inability to fight on. The acting Chancellor, Bauer, brought in after the failure of the previous Cabinet to reach a decision on the Treaty, pledged to 'fulfil the imposed conditions of the peace' but added that these terms went beyond 'the limits of Germany's ability to comply…'

There is no doubt that the Treaty had a profound impact on Germany, although there is disagreement about the extent to which it made an economic collapse in Germany inevitable. More agreement exists on the *psychological* impact. The Treaty was overwhelmingly loathed by the German people, not just for the material losses but also the humiliation of the War–Guilt Clause. The severity of the Treaty played into the hands of the nationalists who accused the Weimar governments of betraying Germany's interests and perpetuating the crimes of the 'November Criminals' who had ended the war too soon.

Was the Treaty of Versailles too harsh?

Reactions at the time

Source 13

[The Treaty of Versailles] seeks to punish one of the greatest wrongs ever done in history, the wrong which Germany sought to do to the world and to civilization, and there ought to be no weak purpose with regard to punishment. She attempted an intolerable thing, and she must be made to pay for the attempt.

Extract from President Wilson's speech at Omaha, September 1919

Source 14

I reach, therefore, the final conclusion that, including all methods of payments …£2,000,000,000 is a safe maximum figure of Germany's capacity to pay. In all the actual circumstances, I do not believe that she can pay as much…the Treaty includes no provisions for the economic rehabilitation [recovery] of Europe…nothing to stabilise the new states.

John Maynard Keynes (economist and a British representative at the Peace Conference). Extract from Keynes, *The Economic Consequences of the Peace*, 1920

Source 15

Our Fatherland finds itself in the most difficult hour of its history….We in our party are aware of the results for our people which a rejection of the peace treaty will entail. ('Very True!' from the right.) The resulting harm, however, will only be temporary, but if we accept this treaty we will abandon countless generations of our people to misery…For us the acceptance of the treaty is impossible for many reasons…In addition to making Germany defenceless, there is also the matter of theft of our territory.

The German National Assembly debate on the Treaty of Versaillles, June 1919

Source 16

This is not Peace. It is an Armistice for twenty years.

Ferdinand Foch, French Marshal

Source 17

I have every hope that Lloyd George, who is fighting like a Welsh terrier, will succeed in…imposing some modification [change] in the terms…Now that we see them as a whole, we realise that they are much too stiff…the real crime is the reparation and indemnity chapter, which is immoral and senseless. There is not a single person among the younger persons here who is not unhappy and disappointed at the terms. The only people who approve are the old fire-eaters.

Harold Nicholson (member of the British delegation to Paris). Extract from Nicholson's letter to his father, June 1919, from *Peacemaking 1919*, 1933

Source 18

GIVING HIM ROPE?

German Criminal (*to Allied Police*). "HERE, I SAY, STOP! YOU'RE HURTING ME! [*Aside*] IF I ONLY WHINE ENOUGH I MAY BE ABLE TO WRIGGLE OUT OF THIS YET."

▲ A cartoon from the British magazine, *Punch* about the terms of the Treaty of Versailles.

The reactions of historians

Source 19

In the first place, it came to be felt that there was a moral taint about treaties signed under duress [pressure]. This feeling attached itself mainly to the Versailles Treaty, signed by Germany under the duress of a five-day ultimatum. German propaganda worked hard to popularise the conception of the Versailles Treaty as a Diktat which had no moral validity....[however] the moral objections most frequently expressed against the Versailles Treaty seem, in fact, to have been based not so much on its signature under duress as on the severity of its contents, and on the fact that the Allied Governments, reversing the procedure followed at all important peace conferences down to and including that of Brest-Litovsk, refused to engage in oral negotiations with the representatives of the defeated power. This act of unwisdom probably discredited the Treaty more than the ultimatum which preceded its signature.

Carr, The Twenty Years' Crisis 1919–1939, 1939

Source 20

Although Germany lost some 13% of her territory and some 6 million subjects, it is no longer acceptable to blame the ultimate failure of the Republic on the Treaty of Versailles, and even its economic effects are disputed, given the economic 'recovery' of Germany in the middle-twenties. For Weimar governments there was a real possibility to work patiently and skilfully in their relations with the foreign powers...Yet there remained the perennial problems for Weimar governments of convincing internal opposition of the validity of this approach....Germany's exclusion from the new peace-keeping organisation, the League of Nations, underlined the arguments of German nationalists against the Diktat of Versailles. This disillusionment made it easier for Germans to accept the false notion propagated by rightist and nationalist circles that such an 'unjust' peace need never have been signed in the first place. To accept this one had to believe, incredibly enough...that Germany had not been militarily defeated but could have fought on had the army not been 'stabbed in the back' by the civilian leaders...The pernicious [destructive] effect of the Versailles Treaty lie thus in the way it created added dimensions to existing internal conflicts...

Hiden, The Weimar Republic, 1974

Source 21

The settlement neither crippled Germany nor reconciled her to the new order; instead it left her with grievances and the latent potential to make trouble. It based its judgements on three premises: that Germany had started the war; that she had fought a dirty war; and that she had lost. Accepting none of these the Germans believed the settlement was unjust.... Foch, the French commander of the Allied armies, condemned the Treaty as 'an Armistice for 20 years'. His verdict proved uncannily accurate but was not inevitable. Any fair judgement must consider the reasons why there had been a war in 1914, the difficult circumstances of 1919, and the performance of those who governed Europe after the peace had been made. Even if the settlement was a 'tragedy of disappointment' it was as much because of its virtues as its faults. It did not destroy Germany, it tried to draw maps around people and, through the League, to create a more just and successful international system.

Sharp, 'Versailles 1919: A Tragedy of Disappointment' in Catterall and Vinen (eds), Europe 1914–1945, 1994

Source 22

For twenty years the public had been led to believe that Germany had been crushed at Versailles...Had not Mr Keynes demonstrated that Germany could not be expected to pay...more than £1,000 million per annum for Reparations? That her annual savings were even likely to fall below that sum? How then could she find many, many times as much to finance rearmament on a scale adequate to beat the combined forces of the Democracies?

Mantoux, The Carthaginian Peace or the Economic Consequences of Mr Keynes, 1946

■ Activity   KEY SKILLS

'The Treaty of Versailles did more harm than good.'
Divide into two groups. Using all the evidence on these two pages and your own knowledge, prepare for a debate on the Treaty of Versailles. One group will be proposing the motion and one will be arguing against it. Once you have read everything and added anything from your own knowledge, write a short introductory speech outlining your arguments.
Try to anticipate the arguments from the other side. Can you pick holes in the evidence they are likely to use? At the end of the debate, try to reach a group decision on the issue.

Conclusions

The final version of the Treaty, ratified by all the represented states except America, was a curious mixture of punishment and peace making. It dealt the new Republic in Germany a severe blow by undermining an already failing economy and confirming the claims of the far right opposition. In *Mein Kampf* Hitler wrote of the souls of the German people 'aflame with a feeling of rage and shame'. He was to use the Treaty to his own advantage in his attempt to stir up nationalist opposition to the Republic.

But did the peacemakers at Versailles make a mistake? Could they have made a better peace? The historian Eric Hobsbawm wrote that the Treaty was 'doomed from the start, and another war was therefore practically certain' (Hobsbawm, 1994). However, there is also a case for arguing that it was the circumstances in which the Treaty was (or was not) implemented that determined its fate. Had the German economic recovery of the mid-1920s continued, had the League of Nations been stronger with American support, had a policy of co-operation between Germany and other states continued in the 1930s, then we would probably not study the Treaty so closely for signs of self-destruction. On the other hand, any treaty which depends on wholly favourable circumstances to be effective might be deemed a weak one. As with so much in history, there is no simple answer. But we do need to guard against making judgements solely in the light of 'what happened next'.

Towards economic collapse

The impact of the Treaty of Versailles

By the end of the war, the national income was two-thirds its pre-war level and both industrial and agricultural production had fallen considerably. Germany had financed the war largely through borrowing and printing more money, both of which continued after 1918 with disastrous consequences. After 1919, the entire Reich budget was needed to pay the interest on the wartime loans. In addition, the government's policy of simply printing more money led to rampant inflation: by 1922, the German mark was worth 1 per cent of its pre-war level and the bad harvest of 1918 forced food prices up further.

This was the situation in which the Treaty of Versailles made its demands. The Treaty deprived Germany of 75 per cent of her iron ore resources, 25 per cent of her coal and 15 per cent of her arable land, and of course the reparations bill came on top of this. The reparations sum of £6,600 million (132,000 million gold marks) was payable over 42 years and opinions differ over whether Germany could have realistically repaid such an amount. Keynes, in his book *The Economic Consequences of the Peace,* calculated that the Allies needed something in the region of £1600–£3000 million to cover war losses and argued forcefully that it was impossible for Germany to repay a larger amount. However, some historians claim that the sum fixed in 1921 might not have been so unrealistic. The government's slowness to act in the face of a growing budget deficit may have been a way of convincing the Allies to reduce reparations repayments.

Nevertheless, there is no doubt that the economy in Germany was spiralling out of control even before the events of 1923.

■ **Activity**   **KEY SKILLS**

This activity is intended to follow the debate on page 85. If you did not take part in the debate, then you must ensure that you have read through the sources on pages 84-85 and familiarised yourself with the issues they raise.

Your task is to produce a detailed analysis of the Treaty of Versailles, which draws on the work you have done so far, the sources in this chapter, other books and information from the Internet. You may also want to read pages 86–8. The focus of your analysis should be on whether the Treaty was fair and provided for a lasting peace. Recommended websites include:

Search.britannica.com/search?query=treaty+of+versailles (this provides a number of useful links)
www.people.virginia.edu/~sas4u/versailles/htm (a recent academic assessment of the treaty)

The format of your analysis is important and must develop your ICT skills. Decide with your teacher what format it should take. Your analysis should include at least one primary source, one image such as a map and one graph, for example showing the scale of Germany's losses.

You should present your findings and judgements to the rest of the group, producing a summarised version of your analysis to illustrate your presentation.

■ **Think about**

▶ Why do you think the government's policy of printing more money would lead to higher prices (inflation)?

The invasion of the Ruhr

At the end of 1921, Germany proclaimed itself unable to meet the reparation payments for the following year. Although it was agreed to halt the payments temporarily, the French were looking for an excuse to take action. The excuse came in the unlikely form of telegraph poles – part of the timber promised to the Allies – which were not delivered to France on time. Delivery of coal was also delayed. The French Prime Minister Poincaré sent 100,000 French and Belgian troops into the Ruhr in January 1923 to collect the coal for themselves. They faced no military opposition – Germany was hardly in a position to fight back – but they did face a workforce ready to back a government policy of passive resistance. As German workers refused to work for the French, leading to the collapse of services such as transport, the French brought in their own workers. Not surprisingly, there was a great deal of ill will between the former enemies and frequent outbreaks of violence and hostility. The worst incident occurred when German workers tried to stop French soldiers taking vehicles belonging to a German business. A total of 13 workers were killed in the gunfire.

This policy of passive resistance might have gone some way to alleviate the feelings of humiliation amongst the Germans, but it had catastrophic consequences on the German economy. The central question was who would pay the striking workers? The government regarded this as its responsibility and paid out millions of marks to the workers and industrialists who were out of pocket. Meanwhile, tax revenue from the Ruhr dried up, as did coal supplies which had to be obtained through imports. The combined cost of all this to the government was twice the annual reparation payments. There were two options open to the government at this point. Firstly, they could raise taxation, rejected on the grounds that the tax burden on the nation was already too high. Secondly, the policy of deficit financing could be continued – in other words to print yet more money. The government opted for the latter and what followed was an unprecedented rise in prices and a dramatic fall in the value of the mark.

Hyperinflation: money gone mad

Note

The Ruhr was the industrial heartland of Germany. It produced 80 per cent of Germany's steel and more than 80 per cent of her coal.

■ **Think about**

▶ What is going on in Source 23? (What do you think the kite is made of?)

Source 23

▶ A practical demonstration of inflation in Germany in the 1920s.

In December 1922, there were 8,000 marks to the US dollar. By April 1923, this figure had risen to 20,000 marks and, by August 1923, there was an incredible 1 million marks to the dollar. People no longer carried their money in purses and wallets. Instead they stuffed banknotes into wheelbarrows. A loaf of bread in Berlin in November 1923 cost you 201,000,000,000 marks, compared with 0.63 marks in 1918.

While not everyone suffered to the same degree, many lost almost everything. The groups that suffered most were those living off a fixed income such as pensioners, students and disabled war veterans. White-collar workers such as teachers and civil servants were also badly affected as they received salaries, which were difficult and time-consuming to negotiate. This latter group had been prominent in its support for the Republic in 1919, but after 1923, began to vote increasingly – and ominously – for more extreme parties. Those with savings saw the value of them wiped out and certain sectors of the population became severely malnourished.

However, some groups were slightly shielded from the worst of the crisis, such as farmers, who despite shrinking markets, did at least have a source of food to eat or barter with. Small tradesmen, shopkeepers and craftsmen all did good business whilst some members of the working class also had union leaders fighting hard on their behalf. In some cases, workers were paid twice daily and allowed time in between to go and spend the money before it depreciated further. Industrial leaders found their debts wiped out and were able to exploit bankruptcies and acquire more holdings.

Nevertheless, the crisis had a significant impact on Germany and brought considerable hardship.

The political consequences of the 1923 crisis

In October and November 1923, both the extreme left and right attempted to exploit the government's difficulties and seize power. The KPD made preparations for revolutionary action in central Germany and tried to use an unusual alliance with the SPD in Saxony to gain the basis for an uprising. The government called a state of emergency and the uprising was finally called off. Similarly, the Nazi Party tried to take advantage of nationalist fury over the ending of passive resistance in September. However, they failed in their attempt to win the support of the Bavarian authorities and march to Berlin. As many as 4000 Nazis, including Hitler, were arrested. Their sentences, as with the Kapp *Putsch*, were mild in the circumstances (they were accused of treason). Hitler was in prison for just nine months.

Dissatisfaction with the government's handling of the crisis was not restricted to the extremes, however. Although it was clear to the more detached observer that the roots of the crisis did not lie exclusively with the Republic's government – the effects of the war, the Treaty and the irresponsible behaviour of German business were at least as much if not more to blame – it nevertheless provided a convenient target to blame. Organizations representing the lower middle class or 'Mittelstand', such as artisans and small traders, accused the Government of violating its responsibility to protect an independent middle class in agriculture, trade and commerce. This resentment did not disappear once the economy had stabilized and members of the *Mittelstand* were to become some of Nazism's most eager supporters.

Note

The effects of hyperinflation were at times bizarre. People burnt paper money because it was cheaper than coal and banknotes were used as wallpaper. There were stories of the price of a cup of coffee doubling in price in the time it took to drink it. A man walking down the street carrying a bag full of money was mugged: the thief emptied the notes onto the pavement and stole the bag.

■ Activity

Draw a summary diagram (possibly a flow chart) explaining as clearly as you can the causes of hyperinflation.

Cross reference

This Nazi uprising became known as the Munich Beer Hall *Putsch*. For more information, see page 119.

■ **Think about**

▶ What do you think is meant in Source 24 by 'the psychological shock' of the experience?

▶ According to Fulbrook, how did the experience of hyperinflation affect people's view of the Weimar Republic? Was this fair?

Source 24

Even when the worst material impact was over, the psychological shock of the experience was to have longer-lasting effects, confirming a deep-seated dislike of democracy – which was thereafter equated with economic distress – and a heightened fear of the possible consequences of economic instability.

Fulbrook, *Germany 1918–1990*, 1991

Document exercise: The Ruhr invasion and hyperinflation

Source A

The impact of hyperinflation

The savings of the middle classes and working classes were wiped out at a single blow with a ruthlessness which no revolution could ever equal; at the same time the purchasing power of wages was reduced to nothing. Even if a man worked till he dropped it was impossible to buy enough clothes for his family – and work, in any case, was not to be found. Whatever the cause of this phenomenon...the result of the inflation was to undermine the foundations of German society in a way which neither the war, nor the revolution of November 1918, nor the Treaty of Versailles had ever done.

Bullock, *Hitler A Study in Tyranny*, 1952

Source B

The impact of hyperinflation on the middle classes

...historians are agreed in their view that the widespread belief as to the 'destruction of the middle class' by the inflation is untrue. The 'middle class' consisted of very different groups which were affected in very different ways by the almost complete devaluation of the currency and consequent wiping out of all debts...While savers, mortgagees and bondholders lost their wealth...small tradesmen, shopkeepers and craftsmen did good business and suffered scarcely at all from the inflation, and farmers were on the whole unaffected...It cannot be denied, however, that the redistribution of wealth within the middle class hastened the dissolution [breaking up] of the German middle class as a social and political factor...

Kolb, *The Weimar Republic*, 1988

Source C

Numbers of American dollars to the German mark

July 1914	4.2
January 1919	8.9
January 1920	64.8
January 1923	17,972.0
July 1923	353,412.0
August 1923	4,620,455.0
September 1923	98,860,000.0
October 1923	25,260,208,000.0
15 November 1923	4,200,000,000,000.0

Source D

Middle classes sell belongings to raise money

■ Examination-style questions

1 Comprehension in context

Was the invasion of the Ruhr the main cause of hyperinflation in Germany? Use Source C and your own knowledge.

2 Comparing the sources

To what extent do Sources A and B agree about the impact of hyperinflation on German society?

3 Assessing the sources

Which of the sources C and D is most useful to a historian researching the impact of hyperinflation in Germany?

4 Making judgements

'Hyperinflation and the invasion of the Ruhr severely undermined the strength of the Weimar Republic.' Using the sources and your own knowledge, to what extent do you agree with this statement?

Conclusions

The early years of the Weimar Republic were extremely unstable. Opposed by many from the very beginning, it faced problems on every front, political, economic, social and foreign. That it managed to survive at all is in many ways remarkable. In answer to the key questions posed at the beginning of the chapter we have seen that:

- Germany's revolution was not particularly violent or radical, but it did turn Germany into a democratic republic
- The new Republic was run according to the Weimar Constitution
- Opposition to the Republic came from both ends of the political spectrum but only once (the Kapp *Putsch*) did it pose a serious threat
- The Treaty of Versailles was hard on Germany, although Germany was not destroyed and was able to rebuild herself in later years
- The Republic was weak from the start – but was it doomed? The following activity invites you to reach your own conclusion.

■ Activity: Was the Weimar Republic doomed from the start?

Some students see the Weimar Republic like the *Titanic*: doomed to fail right from the start. But was the *Titanic* really doomed to sink from the moment she was built, or did it depend on another factor, the iceberg? Maybe she was doomed to sink IF she hit a big iceberg, but that's not quite the same as being doomed to sink no matter what. Can we compare the Weimar Republic with this ill-fated ship? It could be argued that the Republic was not completely doomed to fail, just as Adolf Hitler was not inevitably going to become leader of Germany from birth. In the right circumstances, the new Republic might have survived, but just as the *Titanic* hit an iceberg, so the Republic hit its own series of obstacles. A stronger republic might have survived these blows, it is true, but that itself does not condemn the Weimar Republic.

YOUR TASK

Study the timeline below to refresh your memory of the main events. Then copy out and complete each spider diagram.

Timeline

1918
September: Clear that the war is lost
October: Reforms of the political system
            Mutiny of the German fleet begins
November: Kaiser abdicates
            Ebert becomes Chancellor
            Armistice is signed

1919
January: Spartacist Uprising
            National Assembly elected
June: Treaty of Versailles signed
July: New Weimar Constitution adopted

1920
March: The Kapp *Putsch*
            Communist uprising in the Ruhr

1921
April: Reparations Commission agrees sum for
               Germany to pay
August: Assassination of Matthias Erzberger

1922
June: Assassination of Walter Rathenau

1923
January: Occupation of Ruhr by French and Belgian
               troops
August: Stresemann becomes Chancellor
            Beginning of hyperinflation
September: Passive resistance called off
September – November: Communist, socialist and Nazi
               uprisings

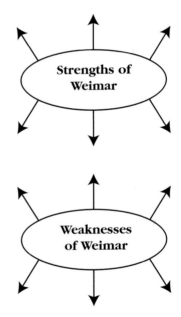

■ Activity

It is November 1923. As editor of *The Times*, you have decided to write an editorial on the future of Germany. Passive resistance has been called off, political uprisings have been crushed and the Allies are considering ways to ease the pressure on Germany. Do you think the Weimar Republic has a future? Or do you believe the new Republic is ultimately too weak to last for much longer? Think back over the previous four years. What are the signs that it will survive or collapse?

Chapter 5

The 'Golden Years' 1924–1929

Introduction

The second half of the 1920s has been described as Weimar's 'Golden Years'. Although not strictly accurate – not everyone prospered and many problems remained – it does at least reflect the way that life in Germany improved compared to the troubles reached by 1923. The economy partially recovered, political threats to the Republic quietened down and better foreign relations were restored. For some, these years offered a welcome distraction from the gloom of war and economic depression. It was the age of cabaret, cinema, theatre – and experimentation. But not everyone approved of the changes taking place. The opposition of the nationalists continued, especially as Germany embarked on a quest to build better relations in Europe and negotiate better peace terms. In addition, the return of some stability in Germany encouraged even the more moderate political parties to act in their own interests rather than in the interests of Germany as a whole. Even the social and cultural changes and experiments brought opposition; not everyone approved of the highlife they witnessed in the cities. They disapproved of what they saw as immoral behaviour in the nightclubs and the way in which issues such as sex were now openly discussed.

■ Think about

The painting shown in Source 1 is 'Big City' by Otto Dix, painted in 1927–1928. It presents mixed messages about Weimar's 'Golden Years'.

▶ What is Dix trying to say about city life?

■ Biography

Gustav Stresemann

Stresemann was born in 1878, the son of an innkeeper. He gained a doctorate with a thesis on the Berlin bottled beer trade in 1902 and went on to enjoy a successful career in business. He entered the Reichstag in 1907 as its youngest member. He supported the monarchy and was a co-founder of the right-wing DVP in 1918. Not a natural supporter of the Weimar Republic at first, he went on to contribute more than almost anyone else to its survival. Appointed Chancellor in 1923 at the height of hyperinflation, he went on to serve as Foreign Minister from 1923 until his death in 1929.

Key questions

● How did the economy recover from hyperinflation?
● Did the economy recover completely?
● Did the Republic continue to face opposition?
● How successful was Stresemann's foreign policy?
● How were society and culture changing?
● How golden were the 'Golden Years'?

The end of the crisis

The appointment of Gustav Stresemann

In August 1923 Gustav Stresemann was appointed to lead a new coalition government as Chancellor. This government was the first to include parties from both the left and the right. Stresemann's own party, the People's Party (DVP), shared power with the Centre Party, the Democrats (DDP) and the Social Democrats (SPD). It was a sign of the crisis of the time and also Stresemann's skill that the SPD were prepared to work in a government headed by a member of the DVP. Stresemann was determined to act in the wider national interest rather than simply in the more narrow interests of his own party.

How did the economy recover?

Stresemann succeeded in solving the two major problems of 1923 in the 103 days that he was Chancellor. Passive resistance in the Ruhr was called off in September and the mark was stabilized. Stresemann knew that Germany had no real option in the Ruhr, but he also realized how unpopular a move it would be. After the humiliation of Versailles, it would seem – correctly – as though Germany was once again being forced to surrender and publicly acknowledge its own weaknesses. As we saw in the last chapter, the political consequences of this were far reaching, involving a threat to the government from the extreme right.

In November, a new currency was issued, the Rentenmark, which was based on a mortgage of all land and industry and therefore relatively secure. Each Rentenmark was exchanged for one trillion old marks; purses and wallets could again be used in place of wheelbarrows. Stresemann was able to enforce the new currency by decree after the Reichstag voted to give the government full power to make decisions in currency matters. The Rentenmark was really just a bluff – 'new banknotes on which only a dozen zeroes had been cancelled' (Heiber, 1966) – but it worked.

Meanwhile, the end of passive resistance in the Ruhr had opened the door to international negotiations. The French invasion had notably lacked any British support and it had helped to deepen distrust between the two countries. The British were alarmed at the heavy-handed tactics of the French and approached America about establishing an international commission of financial experts to regulate any reparations problems. The Americans agreed, despite French objections, and it was from this commission that an important report named after its president, Charles Dawes, emerged in the spring of 1924. This report formed the basis of the Dawes Plan which reorganized the Reichsbank, reduced the total reparations bill and spread out the repayments with annual payments of one billion marks until 1929 and 2.5 billion marks thereafter. Even more crucially, the Plan approved an allied loan to Germany of 800 million gold marks to help her meet the first revised repayment and this opened the floodgates for American capital into Germany. Between 1924 and 1930, loans of up to 25.5 billion marks were received in Germany, mainly from the United States. The Reichstag passed the Dawes Plan in August 1924, but not without opposition from the nationalists who were furious at the idea of Germany's finances being controlled by external powers.

Although the Dawes Plan has generally been regarded as vital to German economic recovery, its long-term effects have not always been seen so positively:

Source 2

While it helped with the immediate problem, the Dawes Plan actually promoted a cycle harmful for international finance. American funds poured into Germany; Germany used the money to pay reparations; Britain and France, who received most of this money, were supposed to pay their war debts to the United States; the United States sent more money into Germany. The Germans fell into the habit of expecting that funds from the United States would flow on indefinitely.

Snyder, *The Weimar Republic*, 1966

How golden were the Golden Years?

Did life get better?

Compared to the years of inflation and hyperinflation, the second half of the 1920s did appear to be golden years. With capital flowing in from America in the form of both short and long-term loans, the economy seemed, on the surface at least, to prosper. Public works schemes provided new stadiums, apartment blocks and opera houses. New welfare schemes were brought in, such as a more comprehensive unemployment insurance system in 1927. Wages increased, particularly for those employed by the state, and working hours continued to be regulated, although some modification was made to the eight hour day in 1923 when a ten hour day could operate as long as a collective

■ Think about

▶ What do you think Snyder means by a 'harmful cycle' in Source 2?

▶ Do you think the Dawes Plan was a good move for Germany or not?

Facts and figures

Average real wages (1936=100):

	Per hour	Per week
1913/14	64.7	76.0
1925	94.6	93.4
1926	100.8	97.1
1927	110.6	109.6
1928	122.9	124.5
1929	129.5	128.2
1930	125.8	118.1
1931	116.3	103.9
1932	97.6	85.8
1933	94.6	87.7

Facts and figures

Average annual working hours

Year	Hours
1913	3,290
1925	2,910
1929	2,770
1938	2,750

■ Think about

Look back at the political parties summarized on page 75.
▶ Which parties might the lower middle class have turned to in a crisis?

Facts and figures

Number of strikes

Year	Strikes
1913	2464
1919	3719
1920	3807
1921	4485
1922	4755
1923	2046
1924	1973
1925	1708
1926	351
1927	844
1928	739
1929	429
1930	353

■ Activity

To what extent do the statistics on wages, working hours and strikes prove the following statements?
● Workers were better off between 1924 and 1929 than before
● Workers worked shorter hours between 1924 and 1929 than before
● There were fewer disputes between workers and employers between 1924 and 1929 than before
● Life was better between 1924 and 1929 than before

Consider the value of statistics as evidence. What CAN they tell us? What CAN'T they tell us? What other information do you need to get the most out of these particular statistics?

agreement had been made. Industrial production increased and, by 1927, Germany was producing at pre-war rates despite her losses at Versailles.

However, it is much too simplistic to view 1924–1929 as the prosperous filling sandwiched between two periods of economic depression. For one thing, the economic recovery did not affect everyone equally. Although hyperinflation had helped big businesses to pay off their debts and make larger profits, it had deepened the divide between the rich and the poor. Amongst those who were never fully to recover during the second part of the decade were the lower middle class – the *Mittelstand*. This group refused to be categorized with the working class, even though their economic position was no better. Instead they prided themselves on a skilled and professional status which set them apart from unskilled manual workers. Their occupations ranged from skilled craftsmen to newer jobs in commerce, the civil service, the service industries and small businesses. They felt their interests were being squeezed between those of big business, which could fend for itself, and the working class, who had trade unions, the SPD and the KPD to defend it.

Farmers were another group who would have been astonished by the term 'golden years'. Affected by a worldwide agricultural depression, farmers needed to modernize in order to remain competitive both on the home and foreign market. However, lack of profit led them further into debt and discouraged investment in new machinery. Agricultural production was patchy and did not keep apace with industry. In 1929, when industrial production had returned to pre-war levels, agricultural production was still 74 per cent of its pre-war total.

Not surprisingly then, farmers were amongst the first group clearly to demonstrate their dissatisfaction with the government by voting for extremist parties, most notably the Nazis in 1928, the same year which saw farmers rioting in protest at their circumstances. Their response was an ominous sign of things to come. The *Mittelstand* also moved towards the political extreme and was to become the Nazis' most loyal group of supporters after 1929, voting for the party in higher proportionate numbers than any other group in Germany.

The industrial workers were in a slightly better position during this period in so far as their wages increased and working hours remained more or less at the eight hours agreed in 1919. However, wages did not go much above the rising cost of living and after the expectations raised by the new Republic, workers were disappointed that their position had not improved further. Superficially, relations between workers and industry improved, with fewer strikes between 1924 and 1929. This was the result of state arbitration which, after 1924, took a fairly middle line in disputes and often defended the rights of the workers. However, the figures concealed a more uneasy relationship between workers and employers; the latter were unhappy at being forced to pay out high wages and were regularly trying to get their workers to work longer hours in return.

Overall, then, experiences between 1924 and 1929 varied widely. Although life for many was much better than it had been in 1923, not everyone prospered to the same extent. For some, their experiences were bad enough to encourage them to cast votes for an extremist party which laid the blame for economic problems at the door of the Jews and the Republic.

Why didn't the economy recover completely?

There were many reasons why the German economy did not make a full recovery between 1924 and 1929. Some of these reasons were to be found outside of the country; others were unique to Germany.

INTERNATIONAL REASONS

The Treaty of Versailles The Dawes Plan certainly helped Germany cope with the demands of reparations, although repayments briefly exceeded 3 per cent of Germany's GNP at the end of the 1920s which was a significant amount. However, the main result of Dawes was a German reliance on American loans which turned sour in 1929 when the American stock market collapsed and loans were recalled.

World economy Germany was not the only European state to experience slow growth in industrial production. In 1925, Germany's industrial production was 95 per cent of its 1913 level; Britain's figure was only 86 per cent and France's was 114 per cent, still only a small improvement. Part of the reason was the growth of other world economies. America profited from the war and her production figure in 1925 was 148 per cent of the 1913 level while Japan's soared to 222 per cent.

World export market In the 1920s conditions were not favourable to an export economy which Germany traditionally had. New competitors such as Japan were undercutting prices and traditional markets were lost. In addition, the export market was shrinking due to a Europe-wide fall in population. Germany's export quota fell from 17.5 per cent in 1910–1913 to 14.9 per cent in 1924–1929.

DOMESTIC REASONS

Industrial production Figures fluctuated and barely exceeded pre-war levels even by 1929. There was some attempt to modernize production methods by bringing in American-style technology, especially in the coal and car manufacture industries. Other industries proved more resistant to change, such as steel. Where successful, the new methods led to a new problem in Germany: long term unemployment. This was the result of attempts to make each individual worker work as productively as possible, therefore reducing the total number of workers required.

Workers' wages and the welfare state Inflation had benefited big businesses. When it ended, industry became less tolerant of its obligations to workers. Germany's workforce had become too expensive compared to other countries and employers were frustrated to lose so much of their profits in wages, not to mention in welfare schemes such as the unemployment insurance scheme.

Trade The knock-on effect of high wages was higher prices for goods, which were therefore less attractive both to foreign and domestic customers (who could buy cheaper imports). Cartels (groups of businesses involved in the same industry) also helped to keep prices high by agreeing between themselves what prices to put on their products. One result was therefore a shortage of foreign trade. German industry had by 1929 increased its production of goods for export, but they could not find adequate markets for these exports. Not surprisingly, industrialists wanted to find a guaranteed market. It was partly this need that made them so supportive of rearmament, which would enable them to sell their goods to the government. This paved the way for an alliance between the Nazis and the big industries in the 1930s.

> **Note**
>
> In November and December 1928, the Ruhr ironworks dispute became the worst industrial dispute of the period. Employers refused to accept the arbitration of the state on wages and prevented 220,000 workers from working until new wage rates were accepted. Eventually a compromise was found.

> **Facts and figures**
>
> **Index of exports and imports (1913=100)**
>
> | | Exports | Imports |
> |------|---------|---------|
> | 1913 | 100 | 100 |
> | 1925 | 66.4 | 82.3 |
> | 1930 | 92.2 | 86.0 |
> | 1932 | 55.6 | 62.5 |

■ Historical debate

The debate about the extent of an economic recovery between 1924 and 1929 is part of a wider debate about exactly when the fate of the Weimar Republic was sealed. If there were serious problems with the economy before the Wall Street Crash in 1929, then this might lend weight to the theory that the Weimar Republic was doomed to fail even before the events of 1930–1933. **James** (1986) stresses the structural weaknesses of the German economy before 1929 and points out that there were signs of economic decline before the American collapse. He writes 'The German economy of the inter-war years was marked by a high degree of instability and low growth rates…'. **Peukert** (1987) similarly focuses on the weaknesses of the pre-1929 economy, describing it as 'The Sick Economy of Weimar'. Several historians such as **Geary** and **Kolb** highlight the deteriorating relations between workers and employers and also the tensions created by an extension of the welfare state. Not all historians paint such a gloomy picture, however. Both **Snyder** (1966) and **Bookbinder** (1996) pay greater attention to recovery, although neither dispute its limitations. Bookbinder, for example, writes 'Although the recovery was not uniform…the period 1924–1929 represented a positive change for many Germans…By 1929 Germany had become the world's second industrial power behind the United States…'

Document exercise: The economic recovery

Source A

Snyder on the economic recovery

The country was still beset by political troubles, but economically the picture was changed. Bolstered by the Dawes Plan, the economy made a surprising recovery. The distressing days of the inflation were forgotten as the people tasted prosperity. It was a spectacular development, to be compared with the equally rapid economic revival of Germany after the nightmare of Hitler's war. True, the coating was thin and the wounds underneath had never completely healed but for the time being at least, happy days were back again.

Snyder, *The Weimar Republic*, 1966

Source B

A cartoon about the rich and the poor

▲ A cartoon by Karl Arnold in 1928. Some are fat by choice, some are thin by choice and some are thin because they have no choice.

Source C

Statistics on the Weimar economy

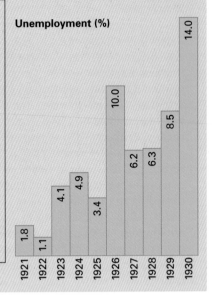

Industrial production

Year	Production (1928=100)
1913	98
1918	56
1919	37
1920	54
1921	65
1922	70
1923	46
1924	69
1925	81
1926	78
1927	98
1928	100
1929	100
1930	87

Unemployment (%)

Year	%
1921	1.8
1922	1.1
1923	4.1
1924	4.9
1925	3.4
1926	10.0
1927	6.2
1928	6.3
1929	8.5
1930	14.0

Source D

James on the economic problems

Germany's economic crisis preceded both the world depression and the political collapse. Weimar's economy suffered from a basic instability and like any unstable structure required only a relatively small push to bring down the whole structure. Some of the causes of Germany's problems stemmed from the world economic setting, but many of them were endogenous [growing from within].

James, 'Economic Reasons for the Collapse of Weimar' in Kershaw (ed),
Weimar – Why did German Democracy Fail?, 1990

■ Examination-style questions

1 Comprehension in context
Using Source C and your own knowledge, explain what was happening to German industry between 1924 and 1929 and how this affected unemployment figures.

2 Comparing the sources
Study Sources A and D. To what extent to they differ in their view of the German economy between 1924 and 1929? Can you suggest any reasons for their differences?

3 Assessing the Sources
Study Source B carefully. Of what use is this source to a historian studying the impact of the economy on the German people between 1924 and 1929?

4 Making judgements
Using all the sources and your own knowledge, how accurate is it to describe the years 1924–1929 as a period of economic recovery?

Foreign policy: an era of fulfilment?

The German acceptance of a reparations repayment plan in 1921 marked the beginning of what we now call the 'Era of Fulfilment'. This basically meant that Germany would show willingness to fulfil the terms of the Versailles Treaty as far as it could. This did not reflect any change of heart by the Germans. They still privately raged against the Treaty and Weimar foreign policy never wavered from its fundamental aim of revising the terms. But it was felt that an appearance of goodwill, together with clear signs that Germany couldn't possibly afford to repay such a large amount, might lead to more revision than an openly hostile attitude. The nationalists, of course, were opposed to such a policy and did their best to sabotage it for the remainder of the decade.

The Treaty of Rapallo, 1922

In April 1922, Germany signed a treaty with its former enemy, Russia, at the World Economic Conference at Genoa. Neither Germany nor Russia gained much from the Conference: the French at this point refused to consider any easing of the Versailles terms and communist Russia was frustrated in its desire to establish trading relations with individual states. The Treaty of Rapallo went some way to compensate. Firstly, Russia offered Germany a new export market whilst Russia stood to benefit from German investment. Secondly, the sheer size of Russia offered Germany the chance to develop weapons and train pilots well away from Allied scrutiny. Thirdly, both states had an active interest in preventing Poland from becoming too powerful with French support: if Poland were sandwiched between two allies, Russia and Germany, its scope for action was limited. General Seekt was a passionate believer in fostering good relations with Russia in order to destroy Poland:

Biography

General Seekt

Known as the 'Sphinx with the monocle' because of his well-dressed appearance. Seekt was the commanding officer of the German army from 1920 until 1926 when he was dismissed for offering a military post to Prince Wilhelm of Prussia, a member of the former royal family. Although he played a major role in suppressing the attempted Nazi *putsch*, he later became a supporter of Hitler during the depression.

Source 3

> Poland's existence is intolerable, incompatible with the survival of Germany. It must disappear, and it will disappear through its own internal weakness and through Russia – with our assistance. For Russia, Poland is even more intolerable than for us; no Russian can allow Poland to exist. With Poland falls one of the strongest pillars of the Treaty of Versailles, the preponderance of France…Poland can never offer any advantage to Germany…The re-establishment of the broad common frontier between Russia and Germany is the precondition for the regaining of strength of both countries.'
>
> Memorandum by Seekt, September 1922

Think about

▶ Why do you think Seekt wanted Poland to 'disappear'?

▶ Why did Seekt support an alliance with Russia?

▶ What might have been the disadvantages of an alliance with Russia?

However, Germany was hardly in a position to launch an offensive against Poland, nor did the Russian alliance help her to develop good relations with the West. France in particular was horrified by Rapallo – it seemed to confirm her worst fears. Rapallo was of no use to Germany in 1923 when the French invaded the Ruhr and would be of little use in any negotiations about the Versailles peace terms. It was this realization that influenced Stresemann's foreign policy in the years he was Foreign Minister.

Stresemann's aims

Gustav Stresemann was Foreign Minister from 1923 to 1929. During that time he did more than anyone else to bring stability to the Weimar Republic, although he earned the anger of the Nationalists, including many in his own party, the DVP. His aims were no different to any other German at that time. He wanted the peace terms revised to enable Germany to regain her great power status in Europe. His methods, however, were more controversial. He realized that Germany needed a policy which looked both east *and* west. It was no good focusing on relations with Russia; the co-operation and support of the West was equally, if not more, crucial. In particular, France needed to be reassured and some trust re-established, as it was France who was proving most stubborn over revision of the peace terms.

Such aims and methods seem to us perfectly sensible and realistic, but at the time, it seemed to the nationalists as if Stresemann was acting more in the interests of European peace and stability than the interests of his own country. They greeted the Dawes Plan with the words 'No new Versailles!'. However, for most of the 1920s, the nationalists were outnumbered by those who supported Stresemann; it was only Stresemann's death in 1929 that removed one of the obstacles to the nationalists' cause.

Stresemann's methods and achievements

In 1923 Stresemann, as Chancellor and Foreign Minister, was responsible for both the ending of hyperinflation and the end of passive resistance. In 1924, the Dawes Plan was the first sign that the Allies were prepared to take Germany's plight seriously and offer some constructive assistance. Furthermore, the last French troops evacuated the Ruhr in July 1925. Stresemann was therefore in a good position to press on with further revision of the Versailles Treaty, but he was aware of the need to reassure France. He returned to an earlier idea of a security pact and in December 1925, in London, the Locarno Pact was signed. This has been regarded by some as Stresemann's greatest achievement.

The pact consisted of several treaties. Germany, France and Belgium signed treaties of mutual guarantee of their shared borders, with Britain and Italy offering further guarantees. Germany was, in effect, accepting her western borders as defined in the Treaty of Versailles. In the east it was a different story. Although Germany signed arbitration treaties with Czechoslovakia and Poland, promising that any future disputes about borders would be submitted for arbitration, she refused to sign a treaty of mutual guarantee of her borders with either country. In other words, Germany was leaving the door open for further revision of the eastern borders as settled at Versailles. Despite this, the Locarno Pact was accepted by the Allies (although France needed a nudge from America and Britain) demonstrating that they were increasingly seeing the western and eastern parts of the Treaty as two separate issues, an approach which would suit Germany just fine.

Locarno was quickly followed by two successes for Germany. The first Rhineland zone was evacuated before the end of 1925 with hopes that a total evacuation would be completed well ahead of 1935. Secondly, Germany gained admission into the League of Nations in August 1926.

Source 4

▶ Gustav Stresemann speaking at the League of Nations in September 1926.

■ Think about

'The euphoria of the 'Age of Locarno' was best illustrated by the ubiquitous [ever present] pictures of Stresemann addressing the League of Nations, a source of pride for many Germans. Pride was in short supply during the Weimar Years.'

Bookbinder, *Weimar Germany*, 1996

▶ Why was Germany's entry into the League of Nations a 'source of pride'?

▶ Do you think everyone in Germany shared this view?

In the summer of 1927, the Allies agreed to reduce the occupation forces in the Rhineland by 10,000 and two years later, as part of the Young Plan, they promised to evacuate the area fully by June 1930, five years earlier than stated in the Treaty of Versailles. The Young Plan also set, for the first time, a time limit for reparation repayments and revised the overall figure to 112,000 million Reichmarks. Germany was to pay an average of 2,000 million Reichsmarks each year for the next 59 years. A key advantage of this for Germany was that the sum they would repay for the next three years would be less than that fixed in the Dawes Plan.

Thus, Germany ended the 1920s in a very different position, not as an outcast in Europe but as a key player.

Document exercise: The Locarno Treaty

Source A

Stresemann defends the treaty against nationalist opposition

Our present purpose is to become an active Great Power once again, and thus to be regarded. I would ask you all to postpone these discussions at least until the result of Locarno is before you as a whole, and in all this conflict over political theories at home, consider the effect that must be produced abroad by the general spectacle now presented by Germany…When we came back from Locarno, at Chamberlain's request, the English Ambassador was there to welcome us and made a speech in which the following sentence appeared: 'The world will never forget that it was Germany that took the initiative towards peace in Europe.'

Extract from Stresemann's speech to the Dresden Press in October 1925

Source B

Rumours of a plot to kill Stresemann

LOCARNO, Switzerland, October 4. – On the eve of the Locarno Conference the preparations have been marred [spoiled] by a persistent rumour that German nationalists have planned to assassinate Dr Stresemann rather than permit him to conclude with the Allies a commitment for the security of Europe laid within the terms of the Treaty of Versailles. Discovery of the plot by the Berlin police is responsible, it is understood, for the strange action of Dr Stresemann and Dr Luther in leaving the special German delegation train at Bellinzona and motoring to Locarno after dark last night.

Extract from *The New York Times*, 5 October 1925

Source C

Locarno was a domestic disaster for Stresemann

...Locarno stands without question as Stresemann's greatest diplomatic triumph. In terms of domestic policy, however, it must be regarded, along with the election of Hindenburg, as a defeat, since it marked the failure of more than a year's efforts to bring the DNVP to accept his foreign policy...Moreover, after the nationalists left the government, their leaders joined the Nazis and other extremist groups in hurling charges of appeasement and fulfilment at Stresemann and the DVP...It deprived him of full recognition for his diplomatic achievement by blinding much of the German public to the gains he had made.

Turner, *Stresemann and the Politics of the Weimar Republic*, 1963

Cross reference

For a profile of Hindenburg, see page 133.

Source D

Locarno was a diplomatic triumph

[The Locarno Treaty] was the turning point of the years between the wars. Its signature ended the First World War... If the object of an international agreement be to satisfy everyone, Locarno was a very good treaty indeed...They had reconciled France and Germany and brought peace to Europe...The Germans could be satisfied too. They were firmly protected against a new occupation in the Ruhr; they were treated as equals, not as the defeated enemy; and they kept the door open for a revision of their eastern frontier. A German statesman of 1919, or even of 1923, would have found no cause for complaint.

Taylor, *The Origins of the Second World War*, 1961

■ **Examination-style questions**

1 Comprehension in context

Using Source B and your own knowledge, explain why German nationalists might have planned to assassinate Stresemann.

2 Comparing the sources

To what extent and why do Sources C and D differ in their views on the success of the Locarno Treaty?

3 Assessing the sources

How useful is Source A for assessing Stresemann's aims?

4 Making judgements

Using all the sources and your own knowledge, explain whether or not you think the Locarno Treaty was a success for Stresemann.

Politics 1923–1929

Although support for anti-Republican parties such as the DNVP and KPD increased in the first election of May 1924, the pro-Weimar parties went on to achieve modest success for the rest of the decade. In the second election of 1924 there was a slight move away from the political extreme and in 1928, the SPD increased its share of the votes from 26 per cent to 29.8 per cent whilst the DNVP's share fell from 20.2 per cent to 14.2 per cent. In addition, there were no significant challenges to the government, a marked contrast to the previous four years.

However, coalition government did not get any easier. In 1923, a grand coalition was put together with no fewer than four political parties. It was a noble attempt, but the differences between the parties were too great. In fact, as stability increased in Germany and the air of crisis was over, parties began to act less in the national interest and more in the interest of their own supporters. The SPD, for example, opted out of 'bourgeois' or middle-class coalitions between 1923-1928 in an attempt to keep the support of the trade unions and prevent the workers from defecting to the KPD. Unfortunately, the SPD remained the largest party in the Reichstag until 1932 and its absence from coalitions was a blow to political stability. It also led the way for a series of Centre-right coalitions which were suspicious of left-wing politics.

The cause of the left-wing was further undermined by the weaknesses of the KPD. After 1923, comparative stability seemed to rob the communist movement of its sense of urgency. Many members and supporters disappeared and those who remained spent much of their time arguing about links with Russia and possible future action. One historian writes 'In 1924–30 the KPD was not a truly significant force within the workers' movement or on the stage of national politics: though conspicuous, it had little real power.' (Kolb, 1988).

One of the biggest blows to the Left, however, came in 1925 with the death of Ebert and the election of a new President. The KPD refused to support the SPD candidate Wilhelm Marx and this failure of the Left to work together brought victory to the right-wing candidate, General Paul von Hindenberg, Field Marshal in the First World War.

Facts and figures

Coalition governments 1923–1930

1923

August – September: SPD, DDP, Centre, DVP (Grand Coalition)

October – November: SPD (until 3 Nov), DDP, Centre, DVP (Grand Coalition)

1924

November – June: DDP, Centre, BVP, DVP (Centre-right coalition)

June – January: DDP, Centre, DVP (Centre-right coalition)

1925

January – December: Centre, DVP, DNVP, BVP (Centre-right coalition)

1926

January – May: Centre, DDP, DVP, BVP (Centre-right coalition)

1927

January – June: Centre, DVP, DNVP, BVP (Centre-right coalition)

1928

June – March 1930: SPD, DDP, Centre, BVP, DVP (Grand Coalition)

Was Stresemann a great statesman?

A SUMMARY OF THE DEBATE

The reputation of Gustav Stresemann has been debated since his death in 1929. Initially, both up to 1933 and after 1945, he was regarded by some as a hero, as someone who abandoned his nationalist, expansionist ambitions and who became a European statesman, fighting for peace and prosperity. This sudden conversion apparently took place around 1920. However, the publication of his letter to the ex-Crown Prince (see Source 7) provided a different view of Stresemann, this time as someone who wanted only to restore German power through expansion. From the 1950s, historians no longer regarded Stresemann as a great European statesman, but a calculating nationalist in the tradition of Kaiser Wilhelm II before him and Hitler after him. More recent appraisals have indeed accepted that Stresemann's methods of co-operation in Europe were a means to an end and that ultimately he wished to see Germany as a great power again. The difference however is that recent historians have not therefore condemned him as a hypocrite. If Stresemann was a 'coolly calculating realist, nationalist and power-politician' then he 'was no different in that respect from other European statesmen of his time…' (Kolb, 1988)

TWO CONTRASTING VIEWS

Source 5

Stresemann's long-term policy was one of preparing for warlike expansion…He worked towards a war, but always kept in view that armed force as a political instrument was, under certain conditions, not calculated to serve the interests of the classes he represented.

Ruge, *Stresemann*, 1965

Source 6

[There was a] great outcry against Stresemann after this death when..his papers revealed clearly his intention to destroy the existing settlement. The outcry was grotesquely unjustified…it was inconceivable that any German could accept the Treaty of Versailles as a permanent settlement…Stresemann wanted to do it peacefully…and this belief entitles him to rank with Bismarck as a great German, even as a great European, statesman. Maybe even greater.

Taylor, *The Origins of the Second World War*, 1961

■ Activity

KEY SKILLS

Consider these questions before completing the task below:

1   How do the two views (Ruge and Taylor) differ?
2   Which of the sources 7 to 11 support each view?
3   Why do you think the two historians differ?

TASK

Your task is to produce three appraisals of Stresemann. Each one should draw on the information about Stresemann in this chapter, paying particular attention to the material presented here. They should also contain evidence of further research, either from other books or the internet, and appropriate images of Stresemann.

● An obituary written immediately after Stresemann's death
● An entry into a biographical dictionary written in 1960
● A summary of his life written for a GCSE textbook in the present time.

Each appraisal should include something about his life, his aims and his achievements.

Source 7

In my opinion there are three great tasks that confront German foreign policy in the more immediate future:

In the first place the solution of the Reparations question in a sense tolerable for Germany…

Secondly, the protection of Germans abroad, those 10 to 12 million of our kindred who now live under a foreign yoke in foreign lands.

The third great task is the readjustment of our eastern frontiers; the recovery of Danzig, the Polish Corridor, and a correction of the frontier in Upper Silesia.

In the background stands the union with German Austria, although I am quite clear that this not merely brings no advantages to Germany, but seriously complicates the problem of the German Reich…[The Locarno Treaty] rules out the possibility of any military conflict with France for the recovery of Alsace-Lorraine…The question of a choice between east and west does not arise as the result of our joining the League. Such a choice can only be made when backed by military force. That, alas, we do not possess…

Letter from Stresemann to the ex-Crown Prince, 7 September 1925, outlining his aims

Source 8

I should like to know how a statesman can pursue a policy if the conditions for maintaining human life are absent. Think of the winter now before us. All these matters, credits, etc., will only be granted to a peaceful Europe, and that is one of the results of Locarno…When I consider, however, the German nationalists voting against us, and the Social Democrats voting against us too…and the whole affair coming to nothing in the end, as a German I can hardly understand it, and a foreigner could not understand it at all. A refusal would have the effect of a hard frost after a succession of lovely May days.

Extract from Stresemann's speech to the Dresden Press, October 1925

Source 9

Germany's relations with the League are not…confined to the possibilities of co-operation in general aims and issues. In many respects the League is the heir and executor of the Treaties of 1919. Out of these Treaties there have arisen in the past, I may say frankly, many differences between the League and Germany. I hope that our co-operation within the League will make it easier to discuss these questions.

Extract from Stresemann's speech to the League of Nations, September 1926

Source 10

In the course of my life I have come to believe that nothing great and permanent has ever been done in the world without give and take, compensation and compromise.

Stresemann, 1927

Source 11

◀ A cartoon by Karl Arnold in 1923, after Stresemann became Chancellor. It is entitled 'Saviour Stresemann'.

Weimar society

The 1920s were a time of social change throughout Europe and this was especially true of Germany. The war had left its mark on society as had the industrial expansion of pre-war years which had led to the growth of cities such as Berlin. In addition, the changing expectations of women, the increased leisure opportunities and the first signs of a relatively new phenomenon, long-term unemployment, were all examples of how society was facing new challenges and inevitable change.

The Weimar Constitution promised freedom and equality to everyone, but not everyone accepted this. The German historian Peukert has described the period as a crisis of modernity. It is true that perhaps the biggest tension was between those who wanted change and a more 'modern' way of life and those who clung on to more traditional values and lifestyles. This type of conflict is hardly unique, but in Germany it was being fought at a time of acute political and economic crisis. It was also used to the advantage of right-wing groups, such as the Nazis, who claimed the moral high ground and promised to protect society against evil modern influences.

Population changes

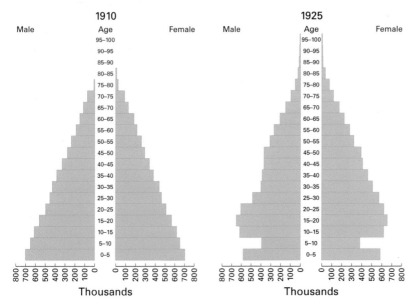

The population changes were partly the result of long-term trends, such as the growing ideal of a smaller family and an extended life expectancy. Added to that was the impact of the First World War and a baby boom between 1900 and 1910. Both of these latter changes had a profound impact on society. There were more single women in need of employment and there was also a large number of adolescents reaching employment age with an economic crisis just around the corner.

Youth

The youth of Germany were pioneer audiences and made the most of new commercial opportunities such as cinema, the radio and the gramophone. They were also active in setting up youth clubs although the presence of alternative groups known as *Wilde Cliquen* (wild bunch) seemed to confirm fears that youths were rejecting authority. It was true that during the war, absent fathers

Source 12

◀ Changes in the German population between 1910 and 1925.

■ **Think about**

▶ How did the population change between 1910 and 1925?

Think about the following areas in particular: Was the population rising or falling? Was the birth rate rising or falling? What was the impact of the First World War? Which age groups were particularly well represented in 1925? What was the balance between men and women?

▶ Now consider what impact the changes might have had on Weimar society.

■ **Further reading**

The best source on Weimar society is Peukert, *The Weimar Republic*, 1991 See also Bookbinder, *Weimar Germany*, 1996

Facts and figures

By 1926, it was claimed that 4.3 million out of a possible 9 million young people belonged to an official youth club or organization.

and increased hardship led to an increase in juvenile delinquency, but on the other hand, in the 1920s increased leisure time and fewer children per family meant that working-class children were receiving greater attention from their parents than before. One thing was certain, however. Higher unemployment hit youths especially hard, and this led to a restlessness which helped to cultivate a hostility to the Weimar system and increase support for extreme political parties. This included support for the Nazis who became the most popular party among university students.

Women

The Weimar Republic appeared, on the surface at least, to welcome the emancipation and equality of women. The Constitution stated that 'All Germans are equal before the law' and women were allowed to vote in national and state elections for the first time. In 1920, 111 women were elected to the Reichstag. In addition, images of the 'new woman' arrived from America, particularly in film. Not only were women now expected to keep a spotless home – the result of new so-called labour-saving inventions – but they were also expected to be glamorous and have a life and even a career of their own.

The reality was somewhat different. Although many women did work, often out of necessity, they did not necessarily gain equal pay and often had to make do with lower status jobs. Despite this, employed women were the target of male resentment, especially in times of economic recession when, ironically, their lower rates of pay shielded them from redundancy. Criticism of the *'Doppelverdiener'* (a married woman bringing home a second wage) was voiced by both men and women and led in 1932 to the 'Law Governing the Legal Status of Female Civil Servants' which allowed women who were second earners to be dismissed from their job.

It isn't entirely clear, however, what women themselves wanted. Whilst some clearly welcomed the opportunity to study and carve out a career, others felt burdened by the expectations placed upon them by the 'new woman' image. The largest woman's group, the BDF (League of German Women's Associations), was moderate in its outlook, stressing the difference between the sexes and encouraging women to take jobs where their 'natural' qualities would be most needed – such as social work. It is in this context that high female support for the Nazis can perhaps be explained.

Jews

Another group which stood to benefit from the social rights enshrined in the Weimar Constitution were the Jews. They made up less than 1 per cent of Germany's population: 570,000 out of a population of 60 million. They were mainly middle class and made a significant contribution to the cultural and professional life of Germany. Eleven per cent of Germany's doctors and 16 per cent of Germany's lawyers were Jewish, for example. Many were involved in trade and commerce but contrary to propaganda at the time, did not control the major industries nor did they control the banks. They generally considered themselves German first and Jewish second.

Although anti-Semitism had existed in Germany, as elsewhere, for a long time, the rise of nationalist right-wing parties in Weimar intensified anti-Semitic behaviour. Jews were made the scapegoats for Germany's humiliating defeat in the First World War and the economic crises of the 1920s. When compared with the horrors that were to come, the position of Jews in Weimar Germany seems good, but it was a long way from total acceptance and toleration.

■ Activity   KEY SKILLS

Either in small groups or individually, choose one of the following areas to research in more detail:
- Youth
- Women
- Jews
- Culture (see pages 108–9)

Use the information in this book as a starting point. Then use other books and the Internet/CD ROMs to research into your chosen area in more detail. Focus your research around the following question: 'Was Weimar society stable and united?' Present your findings to the rest of the group, using at least one image to illustrate your points. After the presentations, discuss the question as a whole group, drawing on all the information which has been shared.

Quotation

We in no way felt we were assimilated [like everyone else] 'Jews', but Germans like other Germans... our whole life was deeply rooted in German life and had no other foundation...

Richard Bendix

Weimar culture

Introduction

This was an era of experimentation. Artists began to experiment with new techniques and rejected traditional, conventional styles. But as with social change, there was a tension between those who welcomed the innovations and those who wanted to stick with the old ways. As in any society there was also a distinction between elite or 'avant-garde' culture and mass culture. The former tended towards modernism whilst the latter was more conservative and even reactionary. Some of the greatest cultural achievements of the Weimar years did not, therefore, help to increase feelings of national pride, nor did they help to unite the people. Nevertheless, these were the roaring twenties, the age of cabaret, Charlie Chaplin, jazz music and theatre. During 1926–1927 alone, nine revues in Berlin attracted audiences totalling 11,000. By 1926, the Charleston had become the most popular dance in Germany.

Source 13

▲ A Bauhaus teapot from 1924.

▶ The Bauhaus building itself, designed by Walter Gropius.

Source 14

BAUHAUS

Source 15

▲ Paul Klee, 'Dramatic landscape', 1928.

Avant-garde culture

One of most famous and influential artistic developments was the founding of the Bauhaus by Walter Gropius in 1919. Primarily a school of architecture (see the original Bauhaus in Weimar, above), the Bauhaus was also active in developing skills such as photography, commercial art and industrial design. Famous artists such as Kandinsky and Klee taught there and it became famous for combining artistic skills and modern engineering, especially after 1922. The term 'functionalism' has been used to describe the way in which members of the Bauhaus were encouraged to consider the function or purpose of an object or building above all else and fully embrace new materials such as steel, concrete and glass, as well as modern methods of production. Tubular steel chairs were invented there along with many other everyday objects such as the teapot shown here.

In terms of painting, the move towards expressionism which began before the war continued, certainly until 1923. Expressionist artists like Kandinsky and Klee rejected the traditional, realistic styles and instead attempted to paint in a way that demonstrated how our emotions and feelings colour the way we see the world and remember it. This led to abstract paintings and an aggressive use of colour, as demonstrated by the Klee painting shown here.

Source 16

▲ George Grosz, 'Pillars of Society', 1926.

George Grosz

Born in 1893, George Grosz studied in Dresden and Berlin before becoming famous for his satirical work which caricatured (made fun of) the 'establishment' including army generals, the middle class, landed aristocrats and industrialists (see 'The Pillars of Society'). He was tried for blasphemy after painting Christ on the Cross wearing a gas mask and army boots. He became a leading member of the Berlin Dada movement and of 'Die Neue Sachlichkeit' (the new realism). Grosz emigrated in 1932 due to the rise of Nazism. Some of his work was later to be displayed in a Nazi exhibition entitled 'Degenerate Art'. He remained in America for most of his life, only returning to Berlin shortly before his death in 1959.

Mass culture

Popular or mass culture flourished in the 1920s. The press expanded, a new medium (radio) began, an existing medium (cinema) grew and spectator sports such as boxing and football became more popular. By the end of the 1920s, Germany had more cinemas than any other European country and made more films in the 1920s and early 1930s than all the other European countries put together. Public radio broadcasting began in 1923 and the number of listeners increased from 10,000 in 1924 to over 4 million by 1932. Radio was potentially very effective as a tool for propaganda, but it wasn't until 1932 that the state established any control over it.

■ Activity

1 Why do you think some people in Weimar were so critical of modern, avant-garde culture? Why did they find it threatening?

2 Compare the modern art shown here with the art on page 209. How is it different?

3 Does the culture of Weimar lend weight to the idea that society was not united in Weimar Germany?

The Roaring Twenties: the life of an aristocrat

Source 17

14 January 1919: Sad to say, our revolution has not been the triumph of a growing body of political opinion, but simply the consequence of the old political structure crumbling away. Had it not been for the war, it would have continued in its jog-trot way a long time yet...

11 February 1919: He [Ebert] is respectable, likeable and efficient, but how much he will contribute to the invigoration of political life is at least questionable...

10 January 1920: Today the Peace Treaty was ratified at Paris; the war is over. A terrible era begins for Europe, like the gathering of clouds before a storm...

18 December 1924: I talked for quite a while to Albert Einstein at a banker's jubilee banquet where we both felt rather out of place. In reply to my question what problems he was working on now, he said that he was engaged in thinking...

22 December 1924: In the evening saw Sternheim's play '1913'...A strong and profound play

29 January 1925: In the evening saw Pirandello's 'Six Persons in Search of an Author' at Reinhardt's theatre....

22 December 1925: Opening night of a series of guest performances by Diaghilev and his ballet company...storms of applause. I went behind the footlights and congratulated him...

19 January 1926: With Max to the first night of Richard Strauss's 'Elektra'. The orchestra...played with splendid, headlong, tempestuous verve...

17 February 1926: In the evening I went again to the Negro revue starring Josephine Baker. All these shows are a mixture of jungle and skyscraper elements. The same holds good for the tone and rhythm of their music, jazz. Ultramodern and ultra primitive...

27 October 1928: Saw Reinhardt's production of 'Romeo and Juliet' at the Berliner Theatre. An incredible muddle. So much intellect and bright ideas that the upshot is an inferior provincial performance...

30 October 1928: An evening at Piscator's attractive bright flat, designed by Gropius [founder of the Bauhaus] without frills but pleasant and providing a good background for people...was introduced to Brecht [famous German playwright] – strikingly degenerate look, almost like a criminal...

7 October 1929: It becomes ever more obvious to what an intense degree the nation as a whole has participated in the obsequies [funeral rites] for Stresemann. Hundreds of thousands paid their last respects to him at his lying-in-state. One newspaper has justly commented that his was a national, not a state, funeral...

Extracts from *The Diaries of a Cosmopolitan: Count Harry Kessler 1918-1937*, 1971

■ Biography

Count Harry Kessler

Kessler was born in 1868, the son of a Hamburg banker and a famous Irish beauty. He was educated in France and England and went to university in Bonn and Leipzig. He went on to fight in the First World War in Belgium and the Eastern Front and became the first German Minister in Warsaw. Kessler hated the Kaiser and welcomed the Republic which earned him the nickname 'Red Count' although he was never a supporter of the KPD or the left in general. Instead he helped to found the DDP. He was never a Reichstag deputy but did serve on various diplomatic missions, combining his two beliefs of patriotism and pacifism. However, Kessler's diaries are not restricted to his political observations. They also provide a fascinating account of the life of a wealthy gentleman living in Berlin in the 1920s.

■ Think about

▶ What can we learn from Kessler's Diaries?

▶ How valuable are Kessler's Diaries as evidence about the Weimar Republic?

The Wall Street Crash

The so-called 'Golden Years' of the Weimar Republic ended abruptly on 24 October 1929. After a few days of wild speculation, the American stock market crashed. No more American loans were granted and Germany had to find a way of repaying the loans she had received in the previous years. The impact on Germany, not surprisingly, was considerable. Banks closed, industry laid-off workers, unemployment soared and foreign trade suffered badly. Between 1929 and 1932, the value of German exports fell from £630 million to £280 million and national income fell by 39 per cent. Unemployment rose from 1.3 million in 1929 to over 3 million by September 1930. By the beginning of 1933, it stood at over 6 million, a figure which does not include those who had been unemployed for too long to claim unemployment benefit.

It is difficult to imagine the impact that this must have had, psychologically as well as physically. At one point, one in three Germans were unemployed and this time they could not turn to America or the rest of Europe for help. Hyperinflation six years before had already robbed many of their savings. Now they had nothing to fall back on. Fear was spreading, not just among the unemployed but amongst those lucky enough to have a job, for who knew when that security would be taken away?

■ Think about

▶ Why was 'the nation on the march'?

▶ Who, according to Hasser, suffered the most from the Depression?

▶ What impact do you think these events had on the Weimar Republic?

Source 18

An almost unbroken chain of homeless men extends the whole length of the great Hamburg-Berlin highway…The only people who shouted and waved at me and ran along beside my automobile…were the newcomers…But most of the hikers paid no attention to me. They walked separately or in small groups with their eyes on the ground. And they had the queer, stumbling gait of barefoot people…some were guild members – carpenters with embroidered wallets, knee breeches, and broad felt hats…but they were in a minority. Far more numerous were…the unskilled young people for the most part who had been unable to find a job and never expected to have one. There was something else that had never been seen before – whole families that had piled all their goods into baby carriages and wheelbarrows that they were pushing along as they plodded forward in dumb despair. It was a whole nation on the march.

Heinrich Hasser *The Unemployed*, 1932

Conclusions

The economy did recover from its terrible state in 1923, although not completely. Higher wages and increased production figures concealed problems such as poor export figures and growing unemployment. Some groups flourished in Germany and many enjoyed a happier and more prosperous time. Others did not share such good fortune and parties such as the Nazis began to make small inroads into groups such as farmers and the lower middle class, though nothing on the scale of 1930–1933.

In foreign policy, Germany was no longer seen as an outcast by the rest of Europe and small gestures towards a revision of the Treaty of Versailles were accomplished. This was at a political cost, however, and the divisions between the parties grew bigger. Despite this, there was less open opposition to the Republic during this period with no attempted coups or assassinations.

Chapter 6

The rise of the Nazi Party

He wore an ancient black overcoat, which had been given him by an old-clothes dealer in the hostel, a Hungarian Jew named Neumann, and which reached down over his knees. From under a greasy, black derby hat, his hair hung long over his coat collar. His thin and hungry face was covered with a black beard above which his large staring eyes were the one prominent feature...He disliked regular work. If he earned a few crowns, he refused to draw for days and went off to a cafe to eat cream cakes and read newspapers. He had none of the common vices. He neither smoked nor drank and was too shy and awkward to have any success with women. His passions were reading newspapers and talking politics.

Hitler in his twenties as described by an acquaintance who knew him in Vienna

Source 2

▲ Hitler (right) as a soldier, 1914.

Source 3

▲ Hitler at Nuremberg Rally, 1929.

How did the down-and-out in the long black coat, who resisted work whenever possible and possessed so few social skills, emerge as the leader of a political party, the leader of Germany and the perpetrator of some of the worst crimes committed against mankind?

■ **Further reading**

The Kershaw biography mentioned in the note below is the best place to start for a detailed but very readable account of Hitler's life up to 1936. Shorter accounts are provided in Laver, *Hitler. Germany's Fate or Germany's Misfortune?* 1995 and Welch, *Hitler*, 1998. Bullock's classic *Hitler: A Study in Tyranny*, 1952, is also well worth looking at.

Note

Hitler's father changed his name from Schicklgruber (a peasant name) to Hitler in 1876. As Kershaw points out in his biography *Hitler: Hubris 1889-1936,* this was fortunate for Hitler. 'Heil Schicklgruber' would not have worked.

▲ Hitler as a child.

Note

Brigitte Hamann has argued in her book *Hitler's Vienna* that there is no evidence to support the view that Hitler developed his anti-Semitism in Vienna. Instead, Hamann suggests, Hitler deliberately chose to spend time with Jews and did not develop his extreme views until he experienced the upheaval of post-war Bavaria.

Introduction

The history of Germany during the first half of the twentieth century has in some ways been replaced by the history of the Nazi Party. It is easy, if mistaken, to regard the Weimar Republic merely as the occasion and partial cause of Hitler's rise to power. This is extraordinary given that the Nazis were in power for just 12 years, but reflects the enormous impact made within those years and the legacy that the Nazis have left, not just in Germany but in the world. Not surprisingly, then, there has been a great deal of interest in the early beginnings of this party. Where did it come from? How was it able to rise from obscurity to such power in 14 years?

Key questions

● Who was Adolf Hitler?
● How did the Nazi Party begin?
● Why had the Nazi Party become so popular by 1930?
● Who joined the Nazi Party?
● Was there anything original about the Nazi Party?
● What did Hitler and the Nazis believe in?
● Was Hitler's rise to power inevitable?

Who was Adolf Hitler?

Adolf Hitler was born in an Austrian town close to the German border called Braunau am Inn. His father, Alois Hitler, was an illegitimate child whose own father is unknown to this day. Rumours that the father (and therefore Adolf Hitler's grandfather) was Jewish were circulating by the 1920s but there is little evidence to support this claim. Alois married his third wife, his niece Klara Polzl, in 1885 and their fourth child, born in 1889, was the first to survive infancy. He was called Adolf.

Alois Hitler overcame his lowly origins to become a customs official in the Austrian civil service. His income provided for a comfortable life, although his personality did not. He was a domineering man, a distant and irritable father and a violent husband and was described by Hitler as someone he 'honoured' but did not love. By contrast, the young Hitler developed a strong attachment to his mother, leading one recent biographer to speculate that she 'may well...have been the only person he genuinely loved in his entire life.' (Kershaw, 1998).

Although Hitler enjoyed school for the first six years, his secondary education was less successful. He left at 16 in 1905 and fell into an idleness which was to characterize the next eight years. In 1907 he left for Vienna to pursue his artistic ambitions and took the entrance exam for the Academy of Fine Arts. Out of 113 candidates, only 28 succeeded and Hitler was not one of them. Later that year his beloved mother died and Hitler was left unsure what to do next. For the next five years, Hitler was in effect a drop-out, never doing a full day's work for a proper wage.

He remained in Vienna, sharing lodgings with a friend before a brief spell in a doss house when his money ran out. As Source 1 suggests, he was hardly a prepossessing figure at this point and there were few clues that he would make any sort of lasting mark during his lifetime. Throughout his time in Vienna his two passions were architecture and opera, especially Wagner. He read books and newspapers avidly and would rant endlessly about politics to his fellow lodgers in the Men's House where he spent his later Vienna years. It was, he later claimed, during this time that he developed his lasting hatred for Jews. It was also the period that crystallized his fierce sense of nationalism. He was convinced that ethnic Germans in Austria should be ruled by Germans and not forced to live side by side with other, 'inferior', ethnic groups from the eastern part of the Austro-Hungarian Empire, such as Czechs and Serbs.

In 1913, Hitler fled to Munich in Germany to avoid conscription into the Austrian army. A few months later he was photographed by chance amongst an excited crowd gathered to hear the news of war against Russia. Hitler volunteered to fight in the German army and became a lance-corporal in the infantry. He was later to write in *Mein Kampf* 'Overpowered by stormy enthusiasm, I fell down on my knees and thanked Heaven from an overflowing heart for granting me the good fortune of being permitted to live at this time...' Although he received the Iron Cross for bravery, he was nevertheless turned down for promotion due to inadequate leadership qualities. Hitler was to describe his experiences in the war as the best in his life. Its end in 1918 aroused great bitterness in him and he maintained that the surrender was the work of 'criminals' rather than a genuine defeat.

After the war, Hitler became an 'instruction officer' in the army and set about instructing soldiers on the evils of socialism and democracy. His abilities as a speaker, no doubt developed during his lectures in the Men's House in Vienna, caught the attention of his superiors. In September 1919 he was ordered to investigate a newly formed nationalist-racist political group, the German Workers' Party.

How did the Nazi Party begin?

The German Workers' Party was founded in Munich in 1919 by a locksmith named Anton Drexler. It was one of over 70 right-wing political sects, and there was no reason at first to suppose that it would be any different from the rest. On the evening of 12 September 1919, Hitler attended his first meeting in a Munich beer-cellar. There could only have been around 20 people there and so it could hardly have been a very inspiring occasion. Nevertheless, Hitler joined the German Workers' Party, becoming its 55th new recruit, and the 7th member of the Party's committee. The very obscurity of the Party was in part its attraction for Hitler: here was a chance for him to make his mark. Hitler was put in charge of propaganda and he set about transforming the party into a mass movement. He was later to write in his autobiography *Mein Kampf*, 'To be a leader means to be able to move the masses' and certainly the membership of the Party did increase rapidly.

There was nothing particularly original about the Nazi Party. Both its nationalism and anti-Semitism built on trends dating from the end of the 1800s. What is more, Hitler's experiences in Vienna had provided him with three different models of political parties which were to shape the Nazi Party's image. (See margin note).

In 1920, the party changed its name to the National Socialist German Workers' Party – NSDAP or Nazi for short – and outlined its programme in 'The Twenty-Five Points' which Hitler played a key role in drawing up (Source 4). It was to remain the only official programme of the Nazi Party as Hitler subsequently resisted attempts to specify his party's policies in a way that could restrict his flexibility. The document combined extreme nationalism, racism and some socialist concepts.

In terms of nationalism, the unification of all ethnic Germans was a central aim, together with the demand for more land and territories and the abolition of the

Quotation

And so it had all been in vain...Did all this happen only so that a gang of wretched criminals could lay hands on the Fatherland?...In these nights hatred grew in me, hatred for those responsible for this deed.

Hitler, *Mein Kampf, 1925*

Note

The influences of political parties in Vienna on the Nazi Party are easy to trace. Three parties had a particular impact:
- The Pan-German Nationalists combined extreme German nationalism with anti-Semitism which were to characterize Hitler's ideology.
- The Christian Socialists inspired Hitler by their political tactics. They succeeded in creating a mass following using propaganda and targeted those groups who were vulnerable and most likely to offer support.
- The Social Democrats, although detested by Hitler in terms of their ideology, again had a mass following and used propaganda effectively. They presented a very strong and uncompromising front and used intimidation.

Quotation

Goebbels regarded the Twenty-Five Points as an embarrassment, saying 'If I had founded the Party, I wouldn't have laid down any programme at all!'

Source 4

A Summary of 'The Twenty-Five Points of the German Workers' Party, 1920'

1. We demand the union of all Germans to form a Great Germany on the basis of the right to self-determination.
2. We demand equal rights for Germans when dealing with other countries and the abolition of the Treaties of Versailles and Saint-Germain.
3. We demand land and territory (colonies) to provide food and living space for our people.
4. Only those of German blood may be citizens of the state. No Jew may be a member of the nation.
5. Non-Germans live in Germany only as guests.
6. Only German citizens may vote or be given an official appointment.
7. The first duty of the state is to provide work for its citizens. Foreign nationals should be excluded from the state if it becomes impossible to feed everyone.
8. The immigration of non-Germans must be stopped.
9. Citizens of the state shall have equal rights.
10. The first duty of every citizen is to work with his mind or body. Each individual must work to the general good of the people.
11. Incomes that are not earned through work must be abolished.
12. No-one is to gain money from war; all war gains must be confiscated.
13. We demand that all businesses be nationalized.
14. We demand that the profits in major industrial enterprises are shared.
15. We demand a generous increase in old-age pensions.
16. We demand that large department stores are divided up and rented out cheaply to small trades people.
17. We demand land reform suitable for our national requirements.
18. We demand that those who work against the common interest should be punished with death, whatever their religion or race.
19. We demand that Roman law should be replaced by German common law.
20. Higher education should be available to all able and hardworking Germans. The concept of citizenship should be taught in schools from the very beginning. Gifted children of poor parents must be educated at the state's expense.
21. The nation's health will be improved by protecting mothers and infants and banning child labour. Gymnastics and sports to be made compulsory.
22. We demand the abolition of a paid army and the formation of a national army.
23. We demand the creation of a German national press. All newspaper editors and their assistants must be German citizens; non-German newspapers shall only be published with the permission of the state and any newspaper which tries to undermine the common welfare shall be banned.
24. We demand freedom for all religious faiths in the state, as long as they do not endanger the state. The party represents the point of view of Christianity and fights against the Jewish materialist spirit within and without.
25. We demand that the state has strong central powers. The government should have unquestioned authority over the entire Reich.

■ Think about

▶ What does Source 4 tell us about the Nazis' policies on:

- social welfare
- Jews
- civil liberties
- economics
- foreign policy
- land
- government

▶ Who do you think the Nazis were trying to appeal to here?

Treaty of Versailles. The notion of a race based on pure German blood was outlined and Jews were specifically singled out as outsiders, unable to be a 'member of the nation'. More socialist aims included the nationalization of industry, the sharing of profits and land reform. Hitler was never committed to these latter aims and many were dropped, such as land reform, when it became clear that they were scaring away potential supporters from the middle and upper classes.

Who were the Nazis?

The party initially attracted young men, many of whom were war veterans, and was seen by many as a party of the left. Even by 1923 the Party membership included a disproportionately high number of manual workers, though this was to change in the second half of the decade. Like Hitler, many of the early leaders were of humble origin, with the exception of Hermann Goering, a war hero with aristocratic connections through marriage. However, the Party did manage to attract the support of some wealthy and influential figures. Dietrich Eckhart, a well-known journalist and playwright, had a big influence on Hitler and people such as the Bechsteins, rich piano manufacturers, helped to finance the Party's activities, as well as giving Hitler a taste of the high life.

Who were the leading Nazis?

Paul Josef Goebbels 1897–1945

The 'intellectual' of the Nazi Party. Born in the Rhineland and the son of a manual worker, Goebbels was unable to fight in the First World War due to a crippled foot and permanent limp. He never recovered from this humiliation and was acutely aware of his short height (fellow Nazis called him the 'little mouse doctor') and physical deformity. He received a doctorate in 1921, having been taught by a Jewish professor, and joined the Nazi Party in 1922. He immediately used his journalistic talent to good effect, editing one of the Party's newspapers. Perhaps the most loyal of all Hitler's followers, he was rewarded for his devotion with the post of Gauleiter of Berlin in 1926 and Reich Propaganda Director in 1929. In 1933 he was appointed Minister of Enlightenment and Propaganda. This gave him immense control over Germany's media, culture and education. He was the master of modern political propaganda, adapting American advertising techniques that he had studied. Shortly after Hitler's own suicide in 1945, Goebbels poisoned his six children and his wife before committing suicide.

Hermann Goering 1893–1946

The 'extrovert' of the Nazi Party. Born in Bavaria and the son of a colonial official, Goering won fame and admiration for his achievements as a pilot during the First World War. The end of the war left him without purpose and in 1922 he joined the Nazi Party. By the following year he was in charge of the SA (Stormtroopers) and was severely wounded during the Munich Putsch (he subsequently became addicted to morphine). In 1933 he was appointed Prime Minister and Interior Minister for Prussia where he established the Gestapo and the first concentration camps. In 1935 he became Commander-in-Chief of the air force, by which time he was the most important man in the Third Reich after Hitler. In 1936 he took control of the Four Year Plan, with responsibility to prepare Germany economically for war. Goering was the most popular Nazi after Hitler. He was fat, charming and enjoyed the high life. His art collection was famous, created from the spoils of Jewish confiscations and conquered territories. His influence waned after 1940, however, and he was expelled from the Party in 1945. Goering was sentenced to death at the Nuremberg war crimes trial but committed suicide in his cell.

Heinrich Himmler 1900–1945

The 'sadist' of the Nazi Party. Born in Munich and the son of a secondary school teacher, Himmler served in the First World War from 1917 after which he became a chicken farmer in Bavaria. He joined the Nazi Party in 1923 and by 1929 was in charge of the SS (Hitler's private bodyguards and the elite branch of the SA) which rose from 300 members in 1929 to over 50,000 by 1933. By 1936, Himmler was in charge of the whole German police apparatus. In 1939, he became the Commissar for the Consolidation of German Nationhood, which gave him ultimate control over the extermination campaign. It was his job to devise methods of mass murder. Himmler believed passionately in the racial doctrine of the Party. His gentle and harmless appearance concealed his sadism and craving for power. Despite this, he was unable to witness murder himself. He committed suicide after his arrest by British troops in 1945.

Ernst Röhm 1887–1934

Born in Munich and the son of a civil servant, Röhm was a professional soldier who fought in the First World War and who provided Hitler with useful army contacts in the Nazi Party's early years. After the war, Röhm was restless and looking for direction. He joined the *Freikorps* and was one of the early followers of Hitler and became a close friend. In 1930 he was put in charge of the SA which expanded to over two million members by the end of 1933 Röhm wanted to enhance the role of his organization and himself by merging the SA with the army. Hitler refused and ordered a purge of SA leaders including Röhm who was murdered in June 1934.

Rudolf Hess 1894–1987

Born in Egypt and the son of a German importer, Hess served in the same regiment as Hitler during the First World War and afterwards joined the *Freikorps*. He became Hitler's secretary in 1920. Imprisoned with Hitler after the failed putsch, he wrote out *Mein Kampf* at Hitler's dictation. In 1932 he became Deputy Party Leader and in 1933 was appointed Minister without Portfolio. In 1941 he made an extraordinary decision to fly single-handedly to Scotland, apparently to negotiate peace. He was imprisoned and spent the next 46 years in prison.

Martin Bormann 1900–1973(?)

Born in central Germany and the son of cavalry sergeant, Bormann served in the First World War, joining the *Freikorps* in 1919. He joined the Nazi Party in 1925 and by 1933 became Chief-of-Staff and Secretary to Hess. His power grew rapidly and was increased by Hess' flight to Scotland in 1941, after which Bormann became the most powerful man in the Third Reich after Hitler. His fate at the end of the war remains a mystery. Either he was killed by a road bomb whilst escaping, or he succeeded in reaching South America.

Reinhard Heydrich 1904–1942

Born in Saxony and the son of a middle-class musician who could well have been Jewish (a claim Heydrich fiercely denied), Heydrich was too young to fight in the First World War but joined the navy in 1922. He joined the Nazi Party and the SS in 1931 after involvement with the *Freikorps*. He became Himmler's deputy in 1933 and in 1939 was appointed head of the Reich Central Office for Jewish Emigration. In 1941 he was given responsibility for the mass murder of Jews. He was assassinated by a member of the Czech resistance in 1942.

Activity

Compare the backgrounds of these senior Nazis and note down any similarities. You may wish to use the following headings:
- Place and date of birth
- Family background
- Experience of war
- Experiences after the war

Compare your findings with others in the class. Together, prepare a short profile of the typical background of a senior member of the Nazi Party.

Note: You may like to then compare this profile with Hitler's own background.

How successful was the Nazi Party up to 1923?

In 1921, Hitler became the leader of the Nazis. He was hardly a unanimous choice and his appointment divided the Party. However, his political talents were too precious to lose, as were his contacts with the army. During 1920, Hitler had made over 30 speeches to audiences of up to 2000 people. By 1921, membership had risen to 3300. Hitler's abilities as an orator are legendary:

Facts and figures

Nazi membership figures

Year	Members
1920	2,000
1921	3,300
1922	20,000
1923	55,000

Source 5

My critical faculty was swept away...he was holding the masses, and me with them, under a hypnotic spell by the sheer force of his conviction...I do not know how to describe the emotions that swept over me as I heard this man...When he spoke of the disgrace of Germany, I felt ready to spring on any enemy. His appeal to German manhood was like a call to arms...I forgot everything but the man; then glancing around, I saw that his magnetism was holding these thousands as one. Of course, I was ripe for this experience. I was a man of thirty-two, weary with disgust and disillusionment, a wanderer seeking a cause, a patriot without a channel for his patriotism, a yearner after the heroic without a hero. The intense will of the man, the passion of his sincerity, seemed to flow from him into me. I experienced an exaltation that could be likened only to religious conversion.

The memories of Kurt Ludecke, one of Hitler's earliest followers

■ Think about

▶ Using Sources 5 and 6, what was it about Hitler that seemed to make him such a compelling speaker?

▶ According to Source 5, what attracted Ludecke to Hitler apart from Hitler himself?

Source 6

There were tears in my eyes, my throat was all tight from crying. A liberating scream of the purest enthusiasm discharged the unbearable tension as the auditorium rocked with applause.

The memory of an aristocrat's first experience of Hitler speaking

Hitler cultivated an impression of a long-established and tightly organized party through the use of uniforms and symbols, such as the swastika, the Nazi flag (black swastika in a white circle on a red background – Hitler laboured over the design) and the raised arm salute. He also realized the potential value of a paramilitary wing which he could use to damage his opponents. In 1921, the *Sturmableitung* (Stormtroopers), or SA, was founded and members quickly became known as Brownshirts because of the colour of their uniform. They were mainly ex-*Freikorps* members, unemployed youths or criminals. To give the group an air of respectability, it was claimed to be the 'Gymnastic and Sports Section' of the Party! Source 7 gives us an idea of who joined the SA:

Note

The swastika

The swastika dates back 3000 years and was used to represent life, power, strength and good luck. German nationalists began to use it in the 1800s to suggest a long German history. The Nazis adopted it in 1920.

Source 7

To the Hitler bands flock youths of the featherbrained, unbalanced type, similar to those involved in the Rathenau assassination; students, flotsam and jetsam of the classes that have lost their footing in the new Germany, having been deprived of economic security; clerks, mechanics, even plain hoodlums, such as could once be seen in the following of the Spartacists, purchasable for a few marks, a square meal and the prospect of a free fight with the odds on their side.

New York Times Current History, November 1923

Quotation

Do you wish to fight? To kill?
To see streams of gold?
Great heaps of gold?
Herds of captive women?
Slaves?

Poem used by Goering when recruiting men for the SA

As you can see, the time was right for the formation of such a movement. Germany's situation was to the Nazis' advantage.

The Munich Beer Hall *Putsch*

By 1923, although membership was increasing, the Nazi Party had not succeeded in establishing itself outside Bavaria (in southern Germany). Hitler was becoming impatient. Hyperinflation and the invasion of the Ruhr in 1923 had weakened support for the Weimar government. What is more, the threat of ending the campaign of passive resistance in September filled nationalists with rage. Here was Hitler's opportunity to challenge the Weimar Republic.

Hitler was fortunate that the Bavarian state government – led by the ultra-conservative Gustav von Kahr – and the army in Bavaria were both sympathetic to the extreme right-wing cause. The Bavarian government declared a state of emergency after communists and socialists united in Thuringia and Saxony and formed paramilitary groups. Both Kahr and General von Lossow, Commander of the Bavarian military district, refused orders from Berlin to suppress the Nazi newspaper *Volkischer Beobachter*. They were now acting in defiance of the Weimar government. Perhaps not surprisingly, Hitler believed he would obtain support from the Bavarian government and army in an attempt to overthrow the government. Inspired by Mussolini's successful take-over in Italy in 1922, Hitler decided that the time was ripe, in the autumn of 1923, for an uprising. What followed was a disaster for the Nazis in which 16 Stormtroopers were killed and Hitler was sent to prison.

Hitler had overestimated Kahr's support for an uprising. The Weimar government had crushed the communist-socialist governments in Saxony and Thuringia and Kahr felt that he could no longer justify a march to Berlin. Hitler could not, crucially, rely on the total support of the Bavarian army. However, Hitler had gone too far, having already worked his supporters up to a fever pitch of excitement. He interrupted a public meeting in the Burgerbraukeller – a large beer cellar in Munich – at which Kahr and Lossow were speaking to announce that 'the national revolution' had begun. Outside 600 armed members of the SA surrounded the building. Kahr was forced to promise Hitler his support, but this support was short-lived. The next day it became clear to Hitler that neither Kahr nor the army were going to support his march. The Bavarian police were sent to stop the few thousand supporters that had gathered and opened fire, killing 16 Nazis. Hitler, suffering from a dislocated shoulder after being thrown to the ground, was driven away. Two days later he and other Nazi leaders were arrested and accused of high treason. The Nazi Party was banned and Hitler was given the minimum sentence of five years' imprisonment, showing the basic right-wing sympathy of the courts.

Source 8

Herr von Kahr had spoken for half an hour. Then there was movement at the entrance as if people were wanting to push their way in…Eventually steel helmets came into sight. From this moment on, the view from my seat was rather obscured. People stood on chairs so that I didn't see Hitler until he had come fairly near along the main gangway; just before he turned to the platform, I saw him emerge between two armed soldiers in steel helmets who carried pistols next to their heads, pointing at the ceiling. They turned towards the platform, Hitler climbed on to a chair on my left. The hall was still restless, and then Hitler made a sign to the man on his right, who fired a shot at the ceiling. Thereupon Hitler called out (I cannot recollect the exact order of his words): 'The national revolution has broken out. The hall is surrounded.' Maybe he mentioned the exact number, I am not sure.

Account given by von Muller, an eye witness

■ Think about

Source 9 is an artist's impression of the meeting in the beer hall in November 1923.

▶ Compare the painting with the eye-witness account above (Source 8). What are the differences and similarities?

▶ Which source do you consider to be most reliable about the events in the beer hall, the eye-witness account or the painting?

Source 9

The Nazi Party after 1924

A change in direction

Hitler was in prison for just nine months, during which time he lived in comfortable surroundings and was able to write his autobiography, *Mein Kampf*. He had plenty of time to reflect on the lessons he had learned from the failed *Putsch* and made important decisions about the future of the Nazi Party:

- *Putschist* (violent) tactics would have to be abandoned and, instead, the Nazis would try to win electoral support.

- Strict organization of the Party was necessary, together with a wider geographical base (up to 1923, the Party's supporters were largely confined to Bavaria) and larger membership which would distinguish the Nazis from other nationalist groups.

- The Führer's will would need to dominate completely to enable the Nazis to appear united.

Winning elections

Source 10

When I resume active work it will be necessary to pursue a new policy. Instead of working to achieve power by armed conspiracy, we shall have to hold our noses and enter the Reichstag against the Catholic and Marxist deputies. If outvoting them takes longer than shooting them, at least the results will be guaranteed by their own Constitution!

Hitler's words to Kurt Ludeck when he visited Hitler in prison

The decision to pursue power legally was a turning point in the history of the Nazi Party. Although it took five years before the Nazis gained good results at the polls, the switch to electoral methods did pay off. However, it must never be forgotten that the Nazis were not actually voted into power as they never received a majority in a free general election. It was also the case that despite Hitler's 'magnetic' appeal, the Party was dependent on the right circumstances for success. Chapter 5 explained how the years 1924–1929 saw a relative improvement in Germany's fortunes. In these circumstances, most people were not desperate enough to cast their vote for such an extreme party.

The Nazis initially tried to win the support of industrial workers. They failed, mainly because the workers already had a choice of parties who claimed to represent them. At the beginning of 1928, the Nazis shifted their attention to the middle class and the rural population. Both groups felt that their interests were being squeezed by the Weimar Republic, and farmers were also badly affected by an agricultural depression. In 1928, although a mere 810,127 electors voted for the Nazis, this disguised the fact that more than 10% were voting for the Nazis in certain rural areas in the north-west.

The breakthrough came in 1930 when the Nazis became the second biggest party in the Reichstag with 107 seats. Not even Hitler had expected such a result! This followed the Wall Street Crash of 1929 which was to leave millions unemployed. The pattern observed by the Nazis in the rural areas spread to the cities. Electoral success was born out of desperate circumstances. That does not explain, however, why the Nazis benefitted more than other extreme groups in the aftermath of the Crash. This is explored more fully in the next chapter.

Note

Mein Kampf ('My Struggle') provides a fascinating insight into the mind of Hitler and his preoccupations. The index alone is revealing – 101 entries under anti-Semitism in one edition, for example. But it was hardly a party programme and the historian Alan Bullock argues that Hitler's use of long words and endless repetitions, intended to give the impression of an educated and intellectual man, made it a dull read and a failure as a political bestseller. Despite this, the book helped to make Hitler a rich man – by 1939 it had sold more than 5 million copies and had been translated into 11 languages.

Obeying the Führer

On Hitler's release from prison he found a party deeply divided both in terms of tactics and policy. There were also regional differences, especially between Catholic Bavarians and Protestant Prussians. He set about rebuilding the Party, which saw rapid increases in membership. Hitler was to be seen as the sole source of authority and he refused to share decision-making with anyone. He only intervened in Party disputes when they had reached crisis point, otherwise he remained aloof, an almost mystical figure. On 19 April 1926, Josef Goebbels wrote in his diary 'Adolf Hitler, I love you.' In the same year, Hitler called a meeting of Party leaders at Bamberg to reassert his authority over those agitating for a new Party programme to replace the rather vague Twenty-Five Points. Hitler, not wanting to be restricted by another written document, emphasized the importance of the Twenty-Five Points and linked any rejection of it to a rejection of Hitler himself. Hitler's appeal was a success.

■ Think about

▶ What are the advantages and disadvantages to a political party of such a dominant leader?

Source 11

By 1929, his [Hitler's] dominance in the movement was absolute, the 'idea' now as good as inseparable from the Leader. The Hitler cult had caught hold among the Party faithful in ways scarcely imaginable before 1923, and was now well on the way to elevating the Leader above the Party.

Kershaw, *Hitler: Hubris 1889–1936*, 1998

Organization and membership

The Party began to organize itself on an impressive scale. Germany was divided into *Gaue* or regions, in line with the 35 Reichstag electoral districts, and each was under the control of the *Gauleiter*. Each *Gaue* was then further subdivided into *Kreis,* under the control of a *Kreisleiter.* The *Kreis* were then divided into *Ortsgruppen*, each covering a town or a city and supervised by a *Ortsgruppenleiter.* The Nazis also organized interest groups such as the Hitler Youth (1926), the National Socialist Teachers' Association (1929) and the Office for Agriculture (1930) which helped to win further support for the Party. The SA was restructured and more highly trained, even receiving some training from the Reichswehr (army) by 1930. In 1926 the *Schutzstaffel* (SS) was formed as an elite group of bodyguards.

Facts and figures

Nazi membership figures

1925	27,000
1926	49,000
1927	72,000

Document exercise: The impact of the Beer Hall *Putsch*

Source A

The failure of the *Putsch*

The police used rubber truncheons and rifle butts and tried to push back the crowd with rifles held horizontally. Their barricade had already been broken several times. Suddenly, a National Socialist fired a pistol at a police officer from close quarters. The shot went past his head and killed Sergeant Hollweg standing behind him. Even before it was possible to give an order, the comrades of the sergeant who had been shot opened fire as the Hitler lot did, and a short gun battle ensued…After no more than thirty seconds the Hitler lot fled, some back to the Maximilienstrasse, some to the Odeonsplatz.

Extract from an official report prepared for the inquiry

Source B

Hitler declares himself not guilty of high treason

I bear the responsibility all alone, but I declare one thing: I am no criminal because of that and I do not feel as if I would be a criminal. I cannot plead guilty, but I do confess the act. There is no such thing as high treason against the traitors of 1918. It is impossible that I should have committed high treason, for this cannot be implicit in the action of November 8th and 9th, but only in the intentions and the actions during all the previous months…I do not consider myself as a man who committed high treason, but as a German, who wanted the best for his people.

Extract from Hitler's speech at his trial following the failed Putsch

Source C

A historian's view

The trial received enormous publicity and Hitler's bravado enabled him to turn the ignominious [humiliating] failure of the *Putsch* into a considerable propaganda victory. For, while asserting that Kahr and the others had pursued a similar goal, he did not deny his own part – but claimed it was a patriotic act. He blamed the failure of the enterprise on the pusillanimity [faintheartedness] of the nationalist leaders. As a result of this stand, Hitler now became a hero to many anti-Semites in other parts of Germany who before had never heard of him. They saw him as the one man who had had the courage and energy to act. This ensured that when the Party was refounded after his release, numerous new branches could be established outside Bavaria.

Noakes and Pridham, Nazism 1919–1945 Vol. I, 1998

Source D

The Munich Beer Hall *Putsch* is celebrated in 1942

You died
Fighting for our Reich
And had to die
So that we could
Live victoriously.

Your death
Was the movement's victory
And your heritage
Is to us eternal obligation!

From material prepared for the 1942 celebrations of the Beer Hall Putsch

■ **Examination-style questions**

1 **Comprehension in context**

Using Source B and your knowledge, explain Hitler's reference to the 'traitors of 1918'.

2 **Comparing the sources**

To what extent and why do Sources A and B offer different interpretations of the Munich *Putsch*?

3 **Assessing the sources**

Source D was produced some time after 1923. Of what use is it in explaining the impact of the Munich Beer Hall *Putsch* on the Nazi Party?

4 **Making judgements**

'The Munich Beer Hall *Putsch* was a success for the Nazis'. Using the sources and your own knowledge, how far do you agree with this view?

What did the Nazis believe in?

The roots of Nazi ideology

Although Hitler was reluctant to commit his party to a programme which could restrict him, there were certain fundamental principles which formed the basis of Hitler's ideology. These principles – racial superiority, extreme nationalism and anti-communism – lay at the heart of Hitler's '*Weltanschauung*' or world view. They were not new, however; they had their roots in pre-war Germany. Towards the end of the nineteenth century there were two distinct but overlapping ideological responses to the rapid industrial change which followed unification:

- Anti-Semitism increased as the lower middle class – people such as artisans, shopkeepers and peasant farmers – felt threatened by changes such as mass production and urbanization. Many of those who seemed to pose the most immediate threat such as department store owners, bankers and cattle dealers happened to be Jews. Jews, whose persecution had a long history in Europe, became easy scapegoats for others' insecurities. Significantly, it was during this period that they were increasingly classed as a race rather than a religious or cultural group. It was impossible under this definition for Jews to claim to be both Jewish and German and therefore possible for others to class them as foreigners, even if Germany had been the home of their family for centuries.

- A more extreme form of nationalism emerged in the 1890s, led by the 'new Right' consisting of successful middle-class groups who felt excluded from Germany's ruling class. Organizations such as the Pan-German League were formed to promote their views. They believed that changes in society which industrialization had created – such as the growth of a more political working class – were leading to instability and a lack of unity. In order to protect the German '*Volk*' (people) it was necessary, they argued, to unite the people behind a common cause: the greatness of the German state. This could be achieved firstly, through expansion and secondly, through attempts to keep the supposedly superior German race pure. 'Foreigners' were not tolerated and as the first point above explains, this term now included Jews. The leader of the Pan-German League, Heinrich Class, acknowledged in 1918 'a satisfactory growth in the anti-Semitic mood which had already reached an enormous extent...Our task will be to bring this movement out on to the national political arena...for the Jews the struggle for existence has begun.'

It was significant that Hitler formed his political views in Austria. Unlike Germany, where Jews formed less than 1% of the population, the presence of Jews in Austria was more marked than in Germany. In addition, there were many more different nationalities living in Austria, most of whom were asserting their rights to greater independence. For German-speakers living in Austria, the claims for a single state to include all 'pure' Germans were expressed in the strongest terms.

In conclusion, the power of Hitler's ideology did not lie in its originality. Instead the power lay in its combination of different influences into a 'world view' and in the conviction with which it was held. After the trauma of losing the First World War and the problems experienced by Weimar, Hitler was offering an explanation of – and a solution to – Germany's problems.

Nazi ideology

VOLKGEMEINSCHAFT (People's Community)

Central to Hitler's idea of the German nation was the idea of a community of people who shared a common race and who would work together as one for the good of each other. Hitler believed that all ethnic Germans should be united and hated the fact that Germans in Austria had to live alongside non-Germans. The concept of a German *Volksgemeinschaft* was important in drawing together different groups whose unity was undermined by rapid industrialization. By stressing the need to work together for the common good of the German people (*volk*) the rich and poor, rural and urban, Prussian or Bavarian Germans would feel as though they all shared a common bond. This 'common good' would involve the promotion of a 'pure' race and the expansion of German boundaries.

A MASTER RACE

Hitler believed that there was a hierarchy of races and that the Aryan race (peoples of Northern Europe, defined in the nineteenth century by their common language, German) were at the top of this pyramid while non-Aryans, such as Slavs and Jews, were at the bottom. He combined this with a belief in Social Darwinism – a theory that only the fittest would survive in any struggle between the races. Hitler wanted to achieve racial purity in Germany – which was in fact entirely impossible given the mythical status of a 'pure Aryan' – and his main victims were Jews, who he defined as a racial and not a religious group. The exact origins of Hitler's fanatical anti-Semitism are unclear. Rumours that the source of his hatred was his own possible Jewish ancestry or the death of his mother at the hands of a Jewish doctor are without evidence. He claimed in *Mein Kampf* to experience a revelation on seeing a Jew in Vienna and asking himself *'Is this a German?'*

HITLER'S 'WORLD VIEW'

NATIONALISM

Hitler had visions of a Greater Germany – a Germany that would include all ethnic Germans and acquire the *lebensraum* (living space) necessary for an expanding master race. The first stage was to abolish the Treaty of Versailles and reclaim the lost territories, followed by the inclusion of Austrian Germans, Sudeten Germans and Baltic Germans into the Reich. Thirdly, further expansion into Eastern Europe was indicated in *Mein Kampf* to provide *lebensraum* and superpower status. Expansion into Russia would also serve the added bonus of destroying the centre of communism. Hitler regarded war as 'part of a natural, indeed self-evident pattern of thorough, well-secured, sustained national development.' It fitted in with his idea that everything was achieved through struggle.

ANTI-COMMUNISM

Hitler's ideology did not focus on Russian communism initially. He was, of course, highly suspicious of the Left in general and despised the democratic nature of the Weimar Republic. For him, socialism was about ensuring the unity of the people rather than about sharing power with them. He gradually, however, began to focus on the 'Jewishness' of communism. Because communism was an international movement which sought to spread communism throughout the world, Hitler began to argue that it was part of a Jewish 'world conspiracy'. Communists were therefore part of the Jewish threat and had to be removed. This belief had a profound effect on Hitler's foreign policy. Instead of pursuing colonial expansion, he decided instead to pursue expansion into Russia. This would have the dual effect of destroying 'Jewish' communism and gaining *lebensraum*.

■ Activity

1 Draw four boxes onto a sheet of A4 and write inside each one the headings above. Now draw and label arrows between the boxes to show how they were connected. The labels should explain *how* they were connected. For example, '*Volksgemeinschaft*' and 'A Master Race' were connected because only pure 'Aryans' were allowed to be members of Germany's 'people's community'.

2 Study Sources 12–17. For each one, work out which strand of Hitler's 'world view' it demonstrates.

3 The ideas behind Hitler's 'world view' were found in many parts of Europe. Using your own knowledge, explain why it was in Germany that these ideas had most support by 1930.

Source 12

The NSDAP is an organisation which does not recognise proletarians, does not recognise bourgeois, farmers, manual workers and so on; instead it is an organisation based in all regions of Germany, composed of all social groups. If you ask one of us; 'Young man, what are you? Bourgeois? Proletarian?', he will smile; 'I am a German! I fight in my brown shirt.' That is indicative of our significance; we do not aspire to be anything else, we are all fighting for the future of a people. We are all equal in our ranks.

A speech given by Hitler at an election meeting in Kiel, 1930

Source 13

The main motivating forces of life are self-preservation and the safeguarding of future generations, and politics is none other than the struggle of peoples for their existence. This urge to live is universal and governs the whole nation. The urge to live must lead to conflict because it is insatiable, while the basis of life, territory, is limited. Thus brutality rather than humanity is the basis of life! Man has become master of the world through conflict and continual struggle...But mankind is not a uniform and equal mass. There are differences between races. The Earth has received its culture from elite peoples; what we see today is ultimately the result of the activity and the achievements of the Aryans.

Hitler in a speech in 1928

Source 14

Don't think that you can combat an illness without killing its causative organ, without destroying the bacillus [bacteria], and don't think that you can combat racial tuberculosis without seeing to it that the people is freed from the causative organ of racial tuberculosis. The impact of Jewry will never pass away, and the poisoning of the people will not end, as long as the causal agent, the Jew, is not removed from our midst.

Hitler's anti-Semitism in a speech of 1920

Source 15

Democracy, as practised in Western Europe today, is the forerunner of Marxism. In fact the latter would not be conceivable without the former. Democracy is the breeding–ground in which the bacilli of the Marxist world pest can grow and spread. By the introduction of parliamentarianism democracy produced an abortion of filth and fire, the creative fire of which, however, seems to have died out.

Hitler, *Mein Kampf*, 1925

Source 16

When home-going workers passed us by, Adolf would grip my arm and say 'Did you hear, Gustl? Czechs!' Another time, we encountered some brickmakers speaking loudly in Italian, with florid gestures. 'There you have your German Vienna', he cried, indignantly. This, too, was one of his oft-repeated phrases: 'German Vienna', but Adolf pronounced it with a bitter undertone. Was this Vienna, into which streamed from all sides, Czechs, Magyars, Croats, Poles, Italians, Slovaks, Ruthenians, and above all Galician Jews, still indeed a German city?

Kubizek, *Young Hitler. The Story of Our Friendship*, 1973

Source 17

Germany has an annual increase in population of nearly 900,000. The difficulty of feeding this army of new citizens must increase from year to year and ultimately end in catastrophe, unless ways and means are found to forestall the danger of starvation and misery in time...when we speak of new land in Europe today we must principally bear in mind Russia...Destiny itself seems to wish to point the way for us here...And the end of the Jewish domination in Russia will also be the end of Russia as a state.

Hitler, *Mein Kampf*, 1925

Document exercise: Nazi ideology

◀ This Nazi poster from 1932 shows the socialist SPD as communists and as the guardian angels of the rich Jewish capitalists.

Source B

Hitler describes his views of Jews

If the Jews were alone in this world, they would stifle in filth and offal; they would try to get ahead of one another in hate–filled struggle and exterminate one another, in so far as the absolute absence of all sense of self–sacrifice, expressing itself in their cowardice, did not turn battle into comedy here too....

...With satanic joy in his face, the black haired Jewish youth lurks in wait for the unsuspecting girl whom he defiles with his blood, thus stealing her from her people. With every means he tries to destroy the racial foundations of the people he has set out to subjugate. Just as he himself systematically ruins women and girls, he does not shrink back from pulling down the blood barriers for others, even on a large scale. It was and it is Jews who bring Negroes into the Rhineland always with the same secret thought and clear aim of ruining the hated white race by the necessarily resulting bastardisation...

Hitler, *Mein Kampf*, 1925

Source C

Socialist ideology

We demand a land reform suitable to our national requirements, the passing of a law for the confiscation of land for communal purposes without compensation; the abolition of ground rent, and the prohibition of all speculation in land.

Point 17 in the Twenty-Five Points of 1920

Source D

Socialist ideology is modified

In view of the false interpretations on the part of our opponents of Point 17 of the Programme of the NSDAP, it is necessary to make the following statement:

Since the NSDAP accepts the principle of private property, it is self-evident that the phrase 'confiscation without compensation' refers simply to the creation of possible legal means for confiscation, when necessary, of land acquired illegally or not managed in the public interest. It is, therefore, aimed primarily against Jewish companies which speculate in land.

A 'clarification' of Point 17 of the Twenty-Five Points issued in 1928

Source E

How popular was Hitler's anti-Semitism?

...modern research has overwhelmingly demonstrated that anti-Semitism was not an important factor in generating votes for the Nazis in the elections of 1930–1933 when they became a mass party...As William Sheridan Allen showed long ago in his classic study of the small town of Northeim, Nazi propaganda deliberately played down the anti-Semitic aspects of the Party's ideology from 1928 onwards because they had been found to be unpopular with the electorate...it is necessary to recall that no more than 37.4 per cent of the voters ever supported the Nazis in a free election, and that even in the elections of March 1933, when faced with massive intimidation by the recently installed Nazi government, the Party still failed to win an overall majority.

Evans, Rereading German History 1800–1996, 1997

■ Examination-style questions

1 Comprehension in context

Using Sources A and B and your own knowledge, explain why Hitler considered Jews to be enemies of the state.

2 Comparing the sources

Explain how and why Sources C and D differ.

3 Assessing the sources

How adequately does Source E support its claim that anti-Semitism was not an important factor in generating votes for the Nazi Party?

4 Making judgements

Using all the sources and your own knowledge, explain how important Nazi ideology was in the growing popularity of the Nazis after 1919.

Propaganda

Source 19

The receptivity of the great masses is very limited, their intelligence is small, but their power of forgetting is enormous. In consequence of these facts, all effective propaganda must be limited to a very few points and must harp on these in slogans until the last member of the public understands what you want him to understand by your slogan'.

Hitler, *Mein Kampf, 1925*

Source 18 illustrates some of the ways in which the Nazis presented themselves publicly. Hitler devoted two chapters to propaganda in *Mein Kampf*. He saw propaganda as the form of communication best suited to the masses and therefore central in his bid to turn his party into a genuinely mass movement. He made little attempt to conceal the contempt he held towards his intended audience (Source 19). Keep the message simple, say it over and over again, and, if you are going to tell a lie, tell a really big lie. These were the central messages given to all Nazi propagandists.

The medium most favoured by Hitler was the spoken word and he used the new forms of transport – aeroplane and car – to his advantage, travelling all over Germany to deliver his speeches. We have already discussed his oratorical skills and although his critics pointed to his lack of an educated vocabulary, his extraordinary presence and ability to capture and hold attention was a key factor in the Nazis' success. None of the other opposition parties had such a charismatic leader. Other forms of propaganda used by Hitler and Goebbels (appointed Head of Party Propaganda in 1928) included posters and newspapers and new technology enabled them, during 1930, to make microphones and loudspeakers a standard feature at Nazi rallies. Goebbels made much use of *Der Angriff*, the newspaper he bought in 1927. In 1930, he wrote an article about the death of a young Nazi named Horst Wessel who was murdered by a communist. The real reason for the murder seems to have been an argument between the two men over the prostitute with whom Wessel lived, but Nazi propaganda made no mention of this. Instead, Wessel became a Nazi hero and a song that he had composed became the Nazi marching song.

Source 20

It is 6.30 Sunday morning. He dies after a hard struggle. As I stand by his bed two hours later, I can not believe that it is Horst Wessel....His mortal remains have given up struggle and conflict. Yet I can feel almost physically his spirit rise, to live on with us. He believed it, he knew it. He himself put it in words: He 'marches in spirit in our ranks'.

Joseph Goebbels in *Der Angriff*, 1930

■ **Think about**

▶ Why do you think Goebbels decided to make Horst Wessel into a Nazi martyr?

Activity

Conclusions

Timeline

Think about

NATIONAL-SOZIALISMUS

DER ORGANISIERTE WILLE DER NATION

Chapter 7

The collapse of the Weimar Republic

▲ A Berlin soup kitchen in 1931

▶ An unemployed man looking for work. The sign round his neck says: 'I will take on any work of any type immediately'.

Introduction

The Wall Street Crash, as Sources 1 and 2 suggest, hit Germany very badly. After a period of relative stability, Germany was once again thrown into turmoil and the Weimar Republic faced its biggest challenge yet. What it urgently needed to provide was strong decisive government action which would address the immediate problem of unemployment and reassure the people that the matter was firmly under control. Unfortunately, this did not happen – but why not? The main political parties disagreed over what action to take, but their views were increasingly ignored by the government in any case. To some extent this was not surprising. Both the Nazis' and the Communists' share of the vote was increasing and it was unlikely that such anti-Weimar parties would be welcomed into government. However, there was a move amongst the German elite to isolate all left-wing parties, including the SPD which remained the biggest political party until 1932. Quite what the right-wing members of this elite wanted is not clear. They certainly wanted to reduce the power of the Reichstag and the left-wing and return Germany to authoritarian rule. Some may have wished to see a return of the monarchy, although others simply wanted to see their own power increase under the favour of President Hindenburg. Whatever their motive, they played a crucial role in ending democracy in Weimar and the appointment of Hitler as Chancellor.

Key questions

- To what extent did the Wall Street Crash contribute to the fall of the Weimar Republic?
- When, why and how did democracy collapse?
- To what extent and why did the Nazis gain success between 1930 and 1932?
- Did Hitler get into power 'through the back door'?
- At what point did the fall of Weimar become most likely?

The impact of the Wall Street Crash

Unemployment

The collapse of the American Stock Exchange in October 1929 had a disastrous effect on the German economy, which had never fully recovered from the battering of war and hyperinflation. In the winter of 1928–1929, unemployment had stood at 2.5 million. By the following winter that figure had risen to over 3 million. Registered unemployment eventually exceeded 6 million and it was estimated that around half the economically active population were without work in the winters of 1931–1932 and 1932–1933. Thousands of small family firms collapsed and smaller farms went bankrupt. Diseases such as tuberculosis and pneumonia reappeared, which had been more familiar during periods of wartime famine. Infant mortality increased. Those fortunate enough to be in work saw their incomes fall, and lived in constant fear of joining the massed ranks of the unemployed.

The 'Grand Coalition'

In these circumstances the critical weaknesses of the Weimar political system became more apparent. In 1928, Hermann Müller, a Social Democrat, was appointed Chancellor of the 'Grand Coalition', representing five political parties ranging from the left (SPD) to the moderate right (DVP). This range of political opinion did not make decision-making easy and the economic crisis highlighted their differences. The fundamental problem facing the government was a deficit in the Reich budget. The government was spending more than it was receiving. This was not helped by the inadequacy of the unemployment scheme which was unable to pay out enough benefits to the growing number of the unemployed. The government was therefore forced to make contributions to the scheme which made the budget deficit worse. The parties began to split along class lines over this issue. The SPD wanted to raise the level of contributions to the scheme whilst protecting the workers and unemployed as far as possible. The right-wing parties, such as the DVP, wanted to lighten the tax burden and reduce the value of unemployment benefits. The result was political deadlock. Parties refused to co-operate with each other to tackle the economic crisis effectively.

Müller was unable to muster enough support in the Reichstag to pass laws and consequently turned to Hindenburg for help. He wanted Hindenburg to grant him the use of Article 48 so that the support of the Reichstag was unnecessary. Hindenburg refused, no doubt partly because Müller belonged to the SPD and therefore represented the left-wing which Hindenburg distrusted. Müller was left with no other option than to resign, which he did in March 1930.

Nationalist opposition

Meanwhile, the government was facing further problems from the right. In 1929, an opportunity arose for the right-wing parties to unite against the Young Plan (see page 101). Although Germany stood to gain from it, the Young Plan was denounced by the DNVP and the Nazis as yet another example of foreign powers dictating Germany's fortunes. The two parties joined together in calling for a plebiscite (popular vote) and proposed a 'Freedom Law' which required the government to end all co-operation with international powers over the Rhineland occupation and to reject any obligations which arose from the War-Guilt Clause of the Versailles Treaty. The plebiscite was a failure as only 13.8 per cent of the electorate voted in support of the law, but the Nazis gained greater political respect and financial backing from their association with the DNVP, as well as free publicity in Hugenberg's newspaper. A stream of vicious anti-Weimar propaganda was unleashed by the Nazis and, during 1929, the Party did well in local elections, an ominous sign of things to come.

Cross reference

See page 76 for a reminder of the terms of Article 48.

■ Biography

Hugenberg

Alfred Hugenberg was born in 1865 in Hanover. Before the First World War, he was a civil servant, banker and successful businessman. After the war, he became a Reichstag deputy, representing the right-wing DNVP. He also made his fortune by taking over newspaper houses and film companies. In 1929, he joined with Hitler to oppose the Young Plan. Hitler gained from Hugenberg's support, not least by having access to Hugenberg's newspapers for his propaganda. In 1933, Hugenberg was appointed Minister for Economics and Food, hoping to gain further influence and power. He was disappointed however, especially when the DNVP did badly in the election of March 1933. He resigned and played no further part in politics.

Frauen!

Adolf Hitler!

Source 3

◀ A Nazi appeal to women voters in 1932. It reminds them of the millions of unemployed men and children without a future, and asks them to 'save our German families' by voting for Adolf Hitler.

The collapse of democracy

The key players

President Paul von Hindenburg 1847–1934

A hero of the First World War, Hindenburg was made supreme military commander in 1916. After the war he retired, but was persuaded in 1925 to stand as the presidential candidate of a right-wing coalition. He succeeded, to the dismay of the German left-wing parties and former allied states within Europe, all of whom feared a return to authoritarian rule. In fact, Hindenburg spent the first five years acting within the limits of the Weimar Constitution. From 1930, however, he was increasingly influenced by aristocratic army officers who wished to weaken the new Republic and gain more power for themselves. Hindenburg was getting old. It was said that no-one dared leave a sandwich paper near him in case he mistook it for an official paper and signed it. Although he distrusted Hitler, he was persuaded to appoint him Chancellor in 1933.

Heinrich Brüning 1885–1970

A member of the Centre Party and a Reichstag deputy from 1924–1933, Brüning became the leader of the Centre Party's Reichstag deputies by 1929. Having caught the attention of Hindenburg, Brüning was appointed Chancellor in 1930 but his two years in office were not happy ones. In attempting to keep the left-wing out of government he found himself unable to get laws passed through the Reichstag. He became the first Chancellor routinely to use Article 48 in order to bypass the Reichstag. His memoirs revealed his intention to reform the Constitution and restore the monarchy. He also failed to resolve the economic crisis, earning him the nickname the 'Hunger Chancellor'. He was forced to resign in 1932 and eventually emigrated to America.

Franz von Papen 1879–1969

Papen was born to a wealthy noble family and joined the army. He became a captain of the General Staff in 1913 and became famous for his incompetent secret service activities in Washington. After the war Papen entered politics, representing the extreme right-wing of the Centre Party. He never achieved a place in the Reichstag but did represent the interests of the landed aristocrats in the Prussian Landtag (state parliament). After supporting Hindenburg in the presidential election of 1932, he was appointed Chancellor in May 1932. This was surprising given his lack of experience and general credibility. Papen failed to gain support in the Reichstag, was dismissed within months and was replaced by Schleicher. As revenge, Papen persuaded Hindenburg to sack Schleicher and appoint Hitler as Chancellor with himself as Vice-Chancellor.

Kurt von Schleicher 1882–1934

It was another aristocratic army man, von Schleicher, who was stage-managing the events between 1930 and 1932. Schleicher was born to an old Prussian military family and joined Hindenburg's old regiment in 1903. He became a close friend of Hindenburg's son, Oskar. During the 1920s he achieved success within the Defence Ministry where he combined interests in politics and the army. From this powerful position he could pursue his own personal ambition. He gained the ear of Hindenburg and persuaded him to appoint both Brüning and Papen. He became Defence Minister under Papen and in December 1932 replaced Papen as Chancellor. His attempt to gain support in the Reichstag backfired, providing Papen with an opportunity for revenge. He was forced to resign within two months. He was murdered by the Nazis in 1934.

Brüning as Chancellor

Following Müller's resignation in March 1930, Heinrich Brüning was appointed Chancellor. This was the first occasion when Hindenburg was heavily influenced by von Schleicher in his choice of minister. Schleicher encouraged the creation of a cabinet which excluded the SPD, despite the fact that it remained the largest party in the Reichstag. This was the first step towards eliminating the left wing from German politics. The problem was that it left Brüning with inadequate support in the Reichstag and, therefore, unable to pass laws. Brüning, as we know from his memoirs, supported a return to a more authoritarian style of government and was content to bypass the Reichstag completely by using Article 48 to enforce laws by Presidential Decree.

> ### Source 4
>
> The Cabinet has been formed for the purpose of resolving as quickly as possible those problems that are widely regarded as crucial to the survival of the Reich. This will be the final attempt to resolve these problems through this Reichstag....The government is able and determined *to employ every constitutional means at its disposal to achieve its ends.*
>
> Governmental declaration by Chancellor Brüning, 1 April 1930

The response of the major political parties to Brüning's government was a clear sign that he would face a deadlock in the Reichstag.

> ### Source 5
>
> #### Reactions to Brüning
>
> **SPD**
> 'The Chancellor wants to put his programme into effect through this, I think you must agree, rather motley collection of cabinet members...he is clearly flirting with Article 48...a beginning leading to the establishment of a dictatorship...'
> **From a Reichstag speech, 2 April 1930**
>
> **DNVP**
> 'The serious differences of opinion over foreign affairs, as well as over internal matters and economic policies, which existed between the DNVP and the Müller government continue to characterize our relationship with the new government.'
> **From a Reichstag speech, 3 April 1930**
>
> **KPD**
> 'We Communists call on the working masses to vigorously oppose this middle-class capitalist-dictatorship government; this government that will rob the masses and enrich the property owning classes. We demand the resignation of this government.'
> **From a Reichstag speech, 2 April 1930**
>
> **NSDAP**
> 'No-one...has dared to point out the real cause of all our misery: the Dawes and Young Plans...Mr Brüning should not take shelter behind the world economic crisis. What has caused our misery is the ineffectiveness of German politics over the last 12 years...'
> **From a Reichstag speech, 18 July 1930**

■ **Activity**

Read through the biographies of the 'key players' on page 133 carefully. Make notes under the following headings:
● Backgrounds
● Attitudes to the Weimar Republic
● Political aims
● Successes/failures

Now consider these questions:
1 What did these men have in common?
2 Why do you think Hitler was distrusted, especially by Hindenburg who called him 'that Bohemian corporal'?
3 Why do you think 1932–1933 are described as years of 'backstairs intrigue'?

■ **Activity**

1 To what extent did Brüning lack support from the main political parties?
2 To what extent are their reasons for opposing Brüning similar or different?
3 Can you explain why each party took the view expressed here? (look back at the summary on page 75 if necessary)
4 What would you have advised Brüning to do in the light of these extracts?

Facts and figures

Laws passed by the Reichstag

1930	98
1931	34
1932	5

Emergency decrees

1930	5
1931	44
1932	66

The first crisis occurred in July 1930, when the Reichstag rejected part of Brüning's finance bill which was intended to balance the budget. Brüning used Article 48 to bypass the Reichstag, the first time that such a step had been taken after a bill had already been defeated. (Ebert had used Article 48 to enforce laws in times of emergency when there was no time to call the Reichstag). The Reichstag passed a motion demanding that the decree be withdrawn and Brüning's response was to dissolve (close down) the Reichstag and call a new election. This was an extremely risky strategy given the Nazi successes in recent local elections. If Brüning had not called for new elections, then the Nazis would not have had the opportunity to increase their number of seats from 12 to 107. Under the Weimar Constitution, there was no need for another election until 1932. If the Nazis had still only had 12 seats by 1932, rather than 107, then the history of Germany might look rather different.

The election of 1930

■ Think about

Study the results in Source 6.

▶ What were the major changes between the two elections?

▶ How do you think the 1930 election result might have changed Weimar politics?

▶ Was the 1930 election result good or bad for Brüning?

Source 6

Party	Election Result in 1928		Election Result in 1930	
	Number of seats	Percentage of votes	Number of seats	Percentage of votes
NSDAP	12	2.6	107	18.3
DNVP	73	14.2	41	7.0
Z	62	15.1	68	14.8
SPD	153	29.8	143	24.5
KPD	54	10.6	77	13.1

■ Think about

▶ Can you explain why some historians see 1930 as the date when democracy in Germany collapsed?

The most significant feature about the 1930 election was the growth of the two extreme parties, the KPD and the Nazis. Both benefited from the electorate's impatience with the government's slow response to the economic crisis. Brüning now faced opposition from at least 64 per cent of the Reichstag deputies. Not only were the two extreme parties withholding support, but the DNVP was also refusing to work with Brüning and the SPD remained outside the government. It was inconceivable that Brüning could look to the Reichstag for any support in these circumstances. Luckily for Brüning, however, the SPD decided to swallow its pride and 'tolerate' Brüning's government even though it was excluded from government. It supported Brüning for the simple reason that if his government fell, it might, given the election results, be replaced with a Nazi-nationalist government which would be much worse. Despite this support, Brüning continued to rely on Article 48 to pass laws.

The Presidential election

In April 1932, President Hindenburg was re-elected for a second term. His main rivals were Hitler and Thalmann, leader of the KPD. In the first round, Hindenburg polled 49 per cent of the votes, just failing to secure an overall majority. The failure of the left to agree a joint candidate created the bizarre situation whereby socialists and Centre Party supporters voted for the right-wing Hindenburg simply to keep Hitler out. Hitler, incidentally, did very well in the election, a further sign of his growing prestige and growing popularity.

Facts and figures

The results of the two Presidential elections of 1932.

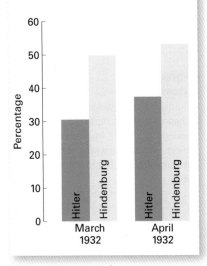

Why did Brüning fall?

Brüning was nicknamed the 'Hunger Chancellor' thanks to an unpopular economic policy. In an attempt to curb public spending and inflation, a series of decrees was issued in December 1931 which reduced wages and public salaries to the level of 1927. In some cases, pensions and benefits fell by 9 per cent. Welfare payments had been reduced and around a third of the unemployed received nothing at all, despite an unemployment figure exceeding 6 million by February 1932. Those lucky enough to be in work faced a falling standard of living and, by the end of 1932, suicide rates in Germany were considerably higher than in the USA, France or Britain. It was, therefore, very serious indeed that Brüning offered no sign of relief to the German people.

Hindenburg's confidence in Brüning was decreasing, not least because Schleicher (see page 133) was urging him to create an even more right-wing government. Schleicher was increasingly of the opinion that the Nazis had to be included in the government if it was to have support at all in the Reichstag and he began secret meetings and negotiations with Hitler. Finally, Hindenburg withdrew his permission for the use of Article 48 and Brüning was forced to resign in May 1932. He apparently retired to bed for days, exhausted and suffering from shock at his treatment.

Source 7

Hurra, Hurra! Der Brüning-Weihnachtsmann ist da!

■ Think about

Source 7 is a photomontage made by John Heartfield in 1930. The title reads 'Hip, Hip, Hurray! Father Christmas Brüning is Here!' Study the photomontage carefully.

▶ Can you find any symbols?

▶ Why do you think Brüning is described as Father Christmas?

▶ What does this tell you about Heartfield's views?

Did Hitler become Chancellor through the back door?

The Cabinet of Barons

Brüning was replaced as Chancellor by the aristocratic Papen (see page 133) with Schleicher as his Defence Minister. None of the members of Papen's rather aristocratic cabinet – nicknamed the 'Cabinet of Barons' – were members of the Reichstag and most had no ties to political parties. Democracy was by now fading fast. Papen's aim was to continue Brüning's policy of ruling by decree, but his position became even more difficult after the election of July 1932. The Nazis achieved their best result so far, becoming the biggest party in the Reichstag with 230 seats, although still without an overall majority. The two parties whose aim it was to destroy the Weimar Republic – the Nazis and the KPD – now controlled more than half the seats between them. This was catastrophic for the survival of democracy.

Note

During Papen's brief spell as Chancellor he attempted to undermine the left by, amongst other things, illegally removing the Prussian government which was led by the SPD.

Despite the lifting of the ban on the SA and SS which Brüning had imposed in April 1932, Hitler refused to work with the Papen government, claiming that with such an election result he should, by rights, be Chancellor himself. In his memoirs, Papen wrote of a meeting he had with Hitler in August 1932. He described Hitler as 'a very different man from the one I had met two months earlier. The modest air of deference had gone, and I was faced by a demanding politician who had just won a resounding electoral success.' By now, it was clear to Papen that the Nazis had to be brought into the government, but he was determined that it should not be wholly on Hitler's terms. Papen urged Hitler to join in a coalition with the DNVP – but Hitler refused, insisting that he be appointed Chancellor or nothing.

In September, the Reichstag passed an overwhelming vote of no confidence in Papen (512 votes to 42) and the election in November brought no further prospects of support for the government. The Nazis, although they lost 34 seats, remained the largest party by some distance. Papen was prepared to dissolve the Reichstag permanently at this stage and, if necessary, use the army to crush opposition. However, Schleicher persuaded President Hindenburg that this would end in civil war and was himself appointed Chancellor in place of Papen on 2 December 1932. Papen was furious and spent much of the next few weeks plotting his revenge.

Schleicher as Chancellor

Schleicher adopted a very risky strategy. He could see that the attempts by Brüning and Papen to rule without the Reichstag had been unsuccessful. In order to make his Chancellorship more successful he wanted to gain more support from the Reichstag and be seen as the man who managed to unite politicians. However, he was deeply suspicious of Hitler and ruled out any deal with the Nazis as a whole. He therefore took a new approach. Firstly, he attempted to split the Nazis by appealing to the more socialist wing of the party led by Gregor Strasser, who was offered the Vice-Chancellorship. Secondly, he tried to gain some support from the left by offering concessions to the trade unions. However, neither strategy worked. The attempt to lure Strasser and his followers away from the Nazis failed due to Hitler's intervention, and the trade unions were too suspicious of Schleicher's motives to offer him support. Not only that, but powerful industrialists and landowners were alarmed at Schleicher's tactics and began to contemplate a toleration of the Nazis as the lesser of two evils.

Papen, aware of Schleicher's failure, seized his chance for revenge. He decided that a government led by Hitler with him as Vice-Chancellor was his best option. This would guarantee him huge support in the Reichstag and he gambled on the fact that a minority of Nazis in the cabinet would be easily controlled. On 4 January, Papen and Hitler moved towards an agreement. Hindenburg needed some persuasion, but pressure from both Papen and his own son, Oskar, finally convinced him. They shared Papen's view that the Nazis could be 'tamed' and saw the Nazis' drop in electoral support in November as a sign that their support was falling. Hindenburg refused Schleicher's request to dissolve the Reichstag and Schleicher resigned on 28 January. Two days later, Hindenburg reluctantly agreed to appoint Hitler as Chancellor and a cabinet was formed consisting of three Nazis and nine other conservatives, including Papen as Vice-Chancellor.

Facts and figures

Election Results: July and November 1932:

Party	July 1932		Nov 1932	
	Seats	% of vote	Seats	% of vote
NSDAP	230	37.3	196	33.1
DNVP	37	5.9	52	8.8
DVP	7	1.2	11	1.9
BVP	20	15.9	18	15.0
DDP	4	1.0	2	1.0
SPD	133	21.6	121	20.4
KPD	89	14.3	100	16.9

■ Summary

Backstairs intrigue

May 1932: Papen appointed Chancellor with Schleicher as Defence Minister.

↓

September 1932: The Reichstag passes a vote of no confidence in Papen. Either he has to go, or Germany could face dangerous instability.

↓

December 1932: Schleicher appointed Chancellor. Papen is furious.

↓

Schleicher is unsuccessful in gaining support in the Reichstag. Papen sees a chance for revenge.

↓

January 1933: Papen strikes a deal with the Nazis which Hindenburg accepts. Hitler is appointed Chancellor with Papen as Vice Chancellor.

■ **Activity**   **KEY SKILLS**

This chapter has so far presented you with a lot of complex information. You now need to review it to make sure you are clear about what happened and why.

1   Read from 'Bruning as Chancellor' on page 134 to the bottom of page 137. Make a note of the **key** events and their consequences using a table like the one below. The timeline should also help you. The table has been started for you.

EVENT	CONSEQUENCE
March 1930 : Müller resigns as Chancellor	*Brüning becomes Chancellor*
July 1930 : Reichstag rejects finance bill	*Brüning uses Article 48 to enforce the bill*

2   Now go though your table and highlight the six events which you think were most important in the collapse of the Weimar Republic. Be prepared to defend your choice to others in a class discussion.

3   Your final task is to write an answer to the question: 'Why did democracy collapse in Germany between 1930 and 1933?' Use the statements below to structure your work. Explain to what extent you agree or disagree with each one.
   ● The main reason why democracy collapsed was because of powers granted to the President by the Weimar Constitution
   ● Brüning should not be blamed for the collapse of democracy
   ● Hitler's appointment as Chancellor was more down to luck than skill

Document Exercise: Who was responsible for Hitler's appointment as Chancellor?

Source A

Papen denies responsibility for Hitler's appointment

I was guest of honour at a dinner given by the Berlin Herrenklub…[and] one of the guests was Schroeder, the Cologne banker. As far as I could make out, he seemed to be of the opinion that the government was still under an obligation to reach some accommodation with Hitler. When he suggested that it might still be possible to make a personal approach to Hitler, I agreed. Schroeder rang me up to ask whether I would be free to meet Hitler during the next few days. I told him that I was going to Berlin, via Düsseldorf, on January 4, and could stop at Cologne on the way if he wished…I thought there was still a possibility of persuading Hitler to join the Schleicher government. I had not the slightest intention of causing Schleicher difficulties…

Extracts from the memoirs of Franz von Papen, 1952

Timeline

1928
June: Hermann Müller appointed Chancellor of the Grand Coalition
1929
June: Publication of the Young Plan
July: Nazis and DNVP unite in opposition to the Young Plan
October: Death of Stresemann
October: US Stock Market crashes
1930
March: Müller resigns and Bruning appointed Chancellor
July: Reichstag dissolved after Bruning uses Article 48
September: Huge Nazi gains in election
1932
February: Unemployment exceeds 6 million
April: Hindenburg re-elected as President
May: Brüning resigns and Papen appointed Chancellor
July: Nazis become the largest party in the Reichstag after election
September: Reichstag passes a vote of no confidence in Papen
November: Nazis lose 34 seats in the election but remain the largest party in the Reichstag
December: Papen resigns and Schleicher appointed Chancellor
1933
January: Secret meeting of Papen and Hitler
January: Schleicher resigns and Hitler is appointed Chancellor

Source B

4 January meeting between Papen and Hitler

On 4 January 1933 Hitler, Papen, Hess, Himmler and Keppler arrived at my house in Cologne...The negotiations took place exclusively between Hitler and Papen...Papen went on to say that he thought it best to form a government in which the conservative and nationalist elements that had supported him were represented together with the Nazis. He suggested that this new government should, if possible, be led by Hitler and himself together...This meeting between Hitler and Papen on 4 January 1933 in my house in Cologne was arranged by me after Papen had asked me for it on about 10 December 1932.

From the account given by Schroeder at the Nuremberg Tribunal after the war

Source C

Papen's continued role in discussions

In the latter part of January, Papen played an increasingly important role in the house of the Reich President, but despite Papen's persuasions, Hindenburg was extremely hesitant, until the end of January, to make Hitler Chancellor. He wanted to have Papen as Chancellor. Papen finally won him over to Hitler with the argument that the representatives of the other right-wing parties which would belong to the government would restrict Hitler's freedom of action. In addition, Papen expressed his misgivings that, if the present opportunity were again missed, a revolt of the National Socialists and civil war were likely.

From the account given by Otto Meissner, State Secretary in Hindenburg's office, to the Nuremberg Tribunal

Source D

Papen openly supports Hitler as Chancellor

I have never seen Hitler in such a state; I proposed to him and Goering that I should see Papen alone that evening and explain the whole situation to him. In the evening I saw Papen and convinced him eventually that the only thing that made sense was Hitler's Chancellorship, and that he must do what he can to bring this about. Papen declared that...he was now absolutely in favour of Hitler becoming Chancellor; this was the decisive change in Papen's attitude.

From the personal notes of Joachim von Ribbentrop, a wealthy member of the Nazi Party since 1931

■ Examination-style questions

1 Comprehension and context

Study Source B. From this source and your own knowledge, explain why negotiations were taking place between Papen and Hitler.

2 Comparing the sources

Study Sources A and B. To what extent and why do the two sources differ in their account of the 4 January meeting?

3 Assessing the sources

Study Source D. How useful is this source as evidence about the role Papen played in Hitler's appointment?

4 Making judgements

Using these sources and your own knowledge, explain who you feel was most responsible for the appointment of Hitler as Chancellor.

Why did the Weimar Republic collapse?

Introduction

We have already considered whether the Weimar Republic was 'doomed from the start' or not (see page 91). The evidence suggests that this is too simplistic a view. After all, there was at least some recovery between 1924 and 1929. However, the fact remains that the Weimar Republic eventually collapsed in 1933. It could even be argued that democracy ended in 1930, when Brüning began to use Article 48 to bypass the Reichstag. Historians have argued about when the collapse of Weimar became most likely (they tend to avoid the term inevitable) with some suggesting 1930 or later and others tracing Weimar's fall back to the 1920s. This section provides you with different historians' views and an opportunity to decide for yourself when and why Weimar's fate was sealed.

■ Activity   KEY SKILLS

1   Read Sources 8–13 carefully. Some of them are complicated and may need reading several times. Then copy out and complete the chart below.

Name of historian	Does the historian suggest a date at which the fall of the Weimar Republic became most likely? If so, which date does he or she choose?	What does the historian feel are the key reasons for the fall of the Weimar Republic?

2   Is there any agreement amongst the historians about when and why Weimar's future collapse became most likely?
3   Can you suggest any reasons why historians differ on this issue?
4   Read the following quotation. To what extent to you agree with what Kolb is saying?

   'What made Hitler possible? Was the Nazi 'seizure of power' inevitable in the circumstances that prevailed? Every discussion of the collapse of Weimar circles round these questions, which have received very different answers from researchers up to the present. Certainly, the monocausal [single cause] explanations which at first prevailed...are by now discarded, as all such simplistic accounts have proved inadequate. Historians today at least agree the collapse of the Republic and the Nazi 'seizure of power' can only be plausibly explained in terms of a very complex range of causes.'

                                                                    Kolb, *The Weimar Republic*, 1988

5   Structured essay question:
   The Weimar Republic collapsed for a variety of reasons, including:
   ● The Weimar Constitution
   ● The Wall Street Crash
   ● The popularity of the Nazis
   ● Backstairs intrigue

   a   Explain how any two of these factors contributed to the collapse of the Weimar Republic.
   b   Compare the importance of at least three of these factors as contributions to the collapse of the Weimar Republic.

Source 8

...the political development that culminated in the overpowering of the Republic by National Socialism was by no means inevitable. In 1923, in similar circumstances, the onslaught of the radical enemy had been successfully repulsed [overcome]. The fact that the crisis of 1929–1933 took a different course cannot be explained by economic factors alone, nor can it be looked upon as a consequence of democracy, for Hitler after all did not come to power via a parliamentary majority. Under the prevailing conditions the political activities of an influential group of critics and enemies of the Republic took on a major importance. Beginning with the well intentioned though mistaken policies of Brüning, Germany became the stage on which a procession of ambitious and misguided men sought to make history, from Schleicher and Papen to Hindenburg.

Bracher, *The German Dictatorship*, 1969

Source 9

Economic constraints, both domestic and international, greatly limited the possibilities for positive political action – regardless of whether or not the actors involved had any correct thoughts. This is not to throw the idea of human agency out the window when discussing why democratic politics collapsed in Weimar Germany, but it is to put the actions of those involved into perspective.

Bessell in *Weimar – Why did German Democracy Fail?* ed. Kershaw, 1990

Source 10

...the survival chances of the Weimar Democracy might be regarded as fairly poor by the end of 1929, very low by the end of 1930, remote by the middle of 1931 and as good as zero by spring 1932.

Kershaw, *Weimar – Why did German Democracy Fail?*, 1990

Source 11

The promise [by the Nazis] of a new, national community, which would make Germany great again...proved a powerful vision to large numbers of desperate, frightened Germans, for whom Weimar democracy had meant only national humiliation, economic disaster, social conflicts and personal uncertainty. Recognising the force of such a mass movement, and recognising their own lack of a popular base, the nationalist, industrial, agrarian and military elites thought they could 'harness', 'tame' and use this movement to give their own schemes for the destruction of democracy a legitimacy [lawfulness] which they could not on their own achieve. Hitler did not need to 'seize' power; the old elites simply opened the door and welcomed him in...In this unique combination of circumstances, Adolf Hitler came to power in Germany.

Fulbrook, *A Concise History of Germany*, 1990

Source 12

Yet the Weimar Republic survived these early crises when the problems of defeat and reparations were at their most urgent. In fact, coalition governments held together in the mid-twenties in Germany when it came to dealing with the problems associated with the Treaty of Versailles. It was a very different issue which sabotaged coalition government once and for all, namely the issue of the level of unemployment benefits and how one was to fund them.

Geary in *Weimar – Why did German Democracy Fail?* ed. Kershaw, 1990

Source 13

The disintegration of the Weimar Republic and the rise of Nazism were two distinct if obviously overlapping historical processes. By 1932, the collapse of Weimar had become inevitable; Hitler's triumph had not.

Stern, *The Failure of Liberalism*, 1972

Why was the Nazi Party so successful, 1930–1932?

Winning elections

Although the Nazi Party never achieved a majority in the Reichstag and was not technically voted into power, it was the extraordinary success of the Nazis at the polls which made them an extremely useful addition to the government. In 1930, they gained a bigger increase in votes than any party in the whole of German history. Learning from the disappointing results of 1928, Hitler paid more attention to winning the middle-class and farming votes and less attention to socialist or anti-Semitic policies. The Nazis, together with the KPD, were the main beneficiaries of the government's failure to address the economic crisis effectively. The Nazis were particularly attractive to those who had lost faith in the Weimar Republic, longed for strong leadership and feared communism. The Nazis prided themselves on presenting the most consistent and effective opposition to communism, a stance which won them a great deal of support from the middle class. Running alongside all of this were Goebbels' propaganda campaigns.

Why did the Nazis achieve power and not the communists?

The economic crisis following the Wall Street Crash could, in theory, have strengthened the communists more than the Nazis. Certainly, unemployed workers were more likely to vote for the KPD than the Nazi Party and the depression could have further undermined confidence in the capitalist system. However, from the very beginning of the Weimar Republic, the communists were weakened by a lack of mass support, the absence of a charismatic leader and a lack of co-operation with the SPD. Furthermore, the increasing influence of Russia on the policies of the KPD did little to endear it to the German people. Although its strength in the Reichstag increased between 1928 and 1932, the KPD continued to suffer from an absence of broad-based support such as that enjoyed by the Nazis. What support they did have came mainly from the weakest section of the working class and even here, they were in competition with the SPD.

Ironically, the growing strength of the communists helped rather than hindered the Nazis. Fear of communism drove many people into the Nazi camp, not least members of the elite for whom co-operation with the Nazis was at least preferable to a growth in the power of the left. This is the final, compelling reason why the Nazis succeeded where the communists failed. The right-wing German elite would have done almost anything to keep the communists out.

Facts and figures

KPD seats in the Reichstag

1928	54
1930	77
1932 (July)	89
1932 (Nov)	100

Who voted for the Nazis?

Historians are in agreement that the group most likely to support the Nazis by the beginning of the 1930s was the *mittelstand* or lower middle class who felt that their interests were being squeezed between big business on the one hand and the rise of communism on the other. There has been a more recent debate, however, about the extent of working-class support for the party. As you will see from the evidence on the next few pages, what characterized the Nazi Party's supporters more than anything was their diversity. They were young and old, rich and poor, Protestant and Catholic. However, some groups of people were more likely to vote for the Nazis than others.

■ Historical debate

Source 14

The mass support of the Nazis in 1932 came from those who had voted in 1928 for the middle-class parties, like the People's Party, the Democrats, and the Economic Party, whose combined vote of 5,582,500 in 1928 had sunk to 954,700 in 1932; from the Nationalist Party, which had lost a million and a half votes; from young people, many of whom without jobs, voting for the first time; and from those who had not voted before, but had been stirred by events and by propaganda to come to the polls this time.

Bullock, *Hitler A Study in Tyranny*, 1952

Source 15

This first mass layer of [middle class] Nazi followers was reinforced by the equally uprooted unemployed, comprising more than one-fifth of the labour force and representing the political driftwood of the late Weimar Republic.

Neumann, *Modern Political Parties*, 1956

Source 16

The NSDAP did not succeed in making inroads among the workers and the trade unions. Despite all efforts of the 'left' wing, the NSDAP claim to being a 'socialist workers' party' remained a propaganda façade. Compared with the early days of the party...the newly formed NSDAP had, sociologically speaking, turned into a middle-class right-wing party without any ties to organized labour...the membership of the NSDAP was composed of the lower middle class, of merchants, artisans, white-collar workers, military adventurers, and youthful romantic activists.

Bracher, *The German Dictatorship*, 1969

Source 17

Although the NSDAP claimed to be a 'workers' party' in its very title...the nucleus of the membership of the Nazi Party was drawn from the *Mittelstand*...However, though never a workers' party as such, the Nazi Party did mobilise an increasingly sizeable membership of blue-collar workers during the 1920s, and by the early 1930s blue collar workers accounted for around 40% of the Party's total membership, making the NSDAP an important force in the political mobilisation of the working-class.

Muhlberger 'A Workers' Party or a Party without Workers?' in Fischer (ed.), *The Rise of Nazism and the Working Classes in Weimar Germany*, 1986

Source 18

The Nazi Party was without doubt a *Volkspartei* (people's party): recruiting its members and its voters across a broad range of social groups, from both sexes and from the older generation...Being Catholic, unemployed or living in a large town significantly reduced the likelihood of voters to opt for Hitler...Conversely, being Protestant in rural Germany greatly increased such a propensity, as did the absence of strong loyalties.

Geary, 'Who Voted for the Nazis?' in *History Today*, October 1998

■ Activity

1 List all the types of people that these historians believed were most likely to vote for the Nazis.

2 How far do the historians agree with each other about Nazi supporters? Give examples of where they agree and disagree.

3 Can you suggest any reasons for the areas of disagreement between historians on this issue? (You may find this question easier to answer after completing the activity on the next page).

Who supported the Nazis?

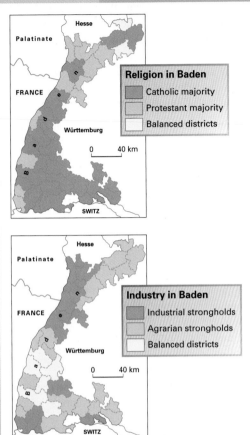

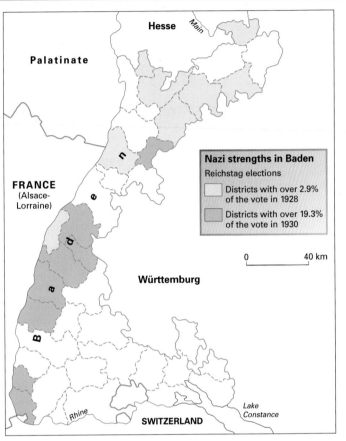

▲ The distribution of Nazi support in one German state. Based on Overy, *The Penguin Historical Atlas of the Third Reich.*

Percentage distribution of Nazi voters, 1928–33

	1928	1930	1932 (July)	1932 (Nov.)	1933
Religious denomination					
Catholic	30	20	17	17	24
Other	70	80	83	83	76
Community size					
0–5,000	39	41	45	47	47
5,000–20,000	14	13	13	12	12
20,000–100,000	16	15	13	13	13
More than 100,000	31	31	29	28	28
Social class					
Working class	40	40	39	40	40
New middle class	23	21	19	19	18
Old middle class	37	39	42	41	42

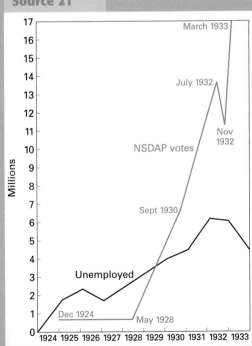

▶ The relationship between unemployment and votes for the Nazis.

Source 22

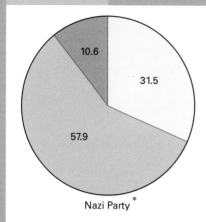

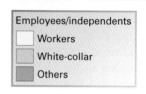

Employees/independents
Workers
White-collar
Others

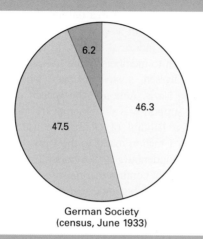

Nazi Party *

German Society
(census, June 1933)

* People who joined the
Nazi Party between February
1925 and January 1933 and
were still members in 1934.

▲ The distribution of support for the Nazis
compared to German society as a whole.

Source 23

Elections for the Reichstag during the Weimar Republic (% of vote)

	1920	1924	1928	1930	1932 July	1932 Nov.	1933
NSDAP	–	3.0	2.6	18.3	37.3	33.1	43.9
DNVP	14.9	20.5	14.2	7.0	5.9	8.8	8.0
DVP	13.9	10.1	8.7	4.5	1.2	1.9	1.1
Z/BVP	17.9	17.3	15.1	14.8	15.9	15.0	14.1
DDP	8.3	6.3	4.9	3.8	1.0	1.0	0.9
SPD	21.6	26.0	29.8	24.5	21.6	20.4	18.2
USPD	17.9	0.3	0.1	–	–	–	–
KPD	2.1	9.0	10.6	13.1	14.3	16.9	12.2
Turnout	79.1	78.8	75.6	81.9	84.0	80.6	88.5

Source 24

Nazi Party membership in 1935

Age in 1935	Percentage of Party membership
18–20	2.1
21–30	41.3
31–40	26.9
41–50	17.1
51–60	9.2
60 & above	3.4

■ **Activity**

Make sure you have completed the activity on page 143.
Copy and complete the following chart:

Type of person identified as most likely to vote Nazi (in the extracts on page 143)	Evidence which supports this view	Evidence which does not support this view	Limitations of the evidence

Using your completed chart, what conclusions can you reach about the types of people who were most likely to support the Nazis after 1928?

Why do you think these types of people supported the Nazis? (You may wish to draw on material from Chapter 6 in this answer)

Note: For inclusion into your key skills portfolio, you should produce an extended analysis of this issue. To support your analysis, you should select and download pre-1933 election posters from the Internet to illustrate the messages and potential appeal of Nazi propaganda. See page 177 for a suggested website.

Did big business support the Nazis?

After the war some left-wing historians claimed that the Nazis got into power because of their support from big business. It is true that the links established with Hugenberg in 1929 provided the Nazis with a source of industrial funds and that Hitler went out of his way to woo industrial leaders. In January 1932 he delivered a two-and-a-half hour speech to members of the Industry Club in Düsseldorf at the invitation of Fritz Thyssen, a steel magnate who was a member and financial supporter of the Nazis. Although the speech received 'tumultuous' applause, further financial support was slow to appear. Until 1933, the Nazis gained support from only a handful of German industrialists – Thyssen was the most significant, giving 1 million marks to the Party. Even the petition sent by leading industrialists to Hindenburg in November 1932, asking him to appoint Hitler as Chancellor, does not confirm that the rise of the Nazis was the *result* of this support. In fact, many big industrialists who became active supporters of the Nazis did so only *after* Hitler's appointment in January 1933.

Document exercise: Big business and the Nazis

Source A

Annual accounts of an east Prussian branch of the Party in 1931

INCOME		EXPENDITURE	
I Subscriptions		**I Subscriptions**	
a) Adoption Dues	100.00	Adoption Dues	104.50
b) Monthly Dues	337.90	Monthly Dues	343.55
c) Publicity Fees	45.90	Publicity Fees	–
d) Documentation Fees	–	Documentation Fees	–
e) SA Insurance Dues	132.30	SA Insurance Dues	170.40
f) Extraordinary Dues	–	Extraordinary Dues	–
II Donations		**II Administrative Expenses**	
a) Voluntary and from		a) Town Group	299.37
Collections	1620.68	b) District Leader	108.20
		c) SA Lieutenant & Colonel	61.40
III Propaganda		**III Propaganda**	
a) Sale of Admission	1203.65	a) Small Ads, Leaflets	1352.10
Tickets to Meetings		Speakers' Fees	
b) Donations to the	754.05	b) Travel, local SA	413.25
Fighting Fund, resp.			
Meetings			
		c) Travel, outside SA	88.00
		d) Rent for Rooms	196.30
		e) Donations to Gau	
		resp. Elections	200.00
IV General		**IV Extraordinary Expenses**	
	475.95	a) For local SA	771.96
		b) For Hitler Youth	22.20
		c) Cover for Damages	
		at Meeting 12.3.30	102.45
		V. General	298.50
Totals	**4670.43**		**4532.18**

Source B

Hitler tries to win support from industrialists, 1932

...our situation in the world...is but the result of our own underestimate of German strength. Only when we have once more changed this fatal valuation of ourselves can Germany take advantage of the political possibilities which, if we look far enough into the future, can place German life once more upon a natural and secure basis – and that means either new living space and the development of a great internal market or protection of German economic life against the world. The labour resources of our people, the capacities, we have them already: no one can deny that we are industrious. But we must first refashion the political pre-conditions: without that, industry...and economy are of no avail...

Baynes (ed.), *The Speeches of Adolf Hitler*, 1942

Source C

A modern historian's view

Hitler's contacts with leaders of business, industry and agriculture had meanwhile deepened without most of them being persuaded that what the solution needed was a Nazi dictatorship. In 1931 the links with Hugenberg had been renewed in the 'Harzburg Front', named after a meeting of nationalist organisations at Bad Harzburg in Lower Saxony...In January 1932 Hitler addressed the influential Düsseldorfer Industrielklub, winning some support but leaving many still unconvinced that he was their man.

Kershaw, *Hitler*, 1991

▶ The poster says 'The meaning of the Hitler saying 'Millions stand behind me''.

■ Examination-style questions

1 Comprehension in context
Study Source A. What can it tell us about the sources of Nazi funding in 1930?

2 Comparing the sources
How far and for what reasons do Sources C and D put forward different views about the extent of industrial support for the Nazis before 1933?

3 Assessing the sources
How could a historian make maximum use out of Source D as evidence about Germany in 1932?

4 Making judgements
Using all the sources and your own knowledge, explain how important you think industrial support was to Nazi success, 1930–1932.

Source D

A 1932 propaganda poster by John Heartfield, an anti-Nazi artist who had close links with the KPD

Conclusions

- The Wall Street Crash was a key factor in the fall of the Weimar Republic
- Democracy in Germany effectively ended in 1930 with the frequent use of Article 48
- The Nazi Party grew considerably in strength between 1930 and 1932 for a number of reasons. These included the economic crisis, fear of communism, the weakness of other radical parties and the tactics and strengths of the Nazi Party itself.
- Hitler did get into power 'through the back door', although success in elections made this possible
- There are a number of points at which the fall of Weimar became most likely. The decision is yours.

Chapter 8

The creation of a Nazi dictatorship

▲ The public reaction to Hitler becoming Chancellor, 30 January 1933.

Source 2

And what did Dr H. bring us? The news that his double, Hitler, is Chancellor of the Reich! And what a Cabinet!!! One we didn't dare dream of in July. Hitler, Hugenberg, Seldte, Papen!!! On each one of them depends part of Germany's hopes... It is so incredibly marvellous that that I am writing it down quickly before the first discordant note comes, for when has Germany ever experienced a blessed summer after a wonderful spring?... Huge torchlight procession in the presence of Hindenburg and Hitler by National Socialists and Stahlhelm... This is a memorable 30 January!

From the diary of Frau Solmitz, 30 January 1933

Source 3

Within two months we will have pushed Hitler so far into the corner that he'll squeak.

Papen, January 1933

Introduction

Hitler's appointment was greeted with an enthusiasm bordering on the hysterical in some quarters of Germany. What we must remember, however, is that at no point, even in the election of March 1933, when propaganda and intimidation reached new heights, did a majority of the German people vote for Adolf Hitler. Some of those who did not support him reassured themselves with the thought that the balance of power lay in the hands of non-Nazis, such as Papen and Hugenberg. Others expected that the Nazi spell in power would be short-lived. These included the communists who believed that a communist revolution would shortly follow. Such hopes help to explain the lack of open opposition to Nazi policies during 1933.

Hitler could hardly have been described as a dictator in January 1933. Papen's claim that 'We have hired him' demonstrated his belief that Hitler had been 'tamed' and could pose little threat. By the end of 1934, however, the Nazi dictatorship was in place. There were three main steps in this transformation:

Step One: January – March 1933. **Control at the centre**
Step Two: April – July 1933. **Control beyond the centre**
Step Three: January – August 1934. **The final stage**

Key questions

- How did the Nazis establish a dictatorship in Germany?
- Why did nobody stop them?
- What impact did this have on the people?

The Nazis in January 1933

Strengths and weaknesses

The Nazis were by far the largest party in the Reichstag in January 1933 and this was their main source of strength. For a nationalist coalition to work, Nazi support was vital. The Nazi Party also held the key positions in the Cabinet. Hitler was, of course, Chancellor whilst Frick was Interior Minister in the Reich and Goering was Interior Minister of Prussia. However, the party also had weaknesses. Despite their numbers in the Reichstag they did not possess an overall majority, even if they were supported by the nationalists. This could prevent Hitler from changing the Weimar Constitution as a two-thirds majority was required for this. In addition, whilst Nazis held the key posts in the Cabinet they still only numbered three out of twelve. Finally, Hitler or any other Nazi Cabinet member could be sacked by the President at any point. Their survival was by no means guaranteed at this stage.

Hitler's aims

Hitler had never made any secret of the fact that, once in power, he wished to destroy the democratic system. In a speech following the Nazis' electoral success of 1930, Hitler declared that 'parliament for us is not the goal, but the means to an end.' This desire to destroy democracy was shared by *all* his fellow Cabinet members and the first step in this direction had already been taken by his predecessors. With regard to his other aims, in his first major speech to the German people as Chancellor, he was careful to tone down both his anti-Semitism and aggressive foreign policy. He focused instead on more reassuring themes such as the importance of the family and the evils of communism.

Source 4

The national government sees as its first and foremost task the restoration of the unity of spirit and will of our people. It will preserve and protect the fundamentals on which the strength of our nation rests. It will preserve and protect Christianity, which is the basis of our system of morality, and the family, which is the germination cell of the body of the people and the state. It will disregard social rankings and classes in order to restore to our people its consciousness of national and political unity and the responsibilities that entails. It will use reverence for our great and glorious past and pride in our ancient traditions as a basis for the education of German youth. In this way it will declare a merciless war upon spiritual, political, and cultural nihilism (absence of belief). Germany shall not and will not sink into anarchistic communism …

The national government will undertake the great task of the reorganisation of the economy of our people through two great four-year plans: rescue of the German farmer to ensure the means of feeding the nation and thereby guaranteeing its existence; rescue of the German worker through a mighty and comprehensive attack on unemployment …

In its foreign policy, the national government regards its highest mission to be in the safeguarding of the right to life of our people and therefore to regain the freedom of our people. As it is determined to end the chaotic conditions of Germany, it will cooperate with other nations in order to establish a state of equal value and equal rights within the community of nations …

Reich President General Field Marshal Von Hindenburg has called on us to employ our courage in order to bring about this re-ascendancy of the nation …

Hitler's appeal to the German people 31 January 1933

The consolidation of power: Step One

The election campaign

Almost immediately, Hitler made it clear that he was not a sleeping partner within the Cabinet. Within days he succeeded in persuading Hindenburg to call for a new election and grant his government powers to suspend meetings and ban newspapers. Thus began a five-week election campaign that witnessed the death of 69 people, the destruction of the Communist Party and a barrage of propaganda and intimidation. Determined as he was to give the *appearance* of legality, Hitler refused to allow state funds to finance the Nazi campaign and instead looked to industrialists for support. This time it was forthcoming. Election posters were produced in bulk and Goebbels made particular use of the radio, ensuring that all Hitler's speeches were broadcast by all stations with his own commentary helping the listener to appreciate the enthusiasm of Hitler's audiences. The 'Goeb', it was suggested by some jokers, should be added to existing weights and measures, signifying the amount of power needed to turn off 100,000 radio sets at the same time.

Political opponents were given short shrift. In Prussia, Goering established control of the police (over half of Germany's entire force) by insisting they serve Nazi interests, sacking them if they did not, and bringing in an extra 50,000 men, mainly SA members. Goering was open about his control over the

■ Think about

▶ In what ways does Hitler seek to reassure the German people in Source 4?

▶ What kinds of people is Hitler trying to appeal to?

▶ Give some examples of how Hitler avoids laying down any specific policies.

▶ How does Hitler try to emphasize the legitimacy or right that he has to be in power?

▶ Give an example of the persuasiveness of Hitler's language.

▶ How useful is this source when examining Hitler's aims and tactics in 1933?

Timeline

Step One: Jan – Mar 1933

30 Jan Hitler becomes Chancellor

31 Jan Hitler's appeal to the German people broadcast over the radio

1 Feb Hitler persuades Hindenburg to dissolve the Reichstag

4 Feb Hitler's government acquires power to ban political meetings and newspapers

6 Feb Decree gives Goering almost full control over Prussia

20 Feb Hitler persuades industrialists to finance election campaign

27 Feb Reichstag Fire

28 Feb Decree for the Protection of People and State repeals civil liberties

3 Mar Thalmann, leader of KPD, and other members arrested

5 Mar Election – Nazis win 43.9% of the votes but still have no majority

8 Mar First concentration camps announced by Interior Minister Frick

13 Mar Goebbels joins Cabinet as Reich Minister of Public Enlightenment and Propaganda

21 Mar Day of Potsdam

23 Mar Enabling Act passed by the Reichstag

police: 'Every bullet that now leaves the mouth of a pistol is my bullet. If you call that murder, then I am the murderer, for I gave the order, and I stand by it.' Goering's forces were amongst those used to intimidate and terrorize Nazi opponents.

The Reichstag fire

On 27 February, a young Dutchman, Marinus van der Lubbe, was caught in the act of burning down the Reichstag. The Nazis immediately claimed that Lubbe was part of a communist conspiracy, although during the trial in Leipzig later that year, no evidence was found to substantiate this claim. Some historians have pointed to the very useful timing of the fire, days before the election, which enabled the Nazis to arrest many communists and undermine their election campaign (they lost 19 seats). General Franz Halder, who attended a birthday lunch for Hitler in 1942, claimed that Goering boasted during the meal 'The only one who really knows the Reichstag is I, for I set fire to it.' During the Nuremberg Trials in 1945–46, however, Goering flatly denied all knowledge of either the lunch or the conversation, claiming that it was complete nonsense, given that 'the Reichstag was known to every representative in the Reichstag.' We still do not know the full truth of the matter. In 1962 an investigation concluded that Lubbe acted alone but eighteen years later, in West Berlin, Lubbe was acquitted altogether! In the end, the question of who started the fire is of limited historical significance. What is significant, however, is the way in which the Nazis exploited it to their advantage. By the following morning, 4000 communists had been arrested and Hitler had alarmed Hindenburg into granting an emergency decree which suspended many civil rights. The Decree for the Protection of People and State gave the government the power to arrest individuals without trial, search private homes, censor post and telephone calls and continue to restrict freedom of assembly and expression. There was nothing *illegal* about the decree. It was enacted according to the Weimar Constitution, at a time when rule by decree was not regarded as unusual, by a President who had been in power for eight years.

Note

The Communist Party was never formally banned. A law was not necessary, given that so many communist deputies had been arrested and members of the KPD had been forced into underground opposition.

Source 5

▶ Marinus van der Lubbe during his trial for masterminding the Reichstag fire.

■ Think about

▶ Of what use is this photograph to a historian researching the Reichstag fire?

Document exercise: The Reichstag fire

Source A

The mystery of the Reichstag fire

Much has been written [about the Reichstag fire] and more will be before the full truth is known – if it ever is. Van der Lubbe was personally involved, but what his motives were, who prompted him, whether he acted alone, is still disputed. Contemporary opinion was in no doubt whatever. It was known that an underground passage connected Goering's office with the Reichstag itself. It was widely believed that the leader of the Berlin SA, Karl Ernst, had led a fire-party through this passage to assist van der Lubbe in his work. Within hours, the wags of Berlin had devised a riddle: 'Why did van der Lubbe take his shirt off?' 'Because' was the answer, 'it was a brown one'. It was also of interest that, at a later date, Karl Ernst and all those allegedly implicated in the fire were executed by Nazi firing-squads...

Adapted from *Knaves, Fools and Heroes,* 1974, the memoirs of Sir John Wheeler-Bennett, a British diplomat, who witnessed the fire himself

Source B

The reactions of the Nazi elite

It so happened that as I drove through the Brandenburg Gate on my way to visit my girlfriend I saw the flames burst through the dome of the Reichstag. Thus I had a ringside seat at a momentous event in European history... Memories of that evening are of the great bulk of Goering, swathed in a trench-coat, dashing into the burning Reichstag, where I already was, and of the bemused expression on the face of Papen, who arrived later and found that, even though he was premier of Prussia, his energetic Interior Minister had on his own responsibility taken measures which meant the end of all constitutional government in Germany....

Adapted from *Insanity Fair*, 1938, by Douglas Reed, a left-wing English journalist

> **Key term**
>
> **Constitutional government**
> Where the government runs the country according to the Constitution.

Source C

The view of the Prussian police

The voluntary confession of van der Lubbe prevented me from thinking that he needed any helpers. Why should not a single match be enough....But this specialist had used a whole knapsack full of inflammable material. He had been so active that he had laid several dozen fires...he had rushed through the big corridor to lay more fires under the old leather sofas. During this hectic activity he was overpowered by Reichstag officials....I reported on the results of the first interrogations of van der Lubbe – that in my opinion he was a maniac. But with this opinion I had come to the wrong man; Hitler ridiculed my childish view: 'That is something really cunning, prepared a long time ago. The criminals have thought all this out beautifully; but they've miscalculated, haven't they, Comrades!'

From an account by Rudolf Diels, head of the Prussian political police, written after the war

Source D

The view of a middle class member of the public

Goering, like an old greying servant, reported gravely the dreadful murder plans of the Communists...They started with the Reichstag. Fire broke out in twenty-eight places...They wanted to send armed gangs to murder and start fires in the villages...Poison, boiling water, all tools from the most refined to the most primitive, were to be used as weapons...If Italy, America and England were wise, they should send us money to fight Bolshevism our ruin will be their ruin!

From the diary of Frau Solmitz

■ Examination-style questions

1 Comprehension in context

Study Source A. Using this source and your own knowledge, explain why some people at the time believed that the Nazis were responsible for the Reichstag fire.

2 Comparing the sources

To what extent do Sources B and C support the view that the Nazis were responsible for the fire?

3 Assessing the sources

To what extent, and why, do Sources A, B, and C provide reliable evidence about the fire?

4 Making judgements

Using these sources and your own knowledge, assess how successfully the Nazis used the Reichstag fire to their own advantage. (*Note:* You may wish to read up to 'Step Two' before answering this question.)

The March election

The election results were surprising, given the circumstances. As you can see from the figures in the margin, the Nazis once more failed to achieve a majority and even with the support of the DNVP, they could not muster the two-thirds support in the Reichstag required to amend the Constitution. Nevertheless, Hitler claimed it as a great victory and a mandate to take forward the 'National Revolution', whilst grass-roots members celebrated by seizing local administrative posts and terrorizing any suspected opponent. Jewish department stores were looted and attacks were made on the Press of the opposition. Hitler, claiming that the local authorities were clearly incapable of maintaining order, promptly replaced legal governments with Reich Commissioners. Nevertheless, he was beginning to feel uneasy at the scale of disorder, mindful of the support he received from big industrialists and army leaders who frowned upon extra-legal, terrorist activity. On 10 March, Hitler appealed for the end to violence, stressing that 'the further progress of the national uprising will be guided and planned from the top'. In an attempt to reassure his more conservative supporters, an elaborate ceremony, known as the Day of Potsdam, was staged in the Potsdam Garrison Church to celebrate the opening of the new Reichstag. Hindenburg, the ex-Crown Prince and several old army generals were present and Hitler's speech stressed the great traditions of Germany for which, he claimed, he stood and represented. It was a propaganda triumph.

The Enabling Act

On 5 March, the Reichstag effectively voted itself out of existence by passing the Enabling Act. This Act gave the Cabinet the power to enact laws without the Reichstag's permission for four years. It effectively killed off the Weimar Constitution and gave Hitler the powers of a dictator. He was no longer dependent on presidential decree; he could enact any law he chose, for four years at least. The Enabling Act was, astonishingly, passed by the Reichstag by 444 votes to 94 – but why?

● **Communists and socialists**: 81 KPD and 26 socialist deputies were refused admission into the Reichstag. In the end, only the remaining SPD deputies voted against the Act.

● **Nazi deal with the Centre Party**: Hitler promised to respect the Catholic Church in return for the support of the Centre Party. They took Hitler at his word and gave him their backing.

Facts and figures

March 1933 Election Results

Party	% of vote	Seats
NSDAP	43.9	288
DNVP	8.0	52
DVP	1.1	2
Z	14.1	74
DDP	0.9	5
SPD	18.2	120
KPD	12.2	81

Quotation

No one can escape the emotion of the moment. Father too is deeply impressed. Mother has tears in her eyes …
[M] is completely unmoved … he considers the whole thing simply a put up job …
'You've got it coming to you', says the 21 year old. I remain silent, ashamed and torn.

Erich Ebermeyer, a dramatist, describes the Day of Potsdam and its impact on him and his family, who were generally unsympathetic to the Nazis

- **Intimidation by the SA**: The Kroll Opera House, where the vote took place, was surrounded by members of the SA and SS, who also lined the walls inside, issuing threats to the deputies.
- **Limiting provisions**: There were provisions in the Act which would limit it e.g. the clause stating that it would become invalid after four years. This encouraged some deputies to vote for the Act, although the limiting provisions were subsequently ignored.

Hitler had established control of the centre of politics. He was filling his Cabinet with Nazis and he could now effectively dispense with the Reichstag. Now Hitler turned to the rest of Germany.

The consolidation of power: Step Two

Why was society 'brought into line?'

Society in the Weimar Republic could be described as *plural*. A number of different interest groups were allowed to exist within the state – interest groups representing all areas of human activity, from jobs to religious beliefs to leisure pursuits. These groups, such as the Church, trade unions and political parties, were potentially quite powerful and could exert pressure on the government in a variety of ways. Think about the following groups and consider how they could have blocked government policies:

> trade unions; the Church; other political parties; the civil service; local government; courts and judges.

To take one of these examples, trade unions could, of course, organize a strike in order to achieve better wages or working conditions. Indeed, they nearly brought Berlin to a standstill during the Kapp Putsch of 1920. In a healthy democracy, these pressures are seen as vital in communicating the will of the people to the government, whose job it is to act in the best interests of the people it represents. Hitler, on the other hand, did not want to see his power limited in such a way. He was not interested in lines of communication from the people to government. His argument was always that he knew what was, in the long run, in the people's best interests and should therefore be allowed to have complete freedom to act in those interests. In reality he wanted to extend his dictatorship across the whole country by eliminating potentially troublesome interest groups and embarking on a process of 'Nazification'. The proper term for this policy was *Gleichschaltung* which literally meant 'bringing into line'.

This process had already started by April 1933, as state governments and police forces were essentially brought under Nazi control. But Hitler was intent on giving his 'National Revolution' an air of legality. All actions had to be defined in legal terms in the form of government acts. Hence the actions in the states were retrospectively legalized in laws issued at the end of March and the beginning of April. The German historian Bracher talks of a 'façade of legality' with reference to the events of 1933, which encouraged Hitler's conservative allies to support him.

How was the *Gleichschaltung* implemented?

- **Trade unions**: On 2 May 1933, members of the SA and the SS occupied union offices and effectively abolished all existing trade unions. A new organization, the German Labour Front (DAF), was set up by the Nazis and led by Robert Ley. Membership was compulsory. Employees lost the right to negotiate with employers over wages and working conditions.

Timeline

Step Two: April – July 1933

31 Mar and 7 Apr Laws for the co-ordination of the states with the Reich

7 Apr Law for the Restoration of the Professional Civil Service

2 May Trade unions dissolved

6 May DAF set up

5 July Centre Party dissolves itself

22 June SPD outlawed

8 July Concordat between Germany and Vatican

14 July Nazi Party the only official party allowed to exist in Germany

Note

Actions similar to *Gleichschaltung* had already been taken by the government before 1933. As you may have read in the margin box on p.136, Papen closed down the left-wing state government of Prussia in the summer of 1932. Its functions were simply absorbed into the national government, making the Nazis' task that much easier when they attempted to do the same throughout Germany after 1933.

- **Political parties**: The Communists were effectively banned after the Reichstag fire. By the time the Enabling Act was introduced, only the SPD were openly opposing Hitler and even they voted in support of Hitler's foreign policy statement in May in an attempt to survive. However, on 22 June 1933, the SPD was outlawed as a 'party hostile to the nation and state'. The other parties dissolved themselves. In July, a decree was passed officially making Germany a one-party state.

- **States**: Immediately after January 1933, Nazis began to infiltrate state governments, which were given the power to issue laws without consulting the Landtage (state parliaments). This was followed up with the appointment of powerful Nazi *Reichstatthalter* (Reich governors). In January 1934, the Landtage were abolished altogether and the state governments were made subordinate to the Reich government in Berlin.

- **Civil service**: Hitler was dependent on an efficient and well-established bureaucracy, and many civil servants retained their posts. Membership of the Nazi Party was not compulsory until 1939. However, a Law for the Restoration of the Professional Civil Service, issued in April 1933, enabled those whose political obedience or racial purity was in question to be dismissed. Most officials of Jewish descent lost their jobs. Twelve and a half per cent of the Prussian civil service was dismissed on political or racial grounds.

Were all groups 'brought into line'?

By the end of July 1933, most of the major interest groups in Germany had been brought under Nazi control. In addition to those outlined above, Nazi organizations absorbed teaching associations, 'intellectual workers', peasant groups and even employers, who became part of the Estate of German Industry. The Reichstag had, of course, already suffered in the first stage of consolidation, as had the press. Only two groups survived the onslaught: the Church and the army. In both cases, Hitler felt he had too much to lose by alienating their support. The German people felt strong loyalty to the Church and Hitler succeeded in neutralizing the role of the Catholic Church in politics by signing a Concordat with the Pope on 8 July. This agreement exchanged a promise from Hitler that the Church would be left to run its own affairs, including Catholic schools, for a promise from the Pope that the Church would not interfere in political matters. Not surprisingly, the Catholic Church was heavily criticized for this policy in subsequent years. In fact, as you will see in Chapter 10, neither the Protestant nor the Catholic Churches escaped *Gleichschaltung* entirely, but they were never completely dismantled.

The other group escaping co-ordination was the army. Hitler was too dependent on its support and mindful that it was the only body who could still force him out of power. He was also dependent on a well-trained and highly disciplined force to implement his ambitious foreign policy. In its turn, the army was grateful for a leader who valued them and wished to expand their size and their role, so this was a relationship based on mutual benefits. It was not until Germany began to lose the Second World War that the army began to turn against Hitler.

How powerful was Hitler by the end of 1933?

■ Activity

Copy and complete the chart below using information from this chapter. The first example has been done for you. Below the chart are other examples to put in the first column. You may be able to think of more.

Who could threaten Hitler's power?	How did the Nazis try to remove this threat?	Were the Nazis successful?
The Cabinet could outvote Hitler because out of 12 members only three were Nazis.	Nazis held the most important posts in the Cabinet and Hitler brought more Nazis in, e.g. Goebbels. Hitler was pursuing policies that the non-Nazi members agreed with, e.g. weakening the Reichstag.	Yes

- The **Reichstag** could refuse to pass laws
- The **Press** could stir up opposition in newspaper articles
- The other **political parties** could stir up opposition
- The **elite** could withdraw their support for Hitler if they disapproved of his methods
- The **state governments and parliaments** could block Nazi policy at a local level
- The **police** could refuse to carry out Nazi orders
- The **trade unions** could arrange strikes
- The **Church** could condemn Nazism from the pulpit
- The **army** could overthrow the Nazis by force

Quotation

Hitler had increased his power at an incredible speed. Even Goebbels was astounded, writing in his diary in April 1933 'The Führer's authority is now completely in the ascendant in the Cabinet. There will be no more voting. The Führer's personality decides. All this has been achieved much more quickly than we had dared to hope . . .'

■ Activity

Using your completed chart, discuss the following questions:

1 What possible threats to Hitler's power had not been removed by the end of 1933? Why?

2 Were all these groups forced to accept Hitler or were some acting out of self interest?

3 How complete was Hitler's power by the end of 1933?

Document Exercise: A legal revolution?

There are two issues here. Firstly, was the Nazi revolution a legal one, and secondly, was it a revolution at all? The document exercise below will focus on the first of these two questions, but you may wish to reflect on the second question yourself. Think about what we mean by revolution. Generally, we use it to describe a period of complete change, usually at a political level. Did everything change in Germany during the Nazi consolidation of power? What changed and what stayed the same?

Source A

The Enabling Act

In addition to the procedure for the passage of legislation outlined in the Constitution, the Reich Cabinet is also authorised to enact laws ... The national laws enacted by the Reich Cabinet may deviate from the Constitution provided they do not affect the position of the Reichstag and the Reichsrat ... This law comes into affect on the day of its publication. It ceases to be valid on 1 April 1937.

Source B

A historian on the legality of the Nazi dictatorship

Rule by decree, which reached its highest point on 28 February, and the conquest of the states were followed by the permanent suspension of the division of powers by virtues of the Enabling Act, which ended the Presidential dictatorship and marked the beginning of the one-man dictatorship. Contrary to the illusions and apologies of professors of public law then and now, the one-man dictatorship had as little legal validity as the rule by decree.

Bracher, The German Dictatorship, 1969

Source C

SA and SS violence in the state of Brunswick

From March 1933 the atmosphere in the town and the countryside became unbearable. One brawl after another. There were growing rumours that the *Volksfreund* – the [SPD] Party, trade union and publishing house building of the workers – was to be raided by National Socialists … There, lorries with SA and SS had driven up at 4.05pm. The porter promptly closed the doors. But the Nazis broke the big display windows and pushed into the building through the holes. They opened fire inside the building with a number of rifles and revolvers. During this, the 28-year-old salesman, Hans Saile, the advertising manager of the Advertising Union, Berlin, was killed by a shot in the stomach. He had received an order from his superiors to leave the threatened district of Brunswick and to travel to Saarbrucken on the same day.

From an account published by the SPD in exile

Source D

Hitler's response to the violence

During these days Hitler indignantly and brusquely rejected complaints voiced by his nationalist partners about the uncertainty over the law of the land and the mounting SA terror…When Papen, too, spoke about SA infringements against foreign citizens during a telephone conversation on 19 March, Hitler reacted the next day with a withering reply to the Vice-Chancellor. He had the impression, Hitler argued in his written response, 'that at the moment there is a systematic barrage aimed at stopping the National Socialist uprising'. Then he enlarged on the fact that the 'regrettable' infringements bore no comparison to the 'high treason' of the November criminals and the suppression of the NSDAP in the Weimar period.

Broszat, The Hitler State, 1981

■ Examination-style questions

1 Comprehension in context

Study Sources A and B. Using these sources and your own knowledge, explain why Bracher claims that the Enabling Act had 'little legal validity'.

2 Comparing the sources

Describe how Sources C and D differ in the views they advance about of the legality of Nazi actions and explain their differences.

3 Assessing the sources

How useful is Source A to an historian studying the Nazi consolidation of power in 1933?

4 Making judgements

Using these sources and your own knowledge, explain whether or not, in your opinion, the Nazi 'revolution' was legal.

Spotlight

The impact of the Nazi take-over on the German people

The diaries of Viktor Klemperer 1933–1941

Viktor Klemperer was a German Jew living in Dresden during the Nazi years. He was professor of Romance languages at Dresden Technical University until he was dismissed in 1935 as a result of Nazi laws. Most Jews living in Dresden had either emigrated during the 1930s or else been deported to camps in 1941. Klemperer survived deportation because he was married to a non-Jew. Even so, he only escaped deportation in 1945 thanks to the British bombing of Dresden, in the confusion of which Klemperer was able to escape to Bavaria where American troops had arrived. Klemperer kept a diary all his life. His intention was not to record events which were recorded in the Press, but instead to focus on what touched him personally. He planned to use this diary to write his memoirs, although only his memoirs from 1881–1918 were ever published. The following extracts focus on the very first months of Nazi rule and illustrate how rapidly the life of this particular German was turned upside down.

▲ Viktor Klemperer and his wife Eva in 1940.

Source 6

10 March Friday evening

30 January: Hitler Chancellor. What, up to election Sunday on 5 March, I called terror, was a mild prelude. Now the business of 1918 is being exactly repeated, only under a different sign, under the swastika. Again it's astounding how easily everything collapses…eight days before the election the clumsy business of the Reichstag fire – I cannot imagine that anyone really believes in communist perpetrators instead of paid Nazi work. Then the wild prohibitions and acts of violence. And on top of that the never-ending propaganda in the street, on the radio etc…No one dares say anything any more, everyone is afraid…How long will I keep my post?

17 March Friday morning

The defeat in 1918 did not depress me as greatly as the present state of affairs. It is shocking how day after day naked acts of violence, breaches of the law, barbaric opinions appear quite undisguised as official decree. The socialist papers are permanently banned. The 'liberals' tremble…And no one stirs; everyone trembles, keeps out of sight.

20 March Monday evening about midnight

At the cinema after a long gap: Hindenburg in front of troops and SA men on Sunday the 12th, the day of the war dead. When I saw him filmed a year ago, the President, his hand on the wrist of his escort, walked somewhat stiffly, but quite firmly…an old but vigorous man. Today: the tiny, laborious steps of a cripple. Now I understand it all…I am now completely certain that Hindenburg is no more than a puppet, that his hand was already being guided on 30 January.

Every new government decree, announcement etc. is more shameful than the previous one…In Breslau Jewish lawyers forbidden to appear in court.

27 March evening

The government is in hot water. 'Atrocity propaganda' from abroad because of the Jewish campaign. It is constantly issuing official denials… But then it openly threatens to proceed against the German Jews if the mischief-making by 'World Jewry' does not stop. Meanwhile there is no bloodshed in the country, but oppression, oppression, oppression. No one breathes freely any more, no free word, neither printed or spoken.

30 March Thursday
During the day the National Socialists' boycott call has been announced. We are hostages...I feel more shame than fear, shame for Germany. I have always felt a German...In a toyshop a children's ball with the swastika.

31 March Friday evening
Ever more hopeless. The boycott begins tomorrow. Yellow placards, men on guard. Pressure to pay Christian employees two months salary, to dismiss Jewish ones.

3 April Monday evening
On Saturday red posters on the shops: 'Recognised German-Christian enterprise'. In between them closed shops, SA men in front of them with triangular boards: 'Whoever buys from the Jew, supports the foreign boycott and destroys the German economy.'

7 April Friday morning
The pressure I am under is greater than in the war, and for the first time in my life I feel political hatred for a group (as I did not during the war), a deadly hatred...No one dares write a letter, no one dares make a telephone call, we visit one another and weigh up our chances.

10 April Monday
The awful feeling of 'Thank God, I'm alive.' The new Civil Service 'law' leaves me, as a front-line veteran, in my post – at least for the time being... Annemarie Kohler was here yesterday

evening. Filled with the greatest bitterness. She tells us how fanatical the male and female nurses in her hospital are. They sit around the loudspeaker. When the Horst Wessel Song is sung (every evening and at other times too), they stand up and raise their arms in the Nazi greeting...

19 June Monday
(after lecture to three people)
On Saturday I read out my 'Afterword'. Shock. How could I keep something like that in the house. Kohler advised: hide it behind a picture – But what shall I do with my diaries? I wait from one day to the next. Nothing stirs. Sometimes I lose all heart and believe that this regime will last after all and outlive me.

1 July Saturday
At the Blumenfelds yesterday evening. Emigrant mentality. Jule Sebba and his family go to Palestine in August.

28 July Friday morning
... the 'Hitler greeting' made obligatory. Obligatory only within 'the place of service'...in offices I saw employees constantly raising their arms to one another.

19 August Saturday
I simply cannot believe that the mood of the masses is really still behind Hitler. Too many signs of the opposite. But everyone literally cringes with fear...Everyone fears the next person may be an informer.

Extracts from Klemperer, *I Shall Bear Witness, The Diaries of Viktor Klemperer 1933-1941*, 1999

Note

The Nazis organized a boycott of Jewish shops and professions on 1 April.

■ Activity

1 What can we learn from these extracts about the impact of Nazism on the lives of the German people?

2 What do the extracts suggest about people's response to the Nazis?

3 How valuable is this diary in finding out about the Nazis' first few months in power?

Note

The 'Law for the Restoration of the Professional Civil Service' in April 1933 excluded officials of 'non-Aryan descent'. Its main purpose was to remove all Jews from the Civil Service. Klemperer was able to keep his job for now, however, because he had fought in the First World War and was therefore given special status.

The consolidation of power: Step Three

By the end of 1933 Hitler's power was extensive but not total. His power was potentially at risk from three sources: the President, the army and his SA (Stormtroopers). Hindenburg could still, in theory, dismiss Hitler and the other Nazis in the Cabinet, the army could use its strength to force Hitler from office and the SA could endanger Hitler's relations with the army by carrying out further acts of hooliganism and demanding more power for themselves. By the end of 1934, all three problems had been largely solved.

The SA and the 'second revolution'

When Hitler became Chancellor in January 1933, the SA, which represented the more working-class element of the Nazi Party, felt that their efforts on the streets had been vindicated. Now Germany would undergo the political *and social* revolution that she so badly needed and members of the SA would be rewarded with positions of authority and a status equivalent to that of the German army. Ernst Röhm, the leader of the SA and long time friend of Hitler, was vehement in his expression of such beliefs. He was determined not to allow the SA to become simply a propaganda tool which took part in 'shining torchlight processions and impressive parades.' Instead, he wanted the SA to merge with the army, with him in overall control, so that the German revolution could be taken forward. He felt badly let down when it became clear that in fact, Hitler had no intention of carrying through a 'second revolution' once his political power had been established, nor was he prepared to reward the SA with a higher status. In fact, the SA was becoming something of an embarrassment to Hitler were, its tactics of street brawls and hooliganism; at odds with Hitler's efforts to appease the German elite and portray his actions as legal. Relations between Röhm and Hitler reached a low point in early 1934, when Röhm declared privately to a friend:

Source 7

Adolf is a swine. He will give us all away. He only associates with the reactionaries now...Getting matey with the East Prussian generals. They're his cronies now...Adolf knows exactly what I want. I've told him often enough. Not a second edition of the old imperial army. Are we revolutionaries or aren't we?...If we are, then something new must arise out of our elan, like the mass armies of the French Revolution. If we're not then we'll go to the dogs. We've got to produce something new, don't you see that? Don't you understand that what's coming must be new, fresh and unused? The basis must be revolutionary. You can't inflate it afterwards. You only get the opportunity once to make something new and big that'll help us lift the world off its hinges. But Hitler puts me off with fair words.

Meanwhile, the army was making clear its opposition to the behaviour of the SA. In February, for example, General von Blomberg alerted Hitler to the growing military activities of the SA in areas that the Treaty of Versailles had demilitarized. Hitler had to make a choice. Either he attempted to win the full backing and trust of the army by effectively removing power from the SA or he risked alienating the army by remaining loyal to the SA. In the end, Hitler chose the army.

Timeline

Step Three: Jan – Aug 1934
January Landtage (state parliaments) abolished
30 June Night of the Long Knives
2 August Death of President Hindenburg. Army swears an oath of allegiance to Hitler.
19 August Hitler proclaims himself both Chancellor and President and adopts the title 'führer' of Germany.

■ Think about

▶ What exactly is Rohm saying in Source 7?

▶ How do you think Hitler would have reacted to this?

The Night of the Long Knives

On the night of 30 June, Röhm and other leaders of the SA were shot by members of the SS. It was clear that the army lent a helping hand by providing transport and weapons, although it was probably unaware that it was supporting what became a bloodbath. Hitler seized the opportunity to remove any old enemies and men such as Strasser and Schleicher were amongst the 400 murdered that night. Afterwards, Hitler claimed that he had responded to a treason plot and was thanked by the Cabinet for his 'determined and courageous action'. Both Blomberg, in the name of the army, and President Hindenburg thanked Hitler publicly for his actions. Thus, Hitler had succeeded in gaining the approval and support of the army which was to be so crucial if he was to achieve his ambitious aims abroad. The SA ceased to be a serious military presence and became what Röhm had feared – a propaganda showpiece which could be displayed at events like the giant Nuremberg rallies. The SA was also wheeled in to carry out acts of vandalism and thuggery against oppressed minorities, in particular the Jews in 1938. But their role as the prime para-military wing of the party was eclipsed by the SS, originally conceived as Hitler's personal bodyguards in 1925. Their role in the Nazi state is considered in more detail in the next chapter.

Cross reference

For more information on the SS, see page 180.

Note

Both Strasser and Schleicher had betrayed Hitler in 1932. In an attempt to split the Nazis, Schleicher persuaded Strasser to offer the government the support of the left wing of the Nazi Party which Strasser represented. It was only with Hitler's direct intervention that Strasser abandoned the plan. Hitler forgave neither of them for such treachery.

Source 8

▷ A British cartoon about the Night of the Long Knives, published on 3 July 1934.

THEY SALUTE WITH BOTH HANDS NOW.

■ Think about

▷ Study Source 8 carefully. Using the information on these two pages to help you, identify:

- The figures standing behind Hitler
- The victims whose feet appear at the bottom of the cartoon
- The men with both arms raised
- The line of men in the top right hand corner

▷ What is meant by 'unkept promises'? Was this a justified accusation?

▷ What is the meaning of the phrase 'They salute with both hands now'

▷ How accurate is this cartoon as a portrayal of the Night of the Long Knives?

Document exercise: The Night of the Long Knives

Source A
Hitler outlines his plans for the army

...a militia as Röhm suggested would not be the least bit suitable for national defence. He sought to establish this by examples from military history. In the course of this he came to his own experience. The hastily and superficially trained division to which he belonged in 1914 as a private, had come to grief at Langemarck with the most heavy losses. Therefore he was resolved to raise a people's army, built up on the *Reichswehr* [army], rigorously trained and equipped with the most modern weapons.....This new army would have to be ready for any defence purposes after five years, and after eight years suitable also for attacking. The SA must confine itself to internal tasks...

An account of Hitler's speech to SA leaders and army generals in February 1934

Source B
Notes concerning the murder of General von Schleicher

...I had a long conversation with Attorney-General Tetzlaff about the motive for the murder....As far as we were concerned, there were only two possibilities. First, that General von Schleicher was murdered by Röhm's henchmen...Or on the other hand, that the same bunch that had taken steps against Röhm...had then also taken the opportunity to eliminate Schleicher. Attorney-General Tetzlaff then expressly cautioned me at the end of our conversation that I should not mention this second possible motive...even though we were both fairly confident that the perpetrators could only have come from the ranks of the SS...The official press release from party headquarters had said that Schleicher committed suicide, but this was changed during the course of the afternoon to read that Schleicher had been shot in self-defence...

A reconstruction of events made by an investigating officer in 1952

Source C
Evidence of Schleicher's cook about the events of 30 June 1934

Today during the noon hour, possibly around 12.30, I was looking through the window toward the street, where I spotted two gentlemen. I asked what they wanted, to which they replied that they 'had to see General von Schleicher'...The gentlemen kept insisting more and more...I replied that 'I would go and see!' I then made my way into the general's study, while being followed by the strangers. Once we had arrived at the study, the strangers stood close behind me and asked Herr von Schleicher...if he were General von Schleicher. The general said yes and turned his body in order to see the men who had asked the question. At that very moment shots rang out. I do not know what happened then, because I was terrified; I screamed and ran out of the room...When I afterward again went back to the room I found Frau von Schleicher and the general, both shot and lying on the floor...

Statement given by Schleicher's cook, a witness

Source D
Hitler justifies his actions to the Reichstag

Without informing me...Chief of Staff Röhm entered into relations with General Schleicher through an utterly corrupt and dishonest go-between... It was General Schleicher who spelt out the secret aims of Chief of Staff Röhm...

The present regime in Germany is not to be tolerated.

Above all, the army and all national associations must be united in a single band. The only man to be considered for such a position is Chief of Staff Röhm

Extract from Hitler's speech to the Reichstag in July 1934

Examination-style questions

1 Comprehension in context

Study Source A. Using the source and your own knowledge, explain why Hitler wanted the SA to confine itself to 'internal tasks'.

2 Comparing the sources

How far, and for what reasons, do Sources B and C differ in their account of Schleicher's death?

3 Assessing the sources

'Source D provides an inaccurate version of events and is, therefore, of little value to the historian.' How far do you agree?

4 Making judgements

Using the sources and your own knowledge, to what extent do you agree that the Night of the Long Knives was necessary for Hitler's survival as dictator of Germany?

Hitler becomes Führer

President Hindenburg died on 2 August. Hitler combined the post of President with that of Chancellor, naming himself 'Führer' (leader) of Germany. This automatically made Hitler the Supreme Commander of the German army. Not only did the army accept this action, but its members also swore an oath of loyalty to their Führer on 2 August. Such an oath was not taken lightly; the soldiers meant what they were saying and believed that it was their duty to uphold it. So Hitler had succeeded in getting the army absolutely on his side. Thus, by 1934, his power was seemingly complete, with all potential challenges to his authority removed. But it is one thing to establish oneself as a dictator and quite another to sustain that role in the long term. The strategies adopted by Hitler and the Nazis are outlined in the next chapter.

Conclusions

By the end of 1934 Hitler and the Nazi Party had succeeded in establishing a powerful dictatorship in Germany. This was achieved through three steps:

- Step One: January – March 1933: control at the centre.
  During this period, Hitler gained the power to bypass the Reichstag and enact laws on the authority of his Cabinet. Civil liberties were suspended to enable him to arrest and imprison political opponents

- Step Two: April – July 1933: control beyond the centre.
  During this period, Hitler attempted to bring any potential enemies under control. Organized opposition was now almost impossible

- Step Three: January – August 1934: the final stage.
  During this period, Hitler brought the SA firmly under his control and won the support of the army. He became the Führer of Germany after Hindenburg's death.

Although opposition to Hitler was never entirely removed, he was now in a strong enough position to begin the transformation of society he wanted and to pursue the foreign policy that lay at the heart of his ambitions.

Quotation

I swear by God this sacred oath: that I will render unconditional obedience to the Führer of the German Reich and people, Adolf Hitler, the Supreme Commander of the Armed Forces, and will be ready as a brave soldier to risk my life at any time for this oath.

Oath taken by the army in 1934

■ Activity   KEY SKILLS

Prepare for a whole-class discussion on the following question: 'How powerful was Hitler by August 1934?' Make notes using this chapter and any other source of information to prepare yourself fully. During the discussion, remember to listen and respond to others' ideas as well as to make your own contributions.

Chapter 9

The Nazi state

▲ Hitler (asleep) and Eva Braun in his mountain retreat, the Berghof in Obersalzberg, before the war.

Source 3

When, I would often ask myself, did he really work? In the eyes of the people Hitler was the Leader who watched over the nation day and night. This was hardly so.

Albert Speer, Hitler's architect and later his Armaments Minister, describes Hitler's attitude to work. From Speer, *Inside the Third Reich*, 1970

Source 2

He knows nothing other than the work that he does as the truest servant of the Reich.

Goebbels describing Hitler in 1935

Think about

▶ How widely do you think Source 1 was distributed during the Third Reich?

Further reading

The classic texts on the Nazi state include:
Bracher, *The German Dictatorship*, 1973
Broszat, *The Hitler State,* 1981
See also Kershaw, *Hitler,* 1991

Introduction

People often assume that the government of the Third Reich was efficient and well organized. The mere sight of a Nuremberg rally on film or photograph creates the impression of order. Of course, this was part of the purpose of such rallies. The Nazis were extremely good at creating false impressions and this was certainly one of them. The reality was, however, very different. The government of Nazi Germany was in fact chaotic and unsystematic. This contrast between propaganda and reality is demonstrated in the sources opposite. Whilst Goebbels was busy creating a public image of Hitler as a hardworking, dedicated 'servant of the Reich', the Führer was in fact spending much of his time sleeping, eating, watching films and ranting endlessly to his circle of admirers.

Key questions

● Why was there chaos in the Nazi state?
● How did the Nazi state manage to function in these circumstances?
● Could this state of chaos help to explain the increasingly barbaric policies of the Nazis, culminating in the murder of 6 million Jews?
● How effectively did the Nazis use propaganda to create a positive image of Hitler and the Nazi state?
● To what extent did the Nazis rely on the use of terror and fear to subdue the German people?

How did the Nazis govern Germany?

Working towards the Führer

If we are to understand the way in which Hitler and the Nazis governed Germany, we must first understand the nature of Hitler's own power. Hitler's power came to be regarded as something above and beyond that of a normal head of state. No matter who you were within the party or the state, you were answerable to Hitler. He was seen to be above party politics and beyond the law. He exercised what we might term a *charismatic leadership* where the source of power does not lie in the law but rather in a single individual.

Think about

▶ What do we mean by the terms 'party' and 'state'?

▶ What is the difference? (This is discussed more fully on pages 172–173.)

Think about

▶ Where, according to Huber, does Hitler's power come from?

▶ How did Huber believe 'Führer power' was different from 'State power'?

Source 4

The office of Führer has developed out of the National Socialist movement. In its origins it is not a State office. This fact must never be forgotten if one wishes to understand the current political and legal position of the Führer... The position of the Führer combines in itself all sovereign power of the Reich; all public power in the State as in the movement is derived from the Führer power....we must not speak of 'State power' but of 'Führer power'...Führer power is comprehensive and total...it embraces all spheres of national life...Führer power is not restricted by safeguards and controls, by autonomous [independent] protected spheres, and by vested individual rigours, but rather it is free and independent, exclusive and unlimited.

Ernst Huber, a leading constitutional theorist of the Third Reich

In his government, Hitler tended to appoint several people to practically the same job. This created chaos in the Nazi state. The only guaranteed way of achieving power and influence was to gain the ear of Hitler and find a way of pleasing him. This was most likely to happen if you were able to present Hitler with a policy which could help to achieve one of his overall aims, especially territorial expansion and the creation of a pure master race. The result was a rather ungainly struggle between ambitious Nazis to gain the approval of their Führer. This struggle has been termed 'working towards the Führer'.

The danger of this struggle between ambitious Nazis was that Hitler's fantasies were taken seriously and policies drawn up to make them a reality. This is the context in which policies of mass extermination were conceived. All it took was a speech by Hitler, which outlined his grand visions, and a group of ambitious Nazis and civil servants who then tried to please Hitler by turning those visions into policies. The most successful Nazi saw his policy put into practice and then enjoyed the power and influence of having pleased the Führer by furthering his most extreme goals. An example of this was the euthanasia programme which began in 1939 and led to the deaths of thousands of Germans, including the mentally and physically handicapped. Hitler had made no secret of his desire for a master race but, as ever, he left the specific policy for others to work out. In fact, the euthanasia programme was partly the result of a letter written by the father of a deformed child, requesting that he be allowed to kill his son and end his misery. Philip Bouhler, an ambitious Nazi, had a senior post in Hitler's personal office and could select which letters to show the Führer. He showed this letter to Hitler and was subsequently given control of the euthanasia project, thereby earning greater power and prestige. That this increased status was at the cost of thousands of lives was all too typical in the period after 1938.

The Hitler myth

A 'Hitler myth' was cultivated which built on people's desire for strong leadership and presented Hitler as an almost God-like figure. Goebbels later claimed that this had been one of his biggest propaganda achievements. Hitler's image was laboured over in a manner not dissimilar to that of pop stars today. What he wore, what he said, what postures he adopted during speeches: all were worked out carefully. Any hint of human failing was covered up and photographs of Hitler wearing glasses were censored. People bought postcards of Hitler and carried them around in their purses. One book, entitled *The Hitler No One Knows* and written in 1932, contained 100 photographs of the Führer and by 1940, had sold 420,000 copies. Later editions, after the Night of the Long Knives, were edited to remove pictures of Hitler and Röhm posing as good friends.

Many people began to separate Hitler from the Nazi Party, enabling Hitler's popularity to remain high whilst the popularity of the Nazi Party fell. This was particularly the case during the Second World War. By 1936, according to the historian Ian Kershaw, the Hitler cult was fully formed.

But this cult or myth was not entirely divorced from reality. It did depend to some extent on successful policies: a sense that life was improving during 1933 was important in the early development of the myth after Hitler's appointment as Chancellor. The Hitler myth was crucial to the success of the regime. Many of those who did not vote for Hitler in March 1933 were later won over.

But crucially, Hitler began to believe in the myth himself after 1936 and this marks the point at which he seriously began to confuse fantasy and reality, mainly in the realm of his foreign ambitions. In the words of Kershaw, 'Hitler himself was a convert to the 'Führer myth', himself a 'victim' of Nazi propaganda.'

Note

The term 'Working towards the Führer' was first used by a Nazi in 1934. The historian Ian Kershaw has made particular use of it more recently.

Cross reference

See page 202 for more information on the euthanasia programme.

▲ A souvenir postcard of Hitler.

Note

There were reports in 1934 of people taking away bits of Hitler's garden fence at his house on the Obersalzberg as mementoes of the Führer.

Document exercise: The Hitler myth

Quotation

I go the way that Providence dictates, with the assurance of a sleepwalker.

Hitler, in a speech
made in March 1936

Source A
Celebrations of Hitler's birthday, April 1933

In a unison of hearts scarcely imaginable a few weeks ago, the people declared its allegiance to Adolf Hitler as Leader of the new Germany… In short: the enthusiastic participation on the personal day of honour of the Chancellor has provided the proof that Adolf Hitler is recognized as Führer in the consciousness of the entire people, and that the heart of Germany belongs to him.

From the middle-class newspaper, *Muncher Neueste Nachrichten*

Source B
Reaction to the reintroduction of military service, 1935

Enthusiasm on 17 March enormous. The whole of Munich was on its feet. People can be forced to sing, but they can't be forced to sing with such enthusiasm. I experienced the days of 1914 and can only say that the declaration of war did not make the same impact on me as the reception of Hitler on 17 March…Trust in Hitler's political talent and honest intentions is getting ever greater, just as generally Hitler has again won extraordinary popularity. He is loved by many…

From a SOPADE (SPD in exile) report

Source C
Goebbels claims the credit

Towards the end of 1941, at the height of Nazi power and domination in Europe, Goebbels claimed the creation of the 'Führer myth' as his greatest propaganda achievement.

Kershaw, *The Hitler Myth*, 1989

Source D
Alan Bullock on the Hitler Myth

…the baffling problem about this strange figure is to determine the degree to which he was swept along by a genuine belief in his own inspiration and the degree to which he deliberately exploited the irrational side of human nature, both in himself and others, with a shrewd calculation. For it is salutary to recall, before accepting the Hitler myth at anything like its face value, that it was Hitler who invented the myth….it was when he began to believe in his own magic, and accept the myth of himself as true, that his flair faltered.

Bullock, *Hitler A Study in Tyranny*, 1952

■ **Examination-style
   questions**

1 Comprehension in context
Study Source B. Using this source and your own knowledge, explain how, and for what reasons, people reacted to the reintroduction of military service.

2 Comparing the sources
Study Sources C and D. How do they differ in their assessment of how the myth developed?

3 Assessing the sources
Study Sources A and B. Which source do you think is more reliable about popular reactions to Hitler?

4 Making judgements
Using these sources and your own knowledge, explain why the Hitler myth was so important to the Nazi regime.

Hitler's personal life

Introduction

As we have seen, Hitler was the ultimate source of authority in the Reich. However, there were two problems. Firstly, the job of governing a population of 70 million could hardly be carried out by one man. And secondly, Hitler made things worse by his intense dislike for routine work, as this spotlight demonstrates.

Source 5

◄ Hitler relaxing with his dog.

Source 6

Fritz Wiedemann, one of Hitler's adjutants, wrote his memoirs after the war. At one point he writes:

In 1935 Hitler kept to a reasonably ordered daily routine… Gradually, this fairly orderly work routine broke down. Later Hitler normally appeared shortly before lunch, quickly read through Reich Press Chief Dietrich's press cuttings, and then went into lunch. So it became more and more difficult to get him to make decisions which he alone could make as Head of State…He disliked the study of documents. I sometimes secured decisions from him, even ones about important matters, without his ever asking to see the relevant files. He took the view that many things sorted themselves out on their own if one did not interfere…

The Berghof

Hitler spent more and more time at his mountain retreat in Obersalzberg in the Alps, known as the Berghof. A typical day's schedule, according to Albert Speer, consisted of:

11am – Hitler got up and went through reports brought by Bormann

Lunch —three courses of simple food, served to around 20 guests

Walk to the teahouse – where Hitler and his guests would consume cakes and hot drinks for 2 hours or so

Supper

After supper – Hitler and his guests would move into the salon to watch one or two films (during the war, they listened to music instead, 'out of sympathy for the privations of the soldiers')

Adapted from Speer, *Inside the Third Reich*, 1970

Source 7

Albert Speer, Hitler's favoured architect and, from 1942, his Armaments Minister, spent 20 years in Spandau prison after pleading guilty at the Nuremberg Trial. His autobiography *Inside the Third Reich* published in 1970, from which this extract is taken, is considered a classic of its kind, providing a unique insight into the workings of the Nazi government:

I myself threw all my strength into my work and was baffled at first by the way Hitler squandered his working time…When, I would ask myself, did he really work? Little was left of the day; he rose late in the morning and conducted one or two official conferences; but from the subsequent dinner on he more or less wasted time until the early hours of the evening…The adjutants often asked me: 'Please don't show any plans today.' Then the drawings I had brought with me would be left by the telephone switchboard at the entrance, and I would reply evasively to Hitler's inquiries. Sometimes he saw through this game and would go to look in the anteroom or the cloakroom for my roll of plans.

Eva Braun

Born in 1912, Braun was Hitler's mistress from 1932 although he went to great lengths to conceal this. She moved into the Berghof where she was often at Hitler's side unless Hitler wished to exclude her from important company – such as Goering – when she had to wait in her rooms. Hitler met her when she was working as an assistant to his favourite photographer, Heinrich Hoffman. She was, according to Hitler's chauffeur, 'the unhappiest woman in Germany'. In April 1945, Hitler married her in his bunker in Berlin as the Allies approached. The following day both Eva and Hitler committed suicide.

Hitler's Private Life

Hitler was a vegetarian and teetotaller

- He ate simple meals and forbade his cook to give him expensive food
- He was a chronic insomniac and as a result was never an early riser
- He appears to have been a hypochondriac, convinced on several occasions that his death was imminent
- He had a number of affairs with women and rumours about his sexual habits were circulated but not confirmed, often put about by his enemies
- He was in love with his niece, Geli Raubal, who committed suicide in 1931 after an argument with Hitler. There were rumours about the circumstances of her death, but no proof, and certainly Hitler appeared devastated by her death, weeping publicly at her graveside

Source 8

▲ Eva Braun.

■ Activity

Every year, Goebbels made a radio broadcast in honour of Hitler's birthday. Study the following extracts from his 1935 speech:

'There is probably no one left on the planet who does not know him as a statesman and as a remarkable popular leader. Only a few…have the pleasure of seeing him as a man each day from close up…One cannot imagine him putting on a front…His daily meals are the simplest, most modest, imaginable…he avoids medals and decorations…His industry and determination in reaching his goal far exceed normal human strength…His Cabinet approves no law that he has not studied…He has sacrificed his personal happiness and private life. He knows nothing other than the work that he does as the truest servant of the Reich.'

1 Which of Goebbels' claims appear from the evidence here to have been true?

2 Why do you think other leading Nazis tolerated Hitler's behaviour?

How chaotic was Nazi government?

Central government

In January 1933 this was the system of government that Hitler inherited:

- Federal government. Individual states could decide their own policies in areas such as education, leaving the central government in Berlin to deal with issues such as the economy and foreign policy.
- Collective government. This meant that policies were discussed amongst Cabinet members and a vote taken to decide on a policy.
- Laws were passed by the Reichstag or sanctioned by the President in times of emergency.

Hitler wasted no time in transforming this system. The power of individual states was removed, collective government ended (the Cabinet rarely met) and laws could be issued on the authority of the Cabinet alone, which in practice meant Hitler himself. Not everything changed, however. Much of the old bureaucracy (civil servants – people who actually put laws into practice) remained the same, largely out of necessity because there were not enough talented Nazis to take their place.

Why was there chaos in government?

■ Activity

In the table below is a list of some of the reasons why Nazi government was chaotic. Copy out the table, summarizing the content in the first column, and in the second column, explain what the consequences of each 'problem' might have been:

Problem	Possible consequences
Cabinet meetings became more infrequent. It met 72 times in 1933, 19 times in 1934, 12 times in 1935 and 4 times in 1936. After 1938 it didn't meet at all.	
Hitler's style of government was to give power to those he trusted and who presented him with good ideas. One consequence was the creation of Supreme Reich Authorities – specialist agencies whose functions often overlapped with existing ministries (see diagram opposite).	
Hitler was the single source of authority for everyone, no matter if you worked in a ministry or an agency. He was therefore in the best position to co-ordinate policy. But he was not interested in the day-to-day affairs of government and neither did he show much interest in directing the specifics of domestic policy.	

Without a Cabinet, there was nowhere for ministers to discuss their policies and keep each other informed. This led to a lack of co-ordination. A lot of time and energy was wasted as people with similar jobs competed with one another to win Hitler's approval for their ideas. Some used the system to their advantage and became extremely powerful, such as Fritz Todt (see diagram). Ambitious Nazis took careful note of Hitler's overall aims, most notably those concerning rearmament, expansion and racial superiority. They then devised specific policies designed to meet Hitler's approval. Much of the legislation of the Third Reich resulted from chance conversations between ministers and the Führer.

An example of how government functions and responsibilities overlapped.

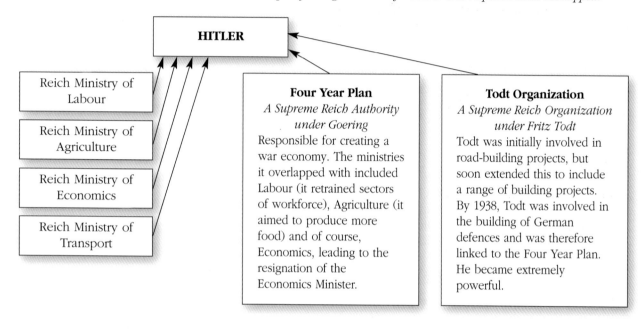

Was this chaos intended?

■ Historical debate

There is a debate amongst historians over whether this state of chaos was intended by Hitler or not. The *Intentionalists* argue that it was intended whilst *Structuralists* or *Functionalists* argue that Hitler was constrained by the 'structure' of the state. The significance of this debate centres on the question of how much power Hitler had. If, as the intentionalists argue, Hitler deliberately pursued a policy of 'divide and rule' to enhance his own power, then this is evidence of the extent to which Hitler was 'master' in the Third Reich. On the other hand, if the state of chaos was the result of 'structural' or outside factors which *prevented* Hitler from acting differently, then this is evidence of 'weak' dictatorship. This debate is largely over now, and historians generally accept that Hitler was not prevented from pursuing his main goals of territorial expansion and the creation of a pure master race and cannot be regarded as a weak dictator. They also accept, however, that Hitler was not involved in the drawing up of actual policy and they accept that certain outside factors, such as the international situation, had a definite impact on Nazi policy. Thus, recent interpretations have tried to *synthesize* or *combine* the intentionalist and the functionalist viewpoints.

■ Think about

▶ Why might a policy of 'divide and rule' have increased Hitler's power?

Cross reference

This debate is discussed more fully in Chapter 14

The Nazi Party

What was the purpose of the Nazi Party after 1933?

The Nazi Party lived an uneasy life alongside the State after 1933. For one thing, its function was now rather unclear. Before 1933, the struggle to win elections and attain power was the Party's prime objective. Once in power, and with the end of party politics, the role of the Nazi Party needed redefining. Many Nazis wanted to see the Party take over State institutions at all levels to ensure a continued involvement in political affairs and to a certain extent this did occur. But the Party and the State never completely merged. The Party's main role after 1933 was to educate the people in Nazi principles. Many Nazi associations were established or existing ones extended covering youth, women, teachers, workers and many more. One historian talks of the way in which German society became 'honeycombed' with Nazi ideas and practices. And, of course, Nazi organizations such as the SS were essential in enforcing the regime's racial policy and stamping out opposition.

Party membership

During 1933 an additional 1.6 million Germans joined the existing Party membership of 849,000. Although there was a ban on further membership, those who joined the SA or other Nazi groups could still become members. By 1939, membership had grown to 5.3 million and by the end of the war stood at around 8 million (only around 10% of the population). Of course, these figures hardly demonstrate in themselves the level of support for the Nazi Party. Many had been forced to join in order to keep their jobs.

Relations between Party and State

As mentioned above, some Nazis wanted to join State and Party together. Hitler ultimately rejected this, although his feelings were not entirely clear. The Law to Ensure the Unity of Party and State, December 1933, described the Nazi Party as being 'inseparably linked with the State'. But in February 1934, at a conference of Gauleiters, Hitler seemed to suggest something rather different, identifying the main tasks of the Party as:

Source 9

...to make the people receptive for the measures intended by the government; to help to carry out the measures which have been ordered by the Government in the nation at large; to support the Government in every way.

In the end, Hitler seemed reluctant to see the Party simply as an instrument of propaganda and his appointment of Hess to the position of Führer's Deputy for Party Affairs suggested that he did in fact want some overlap between Party and State. Hess was also Reich minister without portfolio, thus combining a Party and a State position, and was soon given the right to supervise new legislation and vet the selection of all senior Nazi officials. Hess attempted to establish supremacy within the Party and his successor, Martin Bormann, succeeded in enhancing the role of the Party within the government and the State.

Key term

State institutions

State institutions include groups such as the civil service and the police which, in theory, are run by the same people no matter which party is in power.

Cross reference

See page 180 for information about the SS.

■ Think about

▶ Why do you think that a ban was placed on further membership of the Nazi Party?

Key term

Gauleiters

District leaders of the Nazi Party appointed directly by Hitler

■ Think about

▶ Why would some members of the Party have been dissatisfied with these tasks?

Ways in which the Nazi Party took over State institutions:

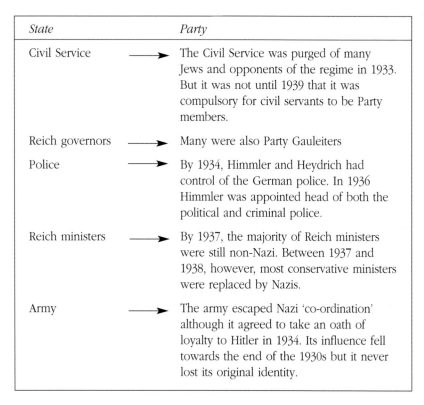

State		*Party*
Civil Service	⟶	The Civil Service was purged of many Jews and opponents of the regime in 1933. But it was not until 1939 that it was compulsory for civil servants to be Party members.
Reich governors	⟶	Many were also Party Gauleiters
Police	⟶	By 1934, Himmler and Heydrich had control of the German police. In 1936 Himmler was appointed head of both the political and criminal police.
Reich ministers	⟶	By 1937, the majority of Reich ministers were still non-Nazi. Between 1937 and 1938, however, most conservative ministers were replaced by Nazis.
Army	⟶	The army escaped Nazi 'co-ordination' although it agreed to take an oath of loyalty to Hitler in 1934. Its influence fell towards the end of the 1930s but it never lost its original identity.

> **Note**
>
> The army was the only institution that stood a realistic chance of overpowering Hitler and its support of the Nazi regime has been condemned by historians. The Nazis appealed to the army's desire for authoritarian rule and military superiority. It was only when the war turned against Germany that certain members of the army mounted any serious opposition.

The army

The army escaped the first phase of *Gleichschaltung* in 1934 and it supported the Nazi policy of rearmament. However, as Hitler's strength grew, and his foreign ambitions became more urgent, a clash of interests became inevitable. In 1937 Hitler outlined his foreign policy ambitions at the Hossbach meeting. The two most senior figures in the German army, Field Marshal von Blomberg (War Minister) and General von Fritsch (Commander-in-Chief) both expressed concerns about the extent of Hitler's plans, believing Germany to be militarily unprepared. A few months later, both men were forced out of office and Hitler himself became Commander-in-Chief of Germany's armed forces. The outbreak of war aroused the army's patriotism and loyalty and it supported Hitler fully. However, as the war turned sour after 1943, opposition grew, culminating in a failed assassination attempt on the Führer.

Persuasion and force in the Nazi state

Propaganda

Terror and fear played a vital role in the Nazi state as we shall shortly see, but it was not seen as desirable in the long term. Ultimately, the aim was to achieve a racially pure state completely in tune with Nazi principles in which concentration camps and spy networks became redundant. Goebbels was particularly of the view that this could be achieved through a concentrated propaganda campaign. Of course, propaganda was not new to the Nazi Party – we have already examined their views and methods in Chapter 6. But in 1933 the Nazis had, for the first time, all the apparatus of the State at their disposal. On 12 March 1933, the Ministry for Popular Enlightenment and Propaganda was set up with Goebbels at its head, providing him with a seat in the Cabinet. In addition to this post, Goebbels was also President of the Reich Chamber of Commerce and Director of the Central Office of the NSDAP. He wasted no time in making his intentions clear, as the following extracts demonstrate.

Source 10

The Press

This Government is, in the truest sense of the word, a People's Government. It derives from the people and it will always execute the people's will...

...The task of the Press cannot be merely to inform; rather, the Press has above and beyond that the much greater task of instructing. It naturally has the task of making clear to the people what the Government is doing, but it must also explain why the Government is doing it, why the Government is forced to act in a certain way and no other... You too will consider ideal a situation in which the Press is so finely tuned that it is, as it were, like a piano in the hands of the Government on which the Government can play...

...you find fault with the Government, you must express yourself in a manner and tone that do not provide the enemy of this Government either at home or abroad with the opportunity of quoting you and thus saying something that he could not otherwise say without risking being banned...You may of course criticise the Government, but in the process you should not lose sight of the Government's interest...

...The word 'propaganda' always has a bitter after-taste. But, if you examine propaganda's most secret causes, you will come to different conclusions...For propaganda is not an end in itself but a means to an end...If we achieve our end through this means, then the means is good...

...we are not going to go away and we shall gradually win the people over in this way completely to our side...We do want to do that not by banning newspapers but by gradually influencing the people while we shape and form public opinion...

...I promise you that I shall stand up for the rights of the Press everywhere and at all times but on one condition: that the Press stands up not just for the rights of the Government but also for the rights of the German people.

The Radio

We make no bones about the fact that the radio belongs to us and to no one else...The radio must subordinate itself to the goals which the Government of the National Revolution has set itself...

...I hold radio to be the most modern and the most important instrument of mass influence that exists anywhere. I am also of the opinion – and one shouldn't say this out loud – I am of the opinion that in the long term radio will replace newspapers...First principle: At all costs avoid being boring...The correct attitudes must be conveyed, but that does not mean that they must be boring.

Extracts from Goebbel's speeches to representatives of the press and radio in March 1933

■ **Activity**

Think about and discuss the questions below as you read through the extracts. Then answer the questions at the bottom of the page more fully.

a How valid was the phrase 'People's Government'? Why do you think Goebbels used it?

b What does Goebbels see as the role of the Press? How would we feel about this view today?

c How far did Goebbels mean what he says about criticizing the government, in your opinion?

d Why do you think Goebbels saw propaganda to be so important for the long-term success of the Nazis?

e Why do you think Goebbels believed radio to be so important? Why was it important for it not to be boring?

■ **Questions**

1 How open was Goebbels about the role of propaganda in the Third Reich?

2 How does he try to overcome any potential opposition to his policies?

3 Why, according to these speeches, was propaganda so important to the Nazis?

Different Nazi speakers had different theme tunes which preceded their radio broadcasts. Hitler's speeches were generally preceded by his favourite march, the Badenweiler, although his speeches on Heroes Day were accompanied by Beethoven's 'Eroica' symphony.

Radio

- Radio was regarded as *the* most important medium for propaganda, reflecting the Nazi preference for the spoken over the written word
- The Reich Radio Company brought all German broadcasting under Nazi control.
- A cheap radio, the *Volksempfanger* ('people's receiver'), was produced and people were able to pay for them in instalments. It had a limited range making it difficult to pick up foreign broadcasts.
- In 1932, less than 25 per cent of German households owned a radio compared to over 70 per cent by 1939.
- Loudspeakers were set up in towns and factories to broadcast important speeches.

Newspapers

- In 1933 there were some 4700 daily newspapers in Germany. By 1944 there were only 1000.
- *Eher Verlag*, the Nazi publishing house, controlled two-thirds of the Press by 1939
- The only news agency allowed was run by the Nazis, who therefore controlled information even before it got into the hands of the journalists.
- Goebbels held a daily press conference for editors who, by the Editors' Law, were solely responsible for the content of their newspapers and liable to punishment if anything unacceptable was printed.
- Although the Nazis preferred the spoken word to the written one, newspapers played an important role in advertising special appeals or anti-Semitic campaigns. The Nazi's own paper, the *Volkischer Beobachter* was at the forefront of the latter campaign.
- Both the number and the quality of newspapers deteriorated. In the five years following 1933, the number of periodicals and learned journals fell by half.

Film

- All films had to undergo a thorough censorship process and 'degenerate' (immoral) artists were not allowed. About half of the best-known film stars emigrated.
- Only about one-sixth of all films could be described as outright Nazi propaganda. Half were simply love stories or comedies and about a quarter were more dramatic, such as thrillers or musicals.
- However, even love stories and the like had to be acceptable to Nazi ideology. Feature films were used to convey ideas such as the master race, the need for more living space and anti-Semitism.

Examples of the weekly quotation during the war:

'Only composure and a heart of iron bring victory'

'No one can get past the German soldier'

Other forms of propaganda

In addition to radio, newspapers and film, there were many other ways in which the Nazis sought to influence people. Stamps bearing a Nazi message were produced; a weekly poster with a quotation was circulated to offices and public buildings and of course, new rituals were created to celebrate the Nazi state. These rituals included the Nazi salute, the *Heil Hitler* greeting, the Nuremberg rallies and days when, for example, the Munich *Putsch* and Hitler's birthday were celebrated. The use made of German art is more fully described in Chapter 10.

How successful was Nazi propaganda?

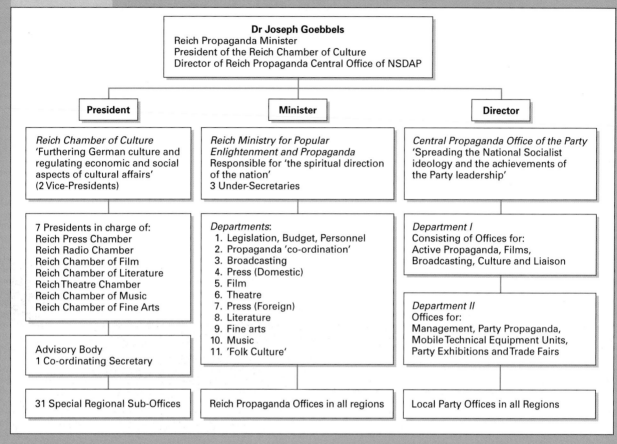

▲ The organisation of the Nazi propaganda machine.

Dr Joseph Goebbels
Reich Propaganda Minister
President of the Reich Chamber of Culture
Director of Reich Propaganda Central Office of NSDAP

President

Reich Chamber of Culture
'Furthering German culture and regulating economic and social aspects of cultural affairs'
(2 Vice-Presidents)

7 Presidents in charge of:
Reich Press Chamber
Reich Radio Chamber
Reich Chamber of Film
Reich Chamber of Literature
Reich Theatre Chamber
Reich Chamber of Music
Reich Chamber of Fine Arts

Advisory Body
1 Co-ordinating Secretary

31 Special Regional Sub-Offices

Minister

Reich Ministry for Popular Enlightenment and Propaganda
Responsible for 'the spiritual direction of the nation'
3 Under-Secretaries

Departments:
1. Legislation, Budget, Personnel
2. Propaganda 'co-ordination'
3. Broadcasting
4. Press (Domestic)
5. Film
6. Theatre
7. Press (Foreign)
8. Literature
9. Fine arts
10. Music
11. 'Folk Culture'

Reich Propaganda Offices in all regions

Director

Central Propaganda Office of the Party
'Spreading the National Socialist ideology and the achievements of the Party leadership'

Department I
Consisting of Offices for:
Active Propaganda, Films, Broadcasting, Culture and Liaison

Department II
Offices for:
Management, Party Propaganda, Mobile Technical Equipment Units, Party Exhibitions and Trade Fairs

Local Party Offices in all Regions

■ Activity

1 Study Source 11. What forms of propaganda were the Nazis planning to use?

2 Were there any gaps in the Nazis' control over the media and the arts?

3 Compare Sources 12 and 13. How do they differ in their accounts of the impact of Nazi propaganda on the German people? Can you suggest any reasons for these differences?

Goebbels the advertising minister is no psychologist. He is boring, people make fun of the boring radio etc...Goebbels does not captivate...The progression of feelings here runs from a deadened indifference to aversion and revolt.

Klemperer, *I Shall Bear Witness: The Diaries of Viktor Klemperer*, 1999

'We are strong and will get stronger', Hitler shouted at them through the microphone, his words echoing across the hushed field from the loudspeakers. And there, in the flood-lit night, jammed together like sardines, the little men of Germany who have made Nazism possible achieved the highest state of being the Germanic man knows: the shedding of their individual souls and mind until under the mystic lights and at the sound of the magic words of the Austrian they were merged completely in the Germanic herd.

William Shirer's account of a rally. Shirer was an American journalist. Shirer, *Berlin Diary: the Journal of a Foreign Correspondent*, 1941

■ **Activity**

1 Compare Sources 14 and 15. To what extent do they support the accounts given in Sources 12 and 13?

2 Why do you think the workers described in Source 14 were so reluctant to see the film and support the collection?

3 Source 15 is itself a piece of propaganda. How does this affect its value as evidence about the impact of propaganda on the people?

Source 14

The lack of interest in (or rejection of) Nazi propaganda was also reflected in the behaviour of the 400 strong staff of a wood-ware factory in Lauf near Nuremberg, which ignored the command of the leader of the Council of Trust to march solidly behind the swastika flag for a communal viewing of a film about the Nazi cult-figure Horst Wessel in the local cinema. Only four workers turned up at the factory gate after work ready to accompany him. The rest disappeared and went home. The proposed visit to the cinema was abandoned and the attempt was not repeated. At another factory in the same town a collection for a wedding present for the young go-ahead Nazi managing director, who had replaced the popular Jewish former head of the firm at the 'seizure of power', totalled only twelve marks from a staff of around 700 persons.

Kershaw, *Popular Opinion and Political Dissent in the Third Reich*, 1984

Source 15

■ **Activity** KEY SKILLS

1 Prepare a presentation on Nazi propaganda using a range of examples, including images downloaded from the Internet. Your presentation should focus on:
● The messages of the propaganda
● The techniques used to get the messages across
● What the examples can tell historians studying the period You may wish to use PowerPoint for the presentation. A useful website to get you started is: www.calvin.edu/academic/cas/gpa/index.htm

2 You have been asked to write a report for SOPADE (SPD in exile) about the effectiveness of Nazi propaganda. The year is 1938. Use the information from your presentation and make sure that you include appropriate images. You may also wish to look at pages 246–7.

▲ The 1934 Nuremberg Rally.

The police state

The Nazi state has been described as 'totalitarian'. This is a term that is also used to describe Stalin's Russia and other one-party dictatorships. More recently, however, historians have questioned the value of such a generalized term, arguing that it glosses over the many differences between the states which it is used to describe. However, it is useful to describe the way in which states such as Hitler's Germany laid a total claim over the behaviour of the people. Almost everything they did was in theory subject to political control and the mildest action could become a punishable offence.

The Nazis created a regime in which many people lived under the constant shadow of fear. Through a network of spies and informers, the mildest of criticisms could lead to arrest, prosecution and a spell (ranging from a few weeks up to a life sentence depending on your 'crime') in a prison or concentration camp. If you were lucky enough to have a trial, you would find yourself faced with lawyers and judges who were themselves part of the Nazi regime and required to enforce a kind of improvised Nazi 'law'.

At the root of all this was a new interpretation of the law. Hitler's view of the law in 1928 (see margin) was a sign of things to come. Again and again, legal experts sympathetic to the Nazi cause defined the law as the will of the Führer, which represented, they argued, the best interests of the German community or *volk*:

> **Quotation**
>
> There is only one kind of law in this world, and that lies in one's own strength.
>
> Hitler, 1928

Source 16

'The law itself is nothing other than the expression of the communal order in which the people live and which derives from the Führer' and 'The individual can be judged by the law only from the point of view of his value for the volkisch community'

Ernst Huber, Professor of Jurisprudence at Kiel

Steps were taken to control all those in a position to interpret and enforce the law. The training of lawyers had to include 'a serious study of National Socialism'. Judges also found their independence under attack. After 1933 it was possible for judges to lose their position as a result of their political beliefs and, in 1937, they could be forced to retire if they 'could not be relied upon to support the National Socialist State'. Special courts were set up for the prosecution of political crimes. Thus, although the law of the land was not rewritten, those in a position to interpret it did so according to the 'will of the Führer'.

Another crucial factor in the attack on civil rights was the Decree for the Protection of People and State, issued in the aftermath of the Reichstag fire in February 1933. Supposedly intended as a means of stamping out a communist conspiracy, the decree allowed anyone, communist or otherwise, to be taken into 'protective custody' to protect the interests of the State. That person could be held for an indefinite period without the right to a trial. Soon afterwards, in March, a new decree was issued against malicious gossip. No wonder Viktor Klemperer wrote in his diary in August 1933: 'No letter, no telephone conversation, no word on the street is safe any more.'

Such a level of intrusion into people's lives required a police network capable of monitoring behaviour on a wide scale. Heinrich Himmler was appointed *Reichsführer SS* in 1936, which enabled him to bring all the different elements

> **Note**
>
> Comments which could lead to punishment:
>
> 'The Hitler Youth is ruining children.'
>
> 'Hitler should get married if he can.'
>
> 'In Dachau concentration camp people get beaten.'

■ Think about

▶ How far do you think the men on the right in Source 17 were dangerous enemies of the state?

▶ Political opponents of the Nazis in Oranienburg concentration camp in August 1933.

of the police state under his control. The agents of terror in the Third Reich were now firmly placed under the control of the Party. Even so, recent research has revealed the extent to which the system of spying and denunciations depended on the contribution of ordinary Germans. There simply were not enough Gestapo officers to monitor everyone's behaviour and the number of cases recorded far exceeded what would have been possible without the public's involvement.

■ Think about

Source 18 reads: 'The old slogan in the new Empire: Blood and Iron.' Bismarck was credited with uniting Germany using blood (i.e. war) and iron (i.e. industrialisation).
▶ What point do you think Heartfield is making about 'Blood and Iron' in the Third Reich?

Der alte Wahlspruch im „neuen" Reich:
BLUT UND EISEN

▶ A John Heartfield poster from 1934.

The Gestapo

- The secret state police
- Set up by Goering in Prussia, 1933
- Soon replaced all the existing political police in Germany
- Himmler in charge after 1933
- By 1936, established as part of Himmler's SS empire
- Main duty was to enforce political conformity
- Made frequent use of 'protective custody'
- Relied on denunciations by ordinary German people
- In Würzberg, 54% of all race-related charges were initiated by private citizens.
- The percentage breakdown of types of cases dealt with by the Gestapo in Düsseldorf, 1933–1945:

30% Continuation of outlawed organizations such as political parties, youth groups, religious sects

29% Non-conforming behaviour such as malicious gossip

4.5% Acquiring or spreading forbidden printed matter

2.3% Listening to foreign radio

0.9% Political passivity

12% Conventional criminality

21.3% Others (unspecified)

The SS

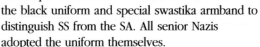

- Full title was *Schutzstaffel* meaning Defence Unit
- Set up in 1925 as Hitler's personal guards
- Himmler appointed leader in 1929. He was responsible for the black uniform and special swastika armband to distinguish SS from the SA. All senior Nazis adopted the uniform themselves.
- Played a key role in carrying out The Night of the Long Knives and thereafter replaced the SA as the main military unit of the Party
- Intended to represent the German elite
- Members carefully screened to ensure racial and biological purity
- By 1935, membership stood at 200,000
- Main duties were to enforce the party's racial policy and run the concentration camps
- Two units were to become particularly notorious: the Death's Head Units who ran the camps and the armed Waffen SS set up in 1940 and intended eventually to replace the army. It had a reputation for brutality and ruthlessness

Himmler's Empire

The police

- All German police under Himmler's control after 1936
- Police divided into the ORPO (municipal police and rural/urban constabularies) and the SIPO (Gestapo and criminal police) which became part of the SD in 1939

The SD (Sicherheitsdienst)

- Set up in 1931 by Himmler as the internal security service for the SS
- Increasingly given the job of intelligence. The reports of the SD, covering issues such as the popularity of the Party, or the situation of the Church, provide us with a valuable source of evidence about the Third Reich

■ **Think about**

▶ Do you think Himmler was the most powerful figure in the Nazi state after Hitler himself?

Himmler's empire

To understand the SS, it is also necessary to understand its leader. Himmler was fanatical in his belief that the Aryan race was superior to all others, particularly the Jews. He firmly believed in the need to expand Germany in order to make it the world power it deserved to be and saw the achievement of racial purity as the necessary first step. His own SS was to be at the vanguard of this crusade.

Cross reference

See page 116 for a biography of Himmler.

Source 19

In politics there are only two possibilities: for Germany or not. Anyone who is not basically for Germany but against Germany does not belong to us and will be eliminated. If he does not emigrate on his own initiative, then he will have to be locked up. If that does not help then we will have to make him a head shorter.

From an article in the SS newspaper, 1939

Quotation

The knowledge of the enormities that the SS perpetrated daily, the knowledge that the camps were always waiting for new inmates, the knowledge that many who entered them were never heard of again was never absent from the minds of the German citizens…

Craig, *Germany 1866–1945, 1981*

Those 'against Germany' included non-Aryans (especially Jews), political enemies (such as communists) and those not conforming to the Nazi 'norm' such as homosexuals, gypsies and alcoholics. All such victims found themselves trapped in the brutal regime of the concentration camps which sprang up almost immediately after January 1933. Initially the location of the camps was improvised – the top floor of a bar, the backyard of a building – but by March 1933 camps such as Dachau were in place. They were originally termed 're-education centres' but the term concentration camp was soon borrowed from the British who had set up camps to 'concentrate' Boer families during the Boer War. There were never fewer than 10,000 Germans in the camps and, according to Nazi statistics, around 225,000 Germans were imprisoned for political crimes between 1933 and 1939. The map below shows the location of these camps:

Source 20

■ Think about

▶ To what extent does this map support the view that the SS was a 'state within a state'?

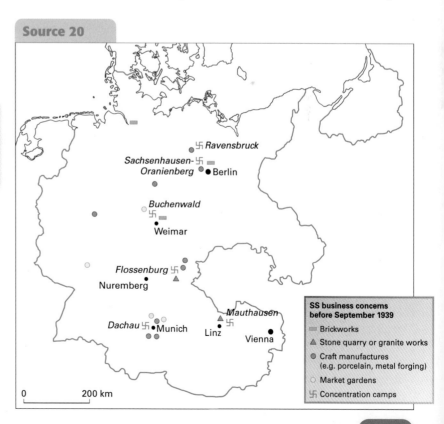

SS business concerns before September 1939

- ▬ Brickworks
- ▲ Stone quarry or granite works
- ● Craft manufactures (e.g. porcelain, metal forging)
- ○ Market gardens
- 卐 Concentration camps

0   200 km

Source 20 demonstrates the breadth of the SS organization. Many historians have termed it a 'state within a state' which reflects its independence from other state organizations. The camps provided a rich source of cheap labour and a number of SS enterprises were established, including road building, metal forging, market gardening and the like. By 1945 the SS was estimated to have a turnover of over 50 million Reichsmarks. Only an organization so dedicated to carrying out the Führer's racial policy was allowed to grow so powerful.

Document exercise: living in a police state

Source A

The speed of Gestapo arrests

In a café a 64-year-old woman remarked to her companion at the table: 'Mussolini has more political sense in one of his boots than Hitler has in his brain.' The remark was overheard by other patrons and five minutes later the woman was arrested by the Gestapo who had been alerted by telephone.

Extract from an SPD report, 1938

Source B

An unusual trial

My client...denied the crime of which he was accused. The appeal judge said 'In that case we can begin with the hearing of the evidence.' At that moment I intervened and asked permission to question my client, before the hearing of the evidence, about the circumstances in which he had signed the statement quoted above, [confessing his guilt after Gestapo interrogation] and in particular as to whether he had been beaten by the officers of the Secret State Police...The appeal judge rose from his chair, leant on his hands on the court table and said to me: 'Council for the defence...a question such as you have asked can lead to your being arrested in the courtroom and taken into custody. Do you wish to sustain the question or not?'...Suddenly, into the dead of silence which followed came the words of the assistant judge 'The defence need not sustain this question, I will take it over on behalf of the court.' I do not know if I would personally have had the courage to stick to my question under the pressure of the situation and the assistant judge saved me this decision. I wholeheartedly admired such courage from a German judge. I also got the impression that only a judge who had been badly wounded in the 1914-18 war could get away with such courage.

Source C

The duty of the judge

His role is to safeguard the concrete order of the racial community, to eliminate dangerous elements, to prosecute all acts harmful to the community......The National Socialist ideology...is the basis for interpreting the law.

Statement issued by a Nazi legal expert

■ **Activity**

Who was more important to the success of the Nazi state: Goebbels or Himmler?

Divide into two groups. One group is to argue that Goebbels was more important to the success of the Nazi state whilst the other group will argue that Himmler contributed more.

After the debate, answer the following question:

'Would Hitler have survived for as long as he did without Goebbels and Himmler?'

Source D

The role of ordinary Germans

The Düsseldorf Gestapo pursued many persons suspected of 'non-conforming everyday behaviour' – 29 per cent of all its cases…Much energy was used to control the spoken word, and the majority of cases of this kind of nonconformity brought to the Gestapo's attention were about airing opinions in public. Many of these kinds of investigations must have been dependent on the observations of people beyond the ranks of the Gestapo, since it simply had too few members to keep watch or to listen in on its own.

Extract from an essay written by Robert Gellately, 1990

■ Examination-style questions

1 Comprehension in context
Study Sources A and D. Using the sources and your own knowledge, explain why the woman in Source A was arrested.

2 Comparing the sources
Study Sources B and C. Why is the behaviour of the assistant judge in Source B surprising in the light of Source C?

3 Assessing the sources
Of what use is Source B to an historian studying the legal system in Nazi Germany?

4 Making judgements
'People had little choice but to conform'. Using these sources and your own knowledge, explain whether this is an accurate view of life in the Third Reich.

Conclusions

The Nazis relied on three sources of power:
● That large numbers of the German people would accept Nazi policies because they stood to gain from them
● That the German people would be persuaded to support the Nazis' policies through propaganda
● That the German people would be forced to accept the Nazis' policies out of fear

The Nazi state was totalitarian in so far as all aspects of peoples' lives were under surveillance and subject to political 'control'. Spies, the Gestapo, the SS, concentration camps: the terror these words conjure up is familiar and their meaning is understood beyond the history books. Of course, it is ultimately impossible to control all aspects of life and pockets of rebellion did exist (see Chapter 13) but generally, the fear of punishment discouraged opposition which was, of course, its very purpose.

In charge of this powerful police state was a government characterized by chaos and a Führer who disliked hard work. Although Goebbels' well-oiled publicity machine created a rather different impression, the Nazi state was in fact governed in a haphazard and ultimately dangerous way. The endless in-fighting between Nazis unsure of their role and ready to exploit the chaos for their own purposes had terrible consequences. Hitler wanted to create a master race in Germany and beyond but did not have the patience to work through specific policies. There were, however, plenty of people waiting in the wings and struggling between themselves to win Hitler's approval. They had plenty of time to develop policies that could deliver Hitler's ambitious and terrible aims.

Social and racial policy in the Third Reich

Source 1

Struggle is always a means for improving a species' health and power of resistance and, therefore, a cause of its higher development.

Adolf Hitler, *Mein Kampf*, 1925

Source 2

▶ A Nazi painting entitled 'We want to see our Fuhrer'.

Source 3

▲ Humiliated Jewish men are forced to scrub the streets clean, August 1938.

■ **Think about**

▶ What is the message of Source 2, do you think?

Introduction

So far we have mainly concentrated on how the Nazis came to power and how they set up a dictatorship in Germany. Now it is time to consider what everyday life was like for those living in Hitler's Germany.

Key questions

- How did everyday life change as a result of Nazi policies?
- To what extent did the Nazis transform society?
- Was there a gap between what the Nazis said and did?

Nazi ideology: what kind of society did the Nazis want?

Hitler wanted to create a society in which every individual saw the purpose of his or her life as contributing towards the greater good of the German *volk* or community. He attacked the idea of individuals having rights, arguing that this would simply damage the national or 'people's' community. For Hitler, all life meant struggle – a struggle to survive and overwhelm enemies. How, he argued, could Germany survive against the threats of Bolshevism, the Jews and other states if its population acted as a group of individuals rather than as a united whole? What Germany needed was a society in which everyone shared the same aims and worked together to achieve them. But of course Hitler did not intend that this united society – the 'people's community' – should include everyone. This is where Hitler's ideal of a 'master race' came into play, with devastating effects. His 'people's community' or *Volksgemeinschaft* would be superior to all other communities because it would be made up of pure Germans. There would be no room for the disabled in Hitler's vision, no room for the social outcast and of course, no room for non-Aryans. If you were Aryan and basically fit in mind and body then you were part of Hitler's *Volksgemeinschaft*. If you were not, then you waited with fear to see what would happen after 1933.

Quotation

There are no more private citizens. The time when anybody could do or not do what he pleased is past.

                                Robert Ley, 1938

Key term

Volksgemeinschaft

Hitler used the term *Volksgemeinschaft* to describe a 'people's community'.

■ **Think about**

▶ What do you think is happening in Source 4?

Source 4

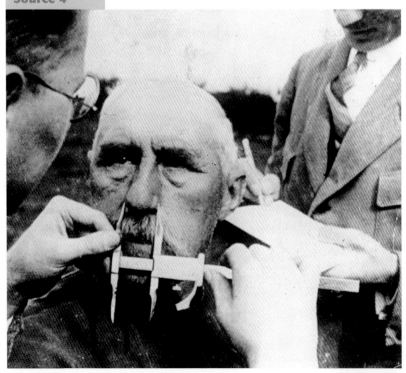

Women and the family

As the figures in the margin indicate, the birth rate in Germany fell during the 1920s. Although this was a Europe-wide phenomenon, the decline in births was more acute in Germany than elsewhere. The possible impact of this on Nazi expansionist ambitions was immense. How could Germany acquire *and populate* more living space *(lebensraum)* if it did not have enough people? Even more worrying in the short term was a population diminishing so fast that Germany would not even be able to maintain its *current* position of strength, let alone extend it. The need to raise the birth rate, therefore, became a key domestic policy during the 1930s. This fitted in neatly with Nazi attacks on the supposed emancipation (freedom) of women during the Weimar Republic. The Nazis rejected moves towards greater female independence and emphasized that a woman's place was in the home. Of course, it is difficult to be sure whether the Nazis really believed this ideology or whether it simply provided the basis for policies that encouraged more reproduction and reduced unemployment figures by removing women from the workplace. Certainly, as time went on and the need for workers increased, the Nazis were prepared to modify their policies about women in the workplace to suit their own needs. As ever, therefore, Nazi ideology was shaped by circumstances.

Birth rates, 1871-1933 (live births)

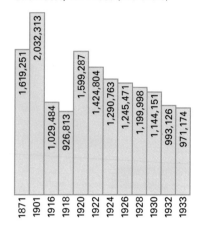

Can you suggest any reasons for the particularly low figures in 1918 and 1932–1933? Why do you think there was a general decrease in the number of births?

Source 5

If one says that man's world is the state, that his world is his struggle, his readiness to devote himself to the community, then one might be able to say that the world of women is a smaller one. For her world is her husband, her family, her children, and her house. (Applause). But where would the larger world be if no one wanted to care for the smaller world? How could the larger world exist if there were no one to make the cares of the smaller world the essence of their lives? No, the larger world is built on this smaller world!...What man offers in heroism on the field of battle, woman equals with unending pain and suffering. Every child she brings into the world is a battle, a battle she wages for the existence of her people...

Hitler speaking at the Nuremberg Rally in 1934

■ Think about

▶ What is Hitler's view on women? In 1935, Hitler stressed that there was equality of rights for women in Germany. Although men and women had different tasks to perform, both sets of tasks were equal in 'dignity and value'. Do you agree that men and women were equal in the Third Reich?

Source 6

■ Think about

▶ What point is this painting trying to make? How successfully do you think the painting gets across its message?

▶ Think back to the experiences of women during the Weimar Republic. Why might some women have welcomed Nazi policies?

◀ A Nazi painting entitled 'The Family', by Wilhelm Haller.

How did the Nazis try to achieve their aims?

Employment

The Nazis took Weimar policies to reduce female employment much further. Married women were often excluded from the civil service and other professions. Employers were encouraged to employ men in favour of women. Numbers of women allowed to enter university were restricted. Many women found themselves forced into part-time work.

Loans and benefits

From 1933, women who left work and married an Aryan man were eligible to receive an interest free marriage loan. The amount to be repaid fell by a quarter with each child born. By having four children, therefore, the repayment would be cancelled altogether. Women with children were also offered generous welfare payments.

Kinder, Kirche und Kuche

This became the Nazi slogan which defined the ideal spheres of female activity. It translates as 'children, church and cooking'. This view was spread by Nazi organizations such as the 'Women's Enterprise' (DFW) which organized training for women in domestic and motherhood skills. By 1939, around 3.5 million women had attended such courses.

Medals

The Nazis tried to raise the status of motherhood. Women were encouraged to play their role in the state by 'donating a baby to the Führer'. As a sign of their appreciation, the Nazis awarded medals to prolific mothers on Mothering Sundays. Those with four or five children received a bronze medal, those with six or seven received silver and those with eight or more received a gold medal from the Führer himself.

Divorce, abortion and contraception

Abortion was restricted and the use of birth control, except for Jews and other 'undesirables', was condemned. Divorce was made easier for those in childless marriages and, indeed, the decision not to have children was regarded as grounds for divorce. Men who were married to non-Aryans were encouraged to divorce them.

A healthy life

Women were encouraged to adopt a healthy lifestyle. Dieting, smoking and late nights were frowned upon and exercise was encouraged. Women were also discouraged from wearing make-up or from dressing in a decadent, 'foreign' way. These ideas were introduced to women at an early age.

As you can see, the Nazis used a combination of tactics in their attempts to raise the birth rate and reduce female employment. But there was another, more sinister, strand to their policies regarding childbirth. It was not simply a question of wanting *more* births, it was also a question of the right *kind* of births. Advice was issued about choosing a partner who was Aryan and healthy and, from 1933, a Sterilization Law forced all those suffering from a hereditary disease to be sterilized. The conditions classed as 'hereditary' included 'chronic alcoholism' and even 'feeble-mindedness'. Between 1934 and 1945, around 320,000 men and women were sterilized, of whom nearly 100 died as a result. The desire for perfection was taken to bizarre extremes. For example, an organisation called the 'Spring of Life' was set up supposedly to provide support for unmarried mothers but in fact it provided opportunities for SS men to father more children.

Source 7

1 Remember that you are a German.

2 If you are genetically healthy you should not remain unmarried.

3 Keep your body pure.

4 You should keep your mind and spirit pure.

5 As a German choose only a spouse of the same or Nordic blood.

6 In choosing a spouse, ask about his ancestors.

7 Health is also a precondition for physical beauty.

8 Marry only for love.

9 Don't look for a playmate but for a companion for marriage.

10 You should want to have as many children as possible.

'Ten Commandments for the Choice of a Spouse', 1934

Spotlight

How successful were Nazi policies towards women?

Source 8

Number of marriages and births

Year	Population (000s)	Number of marriages	Numbers of births
1918	66,811	352,543	926,813
1920	61,797	894,978	1,599,287
1928	64,023	594,631	1,199,998
1932	65,716	516,793	993,126
1933	66,027	638,573	971,174
1934	66,409	740,165	1,198,350
1935	66,871	651,435	1,263,976
1936	67,349	609,770	1,278,583
1937	67,831	620,265	1,277,046
1938	75,396	645,062	1,348,534
1939	86,910	774,163	1,413,230
1940	98,173	612,946	1,402,640

Note: Figures from 1938 onwards include new territory taken by Germany

Source 9

It is generally agreed that from its beginning, the Third Reich treated women in a callous and politically expedient [useful] way. Frau Fischer, however, sees things differently…'Women's emancipation [freedom] in the wide, wide public began fundamentally with National Socialism'. Her reasoning included the extensive membership of German girls in the BDM and German women in the Frauenschaft. Both groups 'now for the first time' were led by their female peers. 'That all really happened in spite of Hitler's wanting the woman to stay with her saucepan.

An interview with Frau Margarete Fischer in Owings, *Frauen*, 1995

Source 10

Employment of women by economic sector (000s)

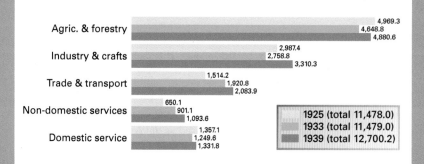

Agric. & forestry — 4,969.3 / 4,648.8 / 4,880.6
Industry & crafts — 2,987.4 / 2,758.8 / 3,310.3
Trade & transport — 1,514.2 / 1,920.8 / 2,083.9
Non-domestic services — 650.1 / 901.1 / 1,093.6
Domestic service — 1,357.1 / 1,249.6 / 1,331.8

1925 (total 11,478.0)
1933 (total 11,479.0)
1939 (total 12,700.2)

Source 11

The evidence suggests that women approved of the regime's glorification of domesticity, since for most women employment in the circumstances of the 1930s was not a particularly attractive proposition. Moreover, men too seem to have approved of this emphasis, which reaffirmed traditional distinctions discriminating between men and women and flattered their male pride.

A historian on the reactions to Nazi policies. From Noakes and Pridham, Nazism 1919–1945 Vol. II, 1984

Source 12

When one had five children, one got an Honourable Mother's Cross, nicht? From the Nazis. Sort of a mark of distinction. And I sent it back to them…I said I won't allow myself to be rewarded. I didn't bear my children for Hitler. But that was bad to say.

An interview with Frau Doktor Margaret Blersch in Owings, *Frauen*, 1995

Source 13

Proportion of women in employment

1933 = 37%	
1937 = 31%	

Source 14

…we can no longer do without the woman doctor, lawyer, economist, and teacher in our professional life.

Extract from the *Volkischer Beobachter* (Nazi newspaper) in 1936

Source 15

◀ Instructing women in Nazi ideas, in about 1935

Source 16

The depression ... gave the National Socialists the excuse to try to put theory into practice by circumscribing [restricting] the activities of professional women, and employed women as a whole. But, again similar to the employment market generally, this soon proved impractical, and the policies which had priority in the Nazi state necessitated warm encouragement to women to enter professional occupations.

Stephenson, *Women in Nazi Society*, 1975

Source 17

...Hitler reluctantly agreed to Saukel [the man responsible for the allocation of labour during the war] issuing a decree on 27 January 1943 'Concerning the Registration of Men and Women for Reich Defence Tasks'. According to the decree, with certain exceptions, all women between the ages of 17 and 45 were obliged to register for work.

Noakes and Pridham, *Nazism 1919–1945 Vol. III*, 1998

Source 18

The conditions which must be filled before the grant of a marriage loan are as follows... That the future wife pledges herself not to take up employment so long as her future husband receives an income...

One of the conditions of receiving marriage loans (1933)

Source 19

I permit wives who have received a marriage loan to take up employment, provided their husbands have been called up for the Labour Service or for training by the armed forces.

The conditions of receiving marriage loans are revised (1937)

■ Activity

1 Using a table like the one below, note down any evidence which suggests that the Nazis did/did not achieve their aims

Nazi Aim	Evidence which suggests the aim was achieved	Evidence which suggests the aim was not achieved
An increased birth rate and bigger population		
An increased number of marriages		
A decrease in female employment		

2 Is there any evidence to suggest that the Nazi policies towards women made them unpopular? Can you suggest some reasons why/why not?

3 Can you see any evidence of Nazi policies changing during the 1930s and early 1940s?

4 'In the end, the only thing that mattered to the Nazis was rearmament and expansion. Their views on women came second'. How far do you agree with this view?

■ **Historical debate**

In 1987, **Claudia Koonz**, in her book *Mothers in the Fatherland*, suggested a new and controversial interpretation of the role of women in the Third Reich. Essentially, she argued that, by providing a loving, stable home environment, women enabled their husbands to carry out the atrocities demanded by the Nazi state. *'Far from remaining untouched by Nazi evil, women operated at its very centre… When the SS man returned home, he entered a doll's house of ersatz goodness in which he could escape from his own evil actions.'* Other historians have accepted that there was a degree of willingness amongst women to go along with many aspects of Nazi Party policy, including its policies towards women and the family, but few share Koonz's ultimate conclusion that women share the guilt of Nazi atrocities by simply being wives and mothers. **Adelheid von Saldern** argued in 1994 that women's role in supporting the Nazi regime *'consisted of passivity and toleration in the face of an action, but not the action itself.'* She suggested that women's traditional roles had not necessarily changed – a warm, loving home environment had long been regarded by many as one of their important duties – but the impact of that role had changed. The fact that women helped to make life seem normal and bearable for those committing daily atrocities was perhaps true. But did that make it women's fault?

■ **Think about**

▶ Compare Koonz's theory with Hitler's speech in Source 5. Are there any similarities?

Conclusions

- The Nazis' emphasis on the 'traditional' role of women found some support amongst the German people, including those for whom the Depression years had removed other opportunities. Many women, especially those from the lower classes, rejected the 'New Woman' image of the Weimar years.
- Despite Nazi policies, female employment remained high, with the overall numbers increasing. In addition, many female professionals, other than those employed in politics or the law, were able to continue their careers. However, many women were forced into badly paid agricultural or part-time work.
- There were several contradictions in Nazi policy. Whilst promoting a stable family life, young men were sent away from home to carry out labour or military service. Similarly, the Nazis were forced, from 1936 onwards, to employ more women to deal with the labour shortage. By 1943, women were being conscripted into war work.
- There were examples of continuity between the Weimar and Nazi years. Attempts were made to reduce the number of working women from as early as 1930.
- Germany was hardly unique in its policies towards women. A falling birth rate was of concern across Europe, and during the 1920s medals were awarded to mothers in France who had several children.

Youth and Education

Source 20 is a summary, written by the Nazis, of a Nazi propaganda film made in 1933. The film, *Hitlerjunge Quex*, contained many clues about the direction which Nazi youth policy would take. The hero of the film, Heini, naturally wishes to belong to the Hitler Youth, not because he agrees with Nazi ideology

Source 20

Heini Volker is a fresh, diligent boy of around 15, an apprentice in a small printers' shop in Beusselkitz. His father, forced into the clutches of the Commune by years of unemployment, enrols his son in the Communist Youth…But Heini's heart belongs to the Nazis, particularly since he went on a weekend camp and had the opportunity to see the contrasting conduct of two youth groups: the clean disciplined, happy comradeship of the Hitler Youth, compared with the atmosphere of the Communists' camp, poisoned by big city life. Heini follows his heart and takes to the Nazi movement, first secretly then openly. He yields to no danger and makes the greatest sacrifice of all, his life.

Note

The film was based on the life of Herbert Norkus, who was a hero and martyr of the Hitler Youth.

Quotation

Those who have the youth on their side control the future.

The leader of the Nazi Teachers' League

Quotation

In 1935, Hitler famously declared that he wanted his youth to be 'swift as the greyhound, tough as leather and hard as Krupp steel'.

■ **Think about**

▶ By what means did Hitler propose to influence the youth of Germany?

(of which he doubtless knows very little), but because of the discipline and comradeship it offers. He has to defy his parents in order to go, but of course he has to 'follow his heart' and in doing so, gives up his life when attacked by communists whilst running an errand for the Nazis. It was this kind of unquestioning, blind loyalty to the Party that the Nazis were aiming for.

Why was German youth so important?

The youth of Germany was the future. Adults could be persuaded or forced into accepting that the Nazis were preferable to other parties but their minds were not as pliable and easily influenced as their children's. The Nazis wanted to raise a generation of Germans who *unquestioningly* obeyed them and were willing to sacrifice their lives on the battlefield in the name of the Fatherland. In 1938, Hitler made no bones about his aims for the youth of Germany:

Source 21

These young people learn nothing else but to think as Germans and to act as Germans; these boys join our organization at the age of ten and get a breath of fresh air for the first time, then, four years later, they move from the jungvolk to the Hitler Youth and there we keep them another four years. And then we are even less prepared to give them back into the hands of those who create our class and status barriers, rather we take them immediately into the Party, into the Labour Front, into the SA or into the SS...And if they are there for eighteen months or two years and have still not become real National Socialists, then they go into the Labour Service and are polished there for six or seven months...and if there are still traces of class consciousness, then the army will take over the further treatment for two years...

Extract from a speech made by Hitler in 1938

As you can see, the Nazis did not want anyone to escape their clutches.

The Hitler Youth

The first stage was to establish an organization which could help to transform children into obedient Nazis. Fortunately for the Nazis, there was already one in place – the *Hitler Jugend* (HJ) or Hitler Youth – which was created in 1925 and by 1933 had 55,000 members. However, as you may remember from Chapter 5, youth groups were very popular in the Weimar Republic and total membership of youth groups was 5 to 6 million. The Hitler Youth therefore represented only 1 per cent of all organized youth. During 1933, most non-Nazi youth groups were forced to join the Hitler Youth as part of the policy of *Gleichschaltung*. The only groups to escape were the Catholic youth groups, temporarily protected by the Concordat signed by Hitler and the Pope. But even they were forced to give up their independence when a law of 1936 incorporated *all* youth groups into the Hitler Youth.

Both boys and girls joined the Hitler Youth. Attendance was, in theory, voluntary until 1939, although membership figures continued to increase during the 1930s and by the beginning of 1939, around 82 per cent of all 11–18 year olds were members.

Why did so many young people join the Hitler Youth?

Children joined for both positive and negative reasons. Many enjoyed the variety of activities offered to them in the Hitler Youth and the chance to mix with people of their own age. For girls in particular, the Hitler Youth offered them a chance to escape from the narrow opportunities that were offered at home. The opportunity for girls to perform sport in public, for example, was quite rare outside of the Hitler Youth. But others joined through peer pressure or sheer intimidation. The following extracts provide us with additional insights into why people joined:

Source 22

There must be many answers to the question – what caused people to become National Socialists at that time…I wanted to follow a different road from the conservative one prescribed for me by family tradition…Whenever I probe the reasons which drew me to join the Hitler Youth, I always come up against this one: I wanted to escape from my childish, narrow life and I wanted to attach myself to something that was great and fundamental…and as my parents would not allow me to become a member of the Hitler Youth I joined secretly.

Melita Maschmann, *Account Rendered: A Dossier on My Former Self*

Source 23

What I liked about the HJ was the comradeship. I was full of enthusiasm when I joined at the age of ten. What boy isn't fired by being presented with high ideals such as comradeship, loyalty and honour… And then the trips! Is there anything nicer than enjoying the splendours of the homeland in the company of one's comrades. We often went off into the countryside round K— to spend Sunday there. What joy we felt when we gathered at some blue lake, collected wood, made a fire, and then cooked pea soup on it…And it always made a deep impression to sit of an evening round a fire outside in a circle and to have a sing-song and tell stories.

The memories of a Hitler Youth leader

Source 24

Teacher A exerts such pressure on the members of the [Catholic] Youth Club that it is almost unbearable for the boys. For example: last Saturday he set those boys concerned the essay: 'Why am I not in the Hitler Youth?', while all the other children in the class had no homework…Another case: a member of the HJ had rejoined the Catholic Youth Club. When Mr A heard of this he threatened he would set him forty sums every time he stayed away from the HJ parade. This was made even worse by his threat of a beating as well. After this, the boy…stayed in the Hitler Youth.

A letter written to the Party district leader by a Catholic priest

Facts and figures

The organization of the HJ

Boys	
Age 10–14	German Young People (DJ)
Age 14–18	Hitler Youth (HJ)

Girls	
Age 10–14	Young Maidens (JM)
Age 15–21	League of German Maidens (BDM)

Facts and figures

Jokes based on the initials BDM (League of German Maidens):
Bubi Druck Mich (Squeeze me laddie)
Brauch Deutsche Madel (Make use of German girls)
Bund Deutscher Milchkuhe (League of German milk cows)

■ **Think about**

► What reason does each source give for joining the Hitler Youth?

► What are the similarities and differences between the sources?

► Why do you think views about the Hitler Youth differed?

What was it like in the Hitler Youth?

As you can see from the photographs below, the emphasis was on preparing each sex for its respective duties in the Third Reich. Boys were trained to be strong and ready for war. Girls, on the other hand, were prepared for their lives as mothers – hence the emphasis on physical fitness – and wives although, ironically, they were also given a taste of freedom and opportunity. However, the Hitler Youth became less popular towards the later 1930s as the activities became increasingly war-oriented and the discipline more strict. Those who had managed to avoid membership were brought in and there was a growing resentment at the way Hitler Youth leaders lorded it over members who were barely younger than they were. Some youths began to kick against the restrictions of both the Hitler Youth and the Nazi state in general. For example, laws were issued in 1940 forbidding under 18-year-olds to walk the streets or attend clubs, cinema and cabarets after 9pm. As a result, alternative youth groups, illegal after the law of 1936, attracted increasing numbers of young people.

▶ Approved activities for boys and girls under the Nazis.

Alternative youth groups

Alternative youth groups were essentially a reaction against the restrictions of the Nazi state. Their intention was not to destroy the Third Reich. However, their attempts to resist the control of the Nazis was seen as a threat and, in the words of a Gestapo report, 'a danger to other young people.' Presumably, the Nazis were worried that the opposition would spread.

The most popular group, the Edelweiss Pirates, included a number of regional groups such as the Kittelbach Pirates from Oberhausen and the Navajos from Cologne. Members were between 14 and 18 years old, were drawn from working-class families and included both girls and boys. All the groups shared a common purpose and that was to make the most of their leisure time and not be forced into spending it in the manner dictated by the Nazis. Their independence was partly the result of leaving school at 14 and entering the world of work as apprentices or, in a time of labour shortage, well-paid unskilled workers. They had the self-confidence to reject the Hitler Youth, which after 1939 was compulsory up to the age of 18, and they were prepared to defend their actions where necessary:

Source 25

Every child knows who the KP [Kittelbach Pirates] are. They are everywhere; there are more of them than there are Hitler Youth. And they all know each other, they stick close together…They beat up the patrols, because there are so many of them. They don't always agree with anything. They don't go to work either, they're always down by the canal, at the lock.'

An Oberhausen mining instructor

The activities of these youths were curiously similar to the Hitler Youth in some respects. They looked forward to weekend hikes and would travel long distances to reach places like the Black Forest, Vienna and the Tyrol, despite restrictions on travel during the war. Once there, the Pirates would swap stories and sing songs, deliberately choosing those which would be frowned upon by the Nazis or rewording more traditional songs to register their protest. One member recalled:

Source 26

It all simply happened in the darkness, in the wasteland which was rather difficult [for the authorities] to supervise. If you wanted, you just joined a group and were accepted. Then we would do the following things: chatted, sang, smoked, had sex – the latter not very often.

The activities of the Pirates rarely became openly political, although a few joined resistance groups during the war. The Nazis found it difficult to suppress them because of the absence of a clear structure or leadership and they were reluctant to react too brutally against the precious youth of the Reich. This did not prevent them, however, from publicly hanging the so-called leaders of the Cologne Pirates in 1944.

A rather different youth group which, like the Edelweiss Pirates, rejected the lifestyle imposed on them by the Nazis, was the Swing Movement. This was a mainly upper-middle-class group which, rather than meeting on street corners and in parks, chose night clubs or parents' homes as their venues. Their passion was 'swing' music, especially American jazz denounced by the Nazis as 'Negro music', to which they would dance, dressed in their English-looking clothes. Although not obviously interested in politics, these youths aroused the anger of the Nazis by embracing the cultures and fashion of wartime enemies such as Britain and America, and by accepting Jews into their groups.

Source 27

The dance music was all English and American. Only swing dancing and jitterbugging took place. At the entrance to the hall stood a notice on which the words 'Swing prohibited' had been altered to 'Swing requested'. Without exception the participants accompanied the dances and songs by singing the English lyrics. Indeed, throughout the evening they attempted to speak only English; and at some tables even French. The dancers made an appalling sight. None of the couples danced normally; there was only swing of the worst sort...When the band played a rumba, the dancers went into wild ecstasy...The band played wilder and wilder numbers; none of the players were sitting any longer, they all 'jitterbugged' on the stage like wild animals.

A Hitler Youth report about a swing festival in Hamburg in 1940

■ Think about

▶ How can we tell that the writers of Source 27 disapproved of the festival?

▶ Does this source tell us more about the Swing Movement or the Nazi regime?

The Nazis came to see the members of the Swing Movement as enemies of the state and Himmler wanted to see the ringleaders put in concentration camps. Overall, the existence of these alternative groups suggested a limit to Nazi control. In the words of the historian, Peukert, 'considerable sections of the younger generation held themselves aloof from National Socialism [which] …even after years in power, still did not have a complete grip on German society…'

Education

For the Nazis, the purpose of education was to make young people loyal and obedient members of the *Volksgemeinschaft*. There was no room for the development of individual ability. In fact, German children were discouraged from thinking too hard about anything. The basic structure of schooling remained largely unchanged and official guidelines and textbooks did not emerge until the later 1930s. However, the teaching profession was quickly brought into line, suffering its first purge in 1933 under the Law for the Restoration of a Professional Civil Service (see page 159). The National Socialist Teachers' League, created in 1929, represented 97 per cent of all teachers by 1937. Many teachers were supportive of the Nazis in 1933, partly because of their experiences during the economic depression. However, they gradually became more disillusioned as promises to improve their status were not kept and their position was undermined by both the Hitler Youth, which challenged the authority of schools, and the Nazi Party itself because of its constant interference.

Facts and figures

60 per cent of lecturers in colleges of education were dismissed, including Viktor Klemperer (see page 158) who lost his job at Dresden Technical University in 1935, on the grounds that he was Jewish.

Quotation

The political task of the school is the education of youth in the service of the nation and state in the National Socialist spirit.

Minister of the Interior, Frick, in 1934

Spotlight

Education in the Third Reich

■ Think about

▶ The timetable opposite will probably be familiar to you. But how might it have looked different in Nazi Germany? Here are some clues:

● More PE was introduced, especially for boys
● Foreign languages were not encouraged
● RE was not encouraged
● History and science were both encouraged
● Practical 'domestic' lessons, such as cookery, were encouraged for girls.

▶ Draw up your own copy of the timetable as it might have looked in Nazi Germany.

■ Think about

▶ Look carefully at the *subject* column in Source 28. What areas of German history are stressed?

▶ What view of German history would a student get from this syllabus?

▶ Study the *Relations to the Jews* column. What are the Jews accused of doing?

▶ What do you notice about the suggested *reading material?*

A typical timetable in a modern British school

	1	2	3	4	5	6
Monday	Maths	English	Art	Drama	PE	French
Tuesday	Geography	Science	Science	Maths	RE	English
Wednesday	History	English	French	Science	Italian	PSHE
Thursday	Science	PE	Music	Geography	Maths	Drama
Friday	Maths	IT	English	History	Art	Italian

Source 28

A Nazi History Syllabus

Weeks	Subject	Relations to the Jews	Reading material
1–4	Pre-war Germany, the Class-war, Profits, Strikes.	The Jew at large!	Hauptmann's The Weavers.
5–8	From Agrarian to Industrial State, Colonies.	The peasant in the claws of the Jews!	Descriptions of the colonies from Hermann Löns.
9–12	Conspiracy against Germany, encirclement, barrage around Germany.	The Jew reigns! War plots.	Beumelburg: Barrage … Life of Hindenburg, Wartime Letters.
13–16	German struggle – German want. Blockade! Starvation!	The Jew Becomes Prosperous! Profit from German want.	Manke: Espionage at the Front. War Reports.
17–20	The Stab in the Back. Collapse!	Jews as Leaders of the November insurrection.	Pierre des Granges: On Secret Service in Enemy Country. Bruno Brehm: That was the End.
21–24	Germany's Golgotha. Erzberger's Crimes! Versailles.	Jews enter Germany from the East. Judah's triumph.	Volkmann: Revolution over Germany. Feder: The Jews. The Stürmer newspaper.
25–28	Adolf Hitler. National Socialism.	Judah's Foe!	Mein Kampf. Dietrich Eckart.
29–32	The bleeding frontiers. Enslavement of Germany. The Volunteer Corps. Schlagter.	The Jew profits by Germany's misfortunes. Loans (Dawes, Young).	Beumelburg: Germany in Chains. Wehner: Pilgrimage to Paris. Schlageter: a German hero.
33–36	National Socialism at grips with crime and the underworld.	Jewish instigators of murder. The Jewish press.	Horst Wessel.
37–40	Germany's Youth at the Helm! The Victory of Faith.	The last fight against Judah.	Herbert Norkus. The Reich Party Congress.

Source 29

New textbooks were brought in in 1933. The existing school libraries were stripped of 'degenerate' literature and stocked with books glorifying nationalism and militarism. Teachers were given lectures laying down the general lines under which history and other sensitive subjects were to be taught. New courses were introduced in 'Racial Theory'. Teachers were careful to get the general line down exactly, since the word was quickly spread that the Hitler Youth would report to the NSDAP on what teachers were doing. In addition to the new subjects and the new approach to old subjects, the schools were required to emphasise sport and physical education, especially shooting and 'defence sport'. In science classes, for example, pupils were put to building model gliders. Nazi propaganda films were used extensively and radios were installed in the classrooms so that propaganda speeches could be heard.

The experience of one German town, from Allen, *The Nazi Seizure of Power*, 1966

Source 30

The construction of a lunatic asylum costs 6 million RM. How many houses at 15,000 RM each could have been built for that amount? To keep a mentally ill person costs approx. 4 RM per day, a cripple 5.50 RM, a criminal 3.50 RM. Many civil servants receive only 4 RM per day, white-collar employees barely 3.50 RM, unskilled workers not even 2 RM per head for their families. (a) Illustrate these figures with a diagram. According to conservative estimates, there are 300,000 mentally ill, epileptics etc. in care. (b) How much do these people cost to keep in total, at a cost of 4 RM per head? (c) How many marriage loans at 1,000 RM each…could be granted from this money?

Maths problems in Nazi textbooks

Source 31

▲ *A page from a Nazi schoolbook published in 1935 called 'Trust no fox on the heath and no Jew on his word'.*

Source 32

▲ Jewish boys are humiliated in their classroom.

■ Activity

1 Study all the sources carefully and make a note of what each one tells you about Nazi education in the form of a chart. Think about what the Nazis were trying to achieve through education and what methods they used.

2 It is 1938. Your task is to write two very different letters about Nazi education. One is to the Führer from the mother of a 14-year-old boy. She is writing to congratulate Hitler on excellent improvements made to her son's education. The other letter is from a teacher who has just been dismissed from his job. The letter is a secret one, written to the British government and smuggled out of the country by the underground SPD movement. In it you explain why Hitler must be stopped immediately because of his education policy which could lead to a new generation of unquestioning Nazis.

Document exercise: The experiences of youth in Nazi Germany

Source A

Memories of Nazi education

No one in our class ever read *Mein Kampf*. I myself had only used the book for quotations. In general we didn't know much about National Socialist ideology. Even anti-Semitism was taught rather marginally at school, for instance through Richard Wagner's essay *The Jews in Music* … Nevertheless, we were politically programmed: programmed to obey orders, to cultivate the soldierly 'virtue' of standing to attention and saying 'Yes, Sir', and to switch our minds off when the magic word 'Fatherland' was uttered and Germany's honour and greatness were invoked.

Peukert, *Inside Nazi Germany*, 1987

Source B

Opposition to the Hitler Youth

A Young people have reason for special disappointment. They were made particularly large promises which for the most part were incapable of fulfilment. The great mass of young people today can see that the well-paying posts in public administration and the Party have been filled by comrades who had the good fortune of being a few years older…In the long run young people too are feeling increasingly irritated by the lack of freedom and the mindless drilling that is customary in the National Socialist organisations.

From a SOPADE (SPD in exile) report, 1938

B The formation of cliques, i.e. groupings of young people outside the Hitler Youth, was on the increase a few years before the war, and has particularly increased during the war, to such a degree that a serious risk of the political, moral and criminal breakdown of youth must be said to exist.

Report from the Reich youth leadership, 1942

Source C

The attractions of the Hitler Youth

Youth is still in favour of the system: the novelty, the drill, the uniform, the camp life, the fact that school and the parental home take a back seat compared to the community of young people – all that is marvellous. A great time without any danger. Many believe that they will find job opportunities through the persecution of Jews and Marxists. The more enthusiastic they get, the easier are the exams and the sooner they will get a position, a job…The parents experience all this too. One cannot forbid the child to do what all children are doing, cannot refuse him the uniform which the others have. One cannot ban it, that would be too dangerous.

SOPADE (SPD in exile) report, 1934

Source D

Membership statistics for the Hitler Youth

	Total	Total population of 10–18 year-olds
End 1932	107,956	
End 1933	2,292,041	7,529,000
End 1934	3,577,565	7,682,000
End 1935	3,943,303	8,172,000
End 1936	5,437,601	8,656,000
End 1937	5,879,955	9,060,000
End 1938	7,031,226	9,109,000
Beg. 1939	7,287,470	8,870,000

■ Examination-style questions

1 Comprehension in context

Study Source A. Using the source and your own knowledge, describe the author's view on his education and explain how far his experience was typical.

2 Comparing the sources

Study Sources B and C. How and why do they differ in their view of the popularity of the Hitler Youth?

3 Evaluating the sources

How useful is Source D to a historian studying the Hitler Youth, *if used by itself?*

4 Making judgements

Using all the sources and your own knowledge, explain how successful the Nazis were at winning the support of the youth of Germany.

Christianity and the Nazis

Germany had a strong Christian tradition, represented largely by Catholicism in the south, west, and east, and Protestantism in the north and centre (see map). There was an obvious gap between Christian beliefs and Nazi ideology which was of course based on war, violence and a lack of compassion to other human beings. One might therefore have expected a united front by the Churches against the regime and open condemnation of its policies. In fact, what open opposition there was often came from individuals within the Churches rather than from the Churches as a whole. But why was this the case? Broadly speaking, the Churches favoured authoritarian rule and also showed some sympathy for anti-Semitism. In addition, the Protestant Church had for a long time identified itself with German nationalism, whilst the Catholic Church regarded Bolshevism, not Nazism, as its main enemy. When the Nazis came to power, the Churches hoped to gain from the apparent support offered by the new regime. In their turn, the Nazis were concerned not to alienate a considerable number of Christians in Germany by an outright attack on the Churches.

The Catholic Church

It was in the Catholic Church's interest to reach an agreement with the Nazis. The Concordat between the Nazis and the Pope, signed in June 1933, guaranteed independence for the Catholic Church in its own affairs in return for a promise that its clergy would not interfere in political matters. This involved the Catholic bishops taking an oath of loyalty to the Nazi state. For the Catholics, this agreement seemed to grant them protection from Nazi interference and a guarantee of their survival. For the Nazis, the advantages of keeping the Catholics happy had already been amply demonstrated when the Centre Party helped to provide the necessary two-thirds majority needed to pass the Enabling Act.

However, as so many were soon to discover, Hitler's promises were not worth the paper they were written on. By the end of 1933, Catholic priests were being harassed and members of Catholic youth groups were intimidated into joining the Hitler Youth. In 1936, the Catholic youth groups were finally forced to merge with the Hitler Youth and the closure of monasteries and convents began. The Pope responded in 1937 with an encyclical *With Burning Concern* which denounced the Nazi state, but this did little to stem the attacks on the Church which in fact increased during the war. In 1941, the Catholic Press was

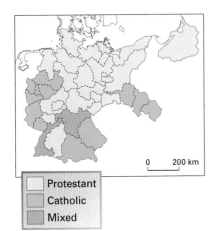

▲ The main distribution of Protestants and Catholics in Germany.

Protestant
Catholic
Mixed

0   200 km

Note

Extracts from the Concordat: 'The German Reich guarantees freedom of belief and of public worship to the Catholic faith... [All bishops] to take an oath...'I swear and promise...loyalty to the German Reich and to the...state'.'

closed down, Church property was destroyed and the activities of the Church restricted. In 1945, the Catholic Church emerged severely weakened but still in existence with the traditional loyalties of the German people largely intact. This was partly due to its agreement with the Nazis in 1933, for which it has been subsequently criticized. Certainly, with the exception of the Pope's encyclical and brave individuals such as Cardinal Galen, who spoke out against the Nazis from the pulpit, there was no concerted programme of opposition led by the Catholic Church.

The Protestant Church

The Nazis adopted a slightly different tactic with the Protestant Church. They tried to infiltrate it and control it from within. There was a nationalist movement within the Protestant Church before 1933 called the 'German Christians', and in 1933 it scored a triumph by winning three-quarters of the votes in the Church elections. A new, more nationalist, Church constitution was drawn up and Ludwig Muller, an ardent Nazi supporter, was made Reich Bishop. Muller was known for wearing 'the cross on his breast and the swastika in his heart'. Thus, it seemed as though the Nazis could count on the Protestant 'Reich' Church to support them. Not all Protestants agreed with the new direction their Church was taking, however. An alternative Church was set up in 1934 for opponents, known as the 'Confessing Church', led by Pastor Martin Niemoller. It attracted a majority of the total Protestant clergy (around 7,000) although many of the members, including Niemoller, were eventually arrested. However, the fact that it attracted so much support led to a dilution of Nazi policy. More orthodox bishops who opposed the policies of the 'German Christians' were allowed back in and they tried to steer a path between the Nazis and the Protestant Church. As in the case of the Catholic Church, the Protestant Church survived the Third Reich, but it was left weakened and deeply divided.

Conclusion

The Nazis never quite had the courage to destroy the established Churches of Germany and risk the level of opposition this might have aroused. Indeed, attendance at church services increased during the war years and, although the Churches were weakened by the Nazi attack, they were to recover their power and influence in the post-war period. In this respect, the relationship between the Churches and the Nazi state reveals the limits of Hitler's powers and provides evidence that the concept of 'totalitarianism' is perhaps a misleading one to apply to the Third Reich. The Nazis certainly, however, tried to *undermine* the influence and independence of the Churches, with mixed results. They were fortunate not to face more united resistance from both Churches, who opted for self-preservation and a defence of their *religious* freedoms as opposed to a strong defence of what we might term *Christian values*.

The creation of a Master Race

We have already seen in the introduction to this chapter how the Nazi idea of *Volksgemeinschaft* was exclusive rather than inclusive. The community was not open to all Germans. Indeed, the very concept of what 'being German' meant was redefined by the Nazis. In 1935, for example, Jews were denied German citizenship. Hence, the concept of a 'people's community' was closely connected with the concept of a 'master race' based on racial and genetic purity, to which a sizeable number did not belong.

Cross reference

See page 202 for more information about Cardinal Galen's sermon.

■ **Biography**

Martin Niemoller
Niemoller was born in 1892 and served as a U-boat commander in the First World War. He was ordained in 1924 and became pastor of a church in Berlin in 1931. He initially supported the Nazis and joined the Party but became disillusioned, especially when they began to interfere with the Church. His sermons attacking the Nazis' religious policies and his leadership of the Confessing Church led to his imprisonment in a series of concentration camps after 1938. He was released by Allied troops in 1945.

Note

Those religious groups unwilling to compromise with the regime fared less well. Jehovah's Witnesses, for example, were sent to concentration camps.

■ **Think about**

▶ How justified is the criticism that the Churches helped Hitler to hold on to power?

▶ What else could they have done?

▶ Do you think it would have made any difference?

■ Further reading

Parts of this section are based on Jeremy Noakes' chapter in the excellent book *Life in the Third Reich* edited by Richard Bessel 1987. Also useful is *The Racial State. Germany 1933-1945* edited by Burleigh and Wippermann 1991.

THE OUTSIDERS:
Those who did not belong to the Nazi's *Volksgemeinschaft*

1 Political enemies e.g. communists, socialists
2 'Asocials' – people who didn't quite fit the 'norm' of society, e.g. gypsies, tramps, homosexuals, alcoholics
3 Biological enemies
   ● people of a different race (according to the Nazis), e.g. Jews, blacks, gypsies
   ● people with hereditary defects (according to the Nazis), such as disabilities, diseases and 'feeble-mindedness'

Dealing with the 'asocials'

Nazi policy towards 'asocials' changed during the course of the 1930s. In 1936 they set up an 'asocial colony', Hashude, for those whose crime it was to be not quite 'normal'. They included those who drank too much, neglected their children or refused to work. The aim of Hashude was to 're-educate' such people so that they could eventually be reintegrated into society. However, as war approached and policy became more brutal, many of the 'asocials' were sent to concentration camps and died there.

Source 33

▶ A Nazi cartoon from 1938 entitled 'Fast Breeders'. It illustrates the menace of fast-breeding 'subhumans', such as criminals and the educationally backward, compared with the ideal German family.

■ Think about

▶ What message do you think this cartoon from 1938 is trying to put across about 'subhumans'?

▶ Is there a contradiction here between different Nazi aims?

Part of the reason for this inconsistent policy was the debate about whether people were *born* asocial or whether they *became* asocial through their experiences. Those advancing the first of these views became more influential during the 1930s. In 1938 there was a round up of those labelled 'work-shy'. An estimated 10,000 tramps were sent to concentration camps and many died there. The gypsies, who suffered the double burden of being labelled both 'asocial' *and* foreign, suffered greatly. Out of a total of 30,000 gypsies living in Germany in 1939, 25,000 died during the war, many of them at Auschwitz. In Europe as a whole, it is estimated that half a million gypsies were murdered.

Dealing with 'hereditary' defects

The first method of eliminating hereditary defects practised by the Nazis was the sterilization of those men and women believed to be carrying some sort of defect in their genes. This was hardly a novel idea by 1933. Eugenics had become increasingly influential during the 1920s, both in Germany and elsewhere, including America. Indeed, in 1932, a draft sterilization law was put forward by the Prussian Health Council, proposing voluntary sterilization in certain cases of hereditary illness. Where the Sterilization Law, introduced by the Nazis in July 1933, differed was in its scale, the fact that it was compulsory and in its rather dubious definition of 'hereditary' (see page 187). The public reaction was not particularly hostile and, of course, Nazi propaganda played a role in this:

Source 34

It is one of the first duties of the community, to see to it, that the increase of those, inferior by heredity, is stopped…the law…gives the right to the national community, to exclude those men and women from propagation with whom it can be expected with certainty through knowledge of the heredity laws, that their offspring will to a great extent be physically, mentally and spiritually inferior. Only comparatively simple medical intervention is necessary for that, which will not affect the well being and ability to live of the person at all.

Extract from Dr Stech, *Textbook on Racial Science, Genetics and Racial Policy* 1937

The policy of sterilization led on to another, more sinister, policy – that of euthanasia. Although this was the term adopted by the Nazis, it was in fact misleading as people had no choice about their 'mercy killing'. In 1939, 5,200 mentally and physically handicapped children were murdered and, in September, the programme was extended to adults. By 1941, the victims numbered 72,000. The Nazis intended to keep the programme secret, and relatives were issued with death certificates from institutions which falsified the cause of death. But the reality soon became public. This was partly the fault of the regime itself: mistakes were made such as claiming that appendicitis had killed people who had already had their appendix removed. Individual lawyers and clergy also protested, most famously Cardinal Count von Galen, Bishop of Munster, whose sermon, printed and circulated to thousands of Germans, publicly condemned the programme.

As a result, the Nazis officially halted the programme (their target figure had in any case been met) although it continued unofficially with the inmates of concentration camps. They also launched a propaganda campaign to overcome public hostility, including the film *Ich Klage An*. In the film, a young doctor and his wife are very happily married. At a party one evening, as she is giving a recital on the piano, her left hand suddenly fails her. Multiple Sclerosis is diagnosed and for weeks, the doctor tries to find a cure, to no avail. He has to watch his beloved wife slowly dying and suffering the greatest pain, knowing he can do nothing to help her. At last he makes a decision and prepares a sleeping draught which gives her release. He has done it at her own request and tells his friend of his action. The friend, however, shows no understanding and denounces him to the police and the doctor is brought to trial. During the trial, the friend pays a visit to a hospital where he sees a ward of small children, all incurably ill and suffering the greatest pain. After much deliberation, he begins to understand his friend and offers himself as main witness for the defence.

Key term

Eugenics

This is the attempt to control who has children in order to eliminate 'undesirables' from the population. Both men and women were sterilized in order to allow the rest to create a 'perfect' race.

■ Think about

▶ How does Dr Stech try to persuade people that sterilization is acceptable and desirable in Source 34?

Quotation

…none of our lives will be safe anymore. Some commission can put us on the list of the 'unproductive' who in their opinion have become worthless life.

Cardinal von Galen, 1941

Note

For the full text of Galen's speech, visit www.historyplace.com/speeches/galen.htm

Note

As many as 18 million Germans saw the film and the reaction was generally positive, although accompanied by demands for legal safeguards.

▶ A still from the 1941 film
Ich Klage An.

■ **Think about**

▶ How did the film distort the reality
of the Nazis' use of euthanasia?

Facts and figures

**Jews as a percentage of the
German population 1871–1933**

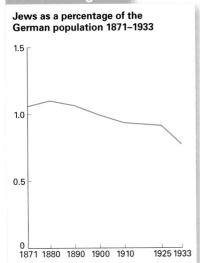

Facts and figures

Whilst representing less than 1 per
cent of the German population,
German Jews in 1933 formed 17 per
cent of all bankers, 10 per cent of all
doctors and dentists and 16 per cent
of all lawyers.

Dealing with the Jews

Anti-Semitism was not invented by the Nazis. The Jews had suffered prejudice
for over a thousand years, especially from the Middle Ages when they were
blamed for anything from food shortages to the plague. The Jews were
scattered across Europe and were therefore always a minority group. This made
them vulnerable to attack, made worse by certain cultural and religious
differences and by the fact that their wealth was often resented. In 1290 they
were expelled from England. Historians have commonly argued that anti-
Semitism increased in Germany during the nineteenth century, as in many parts
of Europe. In Germany, though, a new racial anti-Semitism emerged, based on
ideas of national and racial superiority. In other words, Jews were no longer
simply scapegoats, blamed for Germany's troubles. They were, instead,
opposed on the grounds that they were a *different race*, and an inferior one at
that.

One of the accusations made against Jews, especially during times of economic
hardship, was that they monopolized the cultural and economic life of
Germany. This was hardly a fair accusation, although it was true that their
representation in certain professions was not in proportion to their overall
numbers. Nevertheless, many Jews were also poor and the vast majority was
fully integrated into German culture. Only the 'Eastern Jews' (around 20 per
cent) who emigrated to Germany after the First World War continued to wear
traditional dress and live in certain quarters of the cities. However, the Jew
continued to provide a useful scapegoat – someone to blame for the defeat in
the war, the failure of the economy and the threat of Bolshevism. The
stereotype of Jews as depicted in Nazi propaganda bore no resemblance to the
reality.

The Nazis took anti-Semitism way beyond anything that had gone on before.
Hitler not only portrayed the Jew as the opposite of the Aryan German, but he
also characterized an attack on the Jews as part of a wider cosmic struggle
between the forces of good and evil. He was utterly obsessive in his hatred of
the Jews and there is no doubt that it coloured all his political aims. But it was
not obvious in 1933 exactly what form this attack would take. Certainly he
made it clear even before 1933 that the Jews would have no place in his Reich,
but no one could have foreseen how far he would pursue it.

Anti-Semitic policy

It was the rank and file of the Nazi Party, rather than Hitler, who demanded immediate action against the Jews. Local outbursts, led mainly by the SA, had to be contained during the first delicate months of power in 1933 and the one-day boycott of Jewish shops and professions was intended to serve this very function. The Law for the Restoration of the Professional Civil Service of 1933 excluded many Jews from public service, but until 1935 there were no further large-scale acts of hostility. In 1935, however, Hitler yielded to pressure from within the Party and approved the Nuremberg Laws.

EXTRACTS FROM THE NUREMBURG LAWS

The Reich Citizenship Law, September 1935
● A Citizen of the Reich is only that subject, who is of German or kindred blood and who, through his conduct, shows that he is both desirous and fit to serve faithfully the German people and Reich.

First Regulation to the Reich Citizenship Law, November 1935
● A Jew cannot be a citizen of the Reich. He has no right to vote in political affairs, he cannot occupy a public office.

Law for the Protection of German Blood and German Honour, September 1935
● Marriages between Jews and nationals of German or kindred blood are forbidden.
● Relations outside marriage between Jews and nationals of German or kindred blood are forbidden.
● Jews will not be permitted to employ female nationals of German or kindred blood in their household.
● Jews are forbidden to hoist the Reich and national flag and to present the colours of the Reich.

As you can see, the Nuremberg Laws placed restrictions on who Jews could marry or have sexual relations with. They also made citizenship of Germany conditional on producing a certificate confirming Aryan descent, thereby removing citizenship from all Jews. Although these laws came as a blow to the Jews of Germany, they at least seemed to suggest that the Jews would be allowed to remain in Germany, albeit on unequal terms. One Jewish woman recollected that her parents had welcomed the laws because 'they saw them as a guarantee...which would make it possible for them to remain in their homeland'. It is true that many Jews emigrated and were encouraged to do so by the Nazis; between 1933 and 1939, half of Germany's Jews emigrated, many to Palestine. But not all Jews wanted to leave their home, their family and their country, no matter what it was doing to them. Many clung to the belief that Hitler's days were numbered.

During 1936, outward manifestations of the anti-Semitic campaign were removed for the duration of the Berlin Olympics, but persecution continued, particularly at a local level, where Jews were often refused access to theatres or public swimming pools. The Nazis also tried to encourage an ongoing boycott of Jewish businesses and professionals, although success was mixed. One Gestapo report in 1935 claimed that 'The boycott measures have not had the intended effect. Segments of the population which condemn such measures on principle tend to pity the Jews...'. From 1937, there were signs that the anti-Semitic campaign was escalating. Jewish businesses found their contracts

Timeline

1933 – one-day boycott of Jewish shops and businesses
1935 – Nuremberg Laws
1936 – Berlin Olympics
1938 – Crystal Night (9–10 November) followed by the closure of all Jewish businesses and the removal of Jewish children from schools.
1939 – war begins

■ Think about

▶ Take each clause of the Laws (denoted by bullet points) in turn and discuss the *reasoning* behind it.

▶ What did the Nazis hope to gain from these Laws?

Quotation

Where do I belong? To the 'Jewish nation' decrees Hitler. And I feel...I am nothing but a German...

Viktor Klemperer, October 1935

Quotation

Yesterday, a characteristic scene...A young man, pale, rigid, mad in appearance, shouts without stopping at someone else whom I could not see: 'Whoever buys from the Jew, is a traitor to the nation!'...Everyone is disturbed, embarrassed, no one interferes.

Viktor Klemperer, September 1935

drying up, Jews were no longer allowed to be awarded degrees and in 1938, Jewish doctors, dentists and lawyers were forbidden to work for Aryans. All Jews had to carry an identification card and if their name did not obviously denote their Jewishness, they had to add 'Sara' or 'Israel' to it. By 1938, the Jews of Germany had effectively been squeezed out of public life. But worse was to come.

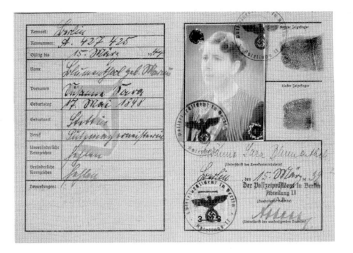

Source 36

▶ A 1939 identity card for a Jewish woman, Susanne 'Sara' Blumenthal.

Reich Kristallnacht (Crystal Night)

On 7 November 1938, a German diplomat was assassinated in Paris by a Jew, Herschel Grunspan. Goebbels seized the opportunity of 'working towards the Führer' by encouraging a group of Party members and SS leaders to lead a campaign of violence against the Jewish community. Hitler gave his consent and a night of terror followed.

Source 37

▶ The location of the main anti-Jewish attacks during Crystal Night.

Ninety-one Jews were murdered that night, 20,000 were sent to concentration camps, over 7,000 Jewish businesses were ruined and 177 synagogues were destroyed. This night of violence took its name from the amount of shattered glass which littered the streets. Further discrimination followed, including the removal of Jewish children from schools, the banning of all Jewish publications and the closure of all Jewish businesses. Jewish cultural and economic life was being extinguished in Germany and the occupied areas. But it was the outbreak of war in 1939 that prompted the beginning of genocide.

Document exercise: German reactions to Crystal Night

Source A

A Nazi Party report on Crystal Night

On the evening of 9 November 1938, Reich Propaganda Director and Party Member Dr Goebbels told the Party leaders assembled at a social evening in the old town hall in Munich that in the districts of Kurhessen and Magdeburg-Anhalt there had been anti-Jewish demonstrations, during which Jewish shops were demolished and synagogues were set on fire. The Führer, at Goebbels' suggestion, had decided that such demonstrations were not to be prepared or organised by the Party, but neither were they to be discouraged if they happened spontaneously... The instructions of Goebbels were probably understood by all Party leaders present to mean that the Party should not appear outwardly as the cause of the demonstrations but that in reality it should organise them and carry them out.

Source B

The reaction of a German girl

Next morning – I had slept well and heard no disturbance – I went into Berlin very early to go to the Reich Youth Leadership office...in order to get to the Lothringerstrasse I had to go down a rather gloomy alley containing many small shops and inns. To my surprise almost all the shop windows were smashed in. The pavement was covered with pieces of glass and fragments of broken furniture. I asked a policeman what on earth had been going on there. He replied: 'In this street they're almost all Jews.' 'Well?' 'You don't read the papers. Last night the National Soul boiled over.'...I went on my way shaking my head. For the space of a second I was clearly aware that something terrible had happened there. Something frighteningly brutal. But almost at once I switched over to accepting what had happened as over and done with...I said to myself: The Jews are the enemies of the New Germany. Last night they had a taste of what that means.

Melita Maschmann, *Account Rendered*

Source C

SOPADE (SPD in exile) report, November 1938

All reports confirm that the steps [taken against Jews] have been heavily criticised by the majority of Germans. During the first few days of the pogrom there were arrests of hundreds of Aryans throughout the Reich because they had publicly expressed their indignation. One can often hear people asking: 'Who will be next after the Jews?' One thing is clear, however, no matter how great the indignation may have been – the brutality of the pogrom has added to the intimidation of the public in general, and has strengthened the feeling that any resistance to the unrestricted National Socialists is useless.

Key term

Pogrom
An organized rampage of destruction and murder

Source D

Two contrasting reactions to Crystal Night

I was coming home late that evening when I saw several thugs beating a man until he collapsed. They dragged him onto the streetcar tracks and left him there. A policeman who happened to come by helped me carry him to the Elizabeth Hospital. He was an old man with white hair – a lawyer I think. On the way back I saw a woman with two small children, with coats over their nightclothes. They were in a state of terror. 'Why are they beating us?' the woman screamed. 'We haven't done anything!' I offered to take them home with me, but she wanted to return to her apartment to look for her husband.

When I described these incidents, my cousin Klaus-Gunter said, 'What are you making such a fuss about! These things are trivial. You have to perceive the larger historical context and accept the idea of political necessity! We annexed Austria and the Sudetenland, we picked up almost half a million more Jews – and they're nothing but parasites! One decisive stroke is preferable to a hundred-year struggle...'

Extract from an interview carried out in 1981

Note

National indignation = the anger of the German people

Source E

Decree issued by Goering on 12 November

All damage which was inflicted on Jewish businesses and dwellings on 9 and 10 November 1938 as a result of the national indignation about the rabble-rousing propaganda of international Jewry against National Socialist Germany must at once be repaired by the Jewish proprietors or Jewish traders.

■ Examination-style questions

1 Comprehension in context

Study Source A. Using the source and your own knowledge, explain the following extract:

'The Führer, at Goebbels' suggestion had decided that such demonstrations were not to be prepared or organized by the Party, but neither were they to be discouraged if they happened spontaneously.'

2 Comparing the sources

Study Sources B and C. To what extent do they offer us different accounts of the reactions to Crystal Night? Can you suggest any reasons why they do/do not differ?

3 Evaluating the sources

Source D provides us with two completely opposite reactions to Crystal Night. What is its value to historians studying the reaction of the German people to Crystal Night?

4 Making judgements

Using all the sources and your own knowledge, explain how accurate Goering was in describing the events of Crystal Night as a result of 'national indignation' (Source E).

Art in the Third Reich

Introduction

Despite his failure to train as an artist in Vienna, Hitler considered himself an expert on art and architecture and attempted to impose his views on the German people. He loathed modern art and instead favoured traditional, realistic art, which contrasted sharply with the creative experiments of the Weimar Republic. Hitler also saw art as a form of propaganda and with Goebbels' help, set out to promote art which contained acceptable images of the Nazi state. These included expressions of anti-Semitism, nationalism, promotion of war, the cult of Hitler, motherhood, the supremacy of the Aryan race, 'Blood and Soil', the power and legitimacy of the Nazi Party, the glorification of the Greek and Roman Empires and a rejection of Christian values. Artists who did not reproduce such images in their paintings were banned and several emigrated as a consequence. Their art was labelled 'degenerate' (immoral). One historian has recently argued, however, that despite the number of artists banned from working, including all Jews, there were many German artists who accepted their loss of independence because they benefited in other ways, for example with guaranteed prices fixed for their work.

Source 38

The artist does not create for the artist. He creates for the people, and we will see to it that the people in future will be called in to judge his art...Before the critics did justice to the genius of a Richard Wagner, he had the people on his side, whereas the people has had nothing to do with so-called 'modern art'...these achievements...might have been produced by untalented children of eight to ten years old [and] could never be considered an expression of our own times or of the German future.

Extract from Hitler's speech in 1937 at the opening of the House of German Art

Source 39

In early 1936 Hitler appointed a purge tribunal of four Nazi artists...to tour all the major galleries and museums of Germany for the purpose of removing all 'decadent' art...On March 31, 1936, these sequestered [confiscated] art works were exhibited in a special display of degenerate art in Munich. Huge crowds came to see the works rejected by Hitler. A concurrent exhibition nearby, the Greater Germany Art Exhibition, at which some 900 works approved by Hitler were shown, drew considerably less enthusiastic crowds.

Snyder, *Encyclopedia of the Third Reich*, 1998

Source 40

NEW YORK. An accord reached between the North Carolina Museum of Art and the family of an Austrian Jew whose possessions were looted during the Nazi era enables the museum to retain "Madonna and Child in a landscape" by Lucas Cranach the Elder, which the museum had returned to the family earlier this year.

The agreement between the museum and the Hainisch family in Vienna means that the painting now returns to Raleigh as a partial purchase by the museum and, according to the museum, a partial gift of the family. The museum will pay the family $600,000 for the work that has been estimated at $800,000 to $1.2 million.

[The picture] will now be part of a travelling exhibition on Nazi art pillaging.

The Art Newspaper, 9 June 2000

■ Think about

▶ What is Hitler arguing in Source 38?

▶ Look back at pages 108–109. Do you think Hitler's opinions would have found any support in Germany?

▶ What does Source 39 tell us about the artistic views of the German people?

▶ Read Source 40. What is meant by 'Nazi loot'?

▶ Why is this family selling their painting back to the museum at half price?

Source 41

■ Activity

Source 41 was painted in 1942 and demonstrates the kind of art approved by the Nazis.

1 Read the Introduction again. How many of the images that the Nazis wanted art to contain are in Source 41?

2 How and why is this painting so different from the painting by Otto Dix on page 92?

3 Of what use is this picture to the historian of the Third Reich?

The 'atomization' of society

Society certainly changed between 1933 and 1945. The experiences of women, children, workers, Christians, Jews, 'asocials' and many others were profoundly influenced by the Nazi regime. But what was the *collective* experience? How was society as a whole altered as a result of Nazi policies? The term *Volksgemeinschaft*, which should now be familiar to you, symbolized Hitler's aim to create a society based around common, nationalist goals. Society would no longer, in Hitler's vision, be composed of individuals or groups of individuals, each pursuing their own particular interests. Instead, people belonged to a much bigger group – the National or People's Community. This was a vision that was not without support; it appealed to those who wished to see the old order based on class differences replaced with a society that was based simply around 'German' values and in which opportunities were equal. This certainly helps to explain the attraction of Nazism to young people.

In reality, the vision of a 'community' working together for a common aim was restricted to Nazi propaganda. People in fact lived in much greater isolation than before. This was partly through fear and partly because the opportunities to take part in collective activities which were not organized and controlled by the Nazis were stopped. In Northeim, described in William Sheridan Allen's book *The Nazi Seizure of Power: The Experience of a Single German Town 1930–1935*, organizations were either taken over by the Nazis or banned. The chess club survived by adding the words 'National Socialist' to its name but clubs which existed for mainly social reasons were either closed down or taken over. In the words of Allen: 'This was partly because of the Nazi desire to keep people from coming together merely for social reasons where discussion prevailed…as one resident put it, 'There was no more social life; you couldn't even have a bowling club." The result was a more isolated way of life based on the individual, rather than on social groups which shared common interests. This was hardly the *Volksgemeinschaft* that Hitler had spoken about.

There were, of course, Nazi organizations to control leisure time, such as the KdF (Strength Through Joy), the purpose of which, according to a SOPADE report in 1935, was 'to make sure that they [the German people] are not left to their own devices and, as far as possible, to see that they do not come to their senses at all…the National Socialists are forever providing excesses of excitement with the express aim of preventing any real communal interests or any form of voluntary association from arising.' In other words, these organizations were to *prevent* the forming of more meaningful groups and did not prevent a more isolated day-to-day existence during the Third Reich. The KdF, for example, although welcomed by many workers as a diversion from everyday life, was not a substitute for the comradeship of the trade unions and other working-class groups which had existed before 1933.

How discontented were the German people, in that case? Although this is explored more fully in chapter 13, it is worth making one important point here. Although in many ways, this 'atomization' or disintegration of society had a negative impact on people's lives, there was still a strong feeling that at least they had jobs and therefore money in their pockets. According to a post war

■ **Activity**   **KEY SKILLS**

Your task is to research and present detailed information on an aspect of life during the Third Reich. You may, for example, wish to focus on women, youth, the master race or art. The outcome of your research will be a document which can be saved onto the school network (or Intranet) for others to consult. The audience of this document will be your peers and your teacher, who will assess it.

● Select the area you wish to research
● Ensure that you are familiar with the relevant material in this book
● Use further reading to expand your knowledge of the topic
● Plan how you are going to use IT
● Search for and select relevant information from the Internet/CD ROMs
● Download any useful information/sources/images and use a range of techniques for displaying the information, such as graphs and charts
● Using a format agreed by the class, write up all your findings from both your further reading and your Internet searches
● Your final document must include text, images and numerical data
● Save your work onto the school network/intranet/website so that others can access it
● Present the key findings of your research to others in the class

www.tau.ac.il/GermanHistory/links.html#TwentiethCentury

www.2.h-net.msu.edu~german/
www.historyplace.com/

survey in West Germany, memories of the positive aspects of the Third Reich included:

Source 42

The guaranteed pay packet, order, KdF and the smooth running of the political machinery…Thus 'National Socialism' makes them think merely of work, adequate nourishment, KdF and the absence of 'disarray' in political life.

Bessell (ed.), *Life in the Third Reich*, 1987

Of course, experiences differed widely, and this short extract is not intended to create the impression that *everyone* was happy living in the Nazi state. But it is a reminder that the experiences of the late Weimar years perhaps made some people more prepared to accept a life that we would now find intolerable. Here is one historian's conclusion about the impact of the Nazis on society:

Think about

▶ What is meant by 'breaking up… the jigsaw of society'?

▶ How did the Nazis destroy 'social bonds'?

▶ What impact does Peukert believe the Nazis had on individuals?

▶ Did the Nazis create a Volksgemeinschaft according to Peukert?

Source 43

…the Nazis, with their terror apparatus, did succeed in breaking up the complex jigsaw of society into its smallest component parts, and changing much of its traditional coherence almost beyond recognition. By the end of the Third Reich, and of the world war the Reich had staged, the vision of a 'national community' had dissolved. Instead, there lay a society in ruins – ruined not only in a material sense but psychologically, morally and in respect of its social bonds. If the Third Reich could boast any achievement, it was the destruction of public contexts [community] and responsibilities and the dislocation of social forms of life, even in traditional environments which provided some measure of refuge and scope for resistance. Private spheres of behaviour were impoverished and isolated, relapsing into self-serving individualism devoid of all potentially dangerous social connections and meanings. The Volksgemeinschaft that had been so noisily trumpeted and so harshly enforced became, in the end, an atomised society.

Peukert, *Inside Nazi Germany*, 1987

A Social Revolution?

A debate began in the 1960s about whether or not the Nazis revolutionized society. Historians such as Ralf Dahrendorf and David Schoenbaum argued that the Nazis modernized society, albeit unintentionally, by breaking down traditional loyalties and creating a classless society in which there was increased social mobility. More recently, however, historians have focused increasingly on the continuities between society before, during, and after the Third Reich. They have concluded that although society certainly underwent some change, this can hardly be described as 'revolutionary'. Even people's attitudes, it is now argued, did not change as much as it might at first have appeared. People were still concerned first and foremost with the comfort and security of their daily lives and much of the Nazi ideology put about in Goebbels' propaganda passed them by.

It is up to you to decide whether you think society underwent a 'revolution' or not and the following activity will help you to reach a conclusion. It may help you to skim through the section on Weimar society in Chapter 5. This will help you to make judgements about whether changes during the Third Reich would have happened regardless of the Nazis. You may even wish to read some more general accounts of society in *Europe* during this period which will help you to analyse whether the changes happening to Nazi society were unique or whether they mirrored what was going on elsewhere.

WERE THE NAZIS RESPONSIBLE FOR A SOCIAL REVOLUTION IN GERMANY?

Yes: Arguments that suggest the Nazis were responsible for a social revolution	Evidence to support this view
● Nazi society was 'classless' and there were equal opportunities for everyone	
● The old elites were no longer in control	
● The Nazis modernized society, even if unintentionally	
● People's views on race and eugenics were altered	
● Society underwent a fundamental change	
● Traditional loyalties and authorities were broken down	
● People were better off under the Nazis (see Chapter 11)	

NO: Arguments that suggest that the Nazis did not bring about social revolution	Evidence to support this view
● The Nazis were still dependent on elite groups	
● The concept of *Volksgemeinschaft* was merely propaganda	
● People still clung to their traditional loyalties	
● People did not accept racial and eugenic policies	
● Many of the changes followed on from the Weimar years and would probably have happened anyway	
● Many of the changes were happening elsewhere in Europe and would probably have happened anyway	
● Many of the changes were due to the war rather than Nazi policy (see Chapter 13)	
● There were no more opportunities than before and most people were no better off than before (See Chapter 11)	

■ **Activity**

To help you reach your own conclusion to the question, consider each of the arguments listed on this page.

1 Draw two tables, each with two columns. In the first column list each argument, and in the second write down any examples or evidence you can find that would appear to support the claim. In most cases you can find the information in this chapter, but some points include specific references to other chapters.

2 When you have completed the tables as fully as you can, you need to weigh one against the other and think carefully about what is meant by 'revolution'.

Note

If you did the activity on page 107, you have already done half the work for this!

■ Activity

'Was German society more united in the Third Reich than it was in the Weimar Republic?'

This is a very difficult question and the following activity provides a possible approach to answering it.

1 Get into four groups or pairs. You will need two sheets of paper, laid out as below.

The Weimar Republic		The Third Reich	
How life changed	Was society united?	How life changed	Was society united?

2 Each group should choose one of the following topics:

  Youth

  Women

  Jews

  Culture

3 Using this chapter and Chapter 5 (see pages 106–110), complete the tables for your topic.

4 Share and discuss the information as a whole group and then reach your conclusion

■ Activity

Now try the following examination-style question:

  Life in Nazi Germany underwent many changes, especially for the following groups of people:

  a. Women   b. Youth   c. Jews   d. Workers

(a) Choose any two of these groups and explain **how** their lives were changed by Nazi policies.

(b) Would you agree that the Nazis totally transformed German society? You must refer to at least three of the groups above in your answer.

Conclusions

The Nazis certainly tried to transform society. They set out to change the way people behaved and thought. Their policies affected the most private spheres and denied many people basic freedoms such as the right to have children, the right to speak one's mind and even the right to live. However, the degree to which the Nazis were successful is difficult to assess. Certainly life changed, but in some areas at least, the Nazis were unable to assert as much control over the people as they would have liked. Some opposition remained, whether open or secretive, and in some areas such as religion, the Nazis were afraid to risk widespread opposition by closing down the Churches altogether. In other areas, such as their policies towards women, what they did and what they said did not always match up. In the end, Hitler's foreign aims came first and social policy was designed to serve these goals.

Despite all this, it would be wrong to deny that the Nazis changed society profoundly. To do so would be to trivialize the thousands who lost their lives because they did not 'fit in'. Hitler may have been building on what had gone before, but he took these ideas to unthinkable and terrible lengths.

Chapter 11

The Nazi economy

▲ Artillery production at the Krupp steelworks in Essen.

▲ Men of the Nazi Labour Service.

▲ Hitler opening a new autobahn in 1935

Introduction

The German economy was just, but only just, beginning to recover from the Wall Street Crash and subsequent depression when Hitler became Chancellor in January 1933. It is estimated that by 1932, 40 per cent of the working population was unemployed. The official unemployment figures were to approach 6 million, though the reality was probably nearer to 8 million. Foreign trade had halved and industrial production had fallen by 40 per cent during the slump. Indeed, by 1932, industry was producing little more than it had done in the 1890s. Hitler staked a great deal of his reputation on solving this economic nightmare. He promised to 'save' the German farmer and the German worker and his popularity rested on this promise.

Key questions

- Did the Nazis solve the economic problems they inherited?
- Did they create a strong economy?
- Did they create new problems?
- To what extent did they create a successful war economy?
- Were people better off under the Nazis?
- Were the Nazis economically prepared for war in 1939?

Nazi economic policy

The Nazis had no great economic strategy up their sleeves in 1933. There was some pressure for Hitler to implement the more socialist-inspired elements of the Twenty-Five Points of 1920, but Hitler resisted such a move as he realized that he would need the support of private enterprise, and especially big business, to achieve his expansionist aims. So Hitler looked to the experts for guidance. Broadly speaking this advice fell into two categories:

A. 'Unorthodox economics'

Hitler was advised to:

- risk *deficit financing* by pumping government money into schemes which would provide employment. In the long run this would help the economy because more employment meant more people with money in their pockets to spend on goods and services.

- develop autarky (self-sufficiency) as far as possible, so that Germany would not have to import as many goods from other countries. This would obviously be useful in a state of war, but was also attractive in the 1930s when the world-wide slump was encouraging greater protectionism in other countries.

- create a trading zone in which Germany could arrange special deals with other countries over those goods which Germany could not produce itself.

B. Wehrwirtschaft (defence economy)

Hitler was advised to:

- base the economy, even in peacetime, around the needs of war. Only by doing this would Germany avoid a repeat of 1914–1918, when the economy proved unfit to sustain a lengthy war.

Key term

Deficit financing
Government borrowing in order to finance the gap between spending and income and to fund schemes that increase employment to boost the economy.

Key term

Protectionism
When countries raise the duties on imports to encourage people to buy home-produced products.

1933–1936: Economic recovery

In March 1933, Dr Hjalmar Schacht was appointed President of the Reichsbank, a post he had held before, in the 1920s. His appointment was a relief to the business community as it signalled a wish by the Nazis to work with big business and not against it. A year later, Schacht became Minister of Economics, thereby exerting an extremely powerful grip on economic policy.

Tackling unemployment

Policies were quickly implemented to tackle unemployment. Over 1 billion Reichmarks were ploughed into public works schemes such as the building of roads, canals and public buildings. Not only did such schemes provide employment, they also provided perfect propaganda opportunities to demonstrate how the Nazis were improving life in Germany.

In 1935, labour service (RAD) was introduced, making it compulsory for all men between the ages of 19 and 25 to work in areas such as farming or public work schemes for 6 months. Together with the introduction of conscription in the same year, these early policies led to a dramatic fall in unemployment. Even if one takes into account a certain massaging of the figures by the Nazis (for example, part-time workers were classed as full-time) this was a significant achievement.

Trade and government controls

In 1934 there was a balance of payments deficit. This means that Germany was importing more than she was exporting, leading to a shortage of foreign exchange with which to buy more imports. This was a situation which was to haunt Schacht up to his resignation in 1937 and its causes are summarized below:

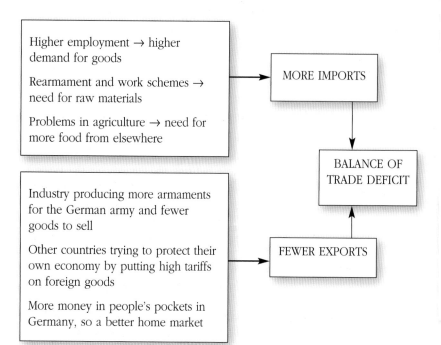

Higher employment → higher demand for goods

Rearmament and work schemes → need for raw materials

Problems in agriculture → need for more food from elsewhere

MORE IMPORTS

BALANCE OF TRADE DEFICIT

Industry producing more armaments for the German army and fewer goods to sell

Other countries trying to protect their own economy by putting high tariffs on foreign goods

More money in people's pockets in Germany, so a better home market

FEWER EXPORTS

Schacht, as part of the 'New Plan' of September 1934, tried to solve the problem by exercising tight government controls over what could and could not be imported. Only vital foodstuffs and materials required by heavy industry,

Facts and figures

Unemployment

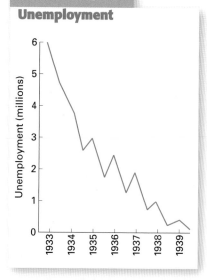

■ Think about

Study the unemployment figures above carefully.

▶ What impact did the Nazis have on the unemployment figures as far as you can tell?

▶ Read the section 'Tackling unemployment' again. Do you think the Nazis were adopting sensible strategies to tackle this problem?

■ Think about

Study the flow diagram carefully.

▶ What was at the root of the problem, do you think?

▶ How might this problem have been solved?

■ Think about

Look back at the two main influences on Hitler's economic thinking on page 215.

▶ Which advice had Hitler taken so far?

Key term

'Blood and Soil' (Blut und Boden)

This Nazi slogan reflected the anti-city and anti-modern ideas of the Party. Aryan farmers were seen as the most racially pure and honest of all Germans, hence the combination of blood and soil.

largely for rearmament, were allowed to be imported in bulk. Non-essential goods such as raw cotton and wool were imported in much smaller quantities than before. In addition, trade agreements were made, particularly with the Balkan states, whereby the money gained from selling raw materials to Germany had to be spent buying back German goods. Schacht succeeded in creating a trade surplus in 1935, but he had hardly tackled the root of the problem.

Agriculture

Farmers had been suffering for longer than most and it was no coincidence that the rural farming population formed the core of Nazi support between 1930 and 1933. The Nazis held the peasant in high regard as a model of racial purity as embodied in their slogan 'blood and soil'. Hitler promised to return prosperity to the farming community, but, as ever, Nazi policy was fraught with contradictions. The strict control of food prices by the Nazis (to avoid inflation which could damage the rearmament programme) hardly brought the farmers greater prosperity. Added to this were the policies followed by the idealistic Minister of Agriculture and Food, Walter Darre, who was a keen proponent of the 'blood and soil' ideology.

Darre set up the Reich Food Estate, with himself in charge, to control all aspects of food production. The result was a lack of freedom which even today's farmers would find intolerable. In September 1933, the Reich Entailed Farm Law placed further restrictions on farmers by making it impossible to sell or divide up any farm of between 7.5 and 10 hectares, which accounted for about 35 per cent of all farms. The purpose was to give peasants security in their jobs, but the result was to hinder modern development on those farms that were not big enough to compete with the larger operations. The inability to divide a farm between more than one son also accelerated the drift to the towns where the attraction of higher wages was already proving irresistible to many. The outcome was a shortage of rural labour.

The situation by 1936

In 1936, there was the threat of another trading deficit and by the summer, munitions factories were only producing 70 per cent as much as they were able to because of a shortage of raw materials. The time had come for Hitler to make a decision about his priorities.

Note

The economic options available in 1936

- Reduce armaments production and instead produce more goods to sell as exports.
- Introduce strict food rationing so that food imports can be cut.
- Become more self-sufficient in raw materials so that arms production can continue to increase and food rationing is avoided.

■ Activity

In the margin box is a list of the economic options available in 1936. Get into small groups and each assume the role of one of the people below. Imagine you are discussing, in 1936, what economic policy the Nazis should now take. What do you agree/disagree about? What decision do you finally take?

- Schacht, whose priority is to keep a balance of trade
- Goebbels, the propaganda chief, whose priority is to keep the German people as happy as possible
- A representative of export industries whose priority is to make profits
- A representative of industries heavily involved in rearmament whose priority is to make profit
- Darre, whose priority is to ensure high levels of food supplies from German farmers
- Hitler, whose priority is foreign expansion

A new direction

Schacht believed that continued rearmament would undermine the whole economy by restricting the production of goods for export and increasing the demand for imported raw materials. This would force Germany into a deeper trade deficit crisis. He was aware that his New Plan was only disguising a deeper problem. He wanted to see exports increase at the expense of arms manufacture, and imports of food decrease through food rationing. However, these were not the words that Hitler wanted to hear. Senior Nazis were hostile to food rationing on the grounds that it would lower public morale. But perhaps more importantly, the reduction of arms manufacture would undermine the whole thrust of Nazi expansionist policy.

It seemed to be a question of guns or butter, neither of which the Nazis wanted to sacrifice. However, there was an alternative route. Experiments with synthetic substitutes for materials such as rubber and fuel had been going on for a number of years and, together with ambitious targets for the production of all armament-related materials, they could provide Hitler with the solution he wanted. This way, the army would still get its guns and the German people would still have their butter. This solution lay at the heart of the Four Year Plan.

Hitler provided a comprehensive statement of his aims in a memo in August 1936. In it, he wrote of the 'historical life struggle of nations' and specifically emphasized the Bolshevik threat which could destroy the German people. Germany, he claimed, was the 'focal point' of Europe's fight against this threat, a fact that he did not welcome but which was nevertheless Germany's 'destiny'. Thus, he succeeded in making Germany's position seem primarily a defensive one. He then elaborated on the necessary means of strengthening Germany's defensive capacity:

Source 4

Hurrah, die Butter ist alle!

This photomontage by Heartfield is suggesting that the German people are being denied butter. In fact, the Nazis were anxious not to restrict foodstuffs and food was only rationed with the outbreak of war.

Source 5

We are overpopulated and cannot feed ourselves from our own resources. The solution ultimately lies in extending the living space of our people, that is, in extending the sources of its raw materials and foodstuffs...Temporary improvement can be brought about only within the framework of our present economy...The increase of our own exports is theoretically possible, but unrealistic in practical terms...it is essential [therefore] to ensure peacetime food supplies and, above all else, the means for the conduct of war; these things can be assured through human energy and activity...[Hitler goes on to identify specific areas in which to achieve self sufficiency such as rubber and fuel] Summarized briefly: I consider it necessary that from now on with iron determination we attain 100% self-sufficiency in all these areas so that we will not be dependent on foreign countries for these most important raw materials, and that thereby we will also be able to save the foreign currency we require during peacetime in order to import our foodstuffs... I therefore set the following tasks: 1. The German army must be operational within four years, and 2. The German economy must be fit for war within four years.

■ Think about

▶ What does Source 5 suggest about Hitler's priorities in 1936?

▶ Why did Hitler believe an increase in exports to be 'unrealistic'?

▶ Read the first sentence again. Using the information from this chapter, how far was this statement true?

▶ A.J.P. Taylor argued that Hitler had a masterplan, a 'blueprint' for his foreign policy. Is this piece of evidence conclusive proof that Hitler was in complete control of events and their timing?

By putting Goering in charge of the Four Year Plan, which was launched in October 1936 at the Nuremberg Rally, Hitler brought the economy under the control of the Nazi Party. As you can see from the memo, Goering was left in no doubt as the nature of his job: to make Germany economically and militarily ready for war in four years. All efforts were henceforth directed towards the creation of a full-scale war economy.

The Four Year Plan

Goering's Four Year Plan was a prime example of a Supreme Reich Authority (see pages 170–171). Its six departments clearly overlapped with several Reich ministries and Schacht found that his decisions as Minister of Economics were overruled by Goering, whose regular contact with the Führer put him in a privileged position. In November 1937, Schacht resigned and was replaced by a weaker man, Walther Funk. Goering assumed the position of economic dictator, but his rash, egocentric temperament was ill-matched to the task. Internal rivalries and bureaucratic inefficiency characterized the Plan and it failed to achieve almost all of its planned targets.

The main priorities of the Four Year Plan were:
● To achieve self-sufficiency in raw materials, especially rubber, oil and metals
● To retrain certain sectors of the labour force
● To regulate imports and exports closely
● To increase agricultural production.

The ultimate goal of self-sufficiency in key areas was not achieved. Output of oil substitutes, rubber, aluminium and iron ore fell short of the planned targets by 1938, and the situation was only partially improved by 1942 (see Source B on p.224). In agricultural production, it was a similar story. However, there was a considerable expansion of industry and important new techniques were developed in the field of synthetic substitutes, especially leather, plastics, silk and rubber. There can be no question that the economy became entirely geared towards the needs of war. Between 1936 and 1939, two-thirds of industrial investment went into war-related sectors, and by 1939, 40–50 per cent of all employees were involved in war-related projects.

■ Think about

▶ When conscription was introduced in 1935, the other major powers did little to stop it, even though it broke the Treaty of Versailles. Why do you think this was the case?

▶ Do you think that this expansion of armaments helped or hindered economic development? Think of short- and long-term development.

 Tanks, sailors and motorised infantry on parade at Nuremberg in 1937.

Source 6

Was there an economic crisis by the late 1930s?

■ Historical debate

Historians have disagreed in their explanations of the *timing* of the Second World War and this is closely related to whether or not they believe that Germany was experiencing an economic crisis by the late 1930s. Historians from the 'structuralist' school, such as Tim Mason, argue that Hitler was forced into a war in 1939 in order to gain more resources from the conquered lands and divert attention away from Germany's domestic problems. They have pointed to the labour shortage as an example, where the decision to expand and thereby gain more foreign workers was preferable to the employment of women or the compulsory civil conscription of workers which would prove unpopular. Other symptoms of the crisis included a falling trade balance and the potential collapse of trade agreements with Eastern Europe. The only escape for Hitler, according to this interpretation, was to fight a short war in which maximum gains were achieved for minimum effort. Obviously, in the context of an economic crisis, Hitler did not want a prolonged war. This therefore explains *Blitzkrieg* or lightning war, where opponents were simply overwhelmed by the might of the German forces. Poland fell within a month in 1939; Norway, the Low Countries and France were all defeated by the spring of 1940.

There is, however, an alternative interpretation which credits Hitler with much more advanced planning. In particular, Richard Overy has argued that Hitler was not simply reacting to a domestic crisis in 1939. On the contrary, he didn't expect there to be a war at all in September 1939 and gravely underestimated the reaction of Britain and France to his invasion of Poland. Overy suggests that the economy, although under a great deal of strain, was not in a state of crisis. It certainly was not facing the problems normally associated with economic crisis, namely growing unemployment and a fall in prices and profits. If there was not an economic crisis, then Hitler was not forced into a war to solve it or distract attention away from it. The fact that Hitler was not even planning war in 1939 is further proof of this, according to Overy.

Cross reference

See page 171 for a summary of the 'Structuralist' school of thought.

Cross reference

See pages 237–239 for more information on whether Hitler planned the outbreak of war in 1939 or not.

Quotation

Overy writes: 'If Hitler did not expect a major war in 1939, it can hardly be argued that he deliberately provoked one to avoid domestic crisis.'

Were people better off under the Nazis?

Mittelstand

The *Mittelstand* expected to benefit from the Nazi regime which was why they had supported Hitler in such large numbers in the years leading up to 1933. An early piece of legislation, the Law for the Protection of the Retail Trade, seemed to fulfil these expectations by forbidding the extension of department stores and thereby protecting the small shopkeeper. However, in reality, the *Mittelstand* was readily sacrificed by the Nazis when its interests conflicted with other, more urgent priorities. In July 1933, over 14 million Reichmarks were invested in a chain of Jewish-owned department stores to avoid their closure and subsequent job losses. Thereafter, the needs of big business began to take precedence over the needs of the *Mittelstand*.

Farmers

In October 1933, Hitler declared that the farmer was vital to the future of the nation and promised 'with all means and under any circumstances, to support this group on whose existence the continuation or destruction of our people depends.' However, as we have already seen, Nazi agricultural policy was not a success. Smaller farm owners were tied to their land, there was a shortage of rural labour, government controls on production were excessive and price restrictions prevented farmers from buying better machinery or paying more competitive wages. A Gestapo report of 1936 claimed that 'the farmer surfaces as the one member of society who is least enamoured of National Socialism'. However, many farmers probably had mixed feelings. They still saw Nazism as preferable to the threat of Bolshevism and some were no doubt flattered by their supposed importance in Nazi ideology.

Workers

It was clear that a war economy would require certain sacrifices by the people. Certain foodstuffs would be in shorter supply, wages were unlikely to increase much and working hours were likely to be longer. Of course, not all workers were affected in the same ways. Wages varied depending on the sector you worked in. But it was true that living standards in general did not rise after 1936. The Nazis used a number of ways of trying to secure the support of the workers during such times. The KdF – 'Strength Through Joy' – was one such example. This organization was an offshoot of the German Labour Front and was set up in 1933 to provide greater leisure opportunities for German workers who normally would not have been able to afford them. Activities included art exhibitions, theatre trips, hikes and even special holiday cruises. Members were offered the chance to pay in instalments for the Volkswagen ('People's car'). The instalments paid were in fact used for rearmament and the onset of war meant that few of the cars were actually produced, but a SOPADE report of 1939 claimed that it had nevertheless met considerable success as a propaganda programme:

Source 7

Kraft durch Freude

Auch Du kannst jetzt reisen!

▲ A Strength through Joy poster from 1938 advertising the new KdF travel pass.

Source 8

'For a great many Germans the announcement of a people's car was a very great and pleasant surprise. A veritable KdF-Wagen psychosis developed. For a long time the KdF-Wagen was the main topic of conversations among all classes of people in Germany. All other pressing problems – both domestic and in foreign policy – were for a time pushed into the background.'

There was also a 'Beauty of Labour' campaign carried out by the KdF which created better working conditions in factories, including 'Good Illumination – Good Light'.

Were workers better off in the Third Reich?

Source 9

The activities of the KdF in 1938

Activity	How many took part
Concerts	2,515,598
Popular entertainments	13,666,015
Theatre	7,478,633
Films	857,402
Exhibitions	1,595,516
Guided tours	58,472
Others	11,118,636

Noakes and Pridham, *Nazism 1919-1945 Vol. II*, 1984

Source 10

The impact of Nazi measures to reduce unemployment in the town of Thalburg, 1933

At the end of January, 1933, Thalburg had 653 registered unemployed…in July, the great campaign began. Some 450 persons were put to work on a great variety of jobs. Roads were repaired, the town's forests were worked over, and the old moat around Thalburg was drained and converted into a ring of swan ponds and parks…By July 24, Kurt Aergeyx was able to call a press conference and make public the news that all unemployed persons previously on the welfare rolls were at work…This was astounding news…some insisted that they be given work suited to their ability and experience, but the Nazi alternative was work on the works projects or no more dole…Nevertheless, many workers were pleased to be gainfully employed again, and Thalburg's middle class was enormously impressed by the Nazi success in this level.

Allen, *The Nazi Seizure of Power*, 1966

Source 11

5 Mark die Woche musst Du sparen – willst Du im eignen Wagen fahren!

KdF-Wagen: Über Anschaffungspreis und Zahlungsweise erteilen Auskunft alle Betriebswarte und Dienststellen der NS-Gemeinschaft „Kraft durch Freude" Gau München-Oberbayern

Source 12

A meeting of the Reich Chamber of Labour, 1938

The Deputy Führer [Hess] began by making the point that he was aware that some employees still hold against us the fact that, whereas we are always talking about the increase in production and the growth in the national product, our wages have not been correspondingly increased, so that in reality the employees are not sharing the fruits of this increase in production: 'I can only reply to them that the swimming pool in his plant, the canteens, the improvements in working conditions…all these things are the result of the increase in production…'

◀ A 1936 poster encouraging people to save five marks a week for a new Volkswagen

Source 13

Average weekly earnings (1936=100)

Year	Actual wages	Real wages (taking inflation into account)
1913/14	76.0	94.6
1925	93.4	83.2
1926	97.1	85.1
1927	109.6	92.3
1928	124.5	102.2
1929	128.2	103.6
1930	118.1	99.2
1931	103.9	95.1
1932	85.8	88.5
1933	87.7	92.5
1934	94.1	96.7
1935	96.4	97.6
1936	100.0	100.0
1937	103.5	103.0
1938	108.5	107.5
1939	112.6	111.1
1940	116.0	111.0

Source 14

Average working hours & cost of living

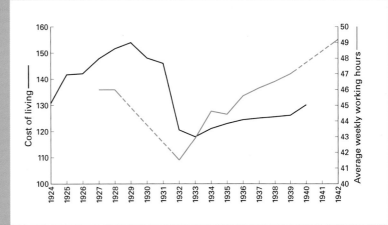

Source 15

Unemployment

1932	29.9%
1935	10.3%
1939	0.5%

■ **Activity**

A Sorting through the evidence

● Get into small groups or pairs. Discuss the question at the top of this section, 'were workers better off in the Third Reich?' What might we mean by 'better off'? What should we be comparing life in the Third Reich to?

● Now sort through the evidence. The easiest way to do this is to divide your page in half with 'Workers were better off' at the top of one half and 'Workers were not better off' at the top of the other. Now summarize the evidence for each point of view (you might find you need another column!).

● Compare your finished chart with others in your group. Should any of the information be discounted on grounds of unreliability? Is there any evidence that you are unsure about?

● Is there anything you can add to your chart from your own knowledge? In addition to this chapter you might like to revisit the information on women on pages 186–190

B Presenting your case

There are lots of ways to do this:

● In your small group, reach a decision about the answer to the 'Big Question' at the top of this spotlight. Summarize your arguments on a sheet of sugar paper to present to the rest of the class. It will be interesting to see how the groups' conclusions differ! **OR**

● Prepare for a class debate, with one half of the class arguing that workers *were* better off in the Third Reich and the other half arguing that they *weren't*. Appoint a person or group of people to judge which side argues most convincingly. **OR**

● Prepare two pieces of propaganda on 'The German Workers and the Nazis'. One produced by the DAF German Labour Front, run by the Nazis, and one produced by the Communist Party in exile. Imagine that both pieces were produced in 1938.

Big business

Big business was the main beneficiary of Nazi economic policy, though some areas benefited more than others. Heavy industry such as coal-mining and steel manufacture benefited hugely from rearmament, and chemical firms such as I.G. Farben prospered after 1936 due to their role in developing synthetic substitutes. Other industries which were more export-oriented did less well in the 1930s. Overall, however, big business saw an increase in undistributed profits from 1.3 billion Reichmarks in 1928 to 5 billion Reichmarks in 1939. And whilst hampered by government controls over production, trade, wages and prices, business was left in the private sector and not taken over by the state. This explains the readiness of industrial leaders such as Thyssen to continue their backing of Hitler even when they disagreed over the route he was taking in economic policy.

Document exercise: How successful was the Nazi economy?

■ **Biography**

Fritz Thyssen

Fritz Thyssen was an extremely rich and powerful industrialist with strong nationalist views. He vigorously opposed the French occupation of the Ruhr in 1923 and became one of the largest benefactors of the Nazi Party, donating over 1 million marks. In 1933 he was elected to the Reichstag and was appointed Prussian State Governor by Goering. However, by 1935 he was beginning to have doubts about the Nazi regime and fled the country in 1939 after making his views public.

Source A

A report by an SPD analyst, 1938

It is true that as long as the German people are prepared to put up with their living standards being held at the lowest of crisis levels, the mechanism by which 12–13 billion Reichmarks are squeezed from the national income for rearmament will keep on functioning. But even then one cannot do everything at once with these billions. One cannot at the same time use them to increase armaments for the land and air forces endlessly, to build up a massive fleet, to build gigantic installations for the production of synthetic substitutes, to construct megalomaniacal buildings and to tear down large parts of cities in order to build them somewhere else. On the basis of the living standards of the German people hitherto, one can either do one or the other or a bit of everything, but not everything at the same time and on an unlimited scale.

Source B

The Four Year Plan

Commodity	1936 output	1938 output	1942 output	Plan target
Mineral oil*	1,790	2,340	6,260	13,830
Aluminium	98	166	260	273
Buna rubber	0.7	5	96	120
Nitrogen	770	914	930	1,040
Explosives	18	45	300	223
Powder	20	26	150	217
Steel	19,216	22,656	20,480	24,000
Iron ore	2,255	3,360	4,137	5,549
Brown coal	161,382	194,985	245,918	240,500
Hard coal	158,400	186,186	166,059	213,000

* Including synthetic petrol · (in thousands of tons)

Source C

Unemployment figures

YEAR	unemployed (000s)	%
1930	3,076	14.0
1931	4,520	21.9
1932	5,603	29.9
1933	4,804	25.9
1934	2,718	13.5
1935	2,151	10.3
1936	1,593	7.4
1937	912	4.1
1938	429	1.9
1939	119	0.5
1940	52	0.2

Source D

Hitler's Four Year Plan memorandum, 1936

I consider it necessary that from now on with iron determination we attain 100 percent self-sufficiency in all these areas [such as steel and coal] so that we will not be dependent on foreign countries for these most important raw materials, and that thereby we will also be able to save the foreign currency we require during peacetime in order to import our foodstuffs.

Source E

A historian's view of the Four Year Plan

The success of the Plan was mixed. On the one hand it fell a long way short of the targets in the vital commodities of rubber and oil, whilst arms production never reached the levels desired by the armed forces and Hitler. On the other hand, production of a number of key materials, such as aluminium and explosives, had expanded greatly and in others it had grown at a respectable rate. All in all Germany's reliance on imports had not been exacerbated further, despite the economic growth.

Layton, *Germany The Third Reich*, 1992

■ Examination-style questions

1 **Comprehension in context**
   Study Source D. Using the source and your own knowledge, explain why Hitler was so keen to develop greater self-sufficiency in Germany.

2 **Comparing the sources**
   Study Sources A and E. To what extent and why do they differ in their views on the Nazi economy?

3 **Assessing the sources**
   How useful are statistics such as Sources B and C to a historian studying the Nazi economy?

4 **Making judgements**
   Using all the sources and your own knowledge, explain whether you think the Nazi economy was successful or not.

Conclusions

Until 1936, economic policy was dominated by attempts to reduce unemployment and maintain a favourable trade balance. Rearmament began in earnest in 1934, but did not initially dominate the economy as much as it was to do after 1936.

After 1936 the economy was dominated by rearmament and the need to prepare for war. The Four Year Plan was a central part of this.

Overall, the success of the Nazi economy was mixed. Unemployment was reduced significantly and industrial production increased. But the Four Year Plan targets were not met and the German people did not, on the whole, find themselves better off by the end of the 1930s, though some groups benefited more than others.

There has been debate, particularly between the historians Richard Overy and the late Tim Mason, over whether the German economy was in crisis or not by the end of the 1930s. It was certainly the case that Germany was not fully prepared for war by 1939. Food rationing, for example, was introduced immediately in September 1939 (rations were not introduced in Britain until 1941). It is far from clear, however, that the Nazis wanted or indeed planned a war in 1939 in order to avoid a worse economic situation. A contrasting argument suggests that war was *not* planned for 1939 and came as an unexpected shock.

■ Further reading

Overy, *The Nazi Economic Recovery*, 1996.

Chapter 12

Nazi foreign policy

▲ Austrians celebrate the Anschluss with Germany.

▲ Czechs watch the arrival of the German army in their country.

Introduction

Hitler's foreign policy lay at the very heart of his ambitions. It was central to his vision of Germany as a world power, perhaps even *the* world power, and to his vision of racial superiority. For Hitler, strength and power were the result of continued struggle and the survival of the fittest. Convinced of the destiny of the Aryan people to become the world's master race and to destroy the evil represented by sub-humans, he never doubted that a successful foreign policy would lead to war. Historians may disagree about the precise nature of Hitler's plans and the extent to which he was able to carry them out as he wished, but none would dispute the fact that Hitler expected and was planning for war from an early stage.

Think about

▶ Why do you think the German troops in Source 1 are being cheered by the Austrian people?

▶ To what extent and why is the reaction of the people in Source 2 different?

Key questions

● What were Hitler's foreign policy aims? Did they remain consistent?
● Did Hitler have a fixed plan or did he react to circumstance?
● Was Hitler planning for a total war?
● Was Hitler limited in his actions by other states or by Germany's economy?
● What was Germany's role in the outbreak of war?
● Did Hitler expect war to break out in September 1939?

The international scene in 1933

Hitler was fortunate in becoming Chancellor at a time when revision of the Treaty of Versailles had already begun. In 1929–1930, Britain and France withdrew all remaining troops from the Rhineland and, in 1932, reparations repayments were effectively written off at the Lausanne Conference. Indeed, the global situation in 1933 worked to Hitler's advantage in a number of ways. The United States, whose entry into the First World War had proved disastrous for Germany, had withdrawn politically from Europe. Her isolation was heightened by the world depression following the Wall Street Crash. Russia was still recovering from the First World War and subsequent internal upheavals and posed no immediate threat to anyone. In Central and Eastern Europe, the peace settlement following the First World War had created a number of small, ill-defended new states who, despite the creation of defensive alliances, remained largely at the mercy of the major powers. In the Far East, Japanese expansion into Manchuria had exposed the weaknesses of the League of Nations and was of particular concern to Britain. Finally, in Italy, the expansionist ambitions of Mussolini held out the possibility of an alliance with Germany.

That was not to say, however, that Hitler had a totally free hand to pursue his ambitions. Alarmed by the aggressive tone of Nazi propaganda before 1933, many European states sought reassurance that Germany posed no threat. Hitler was careful to stress his desire for peace in a speech in May 1933:

Source 3

I desire to declare in the name of the National Government...that we in Germany are filled with deep understanding for the rightful claims to life of the other nations...The French, the Poles etc. are our neighbours, and we know that through no possible development of history can this reality be altered.

Europe in 1933

Great Britain

Britain's main aims in 1933 were to protect her own empire and maintain a balance of power in Europe (which included restraining France if necessary). A greater Germany would threaten the balance of power and Britain was concerned by the Nazis' aggressive talk before 1933. Britain wanted to avoid another war at all costs – she was busy enough attending to her ailing Empire. She supported moves towards a revision of the Treaty of Versailles and was more prepared than France to accept German demands regarding disarmament.

France

France's main aim – as it had been throughout the 1920s – was security from German attack. Dissatisfied with the Treaty of Versailles, she concluded a series of treaties between 1921 and 1927 with the new Eastern European states, designed to provide assistance in the event of an attack from Germany or Russia. The failure of the Ruhr invasion strengthened a move towards a defensive policy and a greater dependence on British support. Forced to accept the evacuation of troops from the Rhineland in 1930, France nevertheless stood firm on the question of disarmament.

Russia

Stalin's main aim in 1933 was to maintain good relations with Germany. Following the Treaty of Rapallo in 1922 [see page 99], the Berlin Treaty was concluded between Germany and Russia in 1926. This treaty promised neutrality in any conflict and reaffirmed the agreements at Rapallo. It was renewed in 1931. Stalin discouraged communist action against Hitler, largely by preventing a communist alliance with the SPD. He did not believe the Nazi regime would last long. Meanwhile, relations between Russia and the rest of Western Europe were not particularly good, largely because of the mutual mistrust between communist and capitalist states.

Italy

In 1922 Mussolini became leader of Italy and established a fascist dictatorship. His aims were: to revise the peace terms of 1919 in order to gain greater spoils for Italy; to construct a defence against possible threats from Germany or France and to pursue colonial expansion. Treaties with Yugoslavia, Albania, Hungary and Austria were concluded between 1924 and 1930. Although Mussolini welcomed the appointment of Hitler in 1933, he was keen to avoid a Nazi take-over of Austria, largely for strategic reasons, and supported the Austrian leader Dollfuss.

Austria

In the peace settlement following the First World War, the Austro-Hungarian Empire was dismantled. Austria became a single state and was significantly weakened. Consequently, she became more dependent on Germany. Most Austrians were hopeful of a union with Germany (*Anschluss*) even though it was forbidden in the Treaty of Versailles. It made sense both from an economic and ethnic point of view. Thus, attempts were made not to offend Germany in any way. Austria was isolated during the 1920s, but in the early 1930s friendships developed with Italy and Hungary.

Czechoslovakia and Poland

Czechoslovakia signed treaties with France and Italy in 1924. She also constructed what became known as the 'Little Entente' with Yugoslavia and Romania in an attempt to build security amongst the newly formed states which emerged from the peace settlement, herself included. The largest minority group in the country were German speakers living in the Sudetenland. Poland was also one of the new national states created by the peace settlement. Her main concern was security and a treaty with France in 1921 was the main focus of this. Polish territory was potentially under threat from Russia and Germany (whose land was divided in half by the 'Polish Corridor' – see map above). The appointment of Hitler was a cause for concern.

Hitler's foreign policy aims

The first three points of the Nazi 'Programme' of 1920 indicated that Nazi foreign policy was no different from that of traditional nationalists. The key aims appeared to be revision of the Treaty of Versailles, the retrieval of the colonies lost in 1919 and the creation of a Greater Germany to embrace all the ethnic Germans of Europe. Britain and France were at this point regarded as the main enemies. Between 1920 and 1924 Hitler modified these aims, however. In *Mein Kampf* he outlined the principles of a foreign policy that endured until his death:

Activity

1 Read Source 4 carefully. As you read it, make notes under the following headings:
 ● The need for living space
 ● Power
 ● Racial superiority
 ● Where to expand and why
 ● Allies

2 How had Hitler's thinking changed since 1920?

Activity

1 Read about Hitler's foreign policy aims on this page.
2 Using the map and the summaries opposite, discuss the following:
 ● What were the potential 'flashpoints' in the Europe of 1933?
 ● What indications were there of future friends and enemies?
 ● Were there any indications of what Hitler's foreign policy might include and how others might respond?

Source 4

Germany has an annual increase in population of nearly 900,000. The difficulty of feeding this army of new citizens must increase from year to year and ultimately end in catastrophe, unless ways and means are found to forestall the danger of starvation and misery in time...The acquisition of new soil for the settlement of our surplus population has an infinite number of advantages, particularly if we turn from the present to the future...The National Socialist movement must seek to eliminate the present disastrous imbalance between our population and the area of our national territory, regarding the latter as the source of food and the basis of our political power...In striving for this it must bear in mind the fact that, as members of the highest species of humanity on this earth, we have a correspondingly high obligation and that we should fulfil this obligation only if we inspire the German people with the racial idea, so that in addition to breeding good dogs and horses and cats, they will also care for the purity of their own blood...The demand for the restoration of the frontiers of 1914 is a political absurdity...the Reich's frontiers in 1914 were anything but logical. In reality they were neither final in the sense of embracing all ethnic Germans, nor sensible with regard to geo-military considerations...However, when we speak of new land in Europe today we must principally bear in mind Russia and the border states subject to her. Destiny itself seems to wish to point the way for us here...The colossal empire in the east is ripe for dissolution. And the end of Jewish domination of Russia will also be the end of Russia as a state...England does not want Germany to be a world power, but France does not want Germany to exist at all; quite a vital difference after all! Today we are not struggling to achieve a position as a world power; we must fight for the existence of our fatherland, for the unity of our nation and the daily bread of our children. If we look round for European allies from this point of view, only two states remain: England and Italy.

Hitler, *Mein Kampf*, 1925

Note

There is a debate amongst historians about whether Hitler had a fixed foreign policy 'programme'. When you study the events of the 1930s, you will see how Hitler was forced to change his plans on a number of occasions and seemed to be improvising his policy as he went along. Most historians now agree however that Hitler's main aims remained constant. This issue is explored in much greater detail on page 237

Two main shifts had occurred in Hitler's thinking. Firstly, he now argued for expansion into Eastern Europe (Russia) rather than the retrieval of lost colonies. This was partly a consequence of Hitler's ideological shift towards seeing the Russian communist movement as part of a Jewish world conspiracy (see page 124). He began to see the destruction of Russia as fundamental to a destruction of world Jewry. Secondly, he now identified Britain as a potential ally rather than as an enemy. This may have been partly as a consequence of the 1923 Ruhr crisis when Britain offered little support to France. Britain subsequently appeared sympathetic to a revision of the Treaty of Versailles. The shift away from colonial aims also made Britain a more likely ally.

1933–1937: Diplomacy and rearmament

Cautious diplomacy

Although *Mein Kampf* had signalled Hitler's clear intention to pursue an aggressive foreign policy, he was not in a position to do so immediately in 1933. Germany's army was far too small, her arms far too limited and her position in Europe too isolated. In any case, with six million Germans unemployed, immediate concerns lay elsewhere. Two months after becoming Chancellor, Hitler made a speech indicating that six years of peace were necessary in order to make Germany strong again. Nevertheless, Hitler was able to make progress towards his ultimate foreign policy aims in ways that avoided war. His short-term aims were:

- To create an economy capable of sustaining a lengthy war
- To rearm
- To avoid war in the short term
- To pursue alliances, especially with Britain and Italy.

The Geneva Disarmament Conference, which had begun before Hitler became Chancellor, presented Hitler with his first opportunity. Weimar politicians, particularly Stresemann, had been keen to see a general reduction of arms in Europe and the purpose of the Disarmament Conference was to reach a common agreement amongst the major powers. However, France refused to allow German forces to equal her own in size and Hitler walked out in protest. In fact, this incident was entirely to Hitler's advantage. He didn't want the size of his army to be dictated by other powers, especially at the figure of 200,000 proposed by Britain. However, the attitude of the French allowed Hitler to represent himself as a victim of injustice and indeed he received some sympathy, particularly from Britain and Italy. This left France more isolated, also to Germany's advantage.

> **Note**
>
> Hitler also used this incident as an excuse to leave the League of Nations.

Although this clever diplomacy appeared successful, Hitler took measures to protect Germany against any possible negative reaction. He concluded a ten-year non-aggression pact with Poland in January 1934 which achieved a number of objectives. Firstly, it was intended to signal that Germany had no intention of invading Poland. Secondly, it weakened the Eastern European defence system created by France. Thirdly, it removed a potential threat from the east. Of course, the pact was entirely cynical; Hitler had no intention of sticking to it. Privately his view was simple: 'All our agreements with Poland have a purely temporary significance'.

The only notable failure in the first two years of Nazi foreign policy was the assassination, by Austrian Nazis, of the Austrian Chancellor Dollfuss. Hitler's aim for Austria was to turn it into a satellite of Germany. He hoped that bullying tactics would bring Austrian Nazis to power. They would then allow Germany to gain her goal of a 'Greater Germany' without having to invade and force the Austrians to unite with her. This would in turn weaken any case brought against Germany by the other powers on the grounds that the *Anschluss* was forbidden in the Treaty of Versailles. However, the violence of an assassination was an embarrassment to Hitler; he could hardly claim that this represented the wishes of the Austrian people as a whole. It also damaged his relations with Italy who had major doubts about a Nazi take-over in Austria given its geographical location. Hitler was, therefore, forced to play down the significance of the assassination and indeed to distance himself from it. His policy in Austria was forced to take a back seat for a while until things cooled down.

> **Key term**
>
> **Satellite**
> This is a country which is entirely dependent on another. It cannot make decisions by itself and is in practice an extension of the 'mother' country.

> **Key term**
>
> **Anschluss**
> The term used to describe a union between Germany and Austria.

Rearmament

The beginning of 1935 saw a victory for the Nazis. The people of the Saar, under the control of the League of Nations for 15 years according to the peace terms, voted in favour of rejoining Germany in a plebiscite. This seemed to mark the beginning of a 'Greater Germany' which embraced all German-speaking people. It also provided the Nazis with excellent propaganda material. This success was quickly followed up with a decision to make Germany's rearmament public. Behind the busy diplomatic activity of the first two years of Nazi rule, rearmament had been gaining pace. It was becoming difficult to disguise the growth of the army and the expansion of the airforce. In March 1935, Hitler publicly announced the existence of a German airforce (banned under the Treaty of Versailles). This was followed by a decree introducing conscription into the peacetime army and a declaration that, henceforth, the Nazis would not obey any of the limitations on German defence contained within the Versailles Treaty.

This time, Hitler provoked a reaction. German rearmament was condemned by the League of Nations and the Prime Ministers of Britain, France and Italy met at Stresa in Italy where they confirmed their support for an independent Austria. This was soon followed by a pact of mutual assistance between France and Russia. This was the high point of German isolation. It was, however, short-lived.

Hitler was still attempting to win the support of Britain and, in June 1935, succeeded in securing an Anglo-German Naval Pact. This allowed Germany to build a navy which was 35 per cent of the size of Britain's and a submarine force which was of equal size. This was not quite the comprehensive agreement that Hitler wanted. Ideally, he wanted Britain to allow Germany a completely free hand in Eastern Europe in return for a promise from Germany not to involve herself in colonial matters. However, the naval agreement was a substantial victory for Germany and a crushing blow to the unity of the Stresa Front.

The Italian invasion of Ethiopia in the same year further improved Germany's fortunes. France and Britain's condemnation of the invasion and subsequent economic sanctions against Italy destroyed what was left of the Stresa Front and convinced Italy of the need to find alternative allies. Germany's neutral position and her continued supply of raw materials to Italy convinced Mussolini of the need to build up a friendship with Hitler. He was even prepared to give Hitler a free hand in Austria. The invasion of Ethiopia did not only provide Germany with a potential new ally, however. It also provided a distraction from German rearmament. Not for the last time Hitler made the most of a good opportunity. In March 1936 he sent troops into the Rhineland, a demilitarized area according to the Treaty of Versailles. It was a risky move with Hitler acting against the advice of his generals. Had the French intervened, the German troops – numbering just 22,000 – would have been hopelessly outnumbered and Hitler would have been forced to withdraw. As it was, however, the French would not mount a challenge without British backing, which was not forthcoming. Hitler had scored a diplomatic and a strategic triumph at France's expense. As ever, in the aftermath of his coup, Hitler attempted to reassure the major powers of his peaceful intentions, stressing the 'purely defensive character of these measures, as well as ... unalterable longing for a real pacification of Europe...'

Cross reference

See page 235 for a map showing the location of the Saar

Note

Locarno Pact

In 1925, Germany signed the Locarno Pact which recognized Germany's western borders as fixed by the Treaty of Versailles. Hitler used the pact between France and Russia in 1935 as an excuse to break the Locarno Pact. He argued that the Franco-Russian agreement was against the spirit of Locarno and put Germany in danger.

Source 5

THE MAN WHO TOOK THE LID OFF.

▲ A British cartoon about Mussolini in October 1935.

Think about

▶ What is the cartoonist predicting here?

Source 6

THE GOOSE-STEP.
"GOOSEY GOOSEY GANDER,
WHITHER DOST THOU WANDER?"
"ONLY THROUGH THE RHINELAND—
PRAY EXCUSE MY BLUNDER!"

◀ A British cartoon about the German military reoccupation of the Rhineland.

■ Think about

▶ Why are German troops represented as a goose?

▶ Explain the significance of the torn piece of paper under the goose's foot.

▶ Why does the goose have an olive branch in its mouth?

▶ What do you think is the overall message of this British cartoon?

Note

Spanish Civil War

Lasting from 1936 to 1939, this war was fought between Republicans and Nationalists led by General Franco. Although the Republicans were in the stronger position initially, the support of Germany and Italy was crucial in securing a victory for Franco. France and Britain, the major democracies of the West, did not offer official support to the Republicans, who instead received most help from Russia and from individuals within the International Brigades. This was the first war in which civilians suffered from air attacks on a large scale. It was also the first war between fascism and democracy and as such anticipated the Second World War. In 1939 Franco established an authoritarian dictatorship.

Germany's friendship with Italy was further cemented by the Spanish Civil War in which they both supported General Franco. In November 1936, the two powers concluded the Rome-Berlin Axis in which co-operation of a non-military nature was secured. Germany had also gained a new and unexpected ally outside of Europe. In the same month as the Rome-Berlin Axis was agreed, Germany and Japan signed the Anti-Comintern (anti-Russian) Pact. Hitler was gradually – though not totally – beginning to accept the absence of a British alliance and focus his efforts elsewhere.

Moving towards war

By the beginning of 1937 Hitler was in a much stronger position than in 1933. Germany was no longer isolated within Europe, she had successfully asserted her right to rearm and she had re-established troops in the Rhineland with no opposition. Although an alliance with Britain remained elusive, Hitler's confidence was growing and he was beginning to make plans based around British opposition rather than support. There were, however, two problems facing Hitler. Firstly, he was aware that his own actions had sparked off an arms race in Europe, a race that he would not ultimately be able to win. Secondly, it was not clear for how long the German economy could sustain the pressure imposed on it by such intensive rearmament. Both developments indicated that war could not be postponed for much longer.

Hitler's thinking at this point is best illustrated in the Hossbach Memorandum. This document consists of minutes taken by Colonel Hossbach at a secret meeting between Hitler and his army advisers. Although it is a personal record of the meeting rather than an official record, it is nevertheless generally regarded as a reasonably accurate account of what was said. Hitler began, according to Hossbach, by stating Germany's right to more living space. It was impossible, he said, for Germany to become self-sufficient, particularly in food, without more land. The question was, however, 'Where could she achieve the greatest gain at the lowest cost?' Hitler went on to outline the destruction of Czechoslovakia and a union with Austria. Both of these, he suggested, could be achieved without too much opposition from Britain and France, both of whom were preoccupied with other matters. Most importantly, Hitler put a time scale to this expansion. He identified 1943–1945 as the latest date by which expansion should have been achieved and stated that 'After this date only a change for the worse, from our point of view, could be expected'.

Historians have disagreed over whether this document represented a serious plan of action. When compared to the actual events which followed it, the memorandum included several inaccurate predictions. Neither the *Anschluss* nor the invasion of Czechoslovakia were carried out as described in the document, the time scale was clearly wrong (war broke out in 1939) and no mention was made of expansion into Russia which was one of Hitler's central aims. It is possible, however, that Hitler was trying to reassure the more conservative generals by playing down the extent of his expansionist ambitions. It is also possible to regard the document as a guide to Hitler's thinking at that particular moment rather than as a blueprint for his subsequent actions. Used in this way – and at the risk of using hindsight – we learn that by 1937, Hitler was identifying Britain as a major enemy and that he was increasingly aware that time was beginning to run out.

1938–1939: The road to war

The end of compromise

Reactions to the Hossbach meeting amongst the army leadership were not wholly positive. Doubts were expressed about Germany's ability to fight a large-scale war as soon as Hitler was suggesting. But Hitler was no longer prepared to tolerate such doubts and made his first move to impose his wishes on the army, itself a sign of his confidence both at home and abroad. The Commander-in-Chief of the Army, General von Fritsch, and Commander-in-Chief of the Armed Forces, von Blomberg, were forced out of office on the ground of personal scandals which were largely fictional. Hitler assumed Blomberg's role himself, in addition to the post of Supreme Commander of the Armed Forces, which he already held. At the same time, Hitler appointed Ribbentrop as Foreign Minister.

Hitler's next step was to establish control in Austria. He had trodden a very careful path since 1934 and it was Goering who pushed for a more assertive policy towards the end of 1937. Hitler continued his diplomatic approach in 1938, bullying the Austrians into conceding considerable rights to the Austrian Nazis. The Austrian Chancellor, Schuschnigg, however, threw the Nazi campaign off course by announcing a plebiscite on the issue of Austria's future.

■ Biography

Ribbentrop

A social climber who pursued his political ambitions by being utterly subservient to Hitler and ensuring he only said and did what the Führer wanted to hear and see. He was intensely disliked by others in the Party. Goebbels wrote of him 'Von Ribbentrop bought his name, he married his money, and he swindled his way into office'. Others renamed him 'Ribbensnob' because of his airs and graces. He joined the Nazi Party in 1932. In contrast to Hitler, who had barely travelled anywhere, Ribbentrop had the air of a well-travelled man. Hitler made him ambassador to Britain in 1936, where he made a series of wrong moves, including greeting the King with the Nazi salute. He made little progress in concluding an alliance with the British and indeed became openly hostile to them after he was snubbed by polite society. He urged Hitler to pursue alliances elsewhere and provided Hitler with misleading information which led him to underestimate the strength of the British and their likelihood to fight over Poland.

Hitler was furious and doubtful of the result. Schuschnigg was forced to resign but the Austrian President refused to appoint a Nazi Chancellor in his place. German troops were sent in, although only at the (forced) invitation of the Austrian government. They were greeted enthusiastically by the crowds (see Source 1) and Hitler, on returning to his childhood town of Linz, made the decision to unite fully with Austria. His strategy had worked. Another step in the direction of a Greater Germany had been made, no opposition from the major powers was forthcoming and Mussolini had not turned a hair. Hitler's grateful response to Mussolini's support bordered on the comical:

Source 7

Hesse: I have just come back from the Palazzo Venezia. The Duce [Mussolini] accepted the whole thing in a very friendly manner. He sends you his regards.

Hitler: Then please tell Mussolini I will never forget him for this.

Hesse: Yes

Hitler: Never, never, never, whatever happens…

Hesse: Yes, my Führer…

Hitler: I will never forget, whatever may happen. If he should ever need any help or be in any danger, he can be convinced that I shall stick to him, whatever may happen, even if the whole world were against him.

Hesse: Yes, my Führer

A telephone conversation between Hitler and Prince Philip of Hesse, 11 March 1938

The next problem: Czechoslovakia

Hitler now turned his attention to Czechoslovakia. He could not pursue expansion into the east without neutralizing any possible threat from the Czechs. He had also, as we saw in Chapter 6, developed ill-feelings towards the Czechs in his youth (see Source 16 page 125) and certainly did not consider them to be a worthy nation. In May 1938 he declared 'I am utterly determined that Czechoslovakia should disappear from the map'. He was still, however, reluctant to risk war so soon and continued the tactic of making his actions appear somehow justified in order to minimize an adverse reaction from the major powers. He did this by exploiting the ethnic situation in Czechoslovakia. The biggest minority group was the three-and-a-quarter million Germans living in the Sudetenland (see map opposite) and who were demanding independence. Hitler used their demands as a bargaining tool with the Czech government, demanding that the Sudetenland be given over to Germany. Hitler did not believe these demands would be met and hoped to turn the Czech refusal into a justification for invading the whole of Czechoslovakia. However, with the encouragement of Britain and France, the Czech government agreed. The matter was formally resolved at the Munich Conference in September 1938. In the Munich Agreement, Hitler was allowed to annexe the Sudetenland. However, the major powers also provided a guarantee of Czechoslovakia's new borders against 'unprovoked aggression'. In other words, Hitler had to be content with what he had been allowed to have.

It was hardly in Hitler's nature, however, to do what he was told. He felt cheated by the Munich Agreement and was determined to secure the collapse of Czechoslovakia. His excuse was the same as before, i.e. that he was supporting the claims of minority groups for independence. In March 1939,

■ Think about

▶ Look at the map on page 228. Why was the union with Austria so important strategically for Germany?

▶ What impression do you get from Source 7 about Hitler's concerns in March 1938?

Key term

Appeasement
The policy of settling disputes using peaceful rather than military methods. Usually associated with Neville Chamberlain, Prime Minister of Britain 1937–1940, who attempted to avoid war through negotiation with Hitler. The policy failed as Hitler interpreted it as weakness and continued to pursue an aggressive foreign policy, leading to war in 1939. It did, however, provide the Allies with time to build up their arms and in this respect was a useful delaying tactic.

Using the Internet, search for and select information about the Munich Conference. In particular, try to find primary evidence and images. What do they suggest about the Munich Agreement? Share your findings with the group.

You may wish to include in your search the following website: www.yale.edu/lawweb/avalon/imt/munich1.htm

Source 8

▶ A cartoon from July 1936. The writing on the last back says 'Boss of the Universe'.

Think about

▶ What point is Low (a British cartoonist) making in this cartoon?

▶ Did Low appear to believe that Hitler had a fixed plan for his foreign policy?

Returned to Germany after a plebiscite, January 1935 (people voted to rejoin Germany)

Remilitarised, March 1936 (troops back in Rhineland)

The Anschluss, March 1938 (Germany and Austria united)

Gained from Czechoslovakia under the Munich Agreement, September 1938

Occupied by Germany and turned into a 'protectorate', March 1939

In name independent, but put under German 'protection' March 1939

Handed over by Lithuania under threat, March 1939

Occupied by Germany after the outbreak of war, September 1939

Invaded by Germany September 1939

German troops entered Czechoslovakia and annexed Bohemia and Moravia. Slovakia became a German protectorate. Britain and France took no military action, despite the Munich Agreement. They did, however, respond with guarantees of Poland's independence. This was the first time that Hitler had been faced with a serious obstacle, as he was clearly setting his sights on Poland next.

STEPPING STONES TO GLORY

The invasion of Poland

Poland was the last obstacle to Hitler's expansionist plans. He initially sought to neutralize Poland and turn it into a satellite of Germany by demanding Danzig and the Polish Corridor (see map). Boosted by the French and British guarantees following the invasion of Czechoslovakia, Poland refused. In May 1939, Hitler concluded the Pact of Steel with Italy which promised military assistance to either power in the event of war. In the same month, Hitler made his intention to crush Poland clear to the heads of his armed forces:

Source 9

There is...no question of sparing Poland and we are left with the decision: *To attack Poland at the first suitable opportunity*. We cannot expect a repetition of Czechoslovakia. There will be a war. Our task is to isolate Poland. Success in isolating her will be decisive...It must not come down to a simultaneous showdown with the West [France and England].

Hitler was about to take his biggest gamble yet. He realized that an invasion of Poland could provoke a European war. He convinced himself however that this was unlikely. This was partly the consequence of misleading intelligence reports on the military preparations of the Allies (Britain and France), which suggested that they were far from ready for such a conflict. In addition, communications between Poland and the Allies suggested that Poland was under pressure to strike a deal with Germany as had happened with Czechoslovakia over the Sudetenland in 1938.

To bolster his position, Hitler concluded a pact with a most unlikely ally, Russia, in August 1939. The Nazi–Soviet Pact included an agreement not to attack each other and to remain neutral in the event of an attack on another country. It was a question of practicalities. Although the conquest of Russia was his long-term goal, Hitler needed her support in order to overcome opposition from the West European countries before he could turn his attention eastwards. He wanted to avoid a war on two fronts, so disastrous in the First World War, at all costs. Once the West was dealt with, the Pact could easily be abandoned. But why did Russia agree to the Pact? Ever since the Munich Conference, Britain and France had been flirting with Russia, but with little conviction. They were deeply suspicious of communism and concluded that, in any case, Russia had little to offer them militarily. This was, in hindsight, a mistake. Stalin, anxious to avoid war, saw the pact as short-term protection against German aggression. He also saw an opportunity to regain territories lost in 1917. The Nazi-Soviet Pact included a 'secret protocol' which promised to divide the spoils of any Nazi expansion into eastern Europe between Germany and Russia.

On 1 September 1939, Hitler made the fateful decision to invade Poland. To his surprise, this was followed by declarations of war by Britain and France. His luck had run out and he was now faced with a war for which he was not wholly prepared. The flaw in his view, according to one historian, 'was the failure to see that the Western Powers had reached their limit in 1939' (Overy, 1987).

■ Activity

Copy out your own version of the chart below. Using the information in this chapter, complete the chart. Use the timeline below to help you. The first event has been filled in for you.

Date	Event	Cause/motive and justification offered	Consequence
October 1933	Hitler walks out of the Disarmament Conference in Geneva	Hitler protests at France's refusal to allow Germany equal military strength. Real reason is Hitler's desire to be free to rearm as much as he wishes.	Sympathy from Italy and Britain. Rearmament begins in earnest. Non-aggression pact with Poland in case of opposition.

October 1933	Disarmament Conference	March 1936	Remilitarization of the Rhineland
January 1934	Ten Year non-aggression pact with Poland	November 1936	Rome–Berlin Axis
		November 1937	Hossbach Memorandum
January 1935	Plebiscite in the Saar	March 1938	Invasion of Austria (Anschluss)
March 1935	Conscription begins	September 1938	Munich Conference
April 1935	Creation of the Stresa Front	March 1939	German troops occupy the rest of Czechoslovakia
June 1935	Anglo-German Naval Agreement	May 1939	Pact of Steel
October 1935	Italian invasion of Ethiopia	August 1939	Nazi–Soviet Pact
		September 1939	Invasion of Poland

Note

The events of the Second World War proved that Hitler had not abandoned his aims to conquer Russia. By the summer of 1940, Germany had defeated Poland, the Low Countries, Norway and France. It had not, however, conquered Britain. Nevertheless, Hitler was becoming impatient to pursue his major goal: expansion into Russia. Formal orders were issued in December 1940 for an invasion. Hitler's advisers suggested that defeat of Russia would take eight weeks. The invasion was launched on 22 June 1941. It was to prove the turning point of the war.

Quotation

Now it is also a great risk. Iron nerves, iron resolution. The following special reasons strengthen my idea. England and France are obligated [to Poland], neither is in a position for it. There is no actual rearmament in England, just propaganda…The enemies are little worms. I saw them at Munich

Hitler's speech to his commanders, 22 August 1939

■ **Think about**

The bias of individual historians affects their interpretation of Hitler's foreign policy. A.J.P. Taylor, by arguing that Hitler had no plan, attributes more blame to the Allies for not stopping him sooner.

▶ Why might British or French historians also argue that Hitler *did* have a definite plan of action?

Quotation

Extract A

For the first two years of the war the degree of economic regulation was no more rigorous than it had been in 1936. The production of armaments did not increase significantly, nor did that of consumer goods decline…Hitler was so pleased with the effectiveness of war on the cheap that he saw no reason to change it when he began to plan his invasion of Russia…He preferred to gamble on a short war, and to do so without allocating enough labour resources to war production…

Craig, *Germany 1866–1945*, 1981

Quotation

Extract B

All the evidence on war preparations and military production plans confirms that the general expectation in Germany before 1939 was that any future war between the major powers…would be a total war from the start. The very nature of modern warfare made this imperative. War was now industrialised: tanks, aircraft, modern communications equipment, all required an industrial effort on a scale hitherto unknown…By the spring of 1940, the German economy was set on the path towards full mobilisation.

Overy, 'Mobilisation for total war in Germany 1939-41' in *English Historical Review*, 103, 1988

Was Hitler in control?

There has been disagreement amongst historians about whether Hitler was in control of his foreign policy or whether he simply made it up as he went along, reacting to events as they happened. This is part of the debate about Hitler as a 'weak dictator' or 'master in the Third Reich' (see page 171). In the immediate aftermath of the Second World War, Hitler was regarded as a 'madman' and opportunist, with no clear plan or set of aims. A.J.P. Taylor, writing in 1961, challenged the idea that Hitler was 'mad' (his only problem, according to Taylor, was that he was German and following the tradition of his predecessors) but agreed that he was basically an opportunist. Hitler's foreign policy, he argued, was essentially a reaction to the absence of firm action by other West European states. It did not follow a preconceived plan or 'blueprint'. This interpretation has since been challenged and through the debates which have followed, two schools of thought have emerged (the 'programme' and 'structuralist' schools).

The 'programme' school

Examples of historians: Hugh Trevor-Roper, Klaus Hildebrand, Gerhard Weinberg
Their argument: All agree that Hitler had a consistent plan which was first outlined in *Mein Kampf*. The key elements of this plan were: achieving greater living space (*lebensraum*), and expanding the German master race. Hitler was definitely in control of foreign policy.
Differences: The main disagreement between programmists lies in the precise extent of Hitler's expansionist ambitions. Did he simply want to conquer Eastern Europe? Or was world conquest the next step?

The 'structuralist' school

Examples of historians: Hans Mommsen, Martin Brosazt, Tim Mason
Their argument: That Hitler did not have a specific plan in foreign policy. Instead, he reacted to events around him, both at home and abroad. Public statements of foreign policy intentions made by Hitler and others are explained in terms of propaganda.
Differences: Not all structuralists believe that Hitler was without a plan. Mason, for example, believes that Hitler did have a plan – but was unable to stick to it in the face of an economic crisis.

Was Hitler really planning for total war?

Despite the priority given to the creation of a war economy during the 1930s, Germany seemed slow to adapt to the demands of war after 1939. Although swift victories in Western Europe did not place huge demands on German industry, the war against Russia forced Hitler to reappraise the organization of the economy and to take measures to increase arms production. This impression of being ill prepared has led to a debate amongst historians. Was Hitler actually planning for total war?

■ **Activity**

1 Read the 'Historical Debate' box on page 220 for important background.

2 Now read extracts A and B in the margin. How do they disagree?

3 Organize yourselves into two groups. Using the information on the next two pages, plus any other information you have, prepare to defend one of these arguments:
'Hitler was clearly planning for total war but was expecting it later than 1939'
'Hitler appeared to have no clear plan. He reacted to events and had to change his tactics when war lasted longer than expected.'

Spotlight

Was Hitler planning for total war?

Source 10

The German labour force, May 1939–May 1943 (millions)

	May 1939	May 1940	May 1941	May 1942	May 1943
All industry		10.9	10.1	10.3	9.9	10.6
Iron and steel		0.35	0.33	0.36	0.36	0.41
Mining		0.59	0.58	0.61	0.62	0.69
Heavy manufacturing industry e.g. chemicals, metals, engineering		3.75	3.87	4.21	4.36	4.81
Building industry		0.91	0.71	0.72	0.51	0.44
Consumer e.g. textiles, food		3.58	2.94	2.84	2.54	2.59

Source 11

With effect from 28 August 1939, four days before the attack on Poland, a number of items of daily diet were rationed so that, as Goebbels insisted, food could be shared out equally among the German people. Ration cards had been printed in 1937 and were kept ready for immediate use.

Kitchen, *Nazi Germany at War*, 1995

Source 12

The Industrial labour force

Year	Index of industrial workers working in military contracts
1939	100
1940	229
1941	249
1942	256
1943	278

Source 13

Throughout the winter of 1939-40 Germany received considerable economic and even military assistance from Soviet Russia. Russia's supplies of vital raw materials, the use of her railway system to transport rubber from the Far East and the protection given to German merchantmen all helped to neutralise the economic consequences of the British blockade... Ironically, it was probably only Russian assistance that prevented an early German economic collapse...

Williamson, *The Third Reich*, 1982

Source 15

Consumption

a. Production of consumer goods
(1928 100)

1938	108
1939	108
1940	102
1941	104
1942	93
1943	98
1944	93

b. Consumption of civilian products (per person) fell by 22% between 1939 and 1941 (In Britain it fell by 15%)

NB: some consumer goods were produced for the armed forces, such as uniforms

Source 14

...the economy must be completely converted...No more place for printing presses, washing machines and the like, they must all make machine tools.

Goering in 1938

Source 16

The fact is that by 1939, women already constituted a very much larger part of the workforce than in other industrialised countries...It would be reasonable to argue that there simply was not a much larger pool of women to be absorbed in the German war effort, that Germany was already close to a ceiling on female employment by the outbreak of war.

Overy, 'Mobilisation for total war in Germany 1939–41' in *English Historical Review*, 103, 1988

Source 17

Foreign workers in Germany, 1938–1944 (000s)

1938/39	435	1942	4,224
1939	301	1943	62,460
1940	1,154	1944 (May)	7,126
1941	3,033	1944 (Sept)	7,487

[Note: statistics on foreign labour are incomplete.]

Source 18

Total income from taxation, 1938-43 (million Rm)

1938	17.72	1941	32.33
1939	23.58	1942	34.71
1940	27.24	1943	34.37

Source 19

Proportion of women in the workforce, 1939–1943

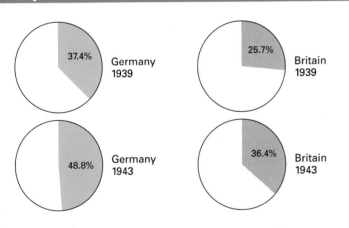

Germany 1939 — 37.4%

Britain 1939 — 25.7%

Germany 1943 — 48.8%

Britain 1943 — 36.4%

Source 20

Percentage of GNP spent on the military in Germany, Britain and the USA, 1933-45

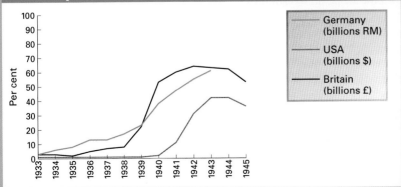

Legend:
- Germany (billions RM)
- USA (billions $)
- Britain (billions £)

Source 21

The turning-point came in December 1941 with the Rationalization Decree. This ordered that the war economy should be simplified and streamlined in order to mass produce. This reorganisation ended the confused planning, poor co-ordination and wasteful duplication of the earlier years. Within two years, the productivity of the workers in the armaments sector almost trebled.

Jenkins, *Hitler and Nazism* 1998

Source 22

...the planners were almost unbelievably lackadaisical in preparing for the attack on the Soviet Union. The army which was thrown against the Soviet Union was only marginally larger and scarcely better equipped than that which invaded France the previous year. In many categories of weapons the losses in the first six months of the campaign greatly exceeded production.

Kitchen, *Nazi Germany at War*, 1995

Did Hitler follow a plan?

As we have seen on the previous pages, there is a debate over the extent to which Hitler was following a plan. Was he in control or was he forced to change his plans due to other 'structural' factors such as domestic pressures? If he didn't have a plan as such, did he have any consistent aims at all? Or was he, as Taylor argued, simply an opportunist?

Interpretations exercise: Hitler's foreign policy

Source A

It is questionable, too, whether National Socialist foreign policy can be considered as an unchanging pursuit of established priorities. Hitler's foreign policy aims, purely dynamic in nature, knew no bounds...to interpret their implementation as in any way consistent or logical is highly problematic...In reality, the regime's foreign policy ambitions were many and varied, without any clear aims and only linked by the ultimate goal: hindsight alone gives them some air of consistency.

Mommsen, 'National Socialism: Continuity and Change' in Laqueur (ed.), *Fascism: A Reader's Guide*, 1976

Source B

He displayed a skill in propaganda and a mastery of deceit, a finesse in exploiting the weaknesses of his opponents and a crudeness in exploiting the strength of his own position which he had learned in the struggle for power in Germany and which he now applied to international relations with even more remarkable results. This is not to suggest that Hitler, any more than Bismarck in the 1860s, foresaw in 1933 exactly how events would develop in the course of the next decade. No man was more of an opportunist, as the Nazi–Soviet Pact shows. No man had more luck. But Hitler knew how to turn events to his advantage. He knew what he wanted and he held the initiative. His principal opponents, Great Britain and France, knew only what they did not want – war – and were always on the defensive. The fact that Hitler was ready to risk war, and started preparing for it from the day he came to power, gave him a still greater advantage.

Bullock, *Hitler A Study in Tyranny*, 1962

Source C

Hitler had no ready-made programme for proceeding [in foreign policy], no blueprint for action. The general thrust of policy was to appear conciliatory, tread warily, but rearm with all speed in order to be ready to seize the main chance when it presented itself. Germany's military weakness and diplomatic isolation offered in any case little alternative to such a strategy...Hitler's hallmark in the early years was less the nature of the foreign policy itself than his capacity to perceive the weakest point of opposition and to push diplomatic relations into completely new terrain through a bold forward move.

Kershaw, *Hitler*, 1991

■ Activity

1 Look back at page 229 on Hitler's aims. What aims did he outline in *Mein Kampf*? Underline what you think were his most important aims.

2 Now compare these aims with what actually happened. Which aims changed? Which aims did he not achieve? Which aims did he achieve?

3 Is it possible to argue that Hitler had consistent foreign policy aims from 1925 onwards?

Source D

Various issues are picked up in the work [*Mein Kampf*] in no thorough or genuinely systematic fashion. One of these is the appropriate diplomatic and foreign aims of the German state. Hitler was always adamant that the humiliation of the Treaty of Versailles had to be overturned and the Reich's lost territories (Alsace, Lorraine, and parts of Poland) returned to Germany. He was also aware that France would never surrender Alsace and Lorraine peacefully. Thus a coming war with France was already implicit in his thinking. However, Hitler's territorial ambitions did not end with the re-creation of the boundaries of Bismarck's Germany. Bismarck, after all, had deliberately excluded Austria and thereby Austrian Germans from the Reich that was created after the victories of 1866 and 1871. In contrast Hitler wanted the pan-German vision of a Reich which would include all ethnic Germans: *ein Volk, ein Reich* (one people, one empire)…Even these pan-German aims, however, were not sufficient to satisfy Hitler. He further believed that the populous German people was being forced to live in a territorial area that was overcrowded and could not meet its needs…What the German people needed was *Lebensraum* (living space). In turn, of course, this then raised the question: where was such living space to be found?…Increasingly…Hitler came to believe that *Lebensraum* would have to be found in the east of Europe and in Russia in particular…

Geary, *Nazism*, 1993

■ Examination-style questions

1 Comprehension in context

Using Source C and your own knowledge, explain the phrase 'his [Hitler's] capacity to perceive the weakest point of opposition'

2 Comparing the sources

Compare Sources A, B, and C. To what extent do they offer similar interpretations about whether or not Hitler followed a plan in his foreign policy?

3 Assessing the sources

Source A's claim that Nazi foreign policy lacked any 'clear aims' seems to be contradicted by Source D. Does this mean that the interpretation in Source A is of limited value?

4 Making judgements

'Hitler did not make plans – for world conquest or anything else. He assumed that others would provide opportunities, and that he would seize them' (Taylor, *The Origins of the Second World War*, 1991). Using all the sources and your own knowledge, explain how far you agree with this statement.

■ Activity   KEY SKILLS

Question 4 can easily be turned into a whole essay. For inclusion into your key skills portfolio, ensure that you have read more extensively from at least two other texts. They could be one of the texts mentioned here, or other ones. Ideally, at least one should include images of some sort. Your teacher will advise you.

■ Activity

Was Hitler in control?

Using the information in this chapter (or the completed table from the activity on page 236), find examples of when Hitler changed his plans. Put your findings into a table:

When did Hitler change his plans	*Why* did Hitler change his plans

Does your table suggest that Hitler was in control of his own foreign policy or not?

Conclusions

Although interpretations differ, it seems relatively safe to suggest that Hitler did have clearly identified aims in his foreign policy, but no fixed plan of how to achieve them. The historian Alan Bullock has described this combination as 'consistency of aim' joined with 'opportunism of method'. Hitler's actions were certainly influenced by circumstances both inside and outside Germany, but there is little evidence to suggest that he was forced to take actions that he did not want. If anything, these constraining or *'structural'* factors, such as the reaction of Britain and France, speeded up his attempt to achieve his aims. But did Hitler expect a war in 1939? Again, this is an area of debate and it is ultimately up to you to decide.

Chapter 13

Popularity and resistance 1933–1945

▲ A group of German women reach out to touch Hitler's hand.

Source 2

For an outsider, a non-German who never experienced Nazism, it is perhaps too easy to criticise, to expect standards of behaviour which it was well-nigh impossible to attain in the circumstances.

Kershaw, *Popular Opinion & Political Dissent in the Third Reich*, 1983

Source 3

One may well assert that the whole nation is convinced that Hitler is a great politician. That is solely attributable to his foreign policy successes, which no one – not even the most confirmed Nazis – would have thought possible before.

A SOPADE report, spring 1939

Introduction

Source 2 provides us with our starting point in this chapter. It is essential that, in examining the ways in which the German people reacted to Nazi rule, we do not make judgements from the comfort and safety of our own position today. This chapter examines the different reactions of the German people to the Nazi state. Before you read on, you need to be familiar with some new terms.

Resistance implies some open form of opposition aimed at bringing down the Nazi state. This type of action was extremely dangerous and mainly limited to the war years.

Dissent is the term used to describe low level opposition aimed at expressing opposition to the Nazis rather than destroying them.

Conformity is used to describe those who, for whatever reason, went along with what the Nazis were doing.

The second part of the chapter considers the impact of the Second World War on the German people and on the popularity of the Nazi Party. It ends with an account of the most serious attempt to assassinate Hitler in 1944.

Key questions

- To what extent did the German people oppose the Nazi regime and on what grounds?
- What impact did this opposition have?
- Why was opposition to the regime limited?
- How did the German people react to the Nazis' anti-Semitism?
- How popular was Hitler personally?
- How did the war affect the German people and the popularity of Hitler and the Nazis?
- How serious was the opposition Hitler faced during the war?

Popular opposition to the Nazis

What did people dislike about living in the Third Reich?

Economic factors

By far the most important factor influencing people's view of the regime was their economic well being. Although the official unemployment statistics suggested overwhelming success by the Nazis, it wasn't until the Four Year Plan launched a massive rearmament programme that unemployment was fully eradicated. In addition, there were other problems. Food shortages and price increases featured in the early years of the regime. The unemployed were sometimes forced to work at wages less than the unemployment benefit they had been receiving, and many of the work creation schemes meant workers leaving home and performing hard labour. Working conditions often deteriorated and there were continued – and largely unsuccessful – efforts by workers to increase their wages. It wasn't just the working class that had cause to complain, however. Peasants and members of the *Mittelstand* (lower middle class) were amongst the most critical of the Nazi regime. Both were similarly hit by price rises and neither felt rewarded for the support they had given the Nazis before 1933.

Intrusion into the private sphere

Not surprisingly, the Nazis' attempt to control the private lives of the German people was often resented. Some people refused to stop listening to banned music, reading banned books and criticizing the regime, though for the most part, great care was taken to do all this in private. More openly, some people refused to stop shopping in Jewish shops or consulting Jewish doctors. Many people were also unhappy with the attack on the Churches.

The coming of war

Every time Hitler acted aggressively in his foreign policy during the 1930s, his popularity dipped. Fortunately for Hitler, each time war was averted up to 1939, the Führer's popularity then increased due to people's enormous relief. But in September 1939, war was not averted and there was little enthusiasm shown by the German people. In June 1939, one observer noted 'The desire for peace is stronger than that for war' and another wrote on the very last day of peace 'Trust in the Führer will now probably be subjected to its hardest acid test. The overwhelming proportion of people's comrades expects from him the prevention of war…'

Conclusion

Of course, there were many other reasons to dislike Nazi rule, depending on your position and experience. That those groups outside Hitler's *Volksgemeinschaft* opposed the regime goes without saying. But as a broad rule of thumb, criticism was at its fiercest when people were affected directly. Opposition to sterilization and even euthanasia was most vehement when a family member or friend was affected. Anti-Semitic policies were generally accepted except when it concerned someone you knew and respected – or until you left your own house to find broken glass on the streets. This is why economic conditions were particularly influential: wages, working hours and availability of food all had an immediate impact on everyday life.

'Everyday' opposition

The basic refusal to conform included:
- Refusal to give the Hitler salute (some people gave the salute but muttered things like 'we should cut the grass when it gets this high' under their breath as they did it)
- Refusal to cook the *Eintopf* ('One pot meal' which people were supposed to cook on certain Sundays in order to save money which could then be donated to the 'Winter Relief Fund')
- Reading of banned literature
- Listening to foreign radio broadcasts
- Listening to banned music
- Continuing to buy goods in Jewish shops
- Telling anti-Nazi jokes

All these expressions of dissent brought risks, however small the gesture. Some people were more aggressive and open in their refusal to conform, such as the alternative youth groups described in Chapter 10. It was very rare for opposition to go beyond this before war broke out.

Did people's opposition have any impact on Nazi policies?

The Nazis were not prevented from pursuing their ultimate goals of racial and territorial mastery until war brought defeat. In this respect opposition to the Nazis failed. However, the Nazis never succeeded in establishing the total control over people which was one of their main domestic goals. Memories of the Revolution in 1918 made them particularly sensitive to the demands of the working class. Hitler banned an increase in food prices in 1938 and abandoned

■ **Further reading**

One of the best sources on everyday life and dissent is Peukert, *Inside Nazi Germany*, 1987.
See also Kershaw, *Popular Opinion and Political Dissent in the Third Reich*, 1983.

Note

A political joke
The Führer, Goering and Mussolini are in a plane above Munich. They discuss how they can make themselves popular with the people of Munich. Goering decides to throw down lard ration coupons. The Führer decides to throw down meat ration coupons. Mussolini goes to the cockpit and asks the pilot for his advice. The pilot advises him to throw the other two passengers down.

Note

Occasionally, an individual was willing to take an enormous risk, such as Goerg Elser, a carpenter. In 1939 he went to the beer hall in Munich, where Hitler was shortly due to deliver his annual speech in memory of the 1923 *Putsch*. During successive evenings, Elser would wait until the beer hall closed, hiding in the toilets so that no-one would throw him out. He would then set to work making a hollow in the platform big enough to hold a time bomb. Through sheer bad luck, the night of the speech was foggy and Hitler left earlier than planned, thus narrowly avoiding his own death and changing the face of history. Elser was arrested on his way to Switzerland and was killed in 1945. What sets Elser and those like him apart from the majority was his willingness to risk his life in order to overthrow the regime. Not surprisingly, very few were so brave.

an attempt to lower wages in 1939 following workers' protests. The Nazis were similarly sensitive to public opinion in 1941, when the euthanasia programme was officially dropped following Galen's speech (see page 202). Overall, however, these responses can hardly be held up as examples of the Nazis being forced to back down over crucial issues.

Why was opposition limited?

Despite these various demonstrations of dissent, opposition was, on the whole, limited in both its size and impact. The most obvious reason for this was, of course, fear. 'Keep quiet or you'll end up in Dachau' [the first concentration camp] was one very good reason not to oppose the regime. Even listening to the wrong music could potentially endanger you in a state that monitored the most private as well as public spheres. But while fear may have been the major disincentive for opposing the Nazis, there were other factors:

Absence of mass organizations to co-ordinate opposition

Potential centres of opposition were quickly dismantled by the Nazis. The SPD was dissolved in June 1933 and its leaders were either imprisoned or had already escaped, establishing headquarters in Prague and, after 1938, in Paris. Its policy after 1933 was to wait for the regime to collapse rather than to force it to do so. The KPD leaders also set up headquarters abroad. Those communists remaining in Germany were a little more active than the SPD in trying to undermine the regime, for example through the distribution of leaflets. But they still faced the problem common to any resistance movement – the inability to meet in large numbers because it was simply too dangerous to do so. Organizing a mass movement of opposition was therefore impossible. Workers also felt the lack of their trade union movement which had provided them with a sense of solidarity. The only mass movement which survived destruction and which was technically outside of the Nazi power structures was the Church. But as we have already seen, the Churches, for various reasons, did not present the Nazis with a united front of opposition.

The attitude of the army

The army was the only institution in a position to mount a serious threat to Hitler (and indeed was the only institution to get close to destroying him in 1944) but they chose to support him in 1934. The ambitious rearmament plans were divisive; older, more traditional officers were concerned about the effects of mass recruitment, while younger officers welcomed the injection of more money into better and more plentiful equipment. Generally the army supported the Nazis in the early years of the regime. By 1938, when a rift appeared between the officers and the Nazis, it was too late to mount a serious challenge, not least because war seemed imminent.

The successes of the Nazi regime

Despite the economic problems already discussed, there was nevertheless a powerful sense that things were gradually getting better, and were certainly better compared to the years of the depression. The grumbles and criticisms of the workers were rarely *political*. In other words, they might complain about low wages and high prices, but that did not automatically imply an attack on the regime as a whole. The Nazis in fact achieved enough successes to win considerable popular support. The general fall in unemployment was a significant factor in this support, as was the return of strong leadership and the destruction of communism. In addition, the increased power and status of Germany following rearmament, conscription and foreign policy coups such as the remilitarization of the Rhineland, helped to convince people that, in the long run, their country stood to gain from Nazi rule, however unpleasant certain aspects of this rule were.

Indifference and apathy

Many people became indifferent about politics. The fact that people felt more isolated increased their sense of helplessness. Even people living in democratic countries today, where they can vote and express their views, still complain that 'nothing will change'. Imagine, then, living in a country where none of this was possible. A SOPADE report from 1936 demonstrates the indifference shown by many German people:

Source 4

Here all life seems to have died out. We have no idea what is going on in the world and most of the time not even what is going on in our town...A large section of the population no longer reads a newspaper. Basically, the population are indifferent to what is in the papers. It is not always the same but, in people's opinion, it is often untrue...Wherever one goes one can see that people accept National Socialism as something inevitable ...I know that this is a gloomy picture which I am giving. It is particularly gloomy because it shows that up to now the Nazis have succeeded in achieving one thing: the depoliticisation of the German people...There can be no doubt that the Nazis have succeeded in persuading the masses to leave politics to the men at the top...

How popular were the Nazis by 1938?

1938 is the year many historians regard as the peak of the Nazi Party's – and especially Hitler's – popularity.

■ Activity

The following activity can be done individually or in small groups. Under each heading list the evidence to support the claims that the Nazis were or were not popular. You may wish to add further headings.

REASONS FOR POPULARITY
● Economic successes (pages 216–221)
● Foreign policy successes (pages 231–235)
● Propaganda (pages 173–177)
● Social policy (pages 185–199)

LIMITS TO THIS POPULARITY
● Groups which didn't benefit Chapter 10, Chapter 11 pages 220–233
● Apathy and indifference rather than support (page 210 and this page)
● Problems in measuring support (page 243)

Document exercise: Popular support for the Nazis, 1935–1938

Source A

A tense political situation

Since the populace in general is timid and takes great care not to express its opinion publicly, it is becoming more and more difficult to observe and assess the public's attitude. Unmistakable, however, is the fact that the internal political situation has lately been considerably tense, which has adversely affected attitudes...one can point to economic factors as a cause for negative attitudes. In this regard the situation of the working class merits special attention in that wage rates are creating increased bitter resentment...The increase in the cost of foodstuffs required on a daily basis, such as potatoes, vegetables, fruit, milk, eggs, and butter, has heightened the dissatisfaction among workers...

Special Report of the State Police in Hannover, August 1935

■ Activity

1 Arrange yourselves into small groups or pairs. Using the information you have studied in this chapter and, if possible, Chapter 10, draw up a list of evidence to support each of the following statements:
● The German people supported the Nazi regime
● The German people opposed the Nazi regime
● The German people were resigned to the Nazi regime

2 When you have done that, discuss either in your group or as a whole class the following statement:

'The German people were terrorized into accepting the Nazi regime.'

■ Activity   KEY SKILLS

When you have completed the activity above, discuss whether or not you agree with the following statement:

'By 1938, most Germans had reason to be grateful to the Nazis.'

In March 1936 Hitler sent German troops into the Rhineland. Under the terms of the Treaty of Versailles, this area was supposed to be demilitarized with no German troops stationed there at all.

Source B

The Germans' reaction to the remilitarization of the Rhineland in 1936

March 13
Here Hitler made his first 'election' speech tonight…Nothing new in it, though he drummed away nicely about his desire for friendship with France. Certainly these Rhinelanders don't want another war with France, but this reoccupation by the German troops has inculcated them with the Nazi bug. They're as hysterical as the rest of the Germans. Later went out…the taxi-driver turned out to be a communist, waxed bitter about the Nazis, and predicted their early collapse. It was a relief to find one German here against the regime. He said there are a lot of others, but I sometimes wonder.

March 29
A fine early spring day for the 'election' and according to Goebbels's figures ninety-five per cent of the German people have approved the reoccupation of the Rhineland. Some of the correspondents…reported irregularities. But there's no doubt, I think, that a substantial majority of the people applaud the action in the Rhineland, regardless of whether they're Nazis or not.

Extracts from William Shirer's *Berlin Diary*. Shirer was an American correspondent in Germany between 1934 and 1940.

Cross reference

See pages 233–234 for information on the *Anschluss*, Germany's unification with Austria in March 1938, which broke the Treaty of Versailles.

Source C

Indifference amongst the German people

The general mood in Germany is characterized by a widespread political indifference. The great mass of the people is completely dulled and does not want to hear anything more about politics. Thus, for example, the *Anschluss* with Austria did not produce anything like the enthusiasm and lasting effect as the reintroduction of conscription three years before. One should not be misled by the general grumbling. Nowadays people grumble everywhere about everything but nobody intends this grumbling to represent a hostile attitude to the regime.

SOPADE (SPD in exile) report, 1938

Source D

Attitude towards war

There is full employment right down the line and, what is more, rising wages which are welcome on social grounds but economically dubious. The theatres are fully booked, the cinemas full, and the cafes are overflowing into the early hours with music and dancing; there are record numbers of outings on Sundays. And yet despite all these signs of a favourable economic situation the mood among large numbers of people is not one appropriate to a boom. It is in many cases depressed about the future…There is serious concern among the broadest sections of the nation that a war will sooner or later put an end to the economic revival and have terrible consequences for Germany.

From a monthly report of the Military Economic Inspectorate, Munich, September 1938

■ Examination-style questions

1 Comprehension in context

Study Source D. Using the source and your own knowledge, explain why there was a 'depressed' mood in Germany in September 1938.

2 Comparing the sources

Study Sources B and C. How and why do they differ in their assessment of the mood of the German people?

3 Assessing the sources

Using Sources A and B, explain why it is difficult to assess popular opinion in Germany during the 1930s.

4 Making judgements

Using all the sources and your own knowledge, examine the view that between 1935 and 1938, popular support for the Nazis was largely superficial.

The Jewish Question

Anyone studying the Third Reich will at some point want the answer to a deceptively simple sounding question. How were the Nazis able to murder 6 million Jews? Behind that question lies another, implicit one. Why were they not stopped? To answer this question we must start by asking 'Who *could* have stopped them?'. Given that the acts of genocide were carried out during the Second World War, the most obvious response is the Allied powers, and indeed, it was only the defeat of Germany in 1945 that halted the extermination programme. However, historians have also examined the degree to which the German people accepted Hitler's anti-Semitism long before war actually broke out. We have already seen that during the 1930s, Hitler was not oblivious to public opinion. If the German people had expressed *strong* opposition to anti-Semitic policies, how far would Hitler have pursued them?

We know that Hitler played down anti-Semitism in election campaigns after 1928 because it was not always well received. Similarly, the architects of the 'Final Solution' went to great lengths to keep their plan secret from the public. It certainly seems that Hitler cared about the popular reaction to his anti-Semitic policies. However, it is virtually unthinkable that he would have ever abandoned them, given their central place in his overall vision. The question is not so much, therefore, whether the German people could have *prevented* the full implementation of Hitler's racial policies but rather, to what extent and why they *accepted* them at all, and by doing so, possibly smoothed the path towards genocide. As ever, there is a fine line to be drawn between *acceptance* and *collaboration*. Not surprisingly, this is still a very sensitive issue in Germany today.

The historian Daniel Goldhagen, whose book *Hitler's Willing Executioners* (1996) prompted great controversy and media interest, argues that the German people were virulently and *uniquely* anti-Semitic and had been since medieval times. Not only did the Germans stand by whilst German Jews were persecuted. They were also, according to Goldhagen, the 'willing executioners' of even the most extreme racial policies conceived by the Nazis. Indeed, according to Goldhagen, some of those responsible for the very worst atrocities of the war positively gained pleasure from their actions. It is true that other historians have tried to fathom why ordinary German men were prepared to execute large numbers of Jews and Poles during the war even when offered the chance to back out. However, Goldhagen's claims that they did it *because they wanted to and because they hated Jews* have on the whole been rejected by historians, not least because they have challenged Goldhagen's selective use

Key term

The Final Solution

The Nazis' attempt to eliminate all European Jews between 1941 and 1945.

■ **Think about**

A university student from Cologne discovered in 1994 that one of her grandmothers who died after the war had been Jewish. The discovery brought relief because the student felt she could now express her opinions about the Nazis freely, without fear of saying the wrong thing.

▶ Why do you think she felt like this?

■ **Think about**

Interestingly, the media's response to Goldhagen's book was more positive. After a series of excellent reviews, Goldhagen's book has sold more copies than most other books on the Third Reich. Most historians, however, dismiss the book.

▶ Why might different audiences have reacted differently to the book?

of evidence. The following section provides an extract from his book, together with some contrasting views of other historians about the degree to which the Germans were anti-Semitic before 1933. You will then have the opportunity to study some primary evidence and reach your own conclusions about the popular reaction to Hitler's anti-Semitic policies.

How anti-Semitic were the German people before 1933?

Note

Anti-Semitism in Eastern Europe

Anti-Semitism was well established even before the depression in countries where there was a big Jewish minority. In Poland, for example, Jews were barred from entering the legal and medical professions and were encouraged to emigrate. By 1939, one-third of Polish Jews were dependent on welfare payments and charity.

■ **Further reading**

For more information about anti-Semitism, see Graml, *Anti-Semitism in the Third Reich,* 1992.

■ **Think about**

▶ To what extent do these extracts offer different interpretations of anti-Semitism in Germany before 1933?

▶ Why might it be possible for historians to hold such different views?

■ **Historical debate**

Source A

Daniel Jonah Goldhagen

the...model of Nazi anti-Semitism had taken shape well before the Nazis came to power, and...this model, throughout the nineteenth and early twentieth centuries, was...extremely widespread in all social classes and sectors of German society, for it was deeply embedded in German cultural and political life and conversation, as well as integrated into the moral structure of society.

Goldhagen, *Hitler's Willing Executioners,* 1996

Source B

Sarah Gordon

It is clear that Germany was in many ways a good place for Jews to live during these [pre–1933] years. Had the German population been uniquely rabid [extreme] in its hatred of Jews, it is inconceivable that Jews could have fared so well, especially compared to Jews in other nations.

Gordon,
Hitler, Germans and the Jewish Question, 1984

Source C

Richard J. Evans

If German nationalism defined Germanness by opposing itself to the negative image of Jews, how was it then that the civil equality and legal emancipation [freedom] of the Jews was one of its demands from the outset, finally implemented in full in the unification of 1871? If the German population and German elites were so deeply anti-Semitic, why did Jews actually gain civil equality by legislative enactment [i.e. laws] all over Germany in the course of the nineteenth century?

Evans, *Rereading Germany History 1800–1996,* 1997

What was the popular reaction to Hitler's anti-Semitism?

These extracts are intended to demonstrate the *variety* of responses to Hitler's anti-Semitism as well as to suggest what might have been the most *typical* response. As you study them, keep the debate on the previous page in your mind. To what extent do these extracts support the historians' views?

Source 5

1936 One always thinks that surely somewhere in Germany voices of shame and fear must be raised, protests must come from abroad, where everywhere there are Jews in the highest positions – nothing!

1937 Zaunick, grammar school teacher...man around fifty, recently came up to the car as we were parked at Bismarckplatz. Party badge. Could easily walk past without acknowledging us...But comes up with evident heartfelt pleasure. How am I, whether I have stayed in Dresden, how sorry he is...

In the **Sturmer** I recently saw a picture: two girls in swimming costumes at a seaside resort. Above it: 'Prohibited for Jews', underneath it: 'How nice that it's just us now!' Then I remembered a long-forgotten incident. September 1900 or 1901...In the lower sixth we were 4 among 16...There was little trace of anti-Semitism among either the teachers or the pupils. More precisely none at all...on the Day of Atonement – Yom Kippur – the Jews did not attend classes. The next day our comrades told us, laughing and without the slightest malice, Kufahl, the mathematician, had said to the class: 'Today it's **just** us.'...to me [these words] confirm the claim of the NSDAP to express the true opinion of the German people. And I believe ever more strongly that Hitler really does embody the soul of the German people...

1939 There is no German Jewish question. Whoever recognises one, only adopts or confirms the false thesis of the NSDAP and serves its cause. Until 1933 and for at least a good century before that, the German Jews were entirely German and nothing else...Jews and Germans lived and worked together without friction in all spheres of life. The anti-Semitism which was always present is not at all evidence to the contrary. Because friction between Jews and Aryans was not half as great as that between Protestants and Catholics...

1940 Yesterday I met Moses, the greengrocer...[and] was given an unfrozen cabbage, a swede and carrots – all rare delicacies. In addition a present of a bread coupon. Moses has already repeatedly given Eva potatoes. It is well known that we are allocated fewer coupons than 'comrades of the people'.

1941 Favourable experiences with the star [of David – all Jews were forced to wear it after 1941 to mark them out publicly]. Only a child of former acquaintances had run out full of fear: 'Ugh, a Jew!' Horrified, the mother apologised, he had not heard it at home – presumably at kindergarten...I myself experienced this whilst shopping. Elderly women, selling from a handcart...I glance longingly at the tomatoes, forbidden 'goods in short supply'. 'They're not to be had without a card, are they?' – 'I'll give you some, I know how things stand.' Makes up a pound. Then reaches under her cart, pulls out a handful of onions, which are very rare...There is no doubt that the people feel the persecution of the Jews to be a sin...

Extracts from the Diaries of Viktor Klemperer, a German Jew living in Dresden during the Third Reich (see page 158)

Source 6

I met my former secretary today. She fixed me sharply with her short-sighted eyes, and then turned away. I was so nauseated I spat into my handkerchief. She was once a patient of mine. Later I met her in the street...I took her on, trained her for years...Now she has changed so much that she can no longer greet me; me, who rescued her from the gutter!

Extract from the diary of a German Jewish Doctor, Hertha Nathorff, October 1935

Source 7

Between 10,000 and 12,000 German Jews went into hiding during the war. They were largely dependent on the help of people like Frau Erna Dubnack who hid her Jewish friend, Hilde Naumann, in her Berlin apartment between 1943 and 1945. When asked about the danger to herself, she replied:
'Ah, Gott, well, I, I...you know, one worked. I don't know. I didn't concern myself with it at all...'
But she must have known that she was risking her life.

Owings, *Frauen*, 1995

Source 8

Source 9

Anti-Semitism cannot, it seems, be allocated a significant role in bringing Hitler to power, though, given the widespread acceptability of the Jewish Question as a political issue – exploited not only by the Nazis – nor did it do anything to hinder his rapidly growing popularity. However, the relative indifference of most Germans towards the Jewish Question before 1933 meant that the Nazis did have a job on their hands after the 'take over of power' to persuade them of the need for active discrimination...The permanent radicalisation of anti-Jewish policies [after 1933] can hardly be said to have been the product of...the strong demands of popular opinion...Popular opinion, largely indifferent and...bolstered by propaganda, provided the climate within which spiralling Nazi aggression towards Jews could take place unchallenged. But it did not provoke the radicalisation in the first place. The road to Auschwitz was built by hate, but paved with indifference.

Kershaw, *Popular Opinion and Political Dissent in the Third Reich*, 1983

Source 10

Social discrimination against Jews was practically non-existent in the town. Jews were integrated along class lines: the two wealthiest Jewish families belonged to upper class circles and clubs, Jews of middling income belonged to the middle class social organisations, and working-class Jews were in the socialist community. Yet abstract anti-Semitism in the form of jokes or expressions of generalised distaste was common...If Nazi anti-Semitism held any appeal for the townspeople, it was in a highly abstract form...unconnected with daily encounters with real Jews in Thalburg ...Thalburgers were drawn to anti-Semitism because they were drawn to Nazism, not the other way round. Many who voted Nazi simply ignored other unpleasant aspects of the Nazi movement.

Allen, *The Nazi Seizure of Power: the Experience of a Single German Town 1922–1945*, 1966

Source 11

I learned from the example of my parents...that one could have anti-Semitic opinions without this interfering in one's personal relations with individual Jews...When I heard that the Jews were being driven from their professions and homes and imprisoned in ghettos, the points switched automatically in my mind to steer me round the thought that such a fate could also overtake you or old Levy. It was only the Jew who was being persecuted and 'made harmless'.

Extract from the memoirs of Melita Maschmann

■ Activity

1 Study all the sources carefully. Then note down any evidence which *proves* or *disproves* the following statements:
  ● The German people were extremely anti-Semitic before 1933
  ● The German people actively supported the Nazis' anti-Semitic policies
  ● The German people were largely indifferent to the Nazis' anti-Semitic policies

2 Can you add any further evidence using your own knowledge? *(you may wish to look back at the document exercise on pages 206–207)*

3 Clearly, there was a degree of *acceptance* amongst the German people with regard to anti-Semitic policies in the Third Reich. Do any of the sources suggest a reason for this? Can you suggest any other reasons, from your own knowledge?

4 What are the difficulties facing the historian who wishes to reach a conclusion about the popular reaction to the Nazis' anti-Semitic policies?

The Impact of the Second World War

Rationing

As you would expect, war brought hardships to the German people, both emotionally, as their loved ones left to fight, and physically, with shortages of goods and an increased work burden. Food was rationed immediately, although the Germans were not faced with chronic shortages of food until 1944. However, certain products such as meat and fats were soon in short supply and food consumption per person fell by 25 per cent between 1939–1941. People were encouraged to use unfamiliar, more exotic products brought in from the conquered territories, such as aubergines, fennel and Jerusalem artichokes, but it proved difficult to change people's tastes. Ingenious recipes were devised by special groups to make use of available products and parks and gardens in the cities were dug up and used as vegetable patches.

It was not only food that was rationed: items such as cigarettes, soap, clothing and shoes were also restricted. By 1941, women were allowed only one and a half cigarettes a day and old shoes had to be given up when new ones were bought. Indeed, any household suspected of harbouring unnecessary footwear was inspected by Nazi officials and the offending items removed.

Bombing

Source 12

◄ The centre of Dresden in 1945.

The workforce

Germany faced a serious shortage of labour during the war. By the autumn of 1944 a total of 13 million men had been drafted into the army, leaving a dwindling number of workers to produce the crucial armaments needed at the front. Despite attempts to redistribute workers, the shortage remained acute.

Note

Wartime recipes
Baked udder with herbs
Stuffed calf's heart
Escalope of kohlrabi
Sorrel cutlets
Nettle soufflé
Daisy salad
Rose-hip soup
Acorn nougat
Acorn coffee

Note

Allied aircraft carried out a total of 1,442,280 missions over Germany, especially from 1943 onwards. 2,700,000 tons of bombs were dropped and an estimated 650,000 civilians were killed.

Note

The Nazis were concerned not to alienate the German workers too much and measures to ban holidays, make overtime compulsory and extend hours of work were delayed until the summer of 1944. Nevertheless, working hours were generally longer and a higher rate of sick leave was evidence enough that the work was hard going.

The solution was to bring in thousands of foreign workers and prisoners of war (POWs) and by the end of 1944, more than 8 million foreigners were working in Germany. The foreign workers were paid very little and were hardly predisposed to hard labour, whilst the POWs were treated so appallingly that many of them never made it into a German factory at all. In January 1943 a register was compiled of all able-bodied men between 16 and 65 and women between 17 and 50 who could contribute to the war effort. Again, this wasn't enough, partly because Hitler's reluctance to mobilize women meant that many exceptions were made, and those who were brought in to work often did so on a part-time basis only.

The persecution of the Jews

During the war, persecution of the Jews intensified. In 1941, all Jews were forced to wear the yellow Star of David on their sleeve, a measure which kept Viktor Klemperer indoors for days, unable to face the world outside with this distinguishing mark on him. Jewish emigration was banned in 1941, leaving a third of the Jewish population of 1933 trapped inside a country where their fate appeared to be increasingly sealed. As the war went on, Jews were either rounded up and sent to camps or went into hiding. Those with Aryan partners or parents were safer until 1945, at which point even their lives were at risk. However, the majority of Germany's Jews survived the Third Reich through emigration before 1941 or through hiding. The same cannot, of course, be said of Jews elsewhere in Europe, for example in Poland.

The response of the Churches

Initially at least, the Churches offered no resistance to the war itself. Martin Niemoller, leader of the Confessional Church, even sent a request from Sachsenhausen concentration camp asking for permission to join the German navy. However, harassment of both Churches increased during the early years of the war until Hitler ordered the attacks to stop in the summer of 1941. The Churches responded vigorously to attacks on their own freedoms although they still refrained from open criticism of the Nazis' policies on the 'Jewish Question'. It was left for individual priests and pastors to voice their opposition to the growing barbarity of Nazi policies. Nazi reports during 1943 claimed that Catholic priests were publicly expressing their outrage over policies of genocide. From the Nazi point of view, this was all the more serious in the light of increased attendance at church services. Hitler made it clear however that the destruction of the Churches would have to wait until the end of the war.

How unpopular was the Nazi Party during the war?

Although the German people did not greet the outbreak of war with enthusiasm, the early victories helped to sustain public confidence in the Party and especially in the Führer himself. The sudden collapse of powerful countries such as France seemed to confirm the belief that Hitler was a military genius. However, by December 1940, when the initial run of victories was over and people were faced with the onset of another winter as well as the first spate of Allied bombing raids, Goebbels described the popular mood as one of 'light depression'. This mood became a permanent one after war was declared on Russia in June 1941 and the hopes of a short war soon disappeared.

People responded to an endless stream of propaganda with increased scepticism for which they had good reason. Letters from soldiers fighting at the front painted a very different picture from official reports. Overall, the Nazi

Party certainly lost support during the war. More and more people were reluctant to participate in Party activities and even loyal members were less inclined to attend Party meetings. Membership of the Party fell and the ban imposed on further membership had to be temporarily lifted. The Battle of Stalingrad in 1942–1943 proved a turning point in the people's tolerance of war. All they now wanted was an end to the war. The regime was obliged to make 'defeatism' a criminal offence and punishable by death. Despite this, by 1945, half a million Germans were held in concentration camps compared with 100,000 in 1942.

However, the vast majority of people remained loyal to their Führer. Despite Hitler's preoccupation with the war (he only made three public speeches in 1943) he remained much more popular then the Party itself. Attempts on his life – especially in 1944 – were condemned by many people, partly because they felt that Hitler was the only one who could get Germany out of the mess she was facing abroad. The Churches also spoke out against assassination attempts.

However, even Hitler was the target of some popular criticism after 1943. One Nazi report in 1943 drew attention to the fact that some people were 'openly risking criticism of the Führer himself' by spreading malicious rumours or telling jokes.

How serious was wartime opposition?

Although many people remained basically loyal to the regime during the war, the number of individuals who began seriously to consider ways of overthrowing the regime increased. In most cases, these were people who had supported the Nazis during their early years in power but had become disillusioned during the war.

The White Rose

The White Rose was a student resistance movement organized in Munich University and led by Hans and Sophie Scholl. Most of the members had been initially attracted to the Nazi regime but became increasingly hostile as they witnessed its brutality. Hans Scholl served as a medical orderly on the Eastern Front in 1942 and returned even more convinced of the need to oppose the Nazis. His sister Sophie, meanwhile, had been collecting information about the gassing of disabled children. Together with friends, the students conducted a leaflet campaign condemning the barbarity of the Nazis and stressing the need for action. In February 1943, the White Rose decided to drop leaflets denouncing Nazis as 'sub-humans' into the university lecture rooms. They were spotted by a porter who immediately called the Gestapo. They were arrested and later that month, Hans and Sophie were sentenced to death and beheaded in the courtyard of Stadelheim prison. At her trial Sophie Scholl said 'What we have written and said is in the mind of all of you, but you lack the courage to say it aloud.'

The communists

During the period of the Nazi–Soviet Pact (1939–1941), underground communist groups were unsure what action to take against the Nazis. The official line from Russia was to support Stalin's foreign policy but to oppose Hitler within Germany. The German attack on Russia in June 1941 clarified the communist position. The German communists increased their attempts to undermine the regime, not least by participating in Soviet spy networks. The

Note

The SD summary reports of public mood were stopped in 1944 because their contents had become too demoralizing for the government.

Quotation

A wartime joke

'What is the difference between India and Germany? In India one man [Gandhi] starves for all, in Germany all starve for one man!'

Quotation

Why do the German people behave so apathetically in face of all these dreadful and inhuman crimes?...It is not only pity that we ought to feel but guilt...Each will declare himself guiltless, each does so and then goes to sleep with an easy conscience. But he cannot declare himself guiltless, he is guilty, guilty, guilty.

Extract from a
White Rose leaflet

most famous of these, the Red Orchestra, was uncovered by the Gestapo in 1942 and its leaders hanged in Berlin. Sabotage action continued but in the aftermath of the Bomb Plot in July 1944, thousands of communist activists were arrested.

Conservative opposition

The main conservative opposition group during the war was the Kreisau Circle. This was a diverse group including aristocrats, socialists, clergymen and foreign office officials. It was named after the Silesian estate of Count Helmuth von Moltke where meetings of the circle took place from 1940. The aim of the group was to draw up plans for the period after Hitler's downfall rather than to orchestrate that event themselves. Von Moltke was arrested in January 1944 for speaking against the regime. After his arrest, some members of the circle continued their work and developed links with Colonel von Stauffenberg, in the German army. Von Moltke was executed early in 1945.

The Bomb Plot, 20 July 1944

In 1943, as hopes of victory seemed lost, plans to assassinate Hitler began to take shape within the army itself. After hearing of mass murders of Jews in May 1942, Colonel Claus von Stauffenberg emerged as a key figure in the co-ordination of 'Operation Valkyrie'. Up until that point, Stauffenberg had supported the Nazis in their war aims, even during the Russian setbacks, but the news of atrocities convinced him that it was the duty of army commanders to overthrow the regime.

In May 1944, Stauffenberg was appointed Chief-of-Staff to the Home Army Commander. This position enabled him to make preparations to lead the Home Army in support of the coup once Hitler was assassinated. It also – and this was crucial – gave Stauffenberg access to Hitler himself. It was for this reason that Stauffenberg, physically unsuited to the task, was given the job of planting the bomb intended to kill Hitler. After the assassination, the conspirators intended to declare martial law, set up a provisional government and negotiate for immediate peace with the allies. They were motivated by a desire to save Germany from total destruction, to end the killing which had become pointless – and to prove that there were some Germans prepared to take a stand.

Why did the Bomb Plot fail?

On 20 July, Stauffenberg took two kilos of plastic explosives to a conference at Obersalzberg. He was disturbed whilst setting the fuses and only carried one kilo of explosives into the meeting which, to his surprise, was taking place in the tea-house, rather than the concrete bunker as usual. Stauffenberg placed the briefcase containing the bomb under the large oak table. A table leg lay between the briefcase and its intended victim. Stauffenberg, making the excuse of a pretended telephone call, left the room and drove off immediately to an airstrip where a plane was waiting to carry him back to Berlin to take charge of events once Hitler was dead. Hitler was leaning across the table studying a map when the bomb exploded. The flimsy walls of the tea-house were not enough to contain the force of the bomb which would have caused more damage had the meeting been carried out in the bunker. One person died immediately and a further three died later, but Hitler, shielded by the solid oak table leg, suffered only bruises and a perforated eardrum.

Although the assassination attempt had failed, the coup might still have succeeded had the response been swift and decisive. However, the time taken

■ **Biography**

Claus von Stauffenberg

Born in 1907 to an aristocratic family, Stauffenberg distinguished himself in the early part of the Second World War, serving as an officer in Poland, France and North Africa. In 1943 he suffered extensive wounds, losing an eye, his right hand and part of his left. Soon afterwards he became more openly opposed to Hitler and the Nazis. He deplored the barbaric practices carried out in Europe and joined fellow conspirators in planning Hitler's death. He was the leader of the 1944 conspiracy.

Quotation

I know that he who will act will go down in German history as a traitor; but he who can and does not, will be a traitor to his conscience. If I did not act to stop this senseless killing, I should never be able to face the widows and orphans of the war.

Claus von Stauffenberg

by Stauffenberg to return to Berlin caused a fatal delay during which time the news of Hitler's survival began to reach the other conspirators. Indecision followed and the failure to cut all communications from Obersalzberg robbed the operation of time in which to gather forces. Stauffenberg was arrested when he reached Berlin and shot. A wave of terror followed in which over 7,000 were arrested and around 5,000 executed by April 1945.

Source 13

◀ Goering surveys the remains of the oak table which saved Hitler's life in July 1944.

■ **Further reading**

For more information on resistance to the Nazis, see Clay Large, *Contending with Hitler,* 1991

Document exercise: Resistance during the war

Source A
The views of a conservative anti-Nazi

Berlin, 21 October 1941
The day is so full of gruesome news that I cannot write in peace, although I retired at 5 and have just had some tea...What affects me most is the inadequacy of the reactions of the military... dreadful new orders are being issued, and nobody seems to see anything wrong in it all. How is one to bear the burden of complicity [going along with everything]? In one area in Serbia two villages have been reduced to ashes, 1,700 men and 240 women from among the inhabitants have been executed....May I know this and yet still sit at my table in my heated flat and have tea? Don't I thereby become guilty too? What shall I say when I am asked: And what did you do during that time?... Since Saturday the Berlin Jews are being rounded up...A women Kiep knows saw a Jew collapse on the street; when she wanted to help him, a policeman stepped in, stopped her, and kicked the body on the ground so that it rolled into the gutter; then he turned to the lady with some shame and said: 'Those are our orders.'

Extracts from *Letters to Freya* by Helmuth James von Moltke (leader of the Kreisau Circle, who was executed early in 1945), 1991

Source B
The Catholic reaction to war and genocide

[From Upper Silesia:] In closing, I point to the fact that the Church knowingly ignores the difference between the races. Priests speak for, and pray for 'Catholics of different languages'...In two districts of the old Reich, the clergy attempted to have their German congregation sing old Polish hymns with a German text. A mass was said by a German congregation for Poles who died in a concentration camp...

From reports of 6–12 June 1943, written by regional Nazi Party leaders

Source C

The resistance of university students

The war is approaching its inevitable end. With mathematical certainty Hitler is leading the German nation to disaster. Now it is time for those Germans to act who want to avoid being lumped with the Nazi barbarians by the outside world...Only in broad-minded co-operation between the peoples of Europe can the basis be established for a new society...Freedom of speech, freedom of belief, protection of the individual citizen against...criminal power – these are the foundations of a new Europe.

From a leaflet written in January 1943 by Hans Scholl, leader of the White Rose

Source D

'What about father?' 'He was executed'

My father was a member of the SPD, and because he felt his duties were in Germany, he refused an offer to emigrate to the United States...In 1938 came a turning point that had a very strange effect on my father's career...During this time, Colonel Graf Stauffenberg came to our house on two occasions...One evening in June 1944, my father let me in on the secret with the words, 'I have to put a burden on your shoulders, since now you are a soldier.' He then told me in great detail about his activities in the civilian resistance movement. He was an absolute supporter of the concept of surrender to the Allies after a successful assassination. That way at least all of the troops, especially those in the east, could be brought back...Inwardly he was a sceptic, an opponent of the assassination. But he saw that in all likelihood we would have no other chance to make clear that there were not only Nazis in Germany.

The memories of Michael Maas, whose father was executed by the Nazis after the Bomb Plot in July 1944

■ Examination-style questions

1 **Comprehension in context**
   Using Source B and your own knowledge, explain why the Nazis were concerned about the behaviour of certain Catholic priests.

2 **Comparing the sources**
   Study all the sources. To what extent do they agree about the reasons for opposing the Nazis during the war?

3 **Assessing the sources**
   Assess the usefulness of Source B to a historian studying the response of the Catholic Church to the Nazi regime during the war.

4 **Making judgements**
   Using all the sources and your own knowledge, explain why resistance to the Nazis during the war was unsuccessful.

Conclusions

Before the war there were few attempts to overthrow the Third Reich. This was not because all Germans were happy with the Nazi regime. What stopped people from acting more aggressively was fear and the lack of an organized opposition. It is true, however, that the Nazis did enjoy some popular support during the 1930s and this contributed to the regime's survival. Only the army had the power and resources to destroy the Nazi regime and it was not until defeat in the Second World War seemed imminent that army generals took action. Their failure in 1944 was a humanitarian disaster. During the final year of the war, thousands of lives were lost, not just of those fighting and living in the battle zones but also of Europe's Jews.

Chapter 14

Interpretations of Nazism

Source 1

▲ Hitler at a Nuremberg rally.

Source 2

In so far as it is unlikely that a political oddity like Hitler will ever again achieve political power, it is a serious mistake to concentrate study of the Nazi tyranny on an analysis of the role which Hitler occupied in it. Dictators are as dependent on the political circumstances which bring them to power as they in turn influence these. The destructive and profoundly inhuman forces which the Nazi system unleashed at all levels may well appear again, though under very different circumstances, with different structures, in a different form and certainly with less forcefulness. This is the context in which the experience of the Third Reich should be analysed thoroughly. The fact that Germany – a civilised and highly developed industrial society – rampaged violently out of control has political implications for us today, and it would be wrong to hide these behind a façade that isolates Hitler as the sole and root cause of it. How Hitler could succeed in securing various degrees of support from considerable sections of the German population must be explained in this context.

Mommsen, *From Weimar to Auschwitz*, 1991

■ **Think about**

▶ What is Mommsen arguing in Source 2?

▶ Do you agree?

■ **Further reading**

By far the best starting point on interpretations of the Third Reich is Ian Kershaw's *The Nazi Dictatorship*, 2000. Some of the major works of the historians mentioned on this page are listed below. Note: only works translated into English have been listed which is why the publication date may not be the same as in the main text.

Fischer, *Germany's Aims in the First World War*, 1967
Wehler, *The German Empire, 1871–1918*, 1985
Broszat, *The Hitler State*, 1981
Mommsen, *From Weimar to Auschwitz*, 1991

Note

Most recently there has been an attempt to synthesize or combine some of these different approaches to Hitler and Nazism, as you will discover.

Introduction: historians and Hitler

In the aftermath of the Second World War there was a desperate attempt by German historians to distance the German people from the appalling crimes of the Nazis. In West Germany this took the form of demonizing Hitler and arguing that it was the unique nature of Hitler's evil which had led the nation astray. This view minimized the responsibility of the German people for Nazism. Meanwhile in America, William Shirer (an American journalist who was in Germany during the Third Reich, was present at the Nuremberg Trials in 1945, and published his massive *The Rise and Fall of the Third Reich* in 1959) claimed to trace the roots of Nazism back through centuries of German history. The Nazis, he argued, were products of the German people themselves. They did bear responsibility for what had happened.

These two different interpretations of Nazism can be clearly related to the time and place in which they were produced. They each attempted to explain Nazism in a way immediately appealing to their respective audiences. This is not, however, where the interpretations ended. In the 1960s, Fritz Fischer (1961), though not claiming that the roots of Nazism could be traced back for centuries, nevertheless questioned the conclusions of the West German historians after the war who argued that Hitler's evilness only bore fruit in the extraordinary circumstances of Germany in the 1920s. Fischer instead drew a comparison between the leaders of Germany immediately before the First World War and Hitler. They all, Fischer argued, held expansionist ambitions and were prepared to engage in war to achieve them. This view led to an examination of those members of the German elite who held positions of incredible influence and power in Germany around the turn of the century. Historians such as Wehler (1973) began to point to continuities amongst this elite, who clung desperately to their power in the early 1900s and even supported a war in 1914 which might prolong their period of supremacy. The aim of this elite was to keep a form of authoritarian rule in Germany. In Wehler's view, this paved the way for Hitler because the pre-war elite anticipated some of Hitler's mass political tactics and helped to create a political culture based on subservience and a vulnerability to the appeal of authoritarian rule. Not only that, but members of this elite were prepared, in desperation, to aid Hitler's rise to power.

Wehler's approach was 'structural': it focused less on the particular individual in power and more on the society and political system in which the individual ruled. However, Wehler did not focus on the Third Reich. It was historians such as Broszat (1969) and Mommsen (1971) who adopted a 'structuralist' approach to the Third Reich. They were interested in *how* Hitler ruled and what light this could shed on *why* he was able to build up such an extraordinary power base. Their conclusions, whilst hardly denying Hitler's importance, nevertheless suggested outside factors which help us to understand the nature of his power. They also encouraged a trend which has continued to gain momentum ever since, and that is the study of 'ordinary' Germans. Studying the Third Reich 'from the bottom up' has revealed the sheer complexities of the German reaction to Nazism.

Running alongside this 'structuralist' interpretation was a more traditional view of the Third Reich which continued to emphasize the role of Hitler. Many of these interpretations stressed the importance of Hitler's own visions and beliefs as first outlined in *Mein Kampf*. Historians such as Trevor-Roper (1960) and Hildebrand (1969) argued that Hitler followed a programme, in foreign policy at least. He imposed his wishes on the nation and most of what happened,

happened because he wished it to. This interpretation has become known as the 'intentionalist' school.

Why have historians differed?

East and West Germany

Between 1949 and 1990 Germany was divided in two. East Germany – formally known as the GDR – was run by communists and dominated by Russia. West Germany – formally known as the FRG – was by contrast run as a modern, capitalist democracy with close relations with the rest of Europe and the United States. The differences between the political systems of these two states had a profound effect on the interpretations of Nazism produced by German historians.

In East Germany, Nazism was characterized as the evil consequence of capitalism. The emphasis was not solely on Hitler himself but on the form of fascism which Nazism was characterized as representing. The role of big business in supporting Hitler was highlighted (although this has been questioned by many, especially regarding the years before Hitler was appointed Chancellor). In addition, the role of communist opposition to Nazism was emphasized by GDR historians. All of this served to legitimize the GDR itself. If Nazism as an extreme capitalist system was the problem, then the opposite system, that of communism, was the solution. Nothing could be more different from Nazism. This was useful propaganda to those seeking to build support for the communist regime.

In the West, more attention was paid to explaining Nazism in such a way as to free the German people of collective guilt. This would enable West Germany once again to play an active role in European affairs and ensure that the hostility that lasted beyond the First World War was not repeated. As time went on, however, and West Germany became more established and accepted in the Western World, this need to exonerate the German nation became less crucial. It was clear that Germany had moved on and historians were freer to pose more difficult questions about, for example, the exact nature of people's response to Nazism.

Historical approach

It should be clear from the introduction that historians have varied considerably in the way they have approached the history of the Third Reich. Some more than others have focused on the role of certain individuals, concentrating on the beliefs and power of Hitler in particular. Others have approached it from the other end of the telescope, arguing that it wasn't simply Hitler that determined what was done and how, but also external, structural factors such as the Nazi system of government and German society. This is a key difference and can influence the way different historians interpret the *same* piece of evidence.

Aims and ideology

As we have already seen, two different ideologies emerged in the two Germanys after 1949. In East Germany, where communist ideology dominated, the aim behind much history of the Third Reich was to highlight the evils of capitalism. In the West, by contrast, much of the early history of the Third Reich was anti-totalitarian. Hitler's Nazism was compared with Stalin's communism. The emphasis was on the promotion of free democracies and on trying to distance West Germany from the evils of Nazism. As time went on, however,

■ **Think about**

▶ Why do you think different historians might favour either a 'structuralist' interpretation or an 'intentionalist' one?

Cross reference

See Chapter 15 on the division of Germany in 1949.

Note

The Marxist view of history interprets the past in terms of economic development. All societies are believed to go through various economic stages of which capitalism is the last straw, leading ultimately to the preferred model of communism. For Marxists, Nazism was seen as a form of fascism, which in itself was seen as an extreme form of capitalism. Fascism, they argued, resulted from capitalism in crisis, when profits began to fall. It involved extreme methods to save the economy and protect the profit-makers: for example, smashing trade unions and expanding abroad to secure cheap raw material and bigger markets.

Note

The move towards more study of 'everyday' life has also shifted the emphasis away from seeing the German people as acting and behaving as one. Instead, regional studies such as Kershaw's in Bavaria reveal the complexity and variety of responses to the Nazi regime.

■ **Think about**

Historians in the West were consciously using their accounts of the Third Reich to sound a warning against the dangers of totalitarianism and to try to ensure that it was never repeated.

▶ Is this a valid use of history?

▶ What effects might such an aim have on the way in which they interpreted the past?

West Germany's need to protect herself from any bad press receded and historians were able to study the Third Reich in its own right, rather than as a means of legitimizing the present.

This has subsequently led to many different interpretations of the Third Reich amongst West German historians – and indeed amongst historians of the western world.

Evidence

Although it might appear to students of Nazism that one thing it does not lack is evidence, there are some significant gaps. Some of these are the product of deliberate action by the Nazis themselves, especially towards the end of the war when material was destroyed. Other gaps, however, are the result of circumstance. Bombing raids by the allies accidentally destroyed evidence, for example. And Hitler's very method of governing, with a minimum of paperwork and few formal meetings, means that the evidence stops short of the key decisions where Hitler – we presume – was involved. One gap, for example, is the order to carry out the Final Solution. There is no actual record of who gave the order to go ahead so it is difficult to be certain how big a role Hitler played in it. This lack of evidence causes problems for those trying to prove that Hitler controlled everything in the Nazi government.

Conclusion

As you can see, there are many factors influencing the way historians have interpreted Nazism. Although we have primarily concentrated on German historians here, these differences extend to historians outside Germany. In conclusion, when assessing an interpretation of Nazism, it is necessary to consider the following:

- When was it written? How soon after the war?
- Where was it written? East Germany? West Germany? Outside of Germany?
- Why was it written? Was there a clear purpose?
- Which approach was used? A 'structural' approach or an 'intentionalist' approach?

Cross reference

Before reading this section, you are advised to re-read Chapter 9, especially pages 165–171.

A weak dictator or master in the Third Reich?

As you know from Chapter 9, the Nazi government was far from the well-organized machine suggested by its propaganda. In reality, Nazi officials worked in isolation, ignorant of what others were doing and often duplicating their work. Hitler was somewhat aloof from the day-to-day business of government and had a dislike for paperwork. He preferred others to present him with ideas to which he could respond. Decisions were not always taken quickly and Nazi policy often lacked the coherence which a more organized government would produce.

Historians have disagreed, however, on whether this was a *deliberate* policy by Hitler. Did he deliberately allow the Nazi state to be governed in such a chaotic fashion because it enhanced his own power? By remaining aloof and appointing several people to the same job, was he deliberately encouraging in-fighting and a complete dependence on him alone? Those historians who advance this argument are part of the 'intentionalist' school. They are also known as 'programmists'. They believe that Hitler *did* intend this chaos and that it is further evidence that Hitler was master in the Third Reich. They argue that Hitler followed a programme as laid out in *Mein Kampf* and that everything which followed was shaped by this. This particular argument has

Note

The historian Hildebrand has gone as far as to say that Nazism was in fact Hitlerism, such was the pivotal role of Hitler in the Party.

been most successfully applied to foreign policy (see Chapter 12, page 237).

Other historians, part of the 'structuralist' school and also known as 'functionalists', argue that Hitler did not set out to create this chaos. It was in fact a consequence of his own laziness. Rather than being in full control of events, Hitler was in fact constrained by various outside, 'structural' factors. These included his dependence on State institutions dominated by traditional elites (such as the civil service), an economy allegedly spiralling out of control by 1939 and the actions of other states. They also included Hitler's own personality which was ill-suited to the governing of a large state. According to this interpretation, Hitler was forced to respond to events more than he was able to shape them. There was an absence of clear planning and Hitler's ideological aims were little more than propaganda devices to unite the people.

■ Think about

The 'structuralist' interpretation shifts some of the emphasis away from Hitler and in doing so highlights the role of the German elites in supporting Nazism. Think back to the issues raised earlier in this chapter.

▶ Why do you think the 'structuralist' interpretation emerged in West Germany in the late 1960s and not before?

Source 3

In the twelve years of his rule in Germany Hitler produced the biggest confusion in government that has ever existed in a civilised state. During his period of government, he removed from the organisation of the State all clarity of leadership and produced a completely opaque network of competencies. It was not laziness or an excessive degree of tolerance which led the otherwise so energetic and forceful Hitler to tolerate this real witch's cauldron of struggles for position and conflicts over competence. It was intentional. With this technique he systematically disorganised the upper echelons of the Reich leadership in order to develop and further the authority of his own will until it became a despotic tyranny.

Otto Dietrich, Hitler's press chief

Source 4

One thing, especially, Hitler never did – he never ran counter to the opinion of his *Gauleiters*, his district commissioners. Each of these men was in his power, but together they held him in theirs...The secret of his leadership lay in knowing in advance what course the majority of his *Gauleiters* would decide on, and in being the first to declare for that course...Hitler was at all times dependent on them – and not on them alone...the result was that his policy continually developed along wholly different lines to those he had envisaged. He maintained his position of supremacy, but he lost his freedom of decision.

From the memoirs of Rauschning, at one time a friend of Hitler's

Note

Rauschning is probably here referring to Hitler in 1934. See page 172 for a definition of *Gauleiter*.

■ Activity

Look at Sources 3 and 4. Source 3 comes from the memoirs of Otto Dietrich, who was Hitler's press chief. Source 4 is from the memoirs of Rauschning, originally a friend and supporter of Hitler but forced to flee Germany in 1936 and subsequently a critic of Nazism. How could these sources be used by both 'intentionalist' and 'structuralist' historians to support their case?

Interpretations exercise: Was Hitler the master of the Third Reich?

Source A

The confusion and conflict of leadership and administrative hierarchy was further complicated by the wide proliferation of leadership positions. The machinery of both Party and State had to be expanded if the all-encompassing supervisory functions of the totalitarian system were to be carried out. The alleged inefficiency and corruption of the Weimar democracy were as nothing compared to the costly expansion of the one-party state and the antagonistic coexistence of overlapping top-level bodies. So long as the Führer did not interfere – and he gave free rein to the policy of divide and conquer – nothing could stop this. On the contrary. Over the years, Hitler, in the consolidation of his leader dictatorship, created a vast special bureaucracy which in turn had to collide with the 'normal' agencies.

Bracher, *The German Dictatorship*, 1970

■ Activity

Would you describe each of these interpretations (Sources A–D) as 'intentionalist', 'structuralist' or a combination of the two? Summarize your conclusions in the form of a chart:

View of historian	Evidence/reasons provided to support view

Source B

Hitler was never as sure of himself and his position as both his enemies and friends thought. He was a man playing in a game of chance, a German roulette...Particularly in his early days in power, until the Röhm murder and the death of Hindenburg, [there is] evidence of real fears of opposition and then real surprise that the opposition had melted away...Like most common men, he overestimated the ability of his 'superiors'. When he himself was the 'superior', he avoided meetings with subordinates who might question a decision, or he flooded them with monologue to prevent their raising any objection. This is a sign of weakness, not strength...The suspicion is strong that Hitler avoided the really difficult decisions and acted only when forced to and then not from a long-considered specific plan, but from simple prejudices and the inspiration of the moment. Possibly he was overrun by circumstance. Precise plans, as against romantic dreams, may have been the concern of his more methodical subordinates, and possibly of more inventive historians who 'discovered' them.

Peterson, *The Limits of Hitler's Power*, 1969

Source C

The notorious insecurity which pervaded the power structures of the Reich was encouraged by Hitler more out of habit than purposefully and to a large extent was simply a logical consequence of the Nazis' inability to settle into a stable institutional framework once they had achieved power. This insecurity was the source of constant competition for the Führer's favour among the regime's potentates [rulers]. It led to the top officials of the regime constantly seeking to excel each other in advocating ever more radical policies, though they were always careful to ensure that these were in line with Hitler's ideological tirades and – very importantly – not a threat to the position of other dominant interests in the system.

Mommsen, *From Weimar to Auschwitz*, 1991

Source D

...in the case of Hitler there was never any question of a *fronde* [uprising] against the leader, and one of the significant features of both National Socialism and the Third Reich is the fact that from the beginning to the very end it stood and fell with this man, with his decisions, his ideological fixations, his purely political way of life, and his need for the grandiose alternative of victory or catastrophe...It influenced not only the ideological goals of the movement but even more the organization of mass meetings displaying overwhelming power and leader-worship. For these reasons, National Socialism can indeed be called Hitlerism. This man and his intentions and actions will always be in the very centre of Nazi history. But at the same time, Hitler himself is to be understood in terms of German and European traditions which formed the framework and feeding ground of a Nationalist Socialist movement that existed well before Hitler.

Bracher, 'The Role of Hitler: Perspectives of Interpretation', in Laqueur, *Fascism A Reader's Guide*, 1976

Synthesis

How are we supposed to reach a conclusion on this issue? As we have already seen, the evidence itself is never going to provide a conclusive answer:

Source 5

The hypothesis that Hitler was the sole author of all the crimes of the Third Reich cannot be proved in the most mundane sense – the source materials are both inadequate both in quantity and quality to prove it. At this elementary level we know less about Hitler's control over German policy, much less about his motives and calculations, than we know about the conduct of most other nineteenth- or twentieth-century political leaders. For this reason alone, an analysis of his choices and of his influence is exceptionally difficult to execute.

Tim Mason 'Intention and Explanation: A Current Controversy about the Interpretation of National Socialism' in Hirschfeld and Kettenacker, *The 'Führer State': Myth and Reality*, 1981

Historians have now begun to see a way through these debates (which were never as polarized as some historians claimed) to reach an interpretation which acknowledges the structural constraints on Hitler whilst maintaining that he was powerful enough to pursue his major aims. In other words, whilst Nazism cannot be seen simply as Hitlerism and Hitler was not quite the 'master' that historians once thought, he was nevertheless far from being a 'weak dictator'.

How popular was Nazi rule in Germany 1933–1939?

As we have seen, in the aftermath of the war, German historians were busy creating an image of the German people being somehow tricked and cruelly manipulated by Hitler. Outside Germany, there were contrasting attempts to share out the blame for the Third Reich among the German people and to blame their particular human nature. Both interpretations were far too simplistic. What has emerged in their place since the 1960s is a much more complex and sensible emphasis on the variety of responses to Nazism. That is not to say, however, that historians have not differed in their overall interpretations.

■ Examination-style questions

1 **Comprehension in context**
Using Source A and your own knowledge, explain what the author means by 'The confusion and conflict of leadership'.

2 **Comparing the sources**
To what extent do Sources A and C differ in their interpretation of the Nazi state?

3 **Assessing the sources**
To what extent should we treat all these interpretations with some caution?

4 **Making judgements**
Using all the sources and your own knowledge, do you agree that Hitler was indeed 'master in the Third Reich' with no real limitations to his power?

Quotation

Men do make their own history, but they do not make it as they please, not under conditions of their own choosing, but rather under circumstances which they find before them, under given and imposed circumstances.

Marx, 18th Brumaire

▶ Could this quotation be applied to Hitler?

■ Think about

▶ How satisfactory is this synthesis in your opinion?

Cross reference

You are advised to read Chapter 13 again before reading this section.

Broadly speaking, historians have differed in their responses to the following questions:

- What do we mean by 'resistance'? What kinds of behaviour did it include?
- Who resisted Nazism and why?
- Did resistance – defined in its broadest sense – have any impact on the Nazis?

What do we mean by resistance?

Resistance to the Nazis, as interpreted in its most narrow sense, means any action intended to destroy the Nazi regime. This would include assassination attempts on Hitler, for example, and is mainly restricted to the war years and to elite groups, such as the army. There have been alternative interpretations of resistance, however. One of the broadest definitions was offered by H.A. Jacobsen in 1969 (see Source 6).

In Jacobsen's definition, resistance encompasses every kind of rejection of Nazism, from a refusal to give the Nazi salute, to the reading of banned literature, to more dangerous acts of public opposition such as criticizing the regime or continuing to shop in Jewish stores. Jacobsen's definition therefore brackets assassination attempts on Hitler with much more low-key, less dangerous refusals to conform. Martin Broszat proposed a similar interpretation by also arguing that resistance should be examined on a much broader scale than outright attempts to bring down Nazism. He uses the term *'Resistenz'* which roughly translates as the kind of resistance you build up against germs. It does not therefore imply wholly active behaviour but could mean a kind of immunity to Nazism. Again, this would include a range of different kinds of behaviour including relatively minor actions about which the Nazis themselves were probably unaware.

Some historians are not happy with such an all-encompassing definition, however. By using the same term to describe a large spectrum of behaviour, you run the risk of blurring the distinction between different responses to Nazism. In other words, you are over-simplifying the issue. The historian Peukert has tried to overcome this by constructing a graph on which an enormous range of different kinds of behaviour can be plotted:

Source 7

Scope of criticism of the system — general / partial

Nonconformist behaviour – Refusal – Protest – Resistance

private ---------- public/political

Sphere within which dissident behaviour takes place

Who resisted, why and how?

Interpretations have differed according to where the historians came from. The chart on the next page summarizes the changing interpretations to come out of West Germany. It is based on chapter eight of Kershaw's book *The Nazi Dictatorship*, 1993.

Source 6

The concept of resistance must comprise all that was done despite the terror of the Third Reich, despite the suffering and martyrdom, for the sake of humanity, for the aid of the persecuted. And the word resistance in some cases applies, too, to certain forms of standing aside in silence.

Jacobsen, *Germans Against Hitler. July 20 1944*, 1969

■ Activity

Firstly, read Kershaw's categories of different kinds of opposition below:

Resistance – active participation in *organized* attempts to work against the regime with the conscious aim of undermining it or planning for the moment of its demise.

Opposition – a wider concept comprising many forms of actions with partial and limited aims, not directed against Nazism as a system and in fact sometimes stemming from individuals or groups broadly sympathetic towards the regime and its ideology.

Dissent – the voicing of attitudes frequently spontaneous and often unrelated to any intended action, which in any way whatsoever ran counter to or were critical of Nazism.

Kershaw, *Popular Opinion and Political Dissent in the Third Reich*, 1983

In pairs, list all the possible kinds of resistance to the Nazis, defined in its broadest sense. Then categorize these according to Peukert's graph and Kershaw's definitions above. Which method of categorizing works best in your opinion?

Date	Interpretation	Context (in West Germany)
1940s	That there were many in Germany – especially amongst the elites – who challenged and resisted Nazism.	Need to respond to interpretations outside Germany accusing the German people of collective guilt.
1950s	That the communists played no real role in fighting Nazism. The fight against Nazism was a fight against totalitarianism.	The onset of the Cold War with the division of Germany into a communist East and a capitalist, democratic West.
1960s	That the conservative opposition to Hitler was not a fight against totalitarianism. Many of the members of the elites involved in opposition wanted to keep authoritarian rule after Hitler had gone.	More sources of evidence available. West Germany more established, so less need to exonerate the German people. A younger generation of historians.
1970s	That opposition to Nazism was much more widespread than a focus on assassination attempts suggests. There were many different ways of registering opposition to the Nazi regime. The Nazis were far from successful in imposing totalitarian rule. However, there was also a degree of acceptance of Nazism amongst the people for various reasons.	Local studies which focused on everyday life and everyday types of opposition.

> **Quotation**
>
> When the German opposition to Hitler first became an object of historical interest, it was in the context of attempts to disprove Allied theories of collective guilt and to construct a bridge of historical continuity to span the twelve years of Nazi rule, which were regarded at the time as a catastrophic and unnatural interruption of the historical process by demonically destructive forces.
>
> Mommsen, *From Weimar to Auschwitz*, 1991

In East Germany, however, it was a different story. Communist opposition was highlighted as a way of giving greater legitimacy to the GDR. If it could be proved that the communists played the biggest role in opposing the Nazis, then the communists could perhaps be seen as the natural replacement of the Nazis in Germany. It was certainly true that the communists were amongst the very first clear opponents of Nazism and continued to oppose it, as an underground movement, until the fall of the regime. However, as we have seen in the previous chapter, there were other important examples of organized opposition.

> **Source 8**
>
> The East German literature concedes that the communists cannot claim sole credit for whatever was done in resisting the Nazis, but it insists that among the varied resistance groups the communists played the most important role in this struggle. This accounts for the minimal attention paid to other resistance groups, such as, for example, the (Protestant) Confessional Church. As for the oppositional forces gathered around the former Mayor of Leipzig, Carl Goerdeler, which had access to such levers of power as the military and high bureaucrats, their efforts are dismissed as constituting mere tactical disagreements within the ruling class.
>
> Dorpalen, *German History in Marxist Perspective: The East German Approach*, 1985

How much impact did opposition to the Nazis have?

On one level, it is possible to argue that the opposition to Nazism had virtually no effect. The Nazis were not prevented from achieving their major aims and it took the combined force of the wartime Allies to overpower them. In this sense, the opposition was a failure. However, historians looking at it from a different perspective, in terms of whether the Nazis were successful in *controlling* the German people and imposing their will on them, reach a rather different conclusion. They argue that in fact the Nazis were prevented from carrying out some of their aims as they wished and also that the Nazis never had total control over the people. Martin Broszat goes as far as to say that the more low-key forms of opposition – 'resistenz' as he terms it – probably presented a bigger irritant to the Nazis than more organized forms of resistance.

One consequence of examining the response to the Nazis amongst ordinary Germans is that the degree of *consensus* or agreement with Nazism is revealed. Or at the very least, indifference. Reports to SOPADE (SPD in exile) headquarters reveal the Left's frustration at the way in which many people appeared to accept Nazism and go along with it:

■ Think about

▶ Why, according to Source 9, were people grumbling about the Nazis?

▶ Why would this weaken opposition to the Nazis?

Source 9

The weakness of its opponents is a strength of the regime. Its opponents are ideologically and organizationally weak. They are ideologically weak because the masses consist only of dissatisfied people, only grumblers; their dissatisfaction is based solely upon economic reasons…their criticism stems from only narrow personal interests.

From a SOPADE report, 1934

Recent historians who have examined the complexity of the German response to Nazism and have acknowledged the complicity of many with the regime, are nevertheless at pains to acknowledge the sacrifice made by many in the fight against Nazism. It would be quite wrong to disregard the German resistance to Nazism. However, there is no longer any need to shield Germany from the reality that alongside the opponents of Nazism were also its supporters. Hitler's foreign policy in the 1930s, for example, was the cause of particular support. Even more important was the economic recovery and general rise in living standards during the 1930s, which provided more stability and prosperity.

Interpretations exercise: opposition to the Nazis

Source A
No serious opposition

The number of those who consciously criticize the political objectives of the regime is very small, quite apart from the fact that they cannot give expression to this criticism. And the fact that discontent [about other matters] makes itself loudly felt on numerous occasions also confirms the 'good conscience' of these people in terms of the National Socialist regime. They do not want to return to the past and if anyone told them that their complaints about this or that aspect threaten the foundations of the Third Reich they would probably be very astonished and horrified.

From a SOPADE report, 1937

Source B

The opposition of the workers

[In September 1939] The government ordered further wage cuts and more civil conscription; hours of work were lengthened and overtime bonuses abolished; paid holidays were suspended. Wage earners lost virtually all their remaining rights. The consequence was a massive wave of resentment. Absenteeism and refusals to do overtime and week-end shifts increased to such an extent that production was seriously disrupted in October...The government was forced to give way and to withdraw most of its war measures, lest the 'home front' collapse. Now it cannot be demonstrated that what occurred in German industry in the first weeks of the war amounted to a general rejection of *the war* by a large section of the working class. While it is true that the war was unpopular throughout Germany at this time, this interpretation cannot actually be proved from the sources. That is to say, we probably cannot speak of *resistance* in the precise sense of the term. But what happened clearly did have a quite different quality from 'bad work discipline': it had the quality of a broad denial of co-operation by the working-class, a denial marked by economic class consciousness in the widest sense, and in which the solidarities of the old working-class movement were still a driving force. This refusal to co-operate was the exactly appropriate method of asserting immediate class interests *within* the dictatorship. More aggressive or decisive actions, the 'riot' or 'rising' which Hitler feared, could hardly be brought about in the absence of organisations, and would, as everyone knew, have been repressed with ruthless brutality. And the denial of co-operation *was* adequate to the situation, in that its scale was sufficient to force the government to change its social and economic policies within 5–12 weeks...Neither resistance nor opposition were able to overthrow the Nazi regime. In the event, the opposition probably caused it more trouble than the resistance.

Mason 'The Workers' Opposition In Nazi Germany'
in *History Workshop Journal* no. 11, 1981

Source C

The limited impact of resistance

The ineffectiveness and failure of German resistance to Nazism had its roots in the strife-torn political climate of the Weimar Republic. The internecine conflict on the Left, the enthusiasm of the conservative Right to act as gravediggers to the Republic, and the massive popular readiness to embrace authoritarianism and reject the only form of democracy then known to Germany explain divisions within, slowness to act of, and lack of popular support for, resistance during the dictatorship. The moral courage of those who stood up to Nazi tyranny remains, and will remain, en example to all subsequent ages. But a historical understanding of the weaknesses and failure of resistance is crucial. Apart from illustrating the self-evident truth that it is easier to prevent a would-be dictator from taking power than to remove such a dictator once he has the might of the State at his disposal, the historiographical and conceptual debates about resistance...have increasingly demonstrated the very complexity of the problem of resistance under Nazism. Perhaps more than all else, it has been their merit to emphasise more and more as time has passed one cardinal aspect of the problem: that the story of dissent, opposition, and resistance in the Third Reich is indistinguishable from the story of consent, approval, and collaboration.

Kershaw, *The Nazi Dictatorship*, 1993

Source D

The resistance of the elite

The majority of those involved in the national conservative resistance, several of whom held unequivocally Nazi views and most of whom either held senior positions of authority or were members of the officer corps, believed, at least up to the beginning of the war, that they would be able to contain the radicalising tendencies in the regime. These tendencies were regarded primarily as a threat to the Reich's external security and it was felt that they could be contained without having to undertake any major changes in the internal structures of the system...the national conservative resistance only gradually and hesitantly developed from seeking merely to correct abuses in the system and impose alternative strategies on to it to the idea of staging a *coup d'etat* and establishing a new social order.

Mommsen, *From Weimar to Auschwitz*, 1991

Source E

Statistics of resistance

By 1939:
● Around 150,000 communists and Social Democrats had been imprisoned in concentration camps
● 40,000 Germans had left the country for political reasons
● 12,000 Germans had been convicted of high treason
● 40,000 Germans had been imprisoned for lesser political offences.

Figures taken from Kershaw, *The Nazi Dictatorship*, 1993

■ Examination-style questions

1 Comprehension in context
Using Source D and your own knowledge, explain how effectively the elite groups in Germany resisted Nazism.

2 Comparing the sources
To what extent do Sources B and C differ in their interpretation of the success of opposition to Nazism? Can you offer any reasons for their differences?

3 Assessing the sources
Of what use is Source E when assessing the effectiveness of resistance to Nazism?

4 Making judgements
'The popularity of the Nazis outweighed the opposition'. Using the sources and your own knowledge, how far do you agree with this statement?

Chapter 15

The division of Germany, 1945–1969

◀ May 1945, American and Soviet soldiers meet at the River Elbe.

Source 2

▲ August 1961, building the Berlin Wall.

Source 3

▶ De Gaulle of France and Adenauer of West Germany.

Introduction

This chapter examines what happened to Germany at the end of the Second World War and how its fortunes changed between 1945 and 1969. When compared to the years following 1918, the aftermath of the Second World War was very different. To what extent this was a case of learning from past mistakes is up to you to judge. Certainly there were more concerted efforts made to rebuild Germany and integrate her into European affairs. However, post-war reconstruction was soon eclipsed by a new world problem, the Cold War, which led, amongst other things, to the division of Germany into two separate states between 1949 and 1990. The other significant influence on Germany's future in 1945 was the legacy of Nazism. What would happen to those who had supported the Nazi Party? How would Germany cleanse itself of such a heavy burden of responsibility? Some of these latter issues are picked up in Chapter 14, which examines the different interpretations of Nazism to emerge in East and West Germany after the war.

Key questions

- What happened to Germany at the end of the Second World War?
- Why was Germany divided in 1949?
- What were the consequences of this division?
- What were the essential differences between East and West Germany? How was each state ruled?
- How did the economies of each state recover?
- Why was the Berlin Wall built and with what consequences?

A defeated Germany

Hitler's last days

On 20 April 1945, as Russian and American troops were closing in around him, Hitler abandoned previous plans to flee to the south of Germany, and decided – against the advice of other high ranking Nazis – to remain in Berlin. Despite holding daily conferences, when Hitler was given reports indicating that Germany was heading for a complete defeat at the hands of the Allies, he refused to believe that his war was lost. When two of Hitler's most trusted Nazi leaders took action that undermined his leadership and implied defeat, Hitler was outraged. Goering issued a decree to Hitler stating that he intended to assume leadership of the state, as he believed that Hitler was not in a position to continue, whilst surrounded by the Russians in Berlin. Hitler learnt a few days later that Himmler had attempted to strike a peace deal with the Allies. Hitler considered both these men to be traitors and defectors. Their actions prompted the Führer to marry Eva Braun in the early hours of 29 April, and to write his will and last political statement to the German people, indicating that he considered his career, and therefore his life, to be over. The documents stated that Admiral Dönitz should become Hitler's successor as President of the Reich, Minister of War and Supreme Commander of the armed forces. Goebbels was to become Chancellor.

The next day, 30 April, Hitler learnt that the Russians had advanced further into the city. He ate lunch with his cook and secretaries at 2pm. He ordered 200 litres of petrol to be brought into the Chancellery garden. Then, with Eva by his side, he spoke for the last time with Goebbels and Bormann and bid goodbye to his staff. Eva and Hitler went into the Führer's suite of rooms and closed the door. Witnesses heard a single shot. The staff entered the bedroom and found Eva dead, having swallowed poison, and Hitler beside her, also dead, from a

■ Think about

Sources 1–3 demonstrate two things:
1 The amount of change and division that Germany continued to experience after 1945
2 The way in which Germany – or at least a part of Germany – became central to European unity after the war.

▶ Do these images support your own ideas of what happened to Germany after the war?

Note

During the final days of the war, Hitler sheltered with staff and some key Nazi members in an air-raid bunker under the Chancellery, known as the 'Führerbunker'. Eva Braun, Hitler's mistress, had also insisted on coming to Berlin and remaining with the Führer.

Quotation

It is untrue that I, or anyone in Germany, wanted the war in 1939. It was desired and instigated solely by those international statesmen who were either of Jewish descent or who worked for Jewish interests…I die with a happy heart, aware of the immeasurable deeds of our soldiers at the front…

Extract from Hitler's last will and testament

self-inflicted gunshot in the head. Hitler's final instructions were carried out to the letter; the couple were burnt in the garden of the Chancellery.

Surrender

Two hundred yards from where Hitler died stood Russian soldiers. Stalin's Red Army advanced from the east into Berlin, forcing German troops to surrender in May 1945. Germany was in ruins. Her cities were a mass of rubble after intensive Allied bombing, and there was a chronic shortage of supplies. The German people focused all their efforts on physical survival; with no government to represent their interests, their fate lay in the hands of the victors. They accepted this with a sense of inevitability. They were, in any case, uninterested in politics, one of the many legacies of the Nazi era.

The question of quite what to do with the defeated Germany was not one to which the Allies had ready answers. Discussion had already taken place between the Allies before the war had ended. The most important of these conferences was held at Yalta in February 1945, where Churchill, Roosevelt and Stalin all met to discuss plans for Germany following imminent victory. It had already been decided to split Germany into occupation zones following her defeat. At Yalta it was decided that Germany should be divided into four zones which would be occupied and run by the United States, the USSR, Great Britain and France. Berlin would itself be divided into four zones, despite lying within the Soviet zone. There were also decisions about territory, for which the participants of the conference have since been fiercely criticized. Stalin was determined to retain much of the territory he had gained during the war, and believed that in any case land east of Germany was his affair and really no one else's. Poland was effectively 'moved' to the west. The USSR annexed Polish land in the east. It was then agreed that the Oder and Neisse rivers would now form Poland's western border and that Poland would gain German territory to the east of these rivers as compensation for the land lost to the USSR in the east. German East Prussia was also divided between Poland and the USSR. One historian describes the actions of the Western powers at Yalta as handing 'Poland to Stalin on a plate' (Davies, 1997). Certainly, they appeared to have accepted that Poland's fate was in the hands of the USSR.

Source 4

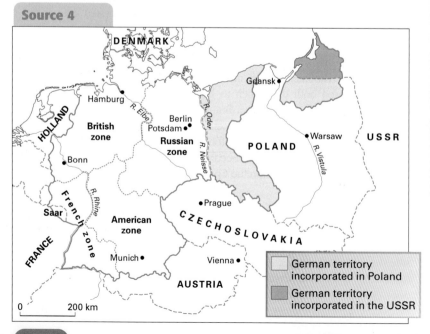

■ Think about

▶ How did Germany's loss of territory compare to the Treaty of Versailles?

▶ Why do you think the Allies decided to occupy Germany following the end of the Second World War?

▶ Berlin was itself divided into four zones. What problems might this have led to?

◀ The fate of Germany after the Second World War.

Beyond the immediate (and supposedly temporary) division of Germany into zones and the settling of the land issue, the Allies had no clear plans. The issue of reparations, for example, provoked disputes between the USSR – who wanted $20 billion – and the other Allies who feared a repeat of the Treaty of Versailles, the demands of which had effectively crippled Germany and prevented a lasting peace. There were also conflicting views about the best way to rebuild Germany and ensure that a Nazi-style dictatorship would never again have the opportunity to flourish there. The USSR wanted to destroy the capitalist economic system which it held as responsible for the Third Reich. The Western Allies, however, wanted gradually to introduce free democracy – firstly at a local level – which would ensure that Germany would become part of the democratic western world.

The Allied occupation

Immediately after the German surrender, the Allies had more pressing matters to deal with than the long-term future of Germany. Supplies had to be brought in to avoid a famine and shelter had to be found for the homeless. One-fifth of Germany's population of 50 million were refugees. In the midst of such chaos, the Allies were forced to entrust much of the administrative work of the country to former Nazis. They were, however, determined to address this issue as soon as possible. At Potsdam, in July–August 1945, the major powers again met to discuss Germany's future. Relatively little of substance was decided, with only general agreements being made. These included confirmation that Germany would one day be a united country again, that Germany would pay reparations of $20 billion (half of which would go to Russia) and that the four allied commanders-in-chief would co-ordinate the 'four Ds' (see margin).

Denazification began in earnest with the Nuremberg trials which began in November 1945. The trials of 22 senior Nazis lasted for 11 months, ending with 12 executions, 7 imprisonments and 3 acquittals. Cleansing Germany of less senior Nazis proved more problematic, particularly as there were potentially 9 million of them. Both the Russians and the Americans vigorously pursued and imprisoned former Nazis until they realized the enormity of the task and also the practical difficulty of imprisoning people who performed valuable functions in the day-to-day running of the country. After 1946, denazification petered out, although prosecution of Nazi criminals has continued intermittently ever since.

Democratization was more contentious, as it was interpreted rather differently in the different zones. In the three western zones, run by America, Britain and France, democracy was established and encouraged at a local level very quickly. At the end of 1947 the local provinces (Länder) had their own local parliaments. Free political parties were also allowed to develop. In the Soviet zone it was rather different. Here, local democracy was distrusted and indeed the Länder were dissolved in 1952 and the political parties were not allowed total freedom. A group of German communists, trained in Moscow and led by Walter Ulbricht, were sent into the Soviet zone and the KPD was encouraged to infiltrate and dominate key administrative posts. It was unable, however, to win enough votes to control the zone completely and consequently the socialists were forced to merge with the KPD to form the Socialist Unity Party (SED). Soviet intentions – to erase all traces of capitalism and instead implement communism – were becoming clear.

■ Think about

The 'Four Ds' that were agreed at Potsdam set out the Allies' most immediate objectives in Germany. They were:
● Denazification
● Democratization
● Demilitarization
● Decartelization (note: cartels were groups of businesses which joined together to protect their own interests)

▶ Take each 'D' in turn. What do you think it would have involved?

▶ Why do you think the Allies decided to implement it?

Facts and figures

Political parties in East Germany:

KPD (communists)
SPD (socialists)
SED (Socialist Unity Party: a combination of KPD and SPD in 1946)
CDU (Christian Democratic Union)
LDPD (liberals)

Political parties in West Germany:

SPD (socialists)
CDU (Christian Democratic Union, which broadened the membership of the old Centre Party to include Protestants. Held conservative views)
CSU (Christian Social Union which was basically the CDU in Bavaria and always supported the CDU)
FDP (Free Democratic Party – the liberals)

A divided nation

The Cold War

Post-war Germany became the first arena within which a new conflict was fought. The boundaries of this conflict stretched beyond Europe. It was a conflict that was essentially ideological. It was a conflict which posed greater physical (nuclear) threats to the globe than any other – and yet it was also a conflict which saw relatively little actual fighting. That conflict was the Cold War.

As we have already seen, the Soviet zone of Germany was immediately run in a different way to the Western zones. Communism, the economic and political system established in Russia in 1917, was soon established as the dominant influence and capitalism eradicated. This seemed to confirm the West's belief that Stalin intended to spread communism as far as possible. To understand much of the history of post-war Europe, it is important to appreciate the fear of communism held by the Western states. It represented an economic and political system at odds with the one that was flourishing in America and Britain and being re-established in much of Western Europe, that of a broadly capitalist economic system and free democracy. America was emerging as the most influential power in post-war Western Europe. She was also the most determined and best-equipped nation to challenge the mighty power of the USSR. The Cold War was therefore also a conflict of the superpowers.

In March 1946 Churchill made the following speech in America:

Source 5

From Stettin on the Baltic to Trieste on the Adriatic, an iron curtain has descended across the continent. Behind that line, lie all the capitals of the ancient states of central and eastern Europe – Warsaw, Berlin, Prague, Vienna, Budapest, Belgrade, Bucharest, and Sofia….This is certainly not the liberated Europe which we fought to build up.

The term 'iron curtain' became well known to describe the way in which Europe was being divided into communist and non-communist spheres of influence. Two months after Churchill's speech, civil war broke out in Greece and the threat of a communist take-over there loomed large. Britain's finances were close to bankruptcy after the strains of war and she appealed to America for assistance. It was really at this point that the USA assumed responsibility for checking the spread of communism in Europe, a principle that was soon extended to the world as a whole. In part, the reason for America's high profile role was economic. America was almost unique in having *gained* economically from the Second World War.

In March 1947 the US President, Truman, outlined what became known as his policy of containment. Any attempt to spread communism further was to be resisted. It was therefore important that Western Europe was in a position to act as one to support the USA. This would involve ensuring that the Western European states were economically stable and therefore less vulnerable to the spread of communism themselves. Shortly after Truman's containment speech the Marshall Plan was approved, which released more than $13 billion from the USA into 16 European states, including the Western zones of Germany. Stalin, however, refused to allow any of the money to be used east of the Iron Curtain. This led to an even greater economic division of Europe.

Timeline

1945–1949
1945
Feb Yalta Conference
May Germany surrenders
July–Aug Potsdam Conference
Nov Nuremburg Trials begin
1946
March Churchill's Iron Curtain speech
April SED formed in the Soviet zone
1947
Jan British and American zones combined to form 'Bizonia'
Mar Truman's policy of containment announced
June Marshall Aid announced
1948
June Decision by the three Western Allies to approve an independent West Germany which would be federal
June Currency reform in the Western zones
June (to May 1949) Berlin Blockade
1949
Aug First elections in West Germany followed by formal declaration of the Federal Republic of Germany (FRG)
Oct The GDR (German Democratic Republic) formally announced. Germany now divided

Note

Although Marshall Aid was extremely significant in the post-war rebuilding of Western Europe, Germany did not do as well from it as might have been expected. Germany received $332.9 billion, whilst Britain received $919.8 billion and France received $673.1 billion.

The division of Germany

> ### Source 6
>
> The economy was the key area for the transformation of Germany into a divided state and diverging societies. Differences in economic policy between the occupying powers both precipitated and symbolized their wider political dissimilarities; and differences in economic policy in the different zones set the pattern for long-term contrasts in the social and political structures of the two Germanys.
>
> M. Fulbrook, *The Fontana History of Germany 1918–1990: The Divided Nation*, 1991

The growing distrust between the USSR and the West did little to help German unity. Economically, the Soviet and the Western zones were becoming more deeply divided as time went on. The Marshall Plan gave an enormous boost to the economy of the Western zones. In the Soviet zone, however, the Soviet policy of dismantling (moving parts of the industrial infrastructure to the USSR) at the start of occupation had reduced the productive capacity of the zone by 26 per cent. In addition, the absence of financial aid meant that economic growth lagged behind the Western zones by some way.

In the Soviet zone, capitalism was eliminated by, for example, dissolving the Junker class and transferring private banks and industries into State ownership. In the Western zones, German industry and enterprise were encouraged. In January 1947 the British and American zones combined to form 'Bizonia'. This was a key step towards a more independent – but divided – Germany. The Bizone was created to enable more effective economic administration to take place, although the Economic Council which was created in fact acted as a kind of government with the power to tax. By February 1948, Bizonia had a central bank and in June, currency reform was introduced into the Western zones creating a much more stable economy. This followed an announcement by the USA, Britain, France, Belgium, Holland and Luxembourg that their intention was to create a separate West German state.

By now, relations with the USSR were reaching their lowest point. Stalin was totally opposed to the creation of a West German state which would be heavily influenced by and economically dependent on the USA. He would have preferred a neutral, non-communist Germany to this division, and accused the other powers of breaking the Potsdam Agreement. A neutral German state was not, however, acceptable to the West. It would still be vulnerable to communist influences and, if forced to choose, they would rather split Germany in two than settle for this. In desperation, the Russians launched the Berlin Blockade. All access to the Western zones of Berlin were blocked by closing all roads and rail links from the West German zones. The policy failed, however, as supplies were airlifted into West Berlin for eleven months, at which point the blockade was called off. It was by now clear that wartime allegiances had changed: the USSR was no longer an ally in the eyes of the West and, what was more, former enemies in the West German zones could provide important assistance against the communists.

Note

Berlin became an anomaly – a state within a state. Despite its location, 120 miles inside the Soviet zone, it was itself divided into four zones. When Germany formally divided into East and West, Berlin also divided along the same lines. Berlin was the scene for some of the most significant and memorable events of 1945–1990 in Germany. The Berlin Blockade in 1948–1949 demonstrated how isolated West Berlin was. Later, in 1961, the Berlin Wall gave new meaning to Churchill's 'iron curtain'. When the Wall came down in 1989, it signified the end of an era, not just in Germany, but in the world.

The creation of East and West Germany

Following the agreement amongst the Western Allies in June 1948 to establish an independent West German state, a constitution was drawn up by a parliamentary council (made up of representatives nominated by the Länder). It aimed to establish a parliamentary government which could never fall victim to the manipulations of the President or a political party set on destroying the political system. The first elections took place in August 1949 and the CDU/CSU won 139 seats, eight more than the SPD. With the backing of the FDP, which had 52 seats, the leader of the CDU, Konrad Adenauer, was elected Chancellor. Theodore Heuss, leader of the FDP, was appointed President, a position that brought little power in the new constitution. In September 1949, the Federal Republic of Germany (FRG) formally came into existence.

The creation of East Germany was slightly delayed, largely because the Soviets were reluctant to commit themselves to an official recognition that Germany was to be split in two, with one half dominated by their Cold War enemies. In October 1949, however, the GDR (German Democratic Republic) was formally announced with a constitution drawn up by the leaders of the SED. Wilhelm Pieck was elected President and Otto Grotewohl became Prime Minister. Real power, however, lay in the hands of Walter Ulbricht, leader of the SED.

Source 7

The Federal Republic, 1949–1966

Adenauer as Chancellor

When Adenauer, leader of the CDU, became Chancellor of the FRG in 1949 he faced a number of problems. Firstly, his party had no electoral majority (the CDU/CSU coalition won 31 per cent of the votes) and he was dependent on the support of the liberals to remain in power. The spectre of Weimar-like coalition governments leading to frequent changes in government and policy

Note

The Occupation Statute ensured that the Western Allies (America, France and Britain) would retain control over West German affairs, even after the creation of the FRG. Foreign policy and trade were two of the areas which the Western Allies controlled, for example. The Statute was only abandoned in 1955 when the FRG gained true independence.

■ **Activity**   **KEY SKILLS**

Who was most responsible for the division of Germany?

Using all the evidence, discuss the role of the following groups in creating a divided Germany.

- The Germans
- The Russians
- The Americans
- All of the Western Allies

Who or what do YOU think was most responsible for the division of Germany?

◀ West Berliners queue at a GDR checkpoint to visit East Berlin.

Timeline

The integration of West Germany into Europe

1949: FRG becomes a member of Organization for European Economic Co-operation (OEEC)

1951: FRG enters the European Coal and Steel Community (ECSC: forerunner of the EEC). FRG becomes a full member of the Council of Europe

1955: FRG recognized as an independent state and becomes member of NATO

1957: FRG becomes a founding member of the EEC in the Treaty of Rome

■ Biography

Konrad Adenauer

One of the oldest leaders in modern Europe, Adenauer was born in January 1876 and was therefore 62 when he became Chancellor of West Germany. Prior to that he had been an active member of the Centre Party and mayor of Cologne. During the Third Reich he was sacked for refusing to fly the swastika from the town hall. He retired and was arrested from time to time by the Nazis between 1934 and 1944. In 1945 he was one of the founders of the CDU.

Facts and figures

Unemployment and growth rates in West Germany

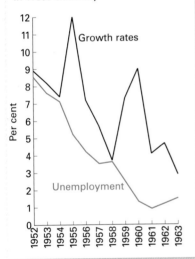

Facts and figures

The GNP of West Germany	
Year	DM millions
1955	181,400
1961	331,400
1965	458,200
1970	679,000
1975	1,034,900
1980	1,485,700
1985	1,844,300
1989	2,260,400

was raised. Fortunately, the liberals were steadfast in their support of Adenauer until around 1961 and, in any case, the CDU/CSU won a majority in the 1957 election. The second problem facing Adenauer was the economy. Over 2 million West Germans were unemployed and prices were rising. A flow of refugees from Eastern Europe added to the pressure and, of course, there was still a good deal of post-war rebuilding to do. The third problem was foreign policy. In 1949 the FRG was not an independent state and there had still not been an official peace treaty to end the Second World War. The Cold War had shifted allegiances, but West Germany's exact position and status within Europe remained unclear.

This last problem was tackled effectively by Adenauer. As the timeline demonstrates, the FRG quickly achieved not only acceptance within Europe but active participation. 1955 was a particularly important year, for it was then that the FRG was recognized as an independent state (although West Berlin was still protected by Allied troops) and the Occupation Statute was abandoned. The key reason for this development was military. Britain was pushing hard for Germany to become a member of NATO (the North Atlantic Treaty Organization designed to provide defence against the Soviet Bloc) and Germany was, therefore, allowed once again to have an army of its own. It made little sense in this context for the FRG to be under the direct political control of the West. From the West's point of view, it was essential to secure the military strength of West Germany – including stationing American bases there – given its close proximity to the Iron Curtain. But not everyone in the FRG was pleased by the decision to remilitarize: it brought back uncomfortable memories.

Economically, West Germany experienced what some have described as a 'miracle'. As we have seen, the economic problems facing Adenauer in 1949 were very real and in 1950, unemployment stood at 8.1 per cent. By the mid-1960s that figure had declined to 0.5 per cent. Economic growth averaged 8 per cent a year, living conditions improved dramatically and disposable income of the average household increased by 400 per cent between 1950 and 1970. So what were the factors behind this success story?

● Ludwig Erhard, the Economics Minister under Adenauer, played an important role in the overall direction of policy. He introduced what became known as the 'social market economy', which combined elements of a free market economy with elements of State intervention to ensure that the weaker sections of the population were protected.

● Much of the industrial infrastructure, such as machinery, somehow survived the bombing raids, providing the FRG with a good base on which to build.

● Raw materials were provided either from the Rühr or from outside Germany at cheap rates due to the undervalued Deutschmark.

● The Marshall Plan.

● Good labour relations, with a low number of strikes and disruption.

● The Korean War, which broke out in 1950, boosted West German industry.

● Refugees from East Germany and elsewhere provided cheap and flexible labour.

All these factors played important roles in the development of the West German economy. Economic success was crucial to the popularity of the Adenauer regime and provided a welcome reassurance that democracy did not inevitably lead to economic crisis as in the Weimar era.

Politically, Adenauer was fortunate that for most of his time in office, the SPD was not functioning very effectively. It was struggling to come to terms both with internal divisions and with a society that was becoming more prosperous and middle class. In 1959 it effectively abandoned its radical stance and aim to dismantle capitalism and this enabled it to emerge as a more viable party of government in the 1960s. At the other end of the scale, denazification was all but abandoned. One estimate puts the number of ex-Nazis in the West German civil service at that time somewhere between 40 and 80 per cent. Adenauer himself included ex-Nazis in his Cabinet, including Hans Globke who was the author of the official commentary which accompanied the Nuremberg Race Laws of 1935. The emphasis of this period was on reconstruction rather than recrimination.

Adenauer's resignation

Despite his successes, Adenauer was forced to resign in 1963. The FDP had split in 1956 and the majority was critical of Adenauer's uncompromising policy towards the GDR. When, in the election of 1961, the FDP's support was crucial for Adenauer's government again, they were able to insist that he eventually be replaced by Erhard. This process was speeded up by the *Spiegel* Affair in 1962, when Adenauer supported the raid on the offices of the magazine *Spiegel* following the publication of an article criticizing the Minister of Defence. The editors of the magazine were subsequently arrested. Outcries followed about the disregard for a free press and methods more reminiscent of the Third Reich than a free democracy. The FDP demanded that Adenauer should step down and he was left with little option but to retire from politics in 1963.

Adenauer's successor as Chancellor was the Economics Minister, Ludwig Erhard, who proved to be less successful in his new role. The main source of his problems was a downturn in the economy. Erhard overreacted to signs of inflation – not surprising in the light of Germany's previous problems with inflation – and proposed to raise taxation and cut government spending. This promoted the resignation of his coalition partners and he was himself forced to resign in 1966.

The GDR 1949–1961

The dominant influence of Walter Ulbricht

The GDR was clearly regarded as part of the Soviet Bloc and the influence of the USSR was everywhere. The SED (Socialist Unity Party) was the USSR's main way of controlling what went on in the GDR and ensuring that communism was established as a political and economic system. The main aim of the SED – and therefore of the USSR – was to achieve a communist state with the level of economic equality that that entailed. This equality was not always achieved in ways that were regarded as fair, however, and Ulbricht, the leader of the SED, never gained the popularity that his West German counterparts enjoyed.

The SED was modelled on the Soviet Communist Party both in the way it organized itself and in the way it set out to control the life of the country. Decisions were taken by a small inner circle but always under the dominant influence of Ulbricht, who became General Secretary of the SED in 1952. Any members suspected of harbouring social-democratic or Western inclinations were not allowed to remain in the Party. In the 1950 election, every candidate on the list had views which the SED found acceptable and those who were not members of the SED were members of parties under its influence. Hence the SED could claim that 99.72 per cent of the votes were cast in favour of its

> **Note**
>
> ### West Germany by 1969
> During the 1960s there was a shift towards the left in politics. Erhard's successor, Kurt-Georg Kiesinger of the CDU, formed a surprising coalition with the SPD, known as the Great Coalition. There was also a move towards more State intervention in the economy. By the end of the decade, the SPD was poised to assume control of the government in coalition with the FDP which had itself shifted towards the left. In the election of 1969, the SPD and FDP polled 48.5% of the vote and Willy Brandt of the SPD became the first socialist Chancellor in Germany since 1930.

> **Note**
>
> Many of the leaders of the SED had spent the war in exile in the USSR. The East German government was really a puppet government which took its orders from Moscow.

policies. The SED also used intimidation tactics and propaganda to establish control. It assumed control of the police and judicial system and used education to reinforce its messages. The West was ridiculed in propaganda and teachers who were not prepared to tow the party line were sacked. It all seemed strangely familiar to those who had lived through the Nazi regime. Yet this was, ironically, the very political system that Hitler had set out to destroy.

Source 8

▶ This East German cartoon entitled 'The Resurrection' shows Adenauer standing in Hitler's place, carrying an American flag and delivering a speech. What is its message?

The unpopularity of the regime came to a head in 1953. Ulbricht was proposing to raise the working hours of the industrial workers whilst also allowing food prices to increase amidst already high taxation. Building workers decided, spontaneously, to protest and a general strike followed on 17 June which brought Berlin to a standstill. Soviet troops were brought in and 21 Germans were killed before the unrest was brought to an end. During the aftermath, thousands of officials and members of the SED were removed and only hardliners within the government were allowed to remain. The unrest did, however, lead to some concessions: working hours were not increased, for example, and food prices were reduced. Ulbricht clung on to power for a further eight years without gaining any more popularity. People continued to resent the repressive policies and the fact that their standard of living did not equal that of West Germany.

The economy of the GDR

The economic situation in East Germany was not initially promising. As we have already seen, during the years of occupation the USSR stripped its zone of much of its economic infrastructure and even by 1950, 25 per cent of industrial goods went directly to the USSR. East Germany's geographical position within Europe was also a disadvantage as it had to trade with more economically backward countries within the Soviet Bloc and was unable to exploit the industrial heartland of the Rühr which of course lay in West Germany.

As with the political system, the economic system in the GDR was modelled on that of the USSR. Plans were frequently drawn up setting quotas for production which either underestimated possible output (enabling quotas to be met) or forced industries to overproduce and ignore capital investment (for example, the purchasing of new machinery) and increase working hours. Industries and banking sectors were largely brought under State control and there was an initial concentration on heavy industry rather than consumer goods, although this balance was redressed to some extent during the 1950s. There was also an attempt to collectivize agriculture during this decade which was extremely unpopular amongst farmers and had disastrous effects on food supplies and, therefore, on prices. The second wave of collectivization in 1959–1960 was largely responsible for the increase in emigration from the GDR to the West as food shortages and rising prices forced people to make difficult decisions.

Despite years of relative success, for example in the latter half of the 1950s when real wages exceeded the 1939 levels and living standards improved, overall the GDR did not really come close to equalling the economic achievement of the FRG. It did not matter to the East Germans that their living standards were the highest in the Soviet Bloc. What mattered to them was that these standards fell behind those of their former countrymen in the West. By 1961 it was estimated that over 1,600,000 had escaped to the West through West Berlin, presenting an incredible drain on the human resources available to the East, especially as many of those who left had valuable skills. Ulbricht persuaded Khrushchev (now the President of the USSR) to allow him to close the border between East and West Berlin. Barbed wire was put in place almost immediately and was eventually replaced by something much more permanent: the Berlin Wall. It was not a question of keeping unwanted visitors out but of keeping unhappy East Germans in.

Facts and figures

The populations of East and West Germany in millions

Year	West Germany	East Germany
1946	46,190	18,388
1961	56,175	17,125
1970	60,651	12,058
1987	61,077	16,641

Note

Although large numbers of East Germans crossed into West Berlin, it was not a straightforward thing to do. After 1952, 200 streets linking East and West Berlin were barricaded and 81 police controls were set up at access points which remained open. The penalty of crossing the border could be between 16 months to 4 years in prison.

Facts and figures

Out of the 2,700,000 East Germans who escaped to the West between 1949 and 1961, 3400 were doctors, 17,000 were teachers and 17,000 were engineers.

Source 9

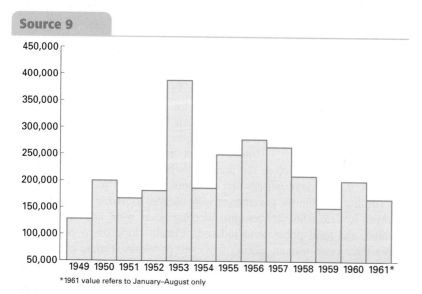

*1961 value refers to January–August only

◄ The numbers of East Germans leaving the GDR 1949–1961.

Source 10

▷ The cover of a West German magazine published on 23 July 1961, less than three weeks before the East Germans began building the Berlin Wall. It shows Chancellor Adenauer and says 'Together with the Chancellor all Germans are anxiously watching their capital city'.

■ **Think about**

▷ What does Source 10 tell you about relations between East and West Germans by 1961?

Conclusion

In 1945 Germany was divided into four occupation zones. There was also an attempt to rebuild Germany, eliminate traces of the Nazi past and reset her boundaries. In 1949, Germany split in two, largely because the West did not trust a neutral Germany to withstand the lure of communism and therefore turned down Stalin's offers for a united but neutral Germany. Stalin, in turn, did not want a united Germany under the control of the West. East and West were run on very different lines, one a communist one-party state and the other a capitalist democracy. The remarkable economic success of West Germany, however, destabilized East Germany. Thousands left in search of the high living standards and consumer delights of the Federal Republic. This was only stopped with the construction of the Berlin Wall.

Spotlight

The Berlin Wall

Key dates

1949 Creation of West and East Germany

1952 Telephone communications between West and East Berlin cut off

1961 13 August: Building of Berlin Wall begins

19 August: First victim of the Wall

24 August: First attempted escapee shot

1962 Death of Peter Fechter

1963 Kennedy's 'Ich bin ein Berliner' speech

1964 57 East Berliners escape through a tunnel dug under the Wall

1971 Telephone communications restored between East and West Berlin

1989 February: The last escapee is shot

November: The border between East and West is reopened

Source 11

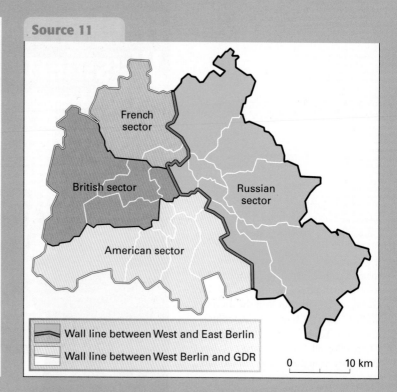

French sector

British sector

Russian sector

American sector

Wall line between West and East Berlin

Wall line between West Berlin and GDR

0   10 km

Facts and figures

Overall length: 155 km (103 miles)

Length in Berlin: 43.1 km (26.8 miles)

Watch towers: 302

Tracks with sliding cables for dogs: 259

Number of dogs: 600

Concrete shelters: 22

Border guards: 14,000

Number of shots fired by border guards: 1693

Successful attempts to scale the Wall: 5043, 574 of whom were border guards

Number of attempted escapees killed: 239

Soldiers and police killed: 27

Number of people wounded: 260

Source 12

▲ The Wall itself and other border defences in East Berlin.

Position of automatic firing system: on Eastern side

Number of streets the Wall cut through: 192

Number of railway lines the Wall cut through: 32

Source 13

▲ West Berliners look over the Berlin Wall in August 1961, as construction begins.

Source 14

▲ In September 1961 it was still possible for a lorry to ram its way through the Berlin Wall, filled with East Germans.

Escapes and tragedies

239 people were killed trying to escape under or over the Wall. They were shot, drowned or killed jumping out of buildings. One of the deaths which caused most outrage was that of Peter Fechter, who lay dying for nearly an hour at the foot of the Wall after being badly injured by a border guard. Nobody came to help him.

Many methods were used to somehow cross the Wall. In the year after it was built, 14 lorries smashed through it. In 1962 the captain of a boat was tied up and 14 East Berliners escaped across the River Spree. In 1965 a whole family used a rope slung from a building in the East and held firm by relatives in the West to pass over the Wall. Nine people managed to hide in a tiny Isetta car by removing the battery and heater. Four men escaped by wearing Soviet uniforms made for them by their girlfriends.

■ Questions

1 Why was the Wall built? Think about the long, medium and short-term reasons.

2 What impact do you think the Wall must have had on the West and East Berliners?

3 The Wall became a powerful symbol for the Western world and featured in songs by, for example, David Bowie and Pink Floyd. Why do you think this was?

Chapter 16

Towards reunification

Source 1

▶ East and West German border guards shake hands through a gap in the Wall as demolition begins.

▼ Jubilant Berliners stand on the Berlin Wall at the Brandenburg Gate in 1989.

Source 2

Introduction

1990 was an extraordinary year for Germany. Towards the end of the previous year the Berlin Wall was opened, an event which captured the imagination of all who witnessed it, either in Berlin itself or on televisions throughout the world. Source 2 demonstrates some of the excitement which accompanied this dramatic event. But even then, no one could have foreseen that East and West Germany would be united once more within one year. One hundred and nineteen years after Germany had first united, it united for a second time.

In 1969, Willy Brandt became Chancellor of West Germany – the first socialist to do so for a long time. He ushered in a new era of co-operation with the GDR which was to ease practical agreements between the two states but made reunification seem even more distant. This was in part a response to the permanence of physical divisions such as the Berlin Wall. It took the collapse of the GDR, triggered by the reforms of the USSR, to bring reunification closer.

Key questions

- What happened to relations between East and West Germany 1969–1990?
- What were the respective fortunes of East and West Germany 1969–1990?
- Why was the Berlin Wall opened in 1989?
- Why was Germany reunited in 1990?

West Germany 1969–1987

Willy Brandt and *Ostpolitik*

As Mayor of Berlin between 1963 and 1969, Brandt had already demonstrated his readiness to negotiate with East Germany in return for practical benefits. During the Christmas of 1963, West Germans were able to visit relatives across the border over a period of 18 days. When he became Chancellor in 1969, Brandt was able to operate this more open policy at a much higher level and he embarked on a policy known as *Ostpolitik* ('Eastern Policy'). Rather than refusing even to acknowledge the existence of the GDR as Adenauer had done, Brandt was prepared to move forward and accept some of the realities Germany now faced. The building of the Berlin Wall had given the division of Germany an air of permanence and both the USA and the USSR were keen to ease the tensions in Eastern Europe as they became more preoccupied with events further afield.

The Moscow Treaty in 1970 was the first of a series of agreements which made *Ostpolitik* a reality. West Germany renounced its claim to represent all German people, a move which anticipated the Basic Treaty of 1972 in which the FRG officially recognized the GDR as a state in its own right. *Ostpolitik* also involved other powers: in 1971 the former wartime Allies and occupiers of Germany concluded the Berlin Agreement in which the USSR promised to respect the right of West Berliners to travel freely to the GDR. In effect, this made another Berlin Blockade unthinkable and was a step towards accepting the status quo. There was, however, considerable opposition to Brandt's policy from right-wing circles in West Germany. They argued that by recognizing the GDR as a separate, independent state, Brandt was not only validating the existence of a repressive, communist regime, but was also making future unification more unlikely (see quotation in margin for Brandt's response). Some members of the FDP (the liberals who were in a coalition with Brandt's party, the SPD) began to vote with the CDU/CSU in protest. Brandt took a gamble by engineering a general election earlier than was required. It was fought almost exclusively on the issue of *Ostpolitik* and it was an impressive victory for Brandt and the SPD

Born in 1913, Brandt became a socialist at the age of 16. He fled Germany in 1933 to escape the Nazis, only returning home after the war. In 1949 he was elected to the Bundestag as a Social Democrat and in 1957, became Mayor of West Berlin, a post he held until 1966. In 1969 he became Chancellor of the FRG, a post he held until 1974. In 1971, Brandt was awarded the Nobel Peace Prize for his success in building more positive relations with East Germany. He was widely admired.

Quotation

The key word "recognition" had been the subject of fierce debate in West Germany in the late 1960s and early 1970s...Willy Brandt quoted a remark of the British Prime Minister, Harold Wilson, to illustrate the difference between the two kinds of recognition. 'If I go into a zoo and see an elephant,' he said, 'I recognize him as an elephant. But that does not mean that I recognize him in the sense that, say, a scientist, writer or athlete receives "recognition" for their achievement.'

Garton Ash,
In Europe's Name, 1993

▶ What point do you think Brandt was trying to make here?

which polled a majority of the votes after an exceptionally high turnout of 91 per cent.

Although *Ostpolitik* was Brandt's most lasting contribution to the future of Germany, his period as Chancellor also saw an expansion of the welfare state and a move towards greater social and sexual equality. By 1973, however, Brandt was dogged by several problems, including signs of inflation in the economy, the beginning of the world oil crisis (see margin) and his own ill health. The final straw was the discovery that his personal assistant, Gunther Guillaume, was an East German spy. Brandt resigned in 1974.

Helmut Schmidt

Brandt was replaced by Schmidt, a member of the SPD who stood on the right wing of the Party. The coalition with the FDP continued, although this was increasingly based solely on *Ostpolitik* which the FDP supported. In other respects the FDP, under the new leadership of the more conservative Genscher, was increasingly attracted by the more right wing CDU/CSU under the leadership of Helmut Kohl. The fragile support of the FDP was not Schmidt's only problem. He was also under attack from the left wing of his own party for moving further towards nuclear power in the wake of the world oil crisis. Not only that, but the decision of the USA to station nuclear missiles in Europe in 1979, including West Germany, led to further protests from the Left.

Schmidt, therefore, faced opposition from both Left and Right, and economic problems arising from a general recession and a rise in unemployment did not help. In 1982, the FDP deserted the SPD and instead entered into a coalition with the CDU. Together they formed a majority and the leader of the CDU, Helmut Kohl, became Chancellor.

Helmut Kohl

Helmut Kohl was to become Germany's longest-serving Chancellor of the twentieth century. Although he was sometimes characterized as rather provincial and capable of public relations blunders, he was to become famous for his enthusiastic support for European co-operation and his role in the unification of Germany in 1990.

One of Kohl's first actions as Chancellor was to call an election so that the West German public would have an opportunity, democratically, to approve the new government. This approval was duly given. Initially, Kohl pursued policies similar to Schmidt. *Ostpolitik* continued and in 1984 there were new financial and travel agreements between East and West Germany. In 1987, the East German President, Erich Honecker, became the first East German leader to visit the FRG. Another example of continuity was Kohl's commitment to allow NATO to site nuclear missiles in West Germany.

Economically, Kohl tightened the government's purse strings as a means of controlling inflation. He earned the opposition of the Left by limiting welfare benefits and funding for social programmes. However, the budget deficit was reduced and despite growth rates which were low compared to earlier years, Germany nevertheless performed better economically than many of her European counterparts, including Britain. The microelectronic industries did well as emphasis moved away from the more traditional heavy industries in the Rühr. One problem Kohl did not solve, however, was unemployment which remained steady at around 8–10 per cent.

Note

Despite the Basic Treaty, the FRG remained committed to eventual reunification and never behaved toward the GDR as if it were an entirely foreign country. For example, West German representatives were sent to the GDR rather than ambassadors.

Note

The world oil crisis began in 1973 when Arab States belonging to OPEC (Organization of Petroleum Exporting Countries) tripled the cost of oil.

Note

The change in government in 1982 was known as *die Wende* – the turning point.

■ Biography

Helmut Kohl

Born in 1930, Kohl lived through the devastation brought by war. It left him determined to do all he could to avoid such a thing ever happening again. He became involved in politics whilst still young, although trained as a lawyer. He joined the CDU in 1946. He became the youngest leader of any West German state in 1969 and in the same year became Vice-Chairman of the CDU. In 1982, Kohl became the youngest Chancellor West Germany had ever had. Since then, he has championed the European Union and overseen dramatic developments in Germany, including the fall of the Berlin Wall and the reunification of Germany. He was replaced as Chancellor of Germany in 1998 by Gerhard Schröder.

The Bitburg Affair was an example of Kohl's occasional public relations blunders which did not help his popularity in the 1980s. A 40th anniversary celebration of the end of the Second World War was planned at a military ceremony at Bitburg and President Reagan of the United States was invited to attend. When it was revealed that SS troops were buried there, pressure was put on Kohl to cancel the ceremony. Defiantly, Kohl insisted it should continue.

■ **Biography**

Erich Honecker

Born in 1912, Honecker was a committed communist from a very early age. He joined communist youth organizations at the age of ten and in 1930 went to Moscow to attend the Lenin School for Young Communists. He spent most of the period of the Third Reich in concentration camps, his punishment for being a communist. After the division of Germany in 1949, Honecker worked his way up the ranks of the SED, becoming Party Secretary in 1958. In 1971, he succeeded Ulbricht as Secretary General of the SED, making him the most powerful figure in the GDR. He remained an old-fashioned, hard-line communist and tried to resist Gorbachev's reforms in the 1980s. He was subsequently forced out of office in 1989 and was later arrested, although soon released. Initially, he moved to the USSR but as it collapsed around him he finally sought refuge in Chile after the case against him for manslaughter (for the killings at the Berlin Wall) was dropped. He died in exile in 1994.

Kohl was fortunate that his main political opponents, the SPD, were in disarray for some of the 1980s, not least because of the success of the Green Party which particularly attracted the younger voters. In 1987, Kohl managed to cling on to power, but he was clearly in difficulties. Unemployment stubbornly refused to go down, the CSU (sister party of the CDU) divided, and the CDU was accused of accepting illegal donations from industry. The result in 1987 was not surprisingly the CDU's worst election result since 1949. In this respect, it could be argued that the unification of Germany in 1990 provided Kohl with a lifeline. Without it, it is unlikely that he would have remained in power until 1998.

The GDR 1971–1989

Honecker

In 1971, Ulbricht was succeeded as Secretary General of the SED by Erich Honecker, who became the GDR's leader at quite a promising time. The GDR was now internationally recognized, largely thanks to Brandt's policy of *Ostpolitik*. Although the economy continued to be under State control, more attention was finally being paid to living standards and material consumer demands. There were also generous loans coming from the FRG and, indeed, in the 1980s, the GDR was becoming dependent on such assistance.

By the mid-1970s, however, it was clear that the GDR was having economic difficulties. The oil crisis had an impact on the foreign trade which was so significant in the GDR's economy. Between 1972 and 1975, the price of imports increased by 34 per cent compared to an increase of only 17 per cent in the price of exports. In addition, the cost of welfare spending outstripped the national income. East Germany's budget simply was not balancing.

Politically, Honecker was hard-line and his policies were heavily influenced by the USSR. In 1961, when the Berlin Wall was built, Honecker was head of East German security forces and many East Germans were shot under his orders while trying to cross the Wall. Even when Mikhail Gorbachev, the new Soviet President in 1985, was implementing reform in the USSR, Honecker resisted and instead began to distance himself from the Russians. Early indications that politically at least, nothing was likely to change under Honecker came in the 1970s when a musician who had been touring the West was refused entry back into the GDR. Several cultural figures in East Germany subsequently left for the West. There were some signs of less repression, however, when in 1978, Christians were allowed greater freedom and toleration. By the 1980s, Christian groups were debating issues of human rights and being publicly critical of the regime. This would not have been tolerated previously.

In its relations with West Germany, the GDR combined a suspicion of closer relations with a growing dependence on financial assistance. *Ostpolitik* was initially greeted with suspicion, although in practical terms the GDR stood to gain international recognition and loans out of it. For nearly 30 years after the beginning of *Ostpolitik*, the GDR allied itself firmly with the USSR in its foreign policy whilst becoming increasingly dependent on the FRG's loans. It is hard to see how these contradictory policies could have lasted indefinitely.

The reformist era swept in by Gorbachev in 1985 was not well received by Honecker. In fact, repression increased in the GDR and the library of the environmental movement was raided and the printing press destroyed. It was Gorbachev, however, who speeded up a sequence of events which was to make German reunification irresistible. The GDR could not ignore what was going on elsewhere in Eastern Europe.

The road to reunification

The reunification of Germany in October 1990 was not the result of years spent planning and negotiating. Its speed took everyone by surprise, not least the man who was to become the Chancellor of a united Germany, Helmut Kohl. What prompted it was the collapse of the GDR. But why did this happen so quickly? The answer lies in three main factors, all of which were superimposed on the existing problems of East Germany, particularly economic, which have been outlined already. These factors were:

- The reform of the USSR under Gorbachev and an end to the Cold War
- The mobilization of reform pressure groups within the GDR which became increasingly insistent that change had to come
- The collapse of authority amongst those who governed the GDR

The impact of Gorbachev

In 1985, Mikhail Gorbachev became the President of the USSR. It was already clear that the USSR was in desperate need of reform and Gorbachev's main contribution was to speed this process up dramatically. He wanted to end the Cold War and seek financial help from the West to avoid economic collapse. He also intended to reform the economy and introduce an era of openness – or *Glasnost* as it became officially known. As we have already seen, Honecker, leader of the GDR, did not respond well to this era of reform. In November 1988, East Germany banned *Sputnik*, a Soviet magazine, on the grounds that it distorted history. In the same month, five Soviet films were banned from a Soviet film festival in East Berlin. Clearly, the GDR was diverging from the reformist intentions of the USSR's new leader. Gorbachev made it plain that he wanted Honecker to adopt a reformist programme. During a visit to East Berlin in October 1989 for the GDR's 40th anniversary celebrations, he made it clear that the GDR could not rely on Soviet troops as they had done before in time of crisis (for example, in 1953). He stressed that 'matters affecting East Germany are decided not in Moscow but in Berlin'.

Meanwhile, Gorbachev was implementing a similar policy in other East European communist states. After his announcement that the USSR would no longer interfere in the matters of other states, Hungary opened its border with Austria, breaching the Iron Curtain and enabling thousands of East Germans to travel to the West via Hungary with Austria's approval. Hundreds of East German tourists camped out in West German embassies in Prague and Warsaw. Honecker had no choice but to grant the tourists in Prague exit visas to the West. His government appeared paralysed in the face of such events and its lack of firm action added significantly to the feeling in East Germany that change was imminent.

> **Quotation**
>
> The Soviet Union effectively renounced the GDR. This was the crucial precondition for its eventual demise.
>
> Fulbrook,
> *Anatomy of a Dictatorship*, 1995

Popular protests

During the summer and autumn of 1989, opposition groups were emerging to demand reform of the GDR from within. The most important of these groups, the New Forum, was founded in September 1989 as a means of promoting free debate which until then only existed in the Church. It was refused legal recognition from the government, however, and this helped to turn it into a more overt pressure group seeking reform within East Germany. It was joined by other groups such as Democratic Awakening and Democracy Now. These

▲ An East German protest march in East Berlin in November 1989.

groups presented a kind of challenge hitherto unknown to the GDR. They wanted official recognition and they wanted a say in how the country was run. Gorbachev's visit to East Berlin in October was preceded by a protest march of around 12,000 protesters in Leipzig. On the day of his visit, between 500 and 700 marchers were arrested in East Berlin. A day later, 30,000 protesters marched in Dresden.

These peaceful protests were met with repression. Protesters were often arrested and at Leipzig, water cannons, batons and dogs were used to disperse demonstrators. However, without the backing of the USSR, the power of the GDR was seriously reduced and there were suspicions that the police forces were reluctant to quash the demonstrations. The turning point came on 9 October, the point at which the will of the people appeared to triumph. A demonstration of around 50,000 protesters in Leipzig was allowed to go ahead peacefully with no intervention. Fulbrook writes that 'from then on, the momentum of growing mass mobilization and the overcoming of fear was to snowball, accompanied by the ever more speedy collapse of authority above.' (1995)

Collapse from above

It was becoming clear, by October 1989, that there was a division amongst the GDR's political leaders. Some wanted to continue Honecker's hard-line approach; others were convinced that reform was the only solution. Honecker finally resigned on 18 October, to be replaced by Egon Krenz who wasted no time in implementing reforms. The New Forum was legalized, for example, and the right to travel in the West for up to 30 days was granted to all East Germans. Meanwhile, Honecker's supporters were ousted. One of the immediate consequences of these events was the escalation of protest marches, including one at Leipzig with as many as 120,000 people. It was clear that the protesters would continue to demand more reform.

Source 4

■ **Think about**

▶ The East Germans had spent years keeping their grumbles to themselves and rarely challenging the political regime. Why do you think this all changed in 1989?

▶ Many of the protesters did not want a united Germany. Instead they wanted East Germany to be run differently. Why do you think this was the case?

▶ East Germans flee their country via Czechoslovakia in October 1989.

Meanwhile, there was a steady stream of East Germans leaving for the West. Egon Krenz suggested that over 100,000 East Germans had recently left. The fact that this information was given out on a television interview was itself a demonstration of how far things had changed. It was clear that the Berlin Wall was no longer serving its purpose and instead had simply become a focus of protests. On 4 November, nearly 1 million people demonstrated in East Berlin, demanding basic freedoms. Four days later, the leaders of the SED all resigned. They did, however, set in motion the right for East Germans to move freely wherever they wanted by announcing that the Berlin Wall was to be taken down. The announcement was made on 9 November. Over the next two days, 2 million East Germans visited West Berlin, although most returned. The celebrations were to eclipse those of a year later when Germany was officially reunited. East Germans were greeted with tears and embraces. Champagne flowed, candles were lit. East Germans flocked to the big department stores on Kurfurstendamm, dazzled by the array of consumer goods and luxuries. Meanwhile, pieces of the wall were hacked off as souvenirs. On television screens the world over, the fall of the Berlin Wall seemed to signal a new era of peace, friendship and unity. Without a doubt, it was one of the defining moments of the twentieth century. The photograph on page 284 shows the drama of these events.

By the beginning of 1990, there were up to 2000 East Germans leaving every day, heading for West Germany and particularly West Berlin. This put an enormous strain on the East German government and on its economy. It also had a big impact on West Germany, which had to cope with this sudden influx of new residents.

Reunification

The new East German Prime Minister, Hans Modrow, brought in further reforms and also moved away from the dominant control of the communist SED. His new government included other party representatives, although the SED remained the biggest presence. This government approved investigations into alleged corruption charges against East German officials and in December, Erich Honecker was put under house arrest, although he was soon released due to his poor health. Modrow also signalled his intention to speed up what was becoming an inevitable process towards unification. In January 1990 he left for Moscow and returned with a four-stage plan for unification.

It was at this stage that the West German Chancellor, Helmut Kohl, became more actively involved in the whole process. In the previous November he had issued a Ten Point Plan for unification which would have taken years to complete. On a visit to East Germany in December 1989, however, he was taken aback by the enthusiasm with which he was received. It convinced him that the moment for reunification had arrived much sooner than expected; the East Germans were themselves ready to unite. Rather than allowing the GDR to determine the nature of the reunification, Kohl started to take the initiative. He rejected the plan put forward by Modrow which insisted that the new united Germany should be militarily neutral. This would have involved severing ties with NATO which Kohl refused to do. By February 1990, Kohl had demonstrated his support for the pro-unification parties in East Germany, including the East German branch of the CDU which had now removed its communist leaders. He had also secured the support of the four Allied powers who had occupied Germany after the war. This became known as the Two-plus-Four agreement – East and West Germany plus America, Britain, France and the USSR. Talks began in May and ended, in favour of unification, in September. This included an acceptance by the USSR that Germany could continue as a member of NATO with the proviso that NATO troops or weapons would not be stationed on what was currently East German soil. The USSR was also softened by pledges of money from West Germany.

Facts and figures

The Berlin Wall had stood for 10,315 days. Within hours, thousands were streaming through the checkpoints to be greeted by ecstatic West Berliners on the other side. The physical dismantling of the Wall took longer to complete. Official demolition of the Wall began in June 1990, when 13 bulldozers, 55 excavators, 65 cranes and 175 lorries were required to complete the task. Most of the Wall was dismantled by November, although certain sections still stand today as a reminder of Germany's past. Many of the concrete blocks were reused to build roads.

Facts and figures

The results of a survey which asked 'Do you personally take a positive or negative view of German reunification?' The figures given are in percentages.

	Very Positive	Rather positive	Rather negative	Very negative	Don't know
FRG	31	49	15	2	3
Spain	48	25	4	2	21
France	17	51	17	6	9
UK	21	40	15	12	12
Italy	41	37	8	5	9
Hungary	23	45	16	6	10
Poland	9	17	26	38	10
USSR	17	34	17	13	19

Glaessner, *The Unification Process in Germany*, 1992

Timeline

1969: Willy Brandt becomes Chancellor of Germany and begins his policy of *Ostpolitik*

1970: The Moscow Treaty: West Germany renounces its claim to represent all the German people

1971: Honecker replaces Ulbricht as General Secretary of the SED and therefore becomes leader of the GDR

1972: The Basic Treaty: West Germany recognizes the GDR as a state in its own right

1974: Brandt resigns and is replaced by Schmidt

1982: Helmut Kohl becomes Chancellor of West Germany

1985: Gorbachev becomes President of the USSR

1987: First visit of an East German leader to the FRG

1989: Gorbachev makes it clear that the USSR will no longer interfere in the affairs of East European states. This includes withdrawing unconditional support of the GDR

1989: Protest marches in East Germany

1989: Honecker resigns

1989: the Berlin Wall is opened

1989: Kohl visits East Germany and is stunned by the warmth with which he is received

1990: Modrow, the new East German Prime Minister, draws up a plan for reunification with the USSR

1990: Two-plus-Four Agreement

1990: Currency union between East and West Germany

1990: Reunification of Germany

■ Activity

Was the reunification of Germany inevitable? To help you answer this question you may find some of the following helpful:

Laver, Rowe and Williamson, *Years of Division*, 1999

Fulbrook, *The Fontana History of Germany 1918–1990*, 1991

Garton Ash, *In Europe's Name*, 1993

Jarausch, *The Rush to German Unity*, 1994

It is also worth looking on the Internet, especially for primary material.

In March, free elections were held in East Germany and were a victory for the CDU, doubtless in part because of the massive support lent to it by its West German equivalent. In July, a currency union between East and West Germany was implemented. After the Two-plus-Four talks concluded in September, the way for unification was clear. On 3 October 1990, East and West Germany were officially reunited and Germany was once again a single state. Helmut Kohl became Chancellor of a united Germany. This time, however, the celebrations were less spontaneous than almost a year previously when the Berlin Wall came down. The realities of a united Germany were beginning to hit home, especially in West Berlin which had experienced the most acute influx of new residents. Reunification was, nevertheless, a momentous occasion and one for which many Germans had waited a long time. For many, the celebrations were real enough.

Source 5

▲ Germans celebrate the reunification of East and West Germany in 1990.

Conclusion

Was the reunification of Germany inevitable? Or to put it a different way, was the GDR doomed to fail? Certainly, the GDR did not experience the economic success enjoyed by the FRG, although its citizens had much higher living standards than elsewhere in the Soviet Bloc. It is also true that the Berlin Wall helped it to survive because it stopped the relentless flow of East Germans into West Germany. The GDR depended on the USSR for military support and the FRG for economic assistance. All these factors hardly encourage historians to claim for certain that the GDR could have lasted indefinitely. However, can we be sure that its collapse was inevitable? In the final analysis, it was the events elsewhere that determined the timing of the GDR's collapse. Like the Weimar Republic before it, one could argue that the GDR was not strong enough to withstand these external factors which crucially undermined it. But whether this in itself means the GDR was doomed to fail is for you to decide.

Chapter 17

The economic modernization of Germany *c.1880–c.1980*

Source 1

▲ German agriculture c.1880.

Source 2

▲ Heavy industry in the 1920s.

Source 3

▲ Modern manufacturing in Germany.

Introduction

This chapter is about the development of the German economy – and more specifically, its modernization. This includes both the extent of modernization and the reasons for it. It is therefore important to be clear about what we mean by the term *economic modernization*.

■ Activity

Discuss what features you would expect to be present in a **modernizing economy**. The list below should provide a prompt for your discussion.

- Industrial production
- Technological change
- Productivity (output per worker)
- Wealth (GNP and per capita)
- Social welfare/living standards
- Capital/investment
- Employment rates
- Distribution of labour (i.e. what sectors – agricultural, industrial, services – were most people employed in)
- Trade/exports

Now write a definition of a *modernizing economy*.
Would your definition need changing if applied to the following three different periods (ignore your own knowledge of Germany here and think more generally):

    1880–1914
    1914–1945
    1945–1980

Does a definition of a *modernizing economy* therefore depend on the period it refers to – or are there certain features you would expect to see in any modernizing economy at any point after 1880?

The concept of a modern economy is a relative one. In 1880, the country which dug the most coal, made the most steel and built the most ships was the most modern. Today, the country which does the least of these things is the most modern. The emphasis has shifted from heavy industries to the chemical and electrical industries, car manufacture, microelectronics and the service industry. There are, however, some features common to a modern economy after 1880. Technological development, relative to the particular period, has been crucial. New forms of power and new kinds of machinery have been central in increasing productivity, which is itself a feature of a modern economy. These are just some of the examples you could use to define a modern economy.

The German economy 1880–1980

A modern and successful economy has played a key role in Germany's development between 1880 and 1980. In fact, even before Germany united in 1871, the economic success of Prussia (the largest and most powerful German state prior to unification) was an important factor in the unification of Germany and its subsequent strength. However, the economy has, like any modern, industrial economy, gone through cycles of growth, stagnation and depression. These are briefly summarized below:

1850–1871

Although not within the time frame of this chapter, it is worth stressing how consistent economic growth was between these years. There was an especially large increase in the output of the industrial sector, which was mainly the result of an expanding rail network.

1873–1895

Economic growth slowed down during this period, partly because the expansion of the railways also slowed down and the easy increases in the productivity of workers had been achieved. Investment fell in 1871, began to increase in the late 1880s and then fell again in 1891.

1895–1913

This period saw very rapid economic growth. Although agriculture grew more slowly, industrial expansion was impressive, with particularly high production of chemicals, metals, machinery and electrical goods. Exports increased and the banks released more money for investment. Investment in education paid off in the quality of the workforce. By the turn of the century, more people were employed in industry than in any other sector. In the years leading up to the First World War, the speed with which industrial production increased outstripped even Britain, the first industrial nation.

1914–1933

The First World War had a devastating impact on the German economy. Although heavy industry expanded, the problems caused by the war long outlasted it. Investment was low for many years and exports fluctuated, partly as a result of higher tariffs and increased competition from elsewhere. In 1913, for example, Germany produced 80 per cent of the world output of dyes. By 1924 that figure had shrunk to 46 per cent. Additional factors, such as the relatively high wages of the 1920s, added to the problems. Within the period, however, there were mini-cycles. In 1921–1922, output in certain industries had begun to recover to pre-war levels and it was only the Rühr invasion and passive resistance in 1923 that caused this output to drop sharply. Similarly, by 1929, manufacturing output had reached new levels, only to be thwarted by the Wall Street Crash in the same year.

1933–1945

Hitler was fortunate to become Chancellor at a time when output and investment had begun to rise after the depression. The Nazis went on to achieve full employment and high rates of growth through big investment in the war-related industries and also in housing and road building. However, productivity did not increase and Nazi economic policies were not conceived with a view to long-term prosperity. They provided short-term solutions to suit Hitler's military aims.

1945–1980

Although Germany after the war was in many ways left in ruins, there were things that had survived. For example, much of the economic infrastructure had miraculously survived the bombing and business and financial institutions remained unchanged. In addition, the flow of refugees from Eastern Europe provided a plentiful supply of cheap labour. Economic growth was rapid in both East and West Germany, particularly between 1950 and 1970. In West Germany, technological advances, record increases in savings and investment and a huge increase in consumer spending all helped to create what has been described as an 'economic miracle'. In East Germany, wages did not match the West, but standards of living were much higher than elsewhere in Eastern Europe and an increase in consumer spending similarly played its part in economic growth. During the 1970s and 1980s, economic growth in both East

■ Activity   **KEY SKILLS**

This is the main activity in this chapter. It will help you to review and reinforce your existing knowledge of the German economy.

Copy out your own version of the chart on the next page. Your chart will need to be much bigger – probably both sides of a sheet of A3 paper.

There is a column under the heading 'Was the economy modernizing?' which has been left blank. Choose a third criterion for measuring how 'modern' an economy is, based on your response to the activity on page 293.

Complete the chart using:
- Previous sections of the book. Page references are provided.
- The overview on pages 293–295.
- The statistical information on pages 296–297.

Note: This is a complex and detailed activity. You may find that working in a pair or small group may help you.

and West Germany slowed down. This was due to a number of factors including the world oil crisis (see page 286) and a general increase in the cost of raw materials.

How modern was Germany's economy?

Page references	Period	Was the economy modernizing?			What factors were influencing the economy?	
		Economic growth	Dominant economic activity (e.g. industrial/ agricultural)	**?**	Internal factors	External factors
Chapter 1 pp. 14–15 Chapter 2 p. 31 pp. 33–34	Bismarck's Germany 1880–1890					
Chapter 2 p. 31 Chapter 3 pp. 54, 55, 56, 57 pp. 59, 60	Wilhelmine Germany 1890–1914					
Chapter 4 p. 71 pp. 14–21 pp. 83–90	Weimar (1) 1918–1923					
Chapter 5 pp. 93–98, 99 p. 111 Chapter 7 p. 131 p. 146–147	Weimar (2) 1924–1933					
All of Chapter 11 Statistics found on pp. 216, 223, 224	The Third Reich 1933–1945					
Chapter 15 pp. 273, 274, 275	Post-war Germany 1945–1948					
Chapter 15 pp. 277, 278 Chapter 16 pp. 286, 287	West Germany 1948–1980					
Chapter 15 pp. 279–280 Chapter 16 p. 287	East Germany 1948–1980					

■ **Think about**

▶ What were the human consequences of the economic changes summarized on your chart?

■ **Activity**

Using all the information, draw a line graph demonstrating your view on the development of the German economy. 'Economic modernization' should run up the Y-axis, whilst the years 1880–1980 should run along the X-axis.

Spotlight

Statistics on the German economy

Distribution of labour, 1852–1987 (per cent)

Date	Agriculture	Industry	Services
1852	55.2	23.2	21.6
1875	49.5	29.2	21.3
1895	41.8	34.0	24.2
1911	35.4	37.9	26.7
1927	30.0	36.9	29.2
1936	25.0	45.9	28.6
West Germany			
1950	24.3	42.1	33.6
1959	15.1	47.4	37.5
1971	8.0	48.4	43.6
1980	5.5	44.1	50.4
1987	5.1	40.5	54.5
East Germany			
1960	17.0	42.1	40.9
1970	12.8	43.7	43.5
1980	10.7	45.1	44.2
1987	10.8	47.4	41.8

Source 5

Exports and imports calculated in 1987 prices (million marks)

Year	Exports	Imports
1880	2,923.0	2,813.7
1885	2,854.0	2,922.6
1890	3,335.1	4,162.4
1895	3,318.0	4,119.0
1900	4,611.2	5,768.6
1905	5,731.6	7,128.8
1910	7,474.7	8,926.9
1913	10,097.5	10,750.9
1923		6,150.1
1925	9,284.0	12,429.2
1930	12,035.6	10,348.7
1932	5,741.1	4,652.8
1935	4,178.0	4,156.2
1940		
1945		
1950	8,363.1	11,373.9
1955	25,716.8	24,461.1
1959	41,062.4	35,485.7
1960	47,900.0	42,700.0
1965	71,700.0	70,400.0
1970	125,300.0	109,600.0
1975	221,600.0	184,300.0
1980	350,300.0	341,400.0
1985	537,100.0	463,800.0

Source 6

Rate of increase in output (per cent)

Date	Agriculture	Industry
1853–73	1.76	4.98
1873–95	1.61	2.16
1895–1911	1.25	5.39
1927–36	2.44	2.21
West Germany		
1950–9	1.82	7.62
1960–70	-1.74	5.29
1970–86	-3.08	1.14
East Germany		
1950–70	1.98	8.00
1979–87	1.67	5.08

Source 7

Rate of increase in output per worker (per cent)

Date	Agriculture	Industry
1853–73	1.15	2.98
1873–95	1.34	0.4
1895–1911	0.73	3.06
1927–36	3.13	-0.25
West Germany		
1950–9	4.61	4.17
1960–70	4.09	4.4
1970–86	-0.16	2.48
East Germany		
1970–87	2.10	3.97

Note: These figures do not provide a completely accurate measure of productivity. For example, working hours and wage increases are not taken into account.

Source 8

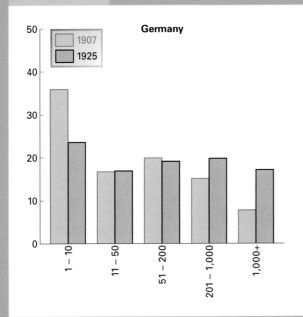

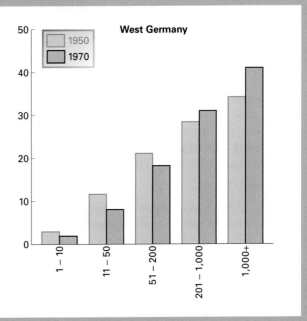

▲ The percentage of the workforce employed in different companies, according to their size (in numbers of staff).

Source 9

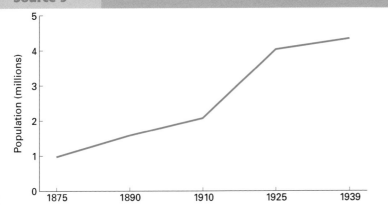

◄ The population growth of Berlin 1875–1939.

Source 11

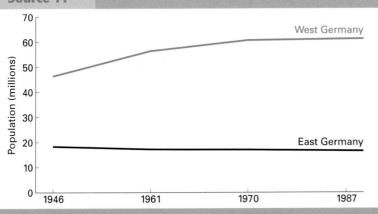

Source 10

The population of Germany 1871–1931	
Year	millions
1871	40.997
1881	45.428
1891	49.762
1901	56.874
1921	62.469
1931	65.084

◄ The population of East and West Germany 1946–1987.

What factors influenced the German economy c.1880–c.1980?

Examples of external factors	Examples of internal factors
War	Growing population
Treaty of Versailles	Preparation for war
Wall Street Crash	Deficit financing (see Ch. 11, p. 215)
Refugees from East Europe	Unification
Marshall Plan	Education
Oil Crisis, 1970s	

Document exercise: How much continuity was there in the German economy 1880–1980?

Source A

Economic expansion in the Wilhelmine era

There were several reasons why Germany forged ahead so dramatically in the industrial field. Her population rapidly increased from 56.7 millions in 1901 to 67.7 millions in 1914…Expansion was [also] encouraged by an abundance of raw materials. The rich iron-ore deposits of Alsace-Lorraine, and the Rühr coalfields, formed the most powerful industrial complex on earth. Credit facilities for expansion were readily available in Germany. German banks, which had always been important in the promotion of trade and industry, expanded their activities enormously at the close of the century and financed practically the whole of industry…The readiness of the State to aid industrial expansion was another factor of importance. Tariffs, subsidies and preferential freight rates were a further extension of the long-established tradition of State intervention. Finally, Germany possessed a skilled working class and an extremely competent managerial class quick to adopt the latest techniques and inventions from other lands, so that industrial expansion was not impeded by out-of-date equipment or outmoded practices.

Carr, *A History of Germany*, 1987

Source B

The dilemmas of the Nazi economy

The Nazis try to persuade the nation that the problem of economic constraints [limitations] is nothing but a foreign exchange problem, whereas in reality it is a problem of the capacity of the economy and of the nation's willingness to make sacrifices. This problem has two aspects: on the one hand, the problem of economic resources, of the maximum level of production and the minimum level of consumption; and, on the other hand, the problem of money, of the financial constraints…The shortage of foreign exchange is, therefore, in reality only a reflection of the overloading of Germany's economic strength through rearmament and the autarky programme.

From a SOPADE report, 1938

■ Activity

1 Add to the lists of external and internal factors using your completed chart and/or your own knowledge. You might want to write your points onto a small piece of card, so that you can move them around later.

2 Are your factors negative or positive influences on the economy?

3 Find evidence to support each one – i.e. what is the evidence that this factor had influence on the German economy?

4 In pairs or small groups, decide which factors have been the most influential in shaping the German economy. Compare your decisions with others in the class and defend your choices.

5 Do different factors play important roles at different times? Are there any factors that are consistently influential throughout the period 1880–1980?

Note

A foreign exchange problem occurs when you are importing more than you are exporting. This causes a balance of trade deficit.

■ Activity

Note: you might find it helpful to complete this activity before attempting the document exercise.

Get into small groups or pairs. Each group should take one of the following features of the German economy between 1880–1980.

● Government economic policies
● Economic growth and productivity
● Social welfare
● Influence of external factors
● Nature of economic activity

Prepare a short presentation on:
'To what extent was there continuity between 1880 and 1980?'

After the presentations, answer the following question:
How much continuity was there in the German economy between 1880 and 1980?

Source C

Index of German industrial production 1913–1974

Year	Total	Year	Total	Year	Total	Year	Total
1913	98	1922	70	1931	70	1940	128
1914	81	1923	46	1932	58	1941	131
1915	66	1924	69	1933	66	1942	132
1916	63	1925	81	1934	83	1944	146
1917	61	1926	78	1935	96	1950	100
1918	56	1927	98	1936	107	1960	248
1919	37	1928	100	1937	117	1965	327
1920	54	1929	100	1938	125	1970	435
1921	65	1930	87	1939	132	1974	486

Note: 1913–1944: 1928=100
1950–1974: 1950=100 (West Germany only)

Source D

The 'Economic Miracle' of West Germany after 1945

West Germany's *Wirtschaftswunder* or 'Economic Miracle' lay at the heart of Western Europe's resurgence. Contrary to popular misconceptions, West Germany did not exceed the performance of all its rivals…But thanks to the sheer size and central location of the West German economy, it was vital to everyone else's success. Its psychological impact was enhanced because the starting-point had been so low. Its author, Dr Erhard, spurned [rejected] government planning of the sort preferred in France and Italy, though certain key sectors were nationalised. The rest was left to efficient organisation, heavy investment, sound training, and hard work. The figures spoke for themselves: in 1948–62 West Germany's foreign trade grew by an annual average of 16 per cent; West German car ownership soared from 200,000 in 1948 to 9 million in 1965; in the same period, 8 million new housing units were constructed – enough to house a minor nation.

Davies, *Europe*, 1996

Conclusion

The German economy certainly did modernize between 1880 and 1980. This was not, however, a straightforward process and the economy went through contrasting phases, not just of boom and bust but also of direction. Perhaps the clearest contrast was between the Nazi economy and the communist economy of East Germany after the Second World War. Nevertheless, there are some features common to the German economy for most of the period. High levels of education, for example, were sustained throughout the period. Similarly, a well-developed banking system was present for much of the period.

■ Examination-style questions

1 Comprehension in context
Study Source B and use your own knowledge.
What does the author of Source B mean when he refers to 'economic constraints' in 1938?

2 Comparing the sources
Study Sources A and D and use your own knowledge.
a   Sources A and D both describe the reasons for rapid economic growth at two different stages in Germany's history. To what extent do they offer similar reasons?
b   Do Sources A and D provide a satisfactory summary of the key factors leading to economic growth and modernization in Germany?

3 Making judgements
Study Sources A, B, C and D and use your own knowledge.
Using these four sources and your own knowledge, to what extent do you agree with the claim that the continuity of the German economy between 1880 and 1980 outweighed the change?

The evolution of Germany

The changes experienced by Germany between 1858 and 1990 were immense. Unification, industrial power, two world wars, a first experiment with democracy followed by a dictatorship, division after the Second World War, communism in East Germany, the Berlin Wall and finally reunification in 1990.

The following maps are intended to provide an overview of how the shape of Germany changed over 100 years. For each one, think about these questions:

● What do you notice about the overall shape of Germany? Where are its borders?
● Why did Germany have those borders at that time?
● What had happened before this to change the shape of Germany?

Then consider these general questions:

1 When did the most significant change in the shape of Germany take place in your view?

2 Can you see any patterns emerging when you compare these maps?

3 To what extent do you think the history of Germany since 1858 has been determined by its geographical location in Europe?

▲ Germany before 1871.

◀ The German Empire in 1871.

▶ The treatment of Germany in the Treaty of Versailles.

Map 1 labels:

Schleswig-Holstein given to Denmark

Southern Schleswig-Holstein

DENMARK

Memel land given to Lithuania

LITHUANIA

East Prussia

HOLLAND

The Polish Corridor given to Poland

Allenstein

• Berlin

Danzig under League of Nations control

GERMANY

BELGIUM

Eupen and Malmedy given to Belgium

Hultschin given to Czechoslovakia

Western Upper Silesia

LUX.

POLAND

Eastern Upper Silesia given to Poland

CZECHOSLOVAKIA

FRANCE

Alsace and Lorraine given to France

AUSTRIA

SWITZERLAND

0   100 km

Land taken from Germany

Area occupied by the Allies

Area from which the German army was banned

Plebiscite areas which voted to remain part of Germany

Map 2 labels:

Memel
Danzig

LITHUANIA

GERMANY

Polish Corridor

GERMANY

POLAND

Sudetenland

The Rhineland

Bohemia-Moravia

Slovakia

Saar

AUSTRIA

0   200 km

Returned to Germany after a plebiscite, January 1935 (people voted to rejoin Germany)

Remilitarised, March 1936 (troops back in Rhineland)

The Anschluss, March 1938 (Germany and Austria united)

Gained from Czechoslovakia under the Munich Agreement, September 1938

Occupied by Germany and turned into a 'protectorate', March 1939

In name independent, but put under German 'protection' March 1939

Handed over by Lithuania under threat, March 1939

Occupied by Germany after the outbreak of war, September 1939

Invaded by Germany September 1939

▲ Germany by September 1939.

Map 3 labels:

DENMARK

Gdansk •

HOLLAND

Hamburg

R. Elbe

British zone

Berlin
Potsdam •

R. Oder

POLAND

• Warsaw

USSR

R. Vistula

Russian zone

R. Neisse

• Bonn

French zone

R. Rhine

Saar

American zone

• Prague

CZECHOSLOVAKIA

FRANCE

Munich •

• Vienna

AUSTRIA

0   200 km

German territory incorporated in Poland

German territory incorporated in the USSR

▲ The treatment of Germany after the Second World War.

Index